SPIRITUALITY
PACK

Yoga Sutras of Patanjali – Translated by Charles
Johnson (1912)

The Bhagavad Gita – Translated by Edwin Arnold
(1885)

The Science of Breath – Yogi Ramacharaka (1904)

Lessons in Mindfulness – Yogi Ramacharaka (1904)

The Dhammapada – Translated by F. Max Muller
(1823)

Table of Contents

THE YOGA SUTRAS OF PATANJALI

Translated by Charles Johnson. Initially Published in 1912.

Introduction to Book I

The Yoga Sutras of Patanjali are in themselves exceedingly brief, less than ten pages of large type in the original. Yet they contain the essence of practical wisdom, set forth in admirable order and detail. The theme, if the present interpreter be right, is the great regeneration, the birth of the spiritual from the psychical man: the same theme which Paul so wisely and eloquently set forth in writing to his disciples in Corinth, the theme of all mystics in all lands.

We think of ourselves as living a purely physical life, in these material bodies of ours. In reality, we have gone far indeed from pure physical life; for ages, our life has been psychical, we have been centred and immersed in the psychic nature. Some of the schools of India say that the psychic nature is, as it were, a looking-glass, wherein are mirrored the things seen by the physical eyes, and heard by the physical ears. But this is a magic mirror; the images remain, and take a certain life of their own. Thus within the psychic realm of our life there grows up an imaged world wherein we dwell; a world of the images of things seen and heard, and therefore a world of memories; a world also of hopes and desires, of fears and regrets. Mental life grows up among these images, built on a measuring and comparing, on the massing of images together into general ideas; on the abstraction of new notions and images from these; till a new world is built up within, full of desires and hates, ambition, envy, longing, speculation, curiosity, self-will, self-interest.

The teaching of the East is, that all these are true powers overlaid by false desires; that though in manifestation psychical, they are in essence spiritual; that the psychical man is the veil and prophecy of the spiritual man.

The purpose of life, therefore, is the realizing of that prophecy; the unveiling of the immortal man; the birth of the spiritual from the psychical, whereby we enter our divine inheritance and come to inhabit Eternity. This is, indeed, salvation, the purpose of all true religion, in all times.

Patanjali has in mind the spiritual man, to be born from the psychical. His purpose is, to set in order the practical means for the unveiling and regeneration, and to indicate the fruit, the glory and the power, of that new birth.

Through the Sutras of the first book, Patanjali is concerned with the first great problem, the emergence of the spiritual man from the veils and meshes of the psychic nature, the moods and vestures of the mental and emotional man. Later will come the consideration of the nature and powers of the spiritual man, once he stands clear of the psychic veils and trammels, and a view of the realms in which these new spiritual powers are to be revealed.

At this point may come a word of explanation. I have been asked why I use the word Sutras, for these rules of Patanjali's system, when the word Aphorism has been connected with them in our minds for a generation. The reason is this: the name Aphorism suggests, to me at least, a pithy sentence of very general application; a piece of proverbial wisdom that may be quoted in a good many sets of circumstance, and which will almost bear on its face the evidence of its truth. But with a Sutra the case is different. It comes from the same root as the word 'sew,' and means, indeed, a thread, suggesting, therefore, a close knit, consecutive chain of argument. Not only has each Sutra a definite place in the system, but further, taken out of this place, it will be almost meaningless, and will by no means be self-evident. So I have thought best to adhere to the original word. The Sutras of Patanjali are as closely knit together, as dependent on each other, as the propositions of Euclid, and can no more be taken out of their proper setting.

In the second part of the first book, the problem of the emergence of the spiritual man is further dealt with. We are led to the consideration of the barriers to his emergence, of the overcoming of the barriers, and of certain steps and stages in the ascent from the ordinary consciousness of practical life, to the finer, deeper, radiant consciousness of the spiritual man.

Book I

1. OM: Here follows Instruction in Union.

Union, here as always in the Scriptures of India, means union of
the individual soul with the Oversoul; of the personal
consciousness with the Divine Consciousness, whereby the
mortal becomes immortal, and enters the Eternal. Therefore,
salvation is, first, freedom from sin and the sorrow which comes
from sin, and then a divine and eternal well-being, wherein the
soul partakes of the being, the wisdom and glory of God.

2. Union, spiritual consciousness, is gained through control of
the versatile psychic nature.

The goal is the full consciousness of the spiritual man, illumined
by the Divine Light. Nothing except the obdurate resistance of
the psychic nature keeps us back from the goal. The psychical
powers are spiritual powers run wild, perverted, drawn from
their proper channel. Therefore our first task is, to regain control
of this perverted nature, to chasten, purify and restore the
misplaced powers.

3. Then the Seer comes to consciousness in his proper nature.

Egotism is but the perversion of spiritual being. Ambition is the
inversion of spiritual power. Passion is the distortion of love.
The mortal is the limitation of the immortal. When these false
images give place to true, then the spiritual man stands forth
luminous, as the sun, when the clouds disperse.

4. Heretofore the Seer has been enmeshed in the activities of the
psychic nature.

The power and life which are the heritage of the spiritual man
have been caught and enmeshed in psychical activities. Instead
of pure being in the Divine, there has been fretful, combative.

9

egotism, its hand against every man. Instead of the light of pure vision, there have been restless senses nave been re and imaginings. Instead of spiritual joy, the undivided joy of pure being, there has been self-indulgence of body and mind. These are all real forces, but distorted from their true nature and goal. They must be extricated, like gems from the matrix, like the pith from the reed, steadily, without destructive violence. Spiritual powers are to be drawn forth from the psychic meshes.

5. The psychic activities are five; they are either subject or not subject to the five hindrances (Book II, 3).

The psychic nature is built up through the image-making power, the power which lies behind and dwells in mind-pictures. These pictures do not remain quiescent in the mind; they are kinetic, restless, stimulating to new acts. Thus the mind-image of an indulgence suggests and invites to a new indulgence; the picture of past joy is framed in regrets or hopes. And there is the ceaseless play of the desire to know, to penetrate to the essence of things, to classify. This, too, busies itself ceaselessly with the mind-images. So that we may classify the activities of the psychic nature thus:

6. These activities are: Sound intellection, unsound intellection, predication, sleep, memory.

We have here a list of mental and emotional powers; of powers that picture and observe, and of powers that picture and feel. But the power to know and feel is spiritual and immortal. What is needed is, not to destroy it, but to raise it from the psychical to the spiritual realm.

7. The elements of sound intellection are: direct observation, inductive reason, and trustworthy testimony.

Each of these is a spiritual power, thinly veiled. Direct observation is the outermost form of the Soul's pure vision. Inductive reason rests on the great principles of continuity and correspondence; and these, on the supreme truth that all life is of the One. Trustworthy testimony, the sharing of one soul in the wisdom of another, rests on the ultimate oneness of all souls.

8. Unsound intellection is false understanding, not resting on a perception of the true nature of things.

When the object is not truly perceived, when the observation is inaccurate and faulty. thought or reasoning based on that mistaken perception is of necessity false and unsound.

9. Predication is carried on through words or thoughts not resting on an object perceived.

The purpose of this Sutra is, to distinguish between the mental process of predication, and observation, induction or testimony. Predication is the attribution of a quality or action to a subject, by adding to it a predicate. In the sentence, 'the man is wise,' 'the man' is the subject; 'is wise' is the predicate. This may be simply an interplay of thoughts, without the presence of the object thought of; or the things thought of may be imaginary or unreal; while observation, induction and testimony always go back to an object.

10. Sleep is the psychic condition which rests on mind states, all material things being absent.

In waking life, we have two currents of perception; an outer current of physical things seen and heard and perceived; an inner current of mind-images and thoughts. The outer current ceases in sleep; the inner current continues, and watching the mind-images float before the field of consciousness, we 'dream.'

Even when there are no dreams, there is still a certain consciousness in sleep, so that, on waking, one says, 'I have slept well,' or 'I have slept badly.'

11. Memory is holding to mind-images of things perceived, without modifying them.

11

Here, as before, the mental power is explained in terms of mind-images, which are the material of which the psychic world is built, Therefore the sages teach that the world of our perception, which is indeed a world of mind-images, is but the wraith or shadow of the real and everlasting world. In this sense, memory is but the psychical inversion of the spiritual, ever-present vision. That which is ever before the spiritual eye of the Seer needs not to be remembered.

12. The control of these psychic activities comes through the right use of the will, and through ceasing from self-indulgence.

If these psychical powers and energies, even such evil things as passion and hate and fear, are but spiritual powers fallen and perverted, how are we to bring about their release and restoration? Two means are presented to us: the awakening of the spiritual will, and the purification of mind and thought.

13. The right use of the will is the steady, effort to stand in spiritual being.

We have thought of ourselves, perhaps, as creatures moving upon this earth, rather helpless, at the mercy of storm and hunger and our enemies. We are to think of ourselves as immortals, dwelling in the Light, encompassed and sustained by spiritual powers. The steady effort to hold this thought will awaken dormant and unrealized powers, which will unveil to us the nearness of the Eternal.

14. This becomes a firm resting-place, when followed long, persistently, with earnestness.

We must seek spiritual life in conformity with the laws of spiritual life, with earnestness, humility, gentle charity, which is an acknowledgment of the One Soul within us all. Only through obedience to that shared Life, through perpetual remembrance of our oneness with all Divine Being, our nothingness apart from Divine Being, can we enter our inheritance.

15. Ceasing from self-indulgence is conscious mastery over the thirst for sensuous pleasure here or hereafter.

Rightly understood, the desire for sensation is the desire of being, the distortion of the soul's eternal life. The lust of sensual stimulus and excitation rests on the longing to feel one's life keenly, to gain the sense of being really alive. This sense of true life comes only with the coming of the soul, and the soul comes only in silence, after self-indulgence has been courageously and loyally stilled, through reverence before the coming soul.

16. The consummation of this is freedom from thirst for any mode of psychical activity, through the establishment of the spiritual man.

In order to gain a true understanding of this teaching, study must be supplemented by devoted practice, faith by works. The reading of the words will not avail. There must be a real effort to stand as the Soul, a real ceasing from self-indulgence. With this awakening of the spiritual will, and purification, will come at once the growth of the spiritual man and our awakening consciousness as the spiritual man; and this, attained in even a small degree, will help us notably in our contest. To him that hath, shall be given.

17. Meditation with an object follows these stages: first, exterior examining, then interior judicial action, then joy, then realization of individual being.

In the practice of meditation, a beginning may be made by fixing the attention upon some external object, such as a sacred image or picture, or a part of a book of devotion. In the second stage, one passes from the outer object to an inner pondering upon its lessons. The third stage is the inspiration, the heightening of the spiritual will, which results from this pondering. The fourth stage is the realization of one's spiritual being, as enkindled by this meditation.

18. After the exercise of the will has stilled the psychic activities, meditation rests only on the fruit of former meditations.

In virtue of continued practice and effort, the need of an external object on which to rest the meditation is outgrown. An interior state of spiritual consciousness is reached, which is called 'the cloud of things knowable' (Book IV, 29).

19. Subjective consciousness arising from a natural cause is possessed by those who have laid aside their bodies and been absorbed into subjective nature.

Those who have died, entered the paradise between births, are in a condition resembling meditation without an external object. But in the fullness of time, the seeds of desire in them will spring up, and they will be born again into this world.

20. For the others, there is spiritual consciousness, led up to by faith, valour right mindfulness, one-pointedness, perception.

It is well to keep in mind these steps on the path to illumination: faith, velour, right mindfulness, one-pointedness, perception. Not one can be dispensed with; all must be won. First faith; and then from faith, velour; from valour, right mindfulness; from right mindfulness, a one-pointed aspiration toward the soul; from this, perception; and finally, full vision as the soul.

21. Spiritual consciousness is nearest to those of keen, intense will.

The image used is the swift impetus of the torrent; the kingdom must be taken by force. Firm will comes only through effort; effort is inspired by faith. The great secret is this: it is not enough to have intuitions; we must act on them; we must live them.

22. The will may be weak, or of middle strength, or intense.

Therefore there is a spiritual consciousness higher than this. For those of weak will, there is this counsel: to be faithful in obedience, to live the life, and thus to strengthen the will to more perfect obedience. The will is not ours, but God's, and we come into it only through obedience. As we enter into the spirit of God, we are permitted to share the power of God.

Higher than the three stages of the way is the goal, the end of the way.

23. Or spiritual consciousness may be gained by ardent service of the Master.

If we think of our lives as tasks laid on us by the Master of Life, if we look on all duties as parts of that Master's work, entrusted to us, and forming our life-work; then, if we obey, promptly, loyally, sincerely, we shall enter by degrees into the Master's life and share the Master's power. Thus we shall be initiated into the spiritual will.

24. The Master is the spiritual man, who s free from hindrances, bondage to works, and the fruition and seed of works.

The Soul of the Master, the Lord, is of the same nature as the soul in us; but we still bear the burden of many evils, we are in bondage through our former works, we are under the dominance of sorrow. The Soul of the Master is free from sin and servitude and sorrow.

25. In the Master is the perfect seed of Omniscience.

The Soul of the Master is in essence one with the Oversoul, and therefore partaker of the Oversoul's all-wisdom and all-power. All spiritual attainment rests on this, and is possible because the soul and the Oversoul are One.

26. He is the Teacher of all who have gone before, since he is not limited by Time.

From the beginning, the Oversoul has been the Teacher of all souls, which, by their entrance into the Oversoul, by realizing their oneness with the Oversoul, have inherited the kingdom of the Light. For the Oversoul is before Time, and Time, father of all else, is one of His children.

27. His word is OM.

OM: the symbol of the Three in One, the three worlds in the Soul; the three times, past, present, future, in Eternity; the three Divine Powers, Creation, Preservation, Transformation, in the one Being; the three essences, immortality, omniscience, joy, in the one Spirit. This is the Word, the Symbol, of the Master and Lord, the perfected Spiritual Man.

28. Let there be soundless repetition of OM and meditation thereon.

This has many meanings, in ascending degrees. There is, first, the potency of the word itself, as of all words. Then there is the manifold significance of the symbol, as suggested above. Lastly, there is the spiritual realization of the high essences thus symbolized. Thus we rise step by step to the Eternal.

29. Thence come the awakening of interior consciousness, and the removal of barriers.

Here again faith must be supplemented by works, the life must be led as well as studied, before the full meaning can be understood. The awakening of spiritual consciousness can only be understood in measure as it is entered. It can only be entered where the conditions are present: purity of heart, and strong aspiration, and the resolute conquest of each sin.

This, however, may easily be understood: that the recognition of the three worlds as resting in the Soul leads us to realize ourselves and all life as of the Soul; that, as we dwell, not in past, present or future, but in the Eternal, we become more at one with the Eternal; that, as we view all organization, preservation, mutation as the work of the Divine One, we shall come more into harmony with the One, and thus remove the barriers in our path toward the Light.

In the second part of the first book, the problem of the emergence of the spiritual man is further dealt with. We are led to the consideration of the barriers to his emergence, of the overcoming of the barriers, and of certain steps and stages in the ascent from the ordinary consciousness of practical life, to the finer, deeper, radiant consciousness of the spiritual man.

30. The barriers to interior consciousness, which drive the psychic nature this way and that, are these: sickness, inertia, doubt, lightmindedness, laziness, intemperance, false notions, inability to reach a stage of meditation, or to hold it when reached.

We must remember that we are considering the spiritual man as enwrapped and enmeshed by the psychic nature, the emotional and mental powers; and as unable to come to clear consciousness, unable to stand and see clearly, because of the psychic veils of the personality. Nine of these are enumerated, and they go pretty thoroughly into the brute toughness of the psychic nature.

Sickness is included rather for its effect on the emotions and mind, since bodily infirmity, such as blindness or deafness, is no insuperable barrier to spiritual life, and may sometimes be a help, as cutting off distractions. It will be well for us to ponder over each of these nine activities, thinking of each as a psychic state, a barrier to the interior consciousness of the spiritual man.

31. Grieving, despondency, bodily restlessness, the drawing in and sending forth of the life-breath also contribute to drive the psychic nature to and fro.

The first two moods are easily understood. We can well see bow a sodden psychic condition, flagrantly opposed to the pure and positive joy of spiritual life, would be a barrier. The next, bodily restlessness, is in a special way the fault of our day and generation. When it is conquered, mental restlessness will be half conquered, too.

The next two terms, concerning the life breath, offer some difficulty. The surface meaning is harsh and irregular breathing; the deeper meaning is a life of harsh and irregular impulses.

32. Steady application to a principle is the way to put a stop to these.

The will, which, in its pristine state, was full of vigour, has been steadily corrupted by self-indulgence, the seeking of moods and sensations for sensation's sake. Hence come all the morbid and sickly moods of the mind. The remedy is a return to the pristine state of the will, by vigorous, positive effort; or, as we are here told, by steady application to a principle. The principle to which we should thus steadily apply ourselves should be one arising from the reality of spiritual life; valorous work for the soul, in others as in ourselves.

33. By sympathy with the happy, compassion for the sorrowful, delight in the holy, disregard of the unholy, the psychic nature moves to gracious peace.

When we are wrapped up in ourselves, shrouded with the cloak of our egotism, absorbed in our pains and bitter thoughts, we are not willing to disturb or strain our own sickly mood by giving kindly sympathy to the happy, thus doubling their joy, or by showing compassion for the sad, thus halving their sorrow. We refuse to find delight in holy things, and let the mind brood in sad pessimism on unholy things. All these evil psychic moods must be conquered by strong effort of will. This rending of the veils will reveal to us something of the grace and peace which are of the interior consciousness of the spiritual man.

34. Or peace may be reached by the even sending forth and control of the life-breath.

Here again we may look for a double meaning: first, that even and quiet breathing which is a part of the victory over bodily restlessness; then the even and quiet tenor of life, without harsh or dissonant impulses, which brings stillness to the heart.

35. Faithful, persistent application to any object, if completely attained, will bind the mind to steadiness.

We are still considering how to overcome the wavering and perturbation of the psychic nature, which make it quite unfit to transmit the inward consciousness and stillness. We are once more told to use the will, and to train it by steady and persistent work: by 'sitting close' to our work, in the phrase of the original.

36. As also will a joyful, radiant spirit.

There is no such illusion as gloomy pessimism, and it has been truly said that a man's cheerfulness is the measure of his faith. Gloom, despondency, the pale cast of thought, are very amenable to the will. Sturdy and courageous effort will bring a clear and valorous mind. But it must always be remembered that this is not for solace to the personal man, but is rather an offering to the ideal of spiritual life, a contribution to the universal and universally shared treasure in heaven.

37. Or the purging of self-indulgence from the psychic nature.

We must recognize that the fall of man is a reality, exemplified in our own persons. We have quite other sins than the animals, and far more deleterious; and they have all come through self-indulgence, with which our psychic natures are soaked through and through. As we climbed down hill for our pleasure, so must we climb up again for our purification and restoration to our former high estate. The process is painful, perhaps, yet indispensable.

38. Or a pondering on the perceptions gained in dreams and dreamless sleep.

For the Eastern sages, dreams are, it is true, made up of images of waking life, reflections of what the eyes have seen and the ears heard. But dreams are something more, for the images are in a sense real, objective on their own plane; and the knowledge that there is another world, even a dream-world, lightens the tyranny of material life. Much of poetry and art is such a solace from dreamland. But there is more in dream, for it may image what is above, as well as what is below; not only the children of men, but also the children by the shore of the immortal sea that brought us hither, may throw their images on this magic mirror: so, too, of the secrets of dreamless sleep with its pure vision, in even greater degree.

39. Or meditative brooding on what is dearest to the heart.

Here is a thought which our own day is beginning to grasp: that love is a form of knowledge; that we truly know any thing or any person, by becoming one therewith, in love. Thus love has a wisdom that the mind cannot claim, and by this hearty love, this becoming one with what is beyond our personal borders, we may take a long step toward freedom. Two directions for this may be suggested: the pure love of the artist for his work, and the earnest, compassionate search into the hearts of others.

40. Thus he masters all, from the atom to the Infinite.

Newton was asked how he made his discoveries. By intending my mind on them, he replied. This steady pressure, this becoming one with what we seek to understand, whether it be atom or soul, is the one means to know. When we become a thing, we really know it, not otherwise. Therefore live the life, to know the doctrine; do the will of the Father, if you would know the Father.

41. When the perturbations of the psychic nature have all been stilled, then the consciousness, like a pure crystal, takes the colour of what it rests on, whether that be the perceiver, perceiving, or the thing perceived.

This is a fuller expression of the last Sutra, and is so lucid that comment can hardly add to it. Everything is either perceiver, perceiving, or the thing perceived; or, as we might say, consciousness, force, or matter. The sage tells us that the one key will unlock the secrets of all three, the secrets of consciousness, force and matter alike. The thought is, that the cordial sympathy of a gentle heart, intuitively understanding the hearts of others, is really a manifestation of the same power as that penetrating perception whereby one divines the secrets of planetary motions or atomic structure.

42. When the consciousness, poised in perceiving, blends together the name, the object dwelt on and the idea, this is perception with exterior consideration.

In the first stage of the consideration of an external object, the perceiving mind comes to it, preoccupied by the name and idea conventionally associated with that object. For example, in coming to the study of a book, we think of the author, his period, the school to which he belongs. The second stage, set forth in the next Sutra, goes directly to the spiritual meaning of the book, setting its traditional trappings aside and finding its application to our own experience and problems.

The commentator takes a very simple illustration: a cow, where one considers, in the first stage, the name of the cow, the animal itself and the idea of a cow in the mind. In the second stage, one pushes these trappings aside and, entering into the inmost being of the cow, shares its consciousness, as do some of the artists who paint cows. They get at the very life of what they study and paint.

43. When the object dwells in the mind, clear of memory-pictures, uncoloured by the mind, as a pure luminous idea, this is perception without exterior or consideration.

We are still considering external, visible objects. Such perception as is here described is of the nature of that penetrating vision whereby Newton, intending his mind on things, made his discoveries, or that whereby a really great portrait painter pierces to the soul of him whom he paints, and makes that soul live on canvas. These stages of perception are described in this way, to lead the mind up to an understanding of the piercing soul-vision of the spiritual man, the immortal.

44. The same two steps, when referring to things of finer substance, are said to be with, or without, judicial action of the mind.

We now come to mental or psychical objects: to images in the mind. It is precisely by comparing, arranging and superposing these mind-images that we get our general notions or concepts. This process of analysis and synthesis, whereby we select certain qualities in a group of mind-images, and then range together those of like quality, is the judicial action of the mind spoken of. But when we exercise swift divination upon the mind images, as does a poet or a man of genius., then we use a power higher than the judicial, and one nearer to the keen vision of the spiritual man.

45. Subtle substance rises in ascending degrees, to that pure nature which has no distinguishing mark.

As we ascend from outer material things which are permeated by separateness, and whose chief characteristic is to be separate, just as so many pebbles are separate from each other; as we ascend, first, to mind-images, which overlap and coalesce in both space and time, and then to ideas and principles, we finally come to purer essences, drawing ever nearer and nearer to unity.

Or we may illustrate this principle thus. Our bodily, external selves are quite distinct and separate, in form, name, place, substance; our mental selves, of finer substance, meet and part, meet and part again, in perpetual concussion and interchange; our spiritual selves attain true consciousness through unity, where the partition wall between us and the Highest, between us and others, is broken down and we are all made perfect in the One. The highest riches are possessed by all pure souls, only when united. Thus we rise from separation to true individuality in unity.

46. The above are the degrees of limited and conditioned spiritual consciousness, still containing the seed of separateness.

In the four stages of perception above described, the spiritual vision is still working through the mental and psychical, the inner genius is still expressed through the outer, personal man. The spiritual man has yet to come completely to consciousness as himself, in his own realm, the psychical veils laid aside.

47. When pure perception without judicial action of the mind is reached, there follows the gracious peace of the inner self.

We have instanced certain types of this pure perception: the poet's divination, whereby he sees the spirit within the symbol, likeness in things unlike, and beauty in all things; the pure insight of the true philosopher, whose vision rests not on the appearances of life, but on its realities; or the saint's firm perception of spiritual life and being. All these are far advanced on the way; they have drawn near to the secret dwelling of peace.

48. In that peace, perception is unfailingly true.

The poet, the wise philosopher and the saint not only reach a wide and luminous consciousness, but they gain certain knowledge of substantial reality. When we know, we know that we know. For we have come to the stage where we know things by being them, and nothing can be more true than being. We rest on the rock, and know it to be rock, rooted in the very heart of the world.

49. The object of this perception is other than what is learned from the sacred books, or by sound inference, since this perception is particular.

The distinction is a luminous and inspiring one. The Scriptures teach general truths, concerning universal spiritual life and broad laws, and inference from their teaching is not less general. But the spiritual perception of the awakened Seer brings particular truth concerning his own particular life and needs, whether these be for himself or others. He receives defined, precise knowledge, exactly applying to what he has at heart.

50. The impress on the consciousness springing from this perception supersedes all previous impressions.

Each state or field of the mind, each field of knowledge, so to speak, which is reached by mental and emotional energies, is a psychical state, just as the mind picture of a stage with the actors on it, is a psychical state or field. When the pure vision, as of the poet, the philosopher, the saint, fills the whole field, all lesser views and visions are crowded out. This high consciousness displaces all lesser consciousness. Yet, in a certain sense, that which is viewed as part, even by the vision of a sage, has still an element of illusion, a thin psychical veil, however pure and luminous that veil may be. It is the last and highest psychic state.

51. When this impression ceases, then, since all impressions have ceased, there arises pure spiritual consciousness, with no seed of separateness left.

The last psychic veil is drawn aside, and the spiritual man stands with unveiled vision, pure serene.

Introduction to Book II

The first book of Patanjali's Yoga Sutras is called the Book of Spiritual Consciousness. The second book, which we now begin, is the Book of the Means of Soul Growth. And we must remember that soul growth here means the growth of the realization of the spiritual man, or, to put the matter more briefly, the growth of the spiritual man, and the disentangling of the spiritual man from the wrappings, the veils, the disguises laid

24

upon him by the mind and the psychical nature, wherein he is enmeshed, like a bird caught in a net.

The question arises: By what means may the spiritual man be freed from these psychical meshes and disguises, so that he may stand forth above death, in his radiant eternalness and divine power? And the second book sets itself to answer this very question, and to detail the means in a way entirely practical and very lucid, so that he who runs may read, and he who reads may understand and practise.

The second part of the second book is concerned with practical spiritual training, that is, with the earlier practical training of the spiritual man.

The most striking thing in it is the emphasis laid on the Commandments, which are precisely those of the latter part of the Decalogue, together with obedience to the Master. Our day and generation is far too prone to fancy that there can be mystical life and growth on some other foundation, on the foundation, for example, of intellectual curiosity or psychical selfishness. In reality, on this latter foundation the life of the spiritual man can never be built; nor, indeed, anything but a psychic counterfeit, a dangerous delusion.

Therefore Patanjali, like every great spiritual teacher, meets the question: What must I do to be saved? with the age-old answer: Keep the Commandments. Only after the disciple can say, These have I kept, can there be the further and finer teaching of the spiritual Rules.

It is, therefore, vital for us to realize that the Yoga system, like every true system of spiritual teaching, rests on this broad and firm foundation of honesty, truth, cleanness, obedience. Without these, there is no salvation; and he who practices these, even though ignorant of spiritual things, is laying up treasure against the time to come.

Book II

1. The practices which make for union with the Soul are: fervent aspiration, spiritual reading, and complete obedience to the Master.

The word which I have rendered 'fervent aspiration' means primarily 'fire'; and, in the Eastern teaching, it means the fire which gives life and light, and at the same time the fire which purifies. We have, therefore, as our first practice, as the first of the means of spiritual growth, that fiery quality of the will which enkindles and illumines, and, at the same time, the steady practice of purification, the burning away of all known impurities. Spiritual reading is so universally accepted and understood, that it needs no comment. The very study of Patanjali's Sutras is an exercise in spiritual reading, and a very effective one. And so with all other books of the Soul. Obedience to the Master means, that we shall make the will of the Master our will, and shall confirm in all wave to the will of the Divine, setting aside the wills of self, which are but psychic distortions of the one Divine Will. The constant effort to obey in all the ways we know and understand, will reveal new ways and new tasks, the evidence of new growth of the Soul. Nothing will do more for the spiritual man in us than this, for there is no such regenerating power as the awakening spiritual will.

2. Their aim is, to bring soul-vision, and to wear away hindrances.

The aim of fervour, spiritual reading and obedience to the Master, is, to bring soul-vision, and to wear away hindrances. Or, to use the phrase we have already adopted, the aim of these practices is, to help the spiritual man to open his eyes; to help him also to throw aside the veils and disguises, the enmeshing psychic nets which surround him, tying his hands, as it were, and bandaging his eyes. And this, as all teachers testify, is a long and arduous task, a steady up-hill fight, demanding fine courage and persistent toil. Fervour, the fire of the spiritual will, is, as we said, two-fold: it illumines, and so helps the spiritual man to see;

26

and it also burns up the nets and meshes which ensnare the spiritual man. So with the other means, spiritual reading and obedience. Each, in its action, is two-fold, wearing away the psychical, and upbuilding the spiritual man.

3. These are the hindrances: the darkness of unwisdom, self-assertion, lust hate, attachment.

Let us try to translate this into terms of the psychical and spiritual man. The darkness of unwisdom is, primarily, the self-absorption of the psychical man, his complete preoccupation with his own hopes and fears, plans and purposes, sensations and desires; so that he fails to see, or refuses to see, that there is a spiritual man; and so doggedly resists all efforts of the spiritual man to cast off his psychic tyrant and set himself free. This is the real darkness; and all those who deny the immortality of the soul, or deny the soul's existence, and so lay out their lives wholly for the psychical, mortal man and his ambitions, are under this power of darkness. Born of this darkness, this psychic self-absorption, is the dogged conviction that the psychic, personal man has separate, exclusive interests, which he can follow for himself alone; and this conviction, when put into practice in our life, leads to contest with other personalities, and so to hate. This hate, again, makes against the spiritual man, since it hinders the revelation of the high harmony between the spiritual man and his other selves, a harmony to be revealed only through the practice of love, that perfect love which casts out fear.

In like manner, lust is the psychic man's craving for the stimulus of sensation, the din of which smothers the voice of the spiritual man, as, in Shakespeare's phrase, the cackling geese would drown the song of the nightingale. And this craving for stimulus is the fruit of weakness, coming from the failure to find strength in the primal life of the spiritual man.

Attachment is but another name for psychic self-absorption; for we are absorbed, not in outward things, but rather in their images within our minds; our inner eyes are fixed on them; our inner desires brood over them; and so we blind ourselves to the presence of the prisoner, the enmeshed and fettered spiritual man.

4. The darkness of unwisdom is the field of the others. These hindrances may be dormant, or worn thin, or suspended, or expanded.

Here we have really two Sutras in one. The first has been explained already: in the darkness of unwisdom grow the parasites, hate, lust, attachment. They are all outgrowths of the self-absorption of the psychical self.

Next, we are told that these barriers may be either dormant, or suspended, or expanded, or worn thin. Faults which are dormant will be brought out through the pressure of life, or through the pressure of strong aspiration. Thus expanded, they must be fought and conquered, or, as Patanjali quaintly says, they must be worn thin,-as a veil might, or the links of manacles.

5 The darkness of ignorance is: holding that which is unenduring, impure, full of pain, not the Soul, to be eternal, pure, full of joy, the Soul.

This we have really considered already. The psychic man is unenduring, impure, full of pain, not the Soul, not the real Self. The spiritual man is enduring, pure, full of joy, the real Self. The darkness of unwisdom is, therefore, the self-absorption of the psychical, personal man, to the exclusion of the spiritual man. It is the belief, carried into action, that the personal man is the real man, the man for whom we should toil, for whom we should build, for whom we should live. This is that psychical man of whom it is said: he that soweth to the flesh, shall of the flesh reap corruption.

6. Self-assertion comes from thinking of the Seer and the instrument of vision as forming one self.

This is the fundamental idea of the Sankhya philosophy, of which the Yoga is avowedly the practical side. To translate this into our terms, we may say that the Seer is the spiritual man; the instrument of vision is the psychical man, through which the spiritual man gains experience of the outer world. But we turn the servant into the master. We attribute to the psychical man, the personal self, a reality which really belongs to the spiritual man alone; and so, thinking of the quality of the spiritual man as belonging to the psychical, we merge the spiritual man in the psychical; or, as the text says, we think of the two as forming one self.

7. Lust is the resting in the sense of enjoyment.

This has been explained again and again. Sensation, as, for example, the sense of taste, is meant to be the guide to action; in this case, the choice of wholesome food, and the avoidance of poisonous and hurtful things. But if we rest in the sense of taste, as a pleasure in itself; rest, that is, in the psychical side of taste, we fall into gluttony, and live to eat, instead of eating to live. So with the other great organic power, the power of reproduction. This lust comes into being, through resting in the sensation, and looking for pleasure from that.

8. Hate is the resting in the sense of pain.

Pain comes, for the most part, from the strife of personalities, the jarring discords between psychic selves, each of which deems itself supreme. A dwelling on this pain breeds hate, which tears the warring selves yet further asunder, and puts new enmity between them, thus hindering the harmony of the Real, the reconciliation through the Soul.

9. Attachment is the desire toward life, even in the wise, carried forward by its own energy.

The life here desired is the psychic life, the intensely vibrating life of the psychical self. This prevails even in those who have attained much wisdom, so long as it falls short of the wisdom of complete renunciation, complete obedience to each least behest of the spiritual man, and of the Master who guards and aids the spiritual man.

The desire of sensation, the desire of psychic life, reproduces itself, carried on by its own energy and momentum; and hence comes the circle of death and rebirth, death and rebirth, instead of the liberation of the spiritual man.

10. These hindrances, when they have become subtle, are to be removed by a countercurrent

The darkness of unwisdom is to be removed by the light of wisdom, pursued through fervour, spiritual reading of holy teachings and of life itself, and by obedience to the Master.

Lust is to be removed by pure aspiration of spiritual life, which, bringing true strength and stability, takes away the void of weakness which we try to fill by the stimulus of sensations.

Hate is to be overcome by love. The fear that arises through the sense of separate, warring selves is to be stilled by the realization of the One Self, the one soul in all. This realization is the perfect love that casts out fear.

The hindrances are said to have become subtle when, by initial efforts, they have been located and recognized in the psychic nature.

11. Their active turnings are to be removed by meditation.

Here is, in truth, the whole secret of Yoga, the science of the soul. The active turnings, the strident vibrations, of selfishness, lust and hate are to be stilled by meditation, by letting heart and mind dwell in spiritual life, by lifting up the heart to the strong, silent life above, which rests in the stillness of eternal love, and needs no harsh vibration to convince it of true being.

12. The burden of bondage to sorrow has its root in these hindrances. It will be felt in this life, or in a life not yet manifested.

The burden of bondage to sorrow has its root in the darkness of unwisdom, in selfishness, in lust, in hate, in attachment to sensation. All these are, in the last analysis, absorption in the psychical self; and this means sorrow, because it means the sense of separateness, and this means jarring discord and inevitable death. But the psychical self will breed a new psychical self, in a new birth, and so new sorrows in a life not yet manifest.

13. From this root there grow and ripen the fruits of birth, of the life-span, of all that is tasted in life.

Fully to comment on this, would be to write a treatise on Karma and its practical working in detail, whereby the place and time of the next birth, its content and duration. are determined; and to do this the present commentator is in no wise fitted. But this much is clearly understood: that, through a kind of spiritual gravitation, the incarnating self is drawn to a home and life-circle which will give it scope and discipline; and its need of discipline is clearly conditioned by its character, its standing, its accomplishment.

14. These bear fruits of rejoicing, or of affliction, as they are sprung from holy or unholy works.

Since holiness is obedience to divine law, to the law of divine harmony, and obedience to harmony strengthens that harmony in the soul, which is the one true joy, therefore joy comes of holiness: comes, indeed, in no other way. And as unholiness is disobedience, and therefore discord, therefore unholiness makes for pain; and this two-fold law is true, whether the cause take effect in this, or in a yet unmanifested birth.

15. To him who possesses discernment, all personal life is misery, because it ever waxes and wanes, is ever afflicted with restlessness, makes ever new dynamic impresses in the mind; and because all its activities war with each other.

31

The whole life of the psychic self is misery, because it ever waxes and wanes; because birth brings inevitable death; because there is no expectation without its shadow, fear. The life of the psychic self is misery, because it is afflicted with restlessness; so that he who has much, finds not satisfaction, but rather the whetted hunger for more. The fire is not quenched by pouring oil on it; so desire is not quenched by the satisfaction of desire. Again, the life of the psychic self is misery, because it makes ever new dynamic impresses in the mind; because a desire satisfied is but the seed from which springs the desire to find like satisfaction again. The appetite comes in eating, as the proverb says, and grows by what it feeds on. And the psychic self, torn with conflicting desires, is ever the house divided against itself, which must surely fall.

16. This pain is to be warded off, before it has come.

In other words, we cannot cure the pains of life by laying on them any balm. We must cut the root, absorption in the psychical self. So it is said, there is no cure for the misery of longing, but to fix the heart upon the eternal.

17. The cause of what is to be warded off, is the absorption of the Seer in things seen.

Here again we have the fundamental idea of the Sankhya, which is the intellectual counterpart of the Yoga system. The cause of what is to be warded off, the root of misery, is the absorption of consciousness in the psychical man and the things which beguile the psychical man. The cure is liberation.

18. Things seen have as their property manifestation, action, inertia. They form the basis of the elements and the sense-powers. They make for experience and for liberation.

Here is a whole philosophy of life. Things seen, the total of the phenomenal, possess as their property, manifestation, action, inertia: the qualities of force and matter in combination. These, in their grosser form, make the material world; in their finer, more subjective form, they make the psychical world, the world of sense-impressions and mind-images. And through this totality of the phenomenal, the soul gains experience, and is prepared for liberation. In other words, the whole outer world exists for the purposes of the soul, and finds in this its true reason for being.

19. The grades or layers of the Three Potencies are the defined, the undefined, that with distinctive mark, that without distinctive mark.

Or, as we might say, there are two strata of the physical, and two strata of the psychical realms. In each, there is the side of form, and the side of force. The form side of the physical is here called the defined. The force side of the physical is the undefined, that which has no boundaries. So in the psychical; there is the form side; that with distinctive marks, such as the characteristic features of mind-images; and there is the force side, without distinctive marks, such as the forces of desire or fear, which may flow now to this mind-image, now to that.

20. The Seer is pure vision. Though pure, he looks out through the vesture of the mind.

The Seer, as always, is the spiritual man whose deepest consciousness is pure vision, the pure life of the eternal. But the spiritual man, as yet unseeing in his proper person, looks out on the world through the eyes of the psychical man, by whom he is enfolded and enmeshed. The task is, to set this prisoner free, to clear the dust of ages from this buried temple.

21. The very essence of things seen is, that they exist for the Seer.

The things of outer life, not only material things, but the psychic man also, exist in very deed for the purposes of the Seer, the Soul, the spiritual man Disaster comes, when the psychical man sets up, so to speak, on his own account, trying to live for himself alone, and taking material things to solace his loneliness.

22. Though fallen away from him who has reached the goal, things seen have not altogether fallen away, since they still exist for others.

When one of us conquers hate, hate does not thereby cease out of the world, since others still hate and suffer hatred. So with other delusions, which hold us in bondage to material things, and through which we look at all material things. When the coloured veil of illusion is gone, the world which we saw through it is also gone, for now we see life as it is, in the white radiance of eternity. But for others the coloured veil remains, and therefore the world thus coloured by it remains for them, and will remain till they, too, conquer delusion.

23. The association of the Seer with things seen is the cause of the realizing of the nature of things seen, and also of the realizing of the nature of the Seer.

Life is educative. All life's infinite variety is for discipline, for the development of the soul. So passing through many lives, the Soul learns the secrets of the world, the august laws that are written in the form of the snow-crystal or the majestic order of the stars. Yet all these laws are but reflections, but projections outward, of the laws of the soul; therefore in learning these, the soul learns to know itself. All life is but the mirror wherein the Soul learns to know its own face.

24. The cause of this association is the darkness of unwisdom.

The darkness of unwisdom is the absorption of consciousness in the personal life, and in the things seen by the personal life. This is the fall, through which comes experience, the learning of the lessons of life. When they are learned, the day of redemption is at hand.

25. The bringing of this association to an end, by bringing the darkness of unwisdom to an end, is the great liberation; this is the Seer's attainment of his own pure being.

When the spiritual man has, through the psychical, learned all life's lessons, the time has come for him to put off the veil and disguise of the psychical and to stand revealed a King, in the house of the Father. So shall he enter into his kingdom, and go no more out.

26. A discerning which is carried on without wavering is the means of liberation.

Here we come close to the pure Vedanta, with its discernment between the eternal and the temporal. St. Paul, following after Philo and Plato, lays down the same fundamental principle: the things seen are temporal, the things unseen are eternal.

Patanjali means something more than an intellectual assent, though this too is vital. He has in view a constant discriminating in act as well as thought; of the two ways which present themselves for every deed or choice, always to choose the higher way, that which makes for the things eternal: honesty rather than roguery, courage and not cowardice, the things of another rather than one's own, sacrifice and not indulgence. This true discernment, carried out constantly, makes for liberation.

27. His illuminations is sevenfold, rising in successive stages.

Patanjali's text does not tell us what the seven stages of this illumination are. The commentator thus describes them;

First, the danger to be escaped is recognized; it need not be recognized a second time. Second, the causes of the danger to be escaped are worn away; they need not be worn away a second time. Third, the way of escape is clearly perceived, by the contemplation which checks psychic perturbation. Fourth, the means of escape, clear discernment, has been developed. This is the fourfold release belonging to insight. The final release from the psychic is three-fold: As fifth of the seven degrees, the dominance of its thinking is ended; as sixth, its potencies, like rocks from a precipice, fall of themselves; once dissolved, they do not grow again. Then, as seventh, freed from these potencies, the spiritual man stands forth in his own nature as purity and light. Happy is the spiritual man who beholds this seven-fold illumination in its ascending stages.

28. From steadfastly following after the means of Yoga, until impurity is worn away, there comes the illumination of thought up to full discernment.

Here, we enter on the more detailed practical teaching of Patanjali, with its sound and luminous good sense. And when we come to detail the means of Yoga, we may well be astonished at their simplicity. There is little in them that is mysterious. They are very familiar. The essence of the matter lies in carrying them out.

29. The eight means of Yoga are: the Commandments, the Rules, right Poise, right Control of the life-force, Withdrawal, Attention, Meditation, Contemplation.

These eight means are to be followed in their order, in the sense which will immediately be made clear. We can get a ready understanding of the first two by comparing them with the Commandments which must be obeyed by all good citizens, and the Rules which are laid on the members of religious orders. Until one has fulfilled the first, it is futile to concern oneself with the second. And so with all the means of Yoga. They must be taken in their order.

30. The Commandments are these: nom injury, truthfulness, abstaining from stealing, from impurity, from covetousness.

These five precepts are almost exactly the same as the Buddhist Commandments: not to kill, not to steal, not to be guilty of incontinence, not to drink intoxicants, to speak the truth. Almost identical is St. Paul's list: Thou shalt not commit adultery, thou shalt not kill, thou shalt not steal, thou shalt not covet. And in the same spirit is the answer made to the young map having great

possessions, who asked, What shall I do to be saved? and
received the reply: Keep the Commandments.

This broad, general training, which forms and develops human
character, must be accomplished to a very considerable degree,
before there can be much hope of success in the further stages of
spiritual life. First the psychical, and then the spiritual. First the
man, then the angel. On this broad, humane and wise foundation
does the system of Patanjali rest.

31. The Commandments, not limited to any race, place, time or
occasion, universal, are the great obligation.

The Commandments form the broad general training of
humanity. Each one of them rests on a universal, spiritual law.
Each one of them expresses an attribute or aspect of the Self, the
Eternal; when we violate one of the Commandments, we set
ourselves against the law and being of the Eternal, thereby
bringing ourselves to inevitable con fusion. So the first steps in
spiritual life must be taken by bringing ourselves into voluntary
obedience to these spiritual laws and thus making ourselves
partakers of the spiritual powers, the being of the Eternal Like
the law of gravity, the need of air to breathe, these great laws
know no exceptions They are in force in all lands, throughout al
times, for all mankind.

32. The Rules are these: purity, serenity fervent aspiration,
spiritual reading, and per feet obedience to the Master.

Here we have a finer law, one which humanity as a whole is less
ready for, less fit to obey. Yet we can see that these Rules are the
same in essence as the Commandments, but on a higher, more
spiritual plane. The Commandments may be obeyed in outer acts
and abstinences; the Rules demand obedience of the heart and
spirit, a far more awakened and more positive consciousness.
The Rules are the spiritual counterpart of the Commandments,
and they have finer degrees, for more advanced spiritual growth.

33. When transgressions hinder, the weight of the imagination should be thrown on the opposite side.

Let us take a simple case, that of a thief, a habitual criminal, who has drifted into stealing in childhood, before the moral consciousness has awakened. We may imprison such a thief, and deprive him of all possibility of further theft, or of using the divine gift of will. Or we may recognize his disadvantages, and help him gradually to build up possessions which express his will, and draw forth his self-respect. If we imagine that, after he has built well, and his possessions have become dear to him, he himself is robbed, then we can see how he would come vividly to realize the essence of theft and of honesty, and would cleave to honest dealings with firm conviction. In some such way does the great Law teach us. Our sorrows and losses teach us the pain of the sorrow and loss we inflict on others, and so we cease to inflict them.

Now as to the more direct application. To conquer a sin. let heart and mind rest, not on the sin, but on the contrary virtue. Let the sin be forced out by positive growth in the true direction, not by direct opposition. Turn away from the sin and go forward courageously, constructively, creatively, in well-doing. In this way the whole nature will gradually be drawn up to the higher level, on which the sin does not even exist. The conquest of a sin is a matter of growth and evolution, rather than of opposition.

34. Transgressions are injury, falsehood, theft, incontinence, envy; whether committed, or caused, or assented to, through greed, wrath, or infatuation; whether faint, or middling, or excessive; bearing endless, fruit of ignorance and pain. Therefore must the weight be cast on the other side.

Here are the causes of sin: greed, wrath, infatuation, with their effects, ignorance and pain. The causes are to be cured by better wisdom, by a truer understanding of the Self, of Life. For greed cannot endure before the realization that the whole world belongs to the Self, which Self we are; nor can we hold wrath against one who is one with the Self, and therefore with ourselves; nor can infatuation, which is the seeking for the happiness of the All in some limited part of it, survive the knowledge that we are heirs of the All. Therefore let thought and imagination, mind and heart, throw their weight on the other side; the side, not of the world,.but of the Self.

35. Where non-injury is perfected, all enmity ceases in the presence of him who possesses it.

We come now to the spiritual powers which result from keeping the Commandments; from the obedience to spiritual law which is the keeping of the Commandments. Where the heart is full of kindness which seeks no injury to another, either in act or thought or wish, this full love creates an atmosphere of harmony, whose benign power touches with healing all who come within its influence. Peace in the heart radiates peace to other hearts, even more surely than contention breeds contention.

36. When he is perfected in truth, all acts and their fruits depend on him.

The commentator thus explains: If he who has attained should say to a man, Become righteous! the man becomes righteous. If he should say, Gain heaven! the man gains heaven. His word is not in vain.

Exactly the same doctrine was taught by the Master who said to his disciples: Receive ye the Holy Ghost: whose soever sins ye remit they are remitted unto them; and whose soever sins ye retain, they are retained.

37. Where cessation from theft is perfected, all treasures present themselves to him who possesses it.

Here is a sentence which may warn us that, beside the outer and apparent meaning, there is in many of these sentences a second and finer significance. The obvious meaning is, that he who has wholly ceased from theft, in act, thought and wish, finds buried treasures in his path, treasures of jewels and gold and pearls. The deeper truth is, that he who in every least thing is wholly honest with the spirit of Life, finds Life supporting him in all things, and gains admittance to the treasure house of Life, the spiritual universe.

38. For him who is perfect in continence, the reward is valour and virility.

The creative power, strong and full of vigour, is no longer dissipated, but turned to spiritual uses. It upholds and endows the spiritual man, conferring on him the creative will, the power to engender spiritual children instead of bodily progeny. An epoch of life, that of man the animal, has come to an end; a new epoch, that of the spiritual man, is opened. The old creative power is superseded and transcended; a new creative power, that of the spiritual man, takes its place, carrying with it the power to work creatively in others for righteousness and eternal life.

One of the commentaries says that he who has attained is able to transfer to the minds of his disciples what he knows concerning divine union, and the means of gaining it. This is one of the powers of purity.

39. Where there is firm conquest of covetousness, he who has conquered it awakes to the how and why of life.

So it is said that, before we can understand the laws of Karma, we must free ourselves from Karma. The conquest of covetousness brings this rich fruit, because the root of covetousness is the desire of the individual soul, the will toward manifested life. And where the desire of the individual soul is overcome by the superb, still life of the universal Soul welling up in the heart within, the great secret is discerned, the secret that the individual soul is not an isolated reality, but the ray, the manifest instrument of the Life, which turns it this way and that until the great work is accomplished, the age-long lesson learned. Thus is the how and why of life disclosed by ceasing from covetousness. The Commentator says that this includes a knowledge of one's former births.

40. Through purity a withdrawal from one's own bodily life, a ceasing from infatuation with the bodily life of others.

As the spiritual light grows in the heart within, as the taste for pure Life grows stronger, the consciousness opens toward the great, secret places within, where all life is one, where all lives are one. Thereafter, this outer, manifested, fugitive life, whether of ourselves or of others, loses something of its charm and glamour, and we seek rather the deep infinitudes. Instead of the outer form and surroundings of our lives, we long for their inner and everlasting essence. We desire not so much outer converse and closeness to our friends, but rather that quiet communion with them in the inner chamber of the soul, where spirit speaks to spirit, and spirit answers; where alienation and separation never enter; where sickness and sorrow and death cannot come.

41. To the pure of heart come also a quiet spirit, one-pointed thought, the victory over sensuality, and fitness to behold the Soul.

Blessed are the pure in heart, for they shall see God, who is the supreme Soul; the ultimate Self of all beings. In the deepest sense, purity means fitness for this vision, and also a heart cleansed from all disquiet, from all wandering and unbridled thought, from the torment of sensuous imaginings; and when the spirit is thus cleansed and pure, it becomes at one in essence with its source, the great Spirit, the primal Life. One consciousness now thrills through both, for the psychic partition wall is broken down. Then shall the pure in heart see God, because they become God.

42. From acceptance, the disciple gains happiness supreme.

One of the wise has said: accept conditions, accept others, accept yourself. This is the true acceptance, for all these things are what they are through the will of the higher Self, except their deficiencies, which come through thwarting the will of the higher Self, and can be conquered only through compliance with that will. By the true acceptance, the disciple comes into oneness of spirit with the overruling Soul; and, since the own nature of the Soul is being, happiness, bliss, he comes thereby into happiness supreme.

43. The perfection of the powers of the bodily vesture comes through the wearing away of impurities, and through fervent aspiration.

This is true of the physical powers, and of those which dwell in the higher vestures. There must be, first, purity; as the blood must be pure, before one can attain to physical health. But absence of impurity is not in itself enough, else would many nerveless ascetics of the cloisters rank as high saints. There is needed, further, a positive fire of the will; a keen vital vigour for the physical powers, and something finer, purer, stronger, but of kindred essence, for the higher powers. The fire of genius is something more than a phrase, for there can be no genius without the celestial fire of the awakened spiritual will.

44. Through spiritual reading, the disciple gains communion with the divine Power on which his heart is set.

Spiritual reading meant, for ancient India, something more than it does with us. It meant, first, the recital of sacred texts, which, in their very sounds, had mystical potencies; and it meant a recital of texts which were divinely emanated, and held in themselves the living, potent essence of the divine.

For us, spiritual reading means a communing with the recorded teachings of the Masters of wisdom, whereby we read ourselves into the Master's mind, just as through his music one can enter into the mind and soul of the master musician. It has been well said that all true art is contagion of feeling; so that through the true reading of true books we do indeed read ourselves into the spirit of the Masters, share in the atmosphere of their wisdom and power, and come at last into their very presence.

45. Soul-vision is perfected through perfect obedience to the Master.

The sorrow and darkness of life come of the erring personal will which sets itself against the will of the Soul, the one great Life. The error of the personal will is inevitable, since each will must be free to choose, to try and fail, and so to find the path. And sorrow and darkness are inevitable, until the path be found, and the personal will made once more one with the greater Will, wherein it finds rest and power, without losing freedom. In His will is our peace. And with that peace comes light. Soul-vision is perfected through obedience.

46. Right poise must be firm and without strain.

Here we approach a section of the teaching which has manifestly a two-fold meaning. The first is physical, and concerns the bodily position of the student, and the regulation of breathing. These things have their direct influence upon soul-life, the life of the spiritual man, since it is always and everywhere true that our study demands a sound mind in a sound body. The present sentence declares that, for work and for meditation, the position of the body must be steady and without strain, in order that the finer currents of life may run their course.

It applies further to the poise of the soul, that fine balance and stability which nothing can shake, where the consciousness rests on the firm foundation of spiritual being. This is indeed the house set upon a rock, which the winds and waves beat upon in vain.

47. Right poise is to be gained by steady and temperate effort, and by setting the heart upon the everlasting.

Here again, there is the two-fold meaning, for physical poise is to be gained by steady effort of the muscles, by gradual and wise training, linked with a right understanding of, and relation with, the universal force of gravity. Uprightness of body demands that both these conditions shall be fulfilled.

In like manner the firm and upright poise of the spiritual man is to be gained by steady and continued effort, always guided by wisdom, and by setting the heart on the Eternal, filling the soul with the atmosphere of the spiritual world. Neither is effective without the other. Aspiration without effort brings weakness; effort without aspiration brings a false strength, not resting on enduring things. The two together make for the right poise which sets the spiritual man firmly and steadfastly on his feet.

48 The fruit of right poise is the strength to resist the shocks of infatuation or sorrow.

In the simpler physical sense, which is also coveted by the wording of the original, this sentence means that wise effort establishes such bodily poise that the accidents of life cannot disturb it, as the captain remains steady, though disaster overtake his ship.

But the deeper sense is far more important. The spiritual man, too, must learn to withstand all shocks, to remain steadfast through the perturbations of external things and the storms and whirlwinds of the psychical world. This is the power which is gained by wise, continuous effort, and by filling the spirit with the atmosphere of the Eternal.

49. When this is gained, there follows the right guidance of the life-currents, the control of the incoming and outgoing breath.

It is well understood to-day that most of our maladies come from impure conditions of the blood. It is coming to be understood that right breathing, right oxygenation, will do very much to keep the blood clean and pure. Therefore a right knowledge of breathing is a part of the science of life.

But the deeper meaning is, that the spiritual man, when he has gained poise through right effort and aspiration, can stand firm, and guide the currents of his life, both the incoming current of events, and the outgoing current of his acts.

Exactly the same symbolism is used in the saying: Not that which goeth into the mouth defileth a man; but that which cometh out of the mouth, this defileth a man. . . . Those things which proceed out of the mouth come forth from the heart . . . out of the heart proceed evil thoughts, murders, uncleanness, thefts, false witness, blasphemies. Therefore the first step in purification is to keep the Commandments.

50. The life-current is either outward, or inward, or balanced; it is regulated according to place, time, number; it is prolonged and subtle.

The technical, physical side of this has its value. In the breath, there should be right inbreathing, followed by the period of pause, when the air comes into contact with the blood, and this again followed by right outbreathing, even, steady, silent. Further, the lungs should be evenly filled; many maladies may arise from the neglect and consequent weakening of some region of the lungs. And the number of breaths is so important, so closely related to health, that every nurse's chart records it.

But the deeper meaning is concerned with the currents of life; with that which goeth into and cometh out of the heart.

51. The fourth degree transcends external and internal objects.

The inner meaning seems to be that, in addition to the three degrees of control already described, control, that is, over the incoming current of life, over the outgoing current, and over the condition of pause or quiescence, there is a fourth degree of control, which holds in complete mastery both the outer passage of events and the inner currents of thoughts and emotions; a condition of perfect poise and stability in the midst of the flux of things outward and inward.

52. Thereby is worn away the veil which covers up the light.

The veil is the psychic nature, the web of emotions, desires, argumentative trains of thought, which cover up and obscure the truth by absorbing the entire attention and keeping the consciousness in the psychic realm. When hopes and fears are reckoned at their true worth, in comparison with lasting possessions of the Soul; when the outer reflections of things have ceased to distract us from inner realities; when argumentative thought no longer entangles us, but yields its place to flashing intuition, the certainty which springs from within; then is the veil worn away, the consciousness is drawn from the psychical to the spiritual, from the temporal to the Eternal. Then is the light unveiled.

53. Thence comes the mind's power to hold itself in the light.

It has been well said, that what we most need is the faculty of spiritual attention; and in the same direction of thought it has been eloquently declared that prayer does not consist in our catching God's attention, but rather in our allowing God to hold our attention.

The vital matter is, that we need to disentangle our consciousness from the noisy and perturbed thraldom of the psychical, and to come to consciousness as the spiritual man. This we must do, first, by purification, through the Commandments and the Rules; and, second, through the faculty of spiritual attention, by steadily heeding endless fine intimations of the spiritual power within us, and by intending our consciousness thereto; thus by degrees transferring the centre of consciousness from the psychical to the spiritual. It is a question, first, of love, and then of attention.

54. The right Withdrawal is the disengaging of the powers from entanglement in outer things, as the psychic nature has been withdrawn and stilled.

To understand this, let us reverse the process, and think of the one consciousness, centred in the Soul, gradually expanding and taking on the form of the different perceptive powers; the one

46

will, at the same time, differentiating itself into the varied powers of action.

Now let us imagine this to be reversed, so that the spiritual force, which has gone into the differentiated powers, is once more gathered together into the inner power of intuition and spiritual will, taking on that unity which is the hallmark of spiritual things, as diversity is the seal of material things.

It is all a matter of love for the quality of spiritual consciousness, as against psychical consciousness, of love and attention. For where the heart is, there will the treasure be also; where the consciousness is, there will the vesture with its powers be developed.

55. Thereupon follows perfect mastery over the powers.

When the spiritual condition which we have described is reached, with its purity, poise, and illuminated vision, the spiritual man is coming into his inheritance, and gaining complete mastery of his powers.

Indeed, much of the struggle to keep the Commandments and the Rules has been paving the way for this mastery; through this very struggle and sacrifice the mastery has become possible; just as, to use St. Paul's simile, the athlete gains the mastery in the contest and the race through the sacrifice of his long and arduous training. Thus he gains the crown.

Introduction to Book III

The third book of the Sutras is the Book of Spiritual Powers. In considering these spiritual powers, two things must be understood and kept in memory. The first of these is this: These spiritual powers can only be gained when the development described in the first and second books has been measurably attained; when the Commandments have been kept, the Rules faithfully followed, and the experiences which are described have been passed through. For only after this is the spiritual man so far grown, so far disentangled from the psychical bandages and veils which have confined and blinded him, that he can use his proper powers and faculties. For this is the secret of all spiritual powers: they are in no sense an abnormal or supernatural overgrowth upon the material man, but are rather the powers and faculties inherent in the spiritual man, entirely natural to him, and coming naturally into activity, as the spiritual man is disentangled and liberated from psychical bondage, through keeping the Commandments and Rules already set forth.

As the personal man is the limitation and inversion of the spiritual man, all his faculties and powers are inversions of the powers of the spiritual man. In a single phrase, his self seeking is the inversion of the Self-seeking which is the very being of the spiritual man: the ceaseless search after the divine and august Self of all beings. This inversion is corrected by keeping the Commandments and Rules, and gradually, as the inversion is overcome, the spiritual man is extricated, and comes into possession and free exercise of his powers. The spiritual powers, therefore, are the powers of the grown and liberated spiritual man. They can only be developed and used as the spiritual man grows and attains liberation through obedience. This is the first thing to be kept in mind, in all that is said of spiritual powers in the third and fourth books of the Sutras. The second thing to be understood and kept in mind is this:

Just as our modern sages have discerned and taught that all matter is ultimately one and eternal, definitely related throughout the whole wide universe; just as they have discerned and taught that all force is one and eternal, so coordinated throughout the whole universe that whatever affects any atom measurably affects the whole boundless realm of matter and force, to the most distant star or nebula on the dim confines of space; so the ancient sages had discerned and taught that all consciousness is one, immortal, indivisible, infinite; so finely correlated and continuous that whatever is perceived by any consciousness is, whether actually or potentially, within the reach of all consciousness, and therefore within the reach of any

48

consciousness. This has been well expressed by saying that all souls are fundamentally one with the Oversoul; that the Son of God, and all Sons of God, are fundamentally one with the Father. When the consciousness is cleared of psychic bonds and veils, when the spiritual man is able to stand, to see, then this superb law comes into effect: whatever is within the knowledge of any consciousness, and this includes the whole infinite universe, is within his reach, and may, if he wills, be made a part of his consciousness. This he may attain through his fundamental unity with the Oversoul, by raising himself toward the consciousness above him, and drawing on its resources. The Son, if he would work miracles, whether of perception or of action, must come often into the presence of the Father. This is the birthright of the spiritual man; through it he comes into possession of his splendid and immortal powers. Let it be clearly kept in mind that what is here to be related of the spiritual man, and his exalted powers, must in no wise be detached from what has gone before. The being, the very inception, of the spiritual man depends on the purification and moral attainment already detailed, and can in no wise dispense with these or curtail them.

Let no one imagine that the true life, the true powers of the spiritual man, can be attained by any way except the hard way of sacrifice, of trial, of renunciation, of selfless self-conquest and genuine devotion to the weal of all others. Only thus can the golden gates be reached and entered. Only thus can we attain to that pure world wherein the spiritual man lives, and moves, and has his being. Nothing impure, nothing unholy can ever cross that threshold, least of all impure motives or self seeking desires. These must be burnt away before an entrance to that world can be gained.

But where there is light, there is shadow; and the lofty light of the soul casts upon the clouds of the mid-world the shadow of the spiritual man and of his powers; the bastard vesture and the bastard powers of psychism are easily attained; yet, even when attained, they are a delusion, the very essence of unreality.

Therefore, ponder well the earlier rules, and lay a firm foundation of courage, sacrifice, selflessness, holiness.

Book III

1. The binding of the perceiving consciousness to a certain region is attention (dharana).

Emerson quotes Sir Isaac Newton as saying that he made his great discoveries by intending his mind on them. That is what is meant here. I read the page of a book while inking of something else. At the end of he page, I have no idea of what it is about, and read it again, still thinking of something else, with the same result. Then I wake up, so to speak, make an effort of attention, fix my thought on what I am reading, and easily take in its meaning. The act of will, the effort of attention, the intending of the mind on each word and line of the page, just as the eyes are focussed on each word and line, is the power here contemplated. It is the power to focus the consciousness on a given spot, and hold it there Attention is the first and indispensable step in all knowledge. Attention to spiritual things is the first step to spiritual knowledge.

2. A prolonged holding of the perceiving consciousness in that region is meditation (dhyana).

This will apply equally to outer and inner things. I may for a moment fix my attention on some visible object, in a single penetrating glance, or I may hold the attention fixedly on it until it reveals far more of its nature than a single glance could perceive. The first is the focussing of the searchlight of consciousness upon the object. The other is the holding of the white beam of light steadily and persistently on the object, until it yields up the secret of its details. So for things within; one may fix the inner glance for a moment on spiritual things, or one may hold the consciousness steadily upon them, until what was in the dark slowly comes forth into the light, and yields up its immortal secret. But this is possible only for the spiritual man, after the

Commandments and the Rules have been kept; for until this is done, the thronging storms of psychical thoughts dissipate and distract the attention, so that it will not remain fixed on spiritual things. The cares of this world, the deceitfulness of riches, choke the word of the spiritual message.

3. When the perceiving consciousness in this meditative is wholly given to illuminating the essential meaning of the object contemplated, and is freed from the sense of separateness and personality, this is contemplation (samadhi).

Let us review the steps so far taken. First, the beam of perceiving consciousness is focussed on a certain region or subject, through the effort of attention. Then this attending consciousness is held on its object. Third, there is the ardent will to know its meaning, to illumine it with comprehending thought. Fourth, all personal bias, all desire merely to indorse a previous opinion and so prove oneself right, and all desire for personal profit or gratification must be quite put away. There must be a purely disinterested love of truth for its own sake. Thus is the perceiving consciousness made void, as it were, of all personality or sense of separateness. The personal limitation stands aside and lets the All-consciousness come to bear upon the problem. The Oversoul bends its ray upon the object, and illumines it with pure light.

4. When these three, Attention, Meditation Contemplation, are exercised at once, this is perfectly concentrated Meditation (sanyama).

When the personal limitation of the perceiving consciousness stands aside, and allows the All-conscious to come to bear upon the problem, then arises that real knowledge which is called a flash of genius; that real knowledge which makes discoveries, and without which no discovery can be made, however painstaking the effort. For genius is the vision of the spiritual man, and that vision is a question of growth rather than present effort; though right effort, rightly continued, will in time infallibly lead to growth and vision. Through the power thus to set aside personal limitation, to push aside petty concerns and cares, and steady the whole nature and will in an ardent love of truth and desire to know it; through the power thus to make way for the All-consciousness, all great men make their discoveries. Newton, watching the apple fall to the earth, was able to look beyond, to see the subtle waves of force pulsating through apples and worlds and suns and galaxies. and thus to perceive universal gravitation. The Oversoul, looking through his eyes, recognized the universal force, one of its own children. Darwin, watching the forms and motions of plants and animals, let the same august consciousness come to bear on them, and saw infinite growth perfected through ceaseless struggle. He perceived the superb process of evolution, the Oversoul once more recognizing its own. Fraunhofer, noting the dark lines in the band of sunlight in his spectroscope, divined their identity with the bright lines in the spectra of incandescent iron, sodium and the rest, and so saw the oneness of substance in the worlds and suns, the unity of the materials of the universe. Once again the Oversoul, looking with his eyes, recognized its own. So it is with all true knowledge. But the mind must transcend its limitations, its idiosyncrasies; there must be purity, for to the pure in heart is the promise, that they shall see God.

5. By mastering this perfectly concentrated Meditation, there comes the illumination of perception.

The meaning of this is illustrated by what has been said before. When the spiritual man is able to throw aside the trammels of emotional and mental limitation, and to open his eyes, he sees clearly, he attains to illuminated perception. A poet once said that Occultism is the conscious cultivation of genius; and it is certain that the awakened spiritual man attains to the perceptions of genius. Genius is the vision, the power, of the spiritual man, whether its possessor recognizes this or not. All true knowledge is of the spiritual man. The greatest in all ages have recognized this and put their testimony on record. The great in wisdom who have not consciously recognized it, have ever been full of the spirit of reverence, of selfless devotion to truth, of humility, as was Darwin; and reverence and humility are the unconscious recognition of the nearness of the Spirit, that Divinity which broods over us, a Master o'er a slave.

6. This power is distributed in ascending degrees.

It is to be attained step by step. It is a question, not of miracle, but of evolution, of growth. Newton had to master the multiplication table, then the four rules of arithmetic, then the rudiments of algebra, before he came to the binomial theorem. At each point, there was attention, concentration, insight; until these were attained, no progress to the next point was possible. So with Darwin. He had to learn the form and use of leaf and flower, of bone and muscle; the characteristics of genera and species; the distribution of plants and animals, before he had in mind that nexus of knowledge on which the light of his great idea was at last able to shine. So is it with all knowledge. So is it with spiritual knowledge. Take the matter this way: The first subject for the exercise of my spiritual insight is my day, with its circumstances, its hindrances, its opportunities, its duties. I do what I can to solve it, to fulfil its duties, to learn its lessons. I try to live my day with aspiration and faith. That is the first step. By doing this, I gather a harvest for the evening, I gain a deeper insight into life, in virtue of which I begin the next day with a certain advantage, a certain spiritual advance and attainment. So with all successive days. In faith and aspiration, we pass from day to day, in growing knowledge and power, with never more than one day to solve at a time, until all life becomes radiant and transparent.

7. This threefold power, of Attention, Meditation, Contemplation, is more interior than the means of growth previously described.

Very naturally so; because the means of growth previously described were concerned with the extrication of the spiritual man from psychic bondages and veils; while this threefold power is to be exercised by the spiritual man thus extricated and standing on his feet, viewing life with open eyes.

8. But this triad is still exterior to the soul vision which is unconditioned, free from the seed of mental analyses.

The reason is this: The threefold power we have been considering, the triad of Attention, Contemplation, Meditation is, so far as we have yet considered it, the focussing of the beam of perceiving consciousness upon some form of manifesting being, with a view of understanding it completely. There is a higher stage, where the beam of consciousness is turned back upon itself, and the individual consciousness enters into, and knows, the All consciousness. This is a being, a being in immortality, rather than a knowing; it is free from mental analysis or mental forms. It is not an activity of the higher mind, even the mind of the spiritual man. It is an activity of the soul. Had Newton risen to this higher stage, he would have known, not the laws of motion, but that high Being, from whose Life comes eternal motion. Had Darwin risen to this, he would have seen the Soul, whose graduated thought and being all evolution expresses. There are, therefore, these two perceptions: that of living things, and that of the Life; that of the Soul's works, and that of the Soul itself.

9. One of the ascending degrees is the development of Control. First there is the overcoming of the mind-impress of excitation. Then comes the manifestation of the mind-impress of Control. Then the perceiving consciousness follows after the moment of Control.

This is the development of Control. The meaning seems to be this: Some object enters the field of observation, and at first violently excites the mind, stirring up curiosity, fear, wonder; then the consciousness returns upon itself, as it were, and takes the perception firmly in hand, steadying itself, and viewing the matter calmly from above. This steadying effort of the will upon the perceiving consciousness is Control, and immediately upon it follows perception, understanding, insight.

Take a trite example. Supposing one is walking in an Indian forest. A charging elephant suddenly appears. The man is excited by astonishment, and, perhaps, terror. But he exercises an effort of will, perceives the situation in its true bearings, and recognizes that a certain thing must be done; in this case, probably, that he must get out of the way as quickly as possible.

Or a comet, unheralded, appears in the sky like a flaming sword. The beholder is at first astonished, perhaps terror-stricken; but he takes himself in hand, controls his thoughts, views the apparition calmly, and finally calculates its orbit and its relation to meteor showers.

These are extreme illustrations; but with all knowledge the order of perception is the same: first, the excitation of the mind by the new object impressed on it; then the control of the mind from within; upon which follows the perception of the nature of the object. Where the eyes of the spiritual man are open, this will be a true and penetrating spiritual perception. In some such way do our living experiences come to us; first, with a shock of pain; then the Soul steadies itself and controls the pain; then the spirit perceives the lesson of the event, and its bearing upon the progressive revelation of life.

10. Through frequent repetition of this process, the mind becomes habituated to it, and there arises an equable flow of perceiving consciousness.

Control of the mind by the Soul, like control of the muscles by the mind, comes by practice, and constant voluntary repetition.

As an example of control of the muscles by the mind, take the ceaseless practice by which a musician gains mastery over his instrument, or a fencer gains skill with a rapier. Innumerable small efforts of attention will make a result which seems well-nigh miraculous; which, for the novice, is really miraculous. Then consider that far more wonderful instrument, the perceiving mind, played on by that fine musician, the Soul. Here again, innumerable small efforts of attention will accumulate into mastery, and a mastery worth winning. For a concrete example, take the gradual conquest of each day, the effort to live that day for the Soul. To him that is faithful unto death, the Master gives the crown of life.

11. The gradual conquest of the mind's tendency to flit from one object to another, and the power of one-pointedness, make the development of Contemplation.

As an illustration of the mind's tendency to flit from one object to another, take a small boy, learning arithmetic. He begins: two ones are two; three ones are three-and then he thinks of three coins in his pocket, which will purchase so much candy, in the store down the street, next to the toy-shop, where are base-balls, marbles and so on,—and then he comes back with a jerk, to four ones are four. So with us also. We are seeking the meaning of our task, but the mind takes advantage of a moment of slackened attention, and flits off from one frivolous detail to another, till we suddenly come back to consciousness after traversing leagues of space. We must learn to conquer this, and to go back within ourselves into the beam of perceiving consciousness itself, which is a beam of the Oversoul. This is the true one-pointedness, the bringing of our consciousness to a focus in the Soul.

12. When, following this, the controlled manifold tendency and the aroused one-pointedness are equally balanced parts of the perceiving consciousness, his the development of one-pointedness.

This would seem to mean that the insight which is called one-pointedness has two sides, equally balanced. There is, first, the manifold aspect of any object, the sum of all its characteristics and properties. This is to be held firmly in the mind. Then there is the perception of the object as a unity, as a whole, the perception of its essence. First, the details must be clearly perceived; then the essence must be comprehended. When the two processes are equally balanced, the true one-pointedness is attained. Everything has these two sides, the side of difference and the side of unity; there is the individual and there is the genus; the pole of matter and diversity, and the pole of oneness and spirit. To see the object truly, we must see both.

13. Through this, the inherent character, distinctive marks and conditions of being and powers, according to their development, are made clear.

By the power defined in the preceding sutra, the inherent character, distinctive marks and conditions of beings and powers are made clear. For through this power, as defined, we get a twofold view of each object, seeing at once all its individual characteristics and its essential character, species and genus; we see it in relation to itself, and in relation to the Eternal. Thus we see a rose as that particular flower, with its colour and scent, its peculiar fold of each petal; but we also see in it the species, the family to which it belongs, with its relation to all plants, to all life, to Life itself. So in any day, we see events and circumstances; we also see in it the lesson set for the soul by the Eternal.

14. Every object has its characteristics which are already quiescent, those which are active, and those which are not yet definable.

Every object has characteristics belonging to its past, its present and its future. In a fir tree, for example, there are the stumps or scars of dead branches, which once represented its foremost growth; there are the branches with their needles spread out to the air; there are the buds at the end of each branch and twig, which carry the still closely packed needles which are the promise of the future. In like manner, the chrysalis has, as its past, the caterpillar; as its future, the butterfly. The man has, in his past, the animal; in his future, the angel. Both are visible even now in his face. So with all things, for all things change and grow.

15. Difference in stage is the cause of difference in development.

This but amplifies what has just been said. The first stage is the sapling, the caterpillar, the animal. The second stage is the growing tree, the chrysalis, the man. The third is the splendid pine, the butterfly, the angel. Difference of stage is the cause of difference of development. So it is among men, and among the races of men.

16. Through perfectly concentrated Meditation on the three stages of development comes a knowledge of past and future.

We have taken our illustrations from natural science, because, since every true discovery in natural science is a divination of a law in nature, attained through a flash of genius, such discoveries really represent acts of spiritual perception, acts of perception by the spiritual man, even though they are generally not so recognized. So we may once more use the same illustration. Perfectly concentrated Meditation, perfect insight into the chrysalis, reveals the caterpillar that it has been, the butterfly that it is destined to be. He who knows the seed, knows the seed-pod or ear it has come from, and the plant that is to come from it. So in like manner he who really knows today, and the heart of to-day, knows its parent yesterday and its child tomorrow. Past, present and future are all in the Eternal. He who dwells in the Eternal knows all three.

17. The sound and the object and the thought called up by a word are confounded because they are all blurred together in the mind. By perfectly concentrated Meditation on the distinction between them, there comes an understanding of the sounds uttered by all beings.

It must be remembered that we are speaking of perception by the spiritual man.

Sound, like every force, is the expression of a power of the Eternal. Infinite shades of this power are expressed in the infinitely varied tones of sound. He who, having entry to the consciousness of the Eternal knows the essence of this power, can divine the meanings of all sounds, from the voice of the insect to the music of the spheres.

In like manner, he who has attained to spiritual vision can perceive the mind-images in the thoughts of others, with the shade of feeling which goes with them, thus reading their thoughts as easily as he hears their words. Every one has the germ of this power, since difference of tone will give widely differing meanings to the same words, meanings which are intuitively perceived by everyone.

18. When the mind-impressions become visible, there comes an understanding of previous births.

This is simple enough if we grasp the truth of rebirth. The fine harvest of past experi ences is drawn into the spiritual nature, forming, indeed, the basis of its development. When the consciousness has been raised to a point above these fine subjective impressions, and can look down upon them from above, this will in itself be a remembering of past births.

19. By perfectly concentrated Meditation on mind-images is gained the understanding of the thoughts of others.

Here, for those who can profit by it, is the secret of thought-reading. Take the simplest case of intentional thought transference. It is the testimony of those who have done this, that the perceiving mind must be stilled, before the mind-image projected by the other mind can be seen. With it comes a sense of the feeling and temper of the other mind and so on, in higher degrees.

20. But since that on which the thought in the mind of another rests is not objective to the thought-reader's consciousness, he perceives the thought only, and not also that on which the thought rests.

The meaning appears to be simple: One may be able to perceive the thoughts of some one at a distance; one cannot, by that means alone, also perceive the external surroundings of that person, which arouse these thoughts.

21. By perfectly concentrated Meditation on the form of the body, by arresting the body's perceptibility, and by inhibiting the eye's power of sight, there comes the power to make the body invisible.

There are many instances of the exercise of this power, by mesmerists, hypnotists and the like; and we may simply call it an instance of the power of suggestion. Shankara tells us that by this power the popular magicians of the East perform their wonders, working on the mind-images of others, while remaining invisible themselves. It is all a question of being able to see and control the mind-images.

22. The works which fill out the life-span may be either immediately or gradually operative. By perfectly concentrated Meditation on these comes a knowledge of the time of the end, as also through signs.

A garment which is wet, says the commentator, may be hung up to dry, and so dry rapidly, or it may be rolled in a ball and dry slowly; so a fire may blaze or smoulder. Thus it is with Karma, the works that fill out the life-span. By an insight into the mental forms and forces which make up Karma, there comes a knowledge of the rapidity or slowness of their development, and of the time when the debt will be paid.

23. By perfectly concentrated Meditation on sympathy, compassion and kindness, is gained the power of interior union with others.

Unity is the reality; separateness the illusion. The nearer we come to reality, the nearer we come to unity of heart. Sympathy, compassion, kindness are modes of this unity of heart, whereby we rejoice with those who rejoice, and weep with those who weep. These things are learned by desiring to learn them.

24. By perfectly concentrated Meditation on power, even such power as that of the elephant may be gained.

This is a pretty image. Elephants possess not only force, but poise and fineness of control. They can lift a straw, a child, a tree with perfectly judged control and effort. So the simile is a good one. By detachment, by withdrawing into the soul's reservoir of power, we can gain all these, force and fineness and poise; the ability to handle with equal mastery things small and great, concrete and abstract alike.

25. By bending upon them the awakened inner light, there comes a knowledge of things subtle, or concealed, or obscure.

As was said at the outset, each consciousness is related to all consciousness; and, through it, has a potential consciousness of all things; whether subtle or concealed or obscure. An understanding of this great truth will come with practice. As one of the wise has said, we have no conception of the power of Meditation.

26. By perfectly concentrated Meditation on the sun comes a knowledge of the worlds.

This has several meanings: First, by a knowledge of the constitution of the sun, astronomers can understand the kindred nature of the stars. And it is said that there is a finer astronomy, where the spiritual man is the astronomer. But the sun also means the Soul, and through knowledge of the Soul comes a knowledge of the realms of life.

27. By perfectly concentrated Meditation on the moon comes a knowledge of the lunar mansions.

Here again are different meanings. The moon is, first, the companion planet, which, each day, passes backward through one mansion of the stars. By watching the moon, the boundaries of the mansion are learned, with their succession in the great time-dial of the sky. But the moon also symbolizes the analytic mind, with its divided realms; and these, too, may be understood through perfectly concentrated Meditation.

28. By perfectly concentrated Meditation on the fixed pole-star comes a knowledge of the motions of the stars.

Addressing Duty, stern daughter of the Voice of God, Wordsworth finely said:

Thou cost preserve the stars from wrong,
And the most ancient heavens through thee are fresh and strong—

thus suggesting a profound relation between the moral powers and the powers that rule the worlds. So in this Sutra the fixed polestar is the eternal spirit about which all things move, as well as the star toward which points the axis of the earth. Deep mysteries attend both, and the veil of mystery is only to be raised by Meditation, by open-eyed vision of the awakened spiritual man.

29. Perfectly concentrated Meditation on the centre of force in the lower trunk brings an understanding of the order of the bodily powers.

We are coming to a vitally important part of the teaching of Yoga: namely, the spiritual man's attainment of full self-consciousness, the awakening of the spiritual man as a self-conscious individual, behind and above the natural man. In this awakening, and in the process of gestation which precedes it, there is a close relation with the powers of the natural man, which are, in a certain sense, the projection, outward and downward, of the powers of the spiritual man. This is notably true of that creative power of the spiritual man which, when embodied in the natural man, becomes the power of generation. Not only is this power the cause of the continuance of the bodily race of mankind, but further, in the individual, it is the key to the dominance of the personal life. Rising, as it were, through the life-channels of the body, it flushes the personality with physical force, and maintains and colours the illusion that the physical life is the dominant and all-important expression of life. In due time, when the spiritual man has begun to take form, the creative force will be drawn off, and become operative in building the body of the spiritual man, just as it has been operative in the building of physical bodies, through generation in the natural world.

Perfectly concentrated Meditation on the nature of this force means, first, that rising of the consciousness into the spiritual world, already described, which gives the one sure foothold for Meditation; and then, from that spiritual point of vantage, not only an insight into the creative force, in its spiritual and physical aspects, but also a gradually attained control of this wonderful force, which will mean its direction to the body of the spiritual man, and its gradual withdrawal from the body of the natural man, until the over-pressure, so general and such a fruitful source of misery in our day, is abated, and purity takes the place of passion. This over pressure, which is the cause of so many evils and so much of human shame, is an abnormal, not a natural, condition. It is primarily due to spiritual blindness, to blindness regarding the spiritual man, and ignorance even of his existence; for by this blind ignorance are closed the channels through which, were they open, the creative force could flow into the body of the spiritual man, there building up an immortal vesture. There is no cure for blindness, with its consequent over-pressure and attendant misery and shame, but spiritual vision, spiritual aspiration, sacrifice, the new birth from above. There is no other way to lighten the burden, to lift the misery and shame from human life. Therefore, let us follow after sacrifice and aspiration, let us seek the light. In this way only shall we gain that insight into the order of the bodily powers, and that mastery of them, which this Sutra implies.

30. By perfectly concentrated Meditation on the centre of force in the well of the throat, there comes the cessation of hunger and thirst.

We are continuing the study of the bodily powers and centres of force in their relation to the powers and forces of the spiritual man. We have already considered the dominant power of physical life, the creative power which secures the continuance of physical life; and, further, the manner in which, through aspiration and sacrifice, it is gradually raised and set to the work

63

of upbuilding the body of the spiritual man. We come now to the dominant psychic force, the power which manifests itself in speech, and in virtue of which the voice may carry so much of the personal magnetism, endowing the orator with a tongue of fire, magical in its power to arouse and rule the emotions of his hearers. This emotional power, this distinctively psychical force, is the cause of 'hunger and thirst,' the psychical hunger and thirst for sensations, which is the source of our two-sided life of emotionalism, with its hopes and fears, its expectations and memories, its desires and hates. The source of this psychical power, or, perhaps we should say, its centre of activity in the physical body is said to be in the cavity of the throat. Thus, in the Taittirîya Upanishad it is written: 'There is this shining ether in the inner being. Therein is the spiritual man, formed through thought, immortal, golden. Inward, in the palate, the organ that hangs down like a nipple,—this is the womb of Indra. And there, where the dividing of the hair turns, extending upward to the crown of the head.'

Indra is the name given to the creative power of which we have spoken, and which, we are told, resides in 'the organ which hangs down like a nipple, inward, in the palate.'

31. By perfectly concentrated Meditation on the centre of force in the channel called the 'tortoise-formed,' comes steadfastness.

We are concerned now with the centre of nervous or psychical force below the cavity of the throat, in the chest, in which is felt the sensation of fear; the centre, the disturbance of which sets the heart beating miserably with dread, or which produces that sense of terror through which the heart is said to stand still.

When the truth concerning fear is thoroughly mastered, through spiritual insight into the immortal, fearless life, then this force is perfectly controlled; there is no more fear, just as, through the control of the psychic power which works through the nerve-centre in the throat, there comes a cessation of 'hunger and thirst.' Thereafter, these forces, or their spiritual prototypes, are turned to the building of the spiritual man.

64

Always, it must be remembered, the victory is first a spiritual one; only later does it bring control of the bodily powers.

32. Through perfectly concentrated Meditation on the light in the head comes the vision of the Masters who have attained.

The tradition is, that there is a certain centre of force in the head, perhaps the 'pineal gland,' which some of our Western philosophers have supposed to be the dwelling of the soul,-a centre which is, as it were, the door way between the natural and the spiritual man. It is the seat of that better and wiser consciousness behind the outward looking consciousness in the forward part of the head; that better and wiser consciousness of 'the back of the mind,' which views spiritual things, and seeks to impress the spiritual view on the outward looking consciousness in the forward part of the head. It is the spiritual man seeking to guide the natural man, seeking to bring the natural man to concern himself with the things of his immortality. This is suggested in the words of the Upanishad already quoted: 'There, where the dividing of the hair turns, extending upward to the crown of the head'; all of which may sound very fantastical, until one comes to understand it.

It is said that when this power is fully awakened, it brings a vision of the great Companions of the spiritual man, those who have already attained, crossing over to the further shore of the sea of death and rebirth. Perhaps it is to this divine sight that the Master alluded, who is reported to have said: 'I counsel you to buy of me eye-salve, that you may see.' It is of this same vision of the great Companions, the children of light, that a seer wrote:

Though inland far we be,
Our souls have sight of that immortal sea
Which brought us hither,
Can in a moment travel thither,
And see the Children sport upon the shore
And hear the mighty waters rolling evermore.

33. Or through the divining power of tuition he knows all things.

This is really the supplement, the spiritual side, of the Sutra just translated. Step by step, as the better consciousness, the spiritual view, gains force in the back of the mind, so, in the same measure, the spiritual man is gaining the power to see: learning to open the spiritual eyes. When the eyes are fully opened, the spiritual man beholds the great Companions standing about him; he has begun to 'know all things.'

This divining power of intuition is the power which lies above and behind the so-called rational mind; the rational mind formulates a question and lays it before the intuition, which gives a real answer, often immediately distorted by the rational mind, yet always embodying a kernel of truth. It is by this process, through which the rational mind brings questions to the intuition for solution, that the truths of science are reached, the flashes of discovery and genius. But this higher power need not work in subordination to the so-called rational mind, it may act directly, as full illumination, 'the vision and the faculty divine.'

34 By perfectly concentrated Meditation on the heart, the interior being, comes the knowledge of consciousness.

The heart here seems to mean, as it so often. does in the Upanishads, the interior, spiritual nature, the consciousness of the spiritual man, which is related to the heart, and to the wisdom of the heart. By steadily seeking after, and finding, the consciousness of the spiritual man, by coming to consciousness as the spiritual man, a perfect knowledge of consciousness will be attained. For the consciousness of the spiritual man has this divine quality: while being and remaining a truly individual consciousness, it at the same time flows over, as it were, and blends with the Divine Consciousness above and about it, the consciousness of the great Companions; and by showing itself to be one with the Divine Consciousness, it reveals the nature of all consciousness, the secret that all consciousness is One and Divine.

35. The personal self seeks to feast on life, through a failure to perceive the distinction between the personal self and the spiritual man. All personal experience really exists for the sake of another: namely, the spiritual man.

By perfectly concentrated Meditation on experience for the sake of the Self, comes a knowledge of the spiritual man.

The divine ray of the Higher Self, which is eternal, impersonal and abstract, descends into life, and forms a personality, which, through the stress and storm of life, is hammered into a definite and concrete self-conscious individuality. The problem is, to blend these two powers, taking the eternal and spiritual being of the first, and blending with it, transferring into it, the self-conscious individuality of the second; and thus bringing to life a third being, the spiritual man, who is heir to the immortality of his father, the Higher Self, and yet has the self-conscious, concrete individuality of his other parent, the personal self. This is the true immaculate conception, the new birth from above, 'conceived of the Holy Spirit.' Of this new birth it is said: 'that which is born of the Spirit is spirit; ye must be born again.'

Rightly understood, therefore, the whole life of the personal man is for another, not for himself. He exists only to render his very life and all his experience for the building up of the spiritual man. Only through failure to see this, does he seek enjoyment for himself, seek to secure the feasts of life for himself; not understanding that he must live for the other, live sacrificially, offering both feasts and his very being on the altar; giving himself as a contribution for the building of the spiritual man. When he does understand this, and lives for the Higher Self, setting his heart and thought on the Higher Self, then his sacrifice bears divine fruit, the spiritual man is built up, consciousness awakes in him, and he comes fully into being as a divine and immortal individuality.

36. Thereupon are born the divine power of intuition, and the hearing, the touch, the vision, the taste and the power of smell of the spiritual man.

67

When, in virtue of the perpetual sacrifice of the personal man, daily and hourly giving his life for his divine brother the spiritual man, and through the radiance ever pouring down from the Higher Self, eternal in the Heavens, the spiritual man comes to birth,—there awake in him those powers whose physical counterparts we know in the personal man. The spiritual man begins to see, to hear, to touch, to taste. And, besides the senses of the spiritual man, there awakes his mind, that divine counterpart of the mind of the physical man, the power of direct and immediate knowledge, the power of spiritual intuition, of divination. This power, as we have seen, owes its virtue to the unity, the continuity, of consciousness, whereby whatever is known to any consciousness, is knowable by any other consciousness. Thus the consciousness of the spiritual man, who lives above our narrow barriers of separateness, is in intimate touch with the consciousness of the great Companions, and can draw on that vast reservoir for all real needs. Thus arises within the spiritual man that certain knowledge which is called intuition, divination, illumination.

37. These powers stand in contradistinction to the highest spiritual vision. In manifestation they are called magical powers.

The divine man is destined to supersede the spiritual man, as the spiritual man supersedes the natural man. Then the disciple becomes a Master. The opened powers of tile spiritual man, spiritual vision, hearing, and touch, stand, therefore, in contradistinction to the higher divine power above them, and must in no wise be regarded as the end of the way, for the path has no end, but rises ever to higher and higher glories; the soul's growth and splendour have no limit. So that, if the spiritual powers we have been considering are regarded as in any sense final, they are a hindrance, a barrier to the far higher powers of the divine man. But viewed from below, from the standpoint of normal physical experience, they are powers truly magical; as the powers natural to a four-dimensional being will appear magical to a three-dimensional being.

38. Through the weakening of the causes of bondage, and by learning the method of passing, the consciousness is transferred to the other body.

In due time, after the spiritual man has been formed and grown stable through the forces and virtues already enumerated, and after the senses of the spiritual man have awaked, there comes the transfer of the dominant consciousness, the sense of individuality, from the physical to the spiritual man. Thereafter the physical man is felt to be a secondary, a subordinate, an instrument through whom the spiritual man works; and the spiritual man is felt to be the real individuality. This is, in a sense, the attainment to full salvation and immortal life; yet it is not the final goal or resting place, but only the beginning of the greater way.

The means for this transfer are described as the weakening of the causes of bondage, and an understanding of the method of passing from the one consciousness to the other. The first may also be described as detachment, and comes from the conquest of the delusion that the personal self is the real man. When that delusion abates and is held in check, the finer consciousness of the spiritual man begins to shine in the background of the mind. The transfer of the sense of individuality to this finer consciousness, and thus to the spiritual man, then becomes a matter of recollection, of attention; primarily, a matter of taking a deeper interest in the life and doings of the spiritual man, than in the pleasures or occupations of the personality. Therefore it is said: 'Lay not up for yourselves treasures upon earth, where moth and rust cloth corrupt, and where thieves break through and steal: but lay up for yourselves treasures in heaven, where neither moth nor rust cloth corrupt, and where thieves do not break through nor steal: for where your treasure is, there will your heart be also.'

39. Through mastery of the upward-life comes freedom from the dangers of water, morass, and thorny places, and the power of ascension is gained.

Here is one of the sentences, so characteristic of this author, and, indeed, of the Eastern spirit, in which there is an obvious exterior meaning, and, within this, a clear interior meaning, not quite so obvious, but far more vital.

The surface meaning is, that by mastery of a certain power, called here the upward-life, and akin to levitation, there comes the ability to walk on water, or to pass over thorny places without wounding the feet.

But there is a deeper meaning. When we speak of the disciple's path as a path of thorns, we use a symbol; and the same symbol is used here. The upward-life means something more than the power, often manifested in abnormal psychical experiences, of levitating the physical body, or near-by physical objects. It means the strong power of aspiration, of upward will, which first builds, and then awakes the spiritual man, and finally transfers the conscious individuality to him; for it is he who passes safely over the waters of death and rebirth, and is not pierced by the thorns in the path. Therefore it is said that he who would tread the path of power must look for a home in the air, and afterwards in the ether.

Of the upward-life, this is written in the Katha Upanishad: 'A hundred and one are the heart's channels; of these one passes to the crown. Going up this, he comes to the immortal.' This is the power of ascension spoken of in the Sutra.

40. By mastery of the binding-life comes radiance.

In the Upanishads, it is said that this binding-life unites the upward-life to the downward-life, and these lives have their analogies in the 'vital breaths' in the body. The thought in the text seems to be, that, when the personality is brought thoroughly under control of the spiritual man, through the life-currents which bind them together, the personality is endowed with a new force, a strong personal magnetism, one might call it, such as is often an appanage of genius.

70

But the text seems to mean more than this and to have in view the 'vesture of the colour of the sun' attributed by the Upanishads to the spiritual man; that vesture which a disciple has thus described: 'The Lord shall change our vile body, that it may be fashioned like unto his glorious body'; perhaps 'body of radiance' would better translate the Greek.

In both these passages, the teaching seems to be, that the body of the full-grown spiritual man is radiant or luminous,—for those at least, who have anointed their eyes with eye-salve, so that they see.

41. From perfectly concentrated Meditation on the correlation of hearing and the ether, comes the power of spiritual hearing.

Physical sound, we are told, is carried by the air, or by water, iron, or some medium on the same plane of substance. But then is a finer hearing, whose medium of transmission would seem to be the ether; perhaps no that ether which carries light, heat and magnetic waves, but, it may be, the far finer ether through which the power of gravity works. For, while light or heat or magnetic waves, travelling from the sun to the earth, take eight minutes for the journey, it is mathematically certain that the pull of gravitation does not take as much as eight seconds, or even the eighth of a second. The pull of gravitation travels, it would seem 'as quick as thought'; so it may well be that, in thought transference or telepathy, the thoughts travel by the same way, carried by the same 'thought-swift' medium.

The transfer of a word by telepathy is the simplest and earliest form of the 'divine hearing' of the spiritual man; as that power grows, and as, through perfectly concentrated Meditation, the spiritual man comes into more complete mastery of it, he grows able to hear and clearly distinguish the speech of the great Companions, who counsel and comfort him on his way. They may speak to him either in wordless thoughts, or in perfectly definite words and sentences.

42. By perfectly concentrated Meditation on the correlation of the body with the ether, and by thinking of it as light as thistle-down, will come the power to traverse the ether.

It has been said that he who would tread the path of power must look for a home in the air, and afterwards in the ether. This would seem to mean, besides the constant injunction to detachment, that he must be prepared to inhabit first a psychic, and then an etheric body; the former being the body of dreams; the latter, the body of the spiritual man, when he wakes up on the other side of dreamland. The gradual accustoming of the consciousness to its new etheric vesture, its gradual acclimatization, so to speak, in the etheric body of the spiritual man, is what our text seems to contemplate.

43. When that condition of consciousness s reached, which is far-reaching and not confined to the body, which is outside the body and not conditioned by it, then the veil which conceals the light is worn away.

Perhaps the best comment on this is afforded by the words of Paul: 'I knew a man in Christ above fourteen years ago, (whether in the body, I cannot tell; or whether out of the body, I cannot tell: God knoweth;) such a one caught up to the third heaven. And I knew such a man, (whether in the body, or out of the body, I cannot tell: God knoweth;) how that he was caught up into paradise, and heard unspeakable [or, unspoken] words, which it is not lawful for a man to utter.'

The condition is, briefly, that of the awakened spiritual man, who sees and hears beyond the veil.

44. Mastery of the elements comes from perfectly concentrated Meditation on their five forms: the gross, the elemental, the subtle, the inherent, the purposive.

These five forms are analogous to those recognized by modern physics: solid, liquid, gaseous, radiant and ionic. When the piercing vision of the awakened spiritual man is directed to the

72

forms of matter, from within, as it were, from behind the scenes, then perfect mastery over the 'beggarly elements' is attained. This is, perhaps, equivalent to the injunction: 'Inquire of the earth, the air, and the water, of the secrets they hold for you. The development of your inner senses will enable you to do this.'

45. Thereupon will come the manifestation of the atomic and other powers, which are the endowment of the body, together with its unassailable force.

The body in question is, of course, the etheric body of the spiritual man. He is said to possess eight powers: the atomic, the power of assimilating himself with the nature of the atom, which will, perhaps, involve the power to disintegrate material forms; the power of levitation; the power of limitless extension; the power of boundless reach, so that, as the commentator says, 'he can touch the moon with the tip of his finger'; the power to accomplish his will; the power of gravitation, the correlative of levitation; the power of command; the power of creative will. These are the endowments of the spiritual man. Further, the spiritual body is unassailable. Fire burns it not, water wets it not, the sword cleaves it not, dry winds parch it not. And, it is said, the spiritual man can impart something of this quality and temper to his bodily vesture.

46. Shapeliness, beauty, force, the temper of the diamond: these are the endowments of that body.

The spiritual man is shapely, beautiful strong, firm as the diamond. Therefore it is written: 'These things saith the Son of God, who hath his eyes like unto a flame of fire, and his feet are like fine brass: He that overcometh and keepeth my works unto the end, to him will I give power over the nations: and he shall rule them with a rod of iron; and I will give him the morning star.'

47. Mastery over the powers of perception and action comes through perfectly concentrated Meditation on their fivefold forms; namely, their power to grasp their distinctive nature, the

element of self-consciousness in them, their inherence, and their purposiveness.

Take, for example, sight. This possesses, first, the power to grasp, apprehend, perceive; second, it has its distinctive form of perception; that is, visual perception; third, it always carries with its operations self-consciousness, the thought: 'I perceive'; fourth sight has the power of extension through the whole field of vision, even to the utmost star; fifth, it is used for the purposes of the Seer. So with the other senses. Perfectly concentrated Meditation on each sense, a viewing it from behind and within, as is possible for the spiritual man, brings a mastery of the scope and true character of each sense, and of the world on which they report collectively.

48. Thence comes the power swift as thought, independent of instruments, and the mastery over matter.

We are further enumerating the endowments of the spiritual man. Among these is the power to traverse space with the swiftness of thought, so that whatever place the spiritual man thinks of, to that he goes, in that place he already is. Thought has now become his means of locomotion. He is, therefore, independent of instruments, and can bring his force to bear directly, wherever he wills.

49. When the spiritual man is perfectly disentangled from the psychic body, he attains to mastery over all things and to a knowledge of all.

The spiritual man is enmeshed in the web of the emotions; desire, fear, ambition, passion; and impeded by the mental forms of separateness and materialism. When these meshes are sundered, these obstacles completely overcome, then the spiritual man stands forth in his own wide world, strong, mighty, wise. He uses divine powers, with a divine scope and energy, working together with divine Companions. To such a one it is said: 'Thou art now a disciple, able to stand, able to hear, able to see, able to speak, thou hast conquered desire and attained to self-knowledge, thou hast seen thy soul in its bloom and recognized it, and heard the voice of the silence.'

50. By absence of all self-indulgence at this point, when the seeds of bondage to sorrow are destroyed, pure spiritual being is attained.

The seeking of indulgence for the personal self, whether through passion or ambition, sows the seed of future sorrow. For this self indulgence of the personality is a double sin against the real; a sin against the cleanness of life, and a sin against the universal being, which permits no exclusive particular good, since, in the real, all spiritual possessions are held in common. This twofold sin brings its reacting punishment, its confining bondage to sorrow. But ceasing from self-indulgence brings purity, liberation, spiritual life.

51. There should be complete overcoming of allurement or pride in the invitations of the different realms of life, lest attachment to things evil arise once more.

The commentator tells us that disciples, seekers for union, are of four degrees: first, those who are entering the path; second, those who are in the realm of allurements; third, those who have won the victory over matter and the senses; fourth, those who stand firm in pure spiritual life. To the second, especially, the caution in the text is addressed. More modern teachers would express the same truth by a warning against the delusions and fascinations of the psychic realm, which open around the disciple, as he breaks through into the unseen worlds. These are the dangers of the anteroom. Safety lies in passing on swiftly into the inner chamber. 'Him that overcometh will I make a pillar in the temple of my God, and he shall go no more out.'

52. From perfectly concentrated Meditation on the divisions of time and their succession comes that wisdom which is born of discernment.

The Upanishads say of the liberated that 'he has passed beyond the triad of time'; he no longer sees life as projected into past, present and future, since these are forms of the mind; but beholds all things spread out in the quiet light of the Eternal. This would seem to be the same thought, and to point to that clear-eyed spiritual perception which is above time; that wisdom born of the unveiling of Time's delusion. Then shall the disciple live neither in the present nor the future, but in the Eternal.

53. Hence comes discernment between things which are of like nature, not distinguished by difference of kind, character or position.

Here, as also in the preceding Sutra, we are close to the doctrine that distinctions of order, time and space are creations of the mind; the threefold prism through which the real object appears to us distorted and refracted. When the prism is withdrawn, the object returns to its primal unity, no longer distinguishable by the mind, yet clearly knowable by that high power of spiritual discernment, of illumination, which is above the mind.

54. The wisdom which is born of discernment is starlike; it discerns all things, and all conditions of things, it discerns without succession: simultaneously.

That wisdom, that intuitive, divining power is starlike, says the commentator, because it shines with its own light, because it rises on high, and illumines all things. Nought is hid from it, whether things past, things present, or things to come; for it is beyond the threefold form of time, so that all things are spread before it together, in the single light of the divine. This power has been beautifully described by Columba: 'Some there are, though very few, to whom Divine grace has granted this: that they can clearly and most distinctly see, at one and the same moment, as though under one ray of the sun, even the entire circuit of the whole world with its surroundings of ocean and sky, the inmost part of their mind being marvellously enlarged.'

76

55. When the vesture and the spiritual man are alike pure, then perfect spiritual life is attained.

The vesture, says the commentator, must first be washed pure of all stains of passion and darkness, and the seeds of future sorrow must be burned up utterly. Then, both the vesture and the wearer of the vesture being alike pure, the spiritual man enters into perfect spiritual life.

Introduction to Book IV

The third book of the Sutras has fairly completed the history of the birth and growth of the spiritual man, and the enumeration of his powers; at least so far as concerns that first epoch in his immortal life, which immediately succeeds, and supersedes, the life of the natural man.

In the fourth book, we are to consider what one might call the mechanism of salvation, the ideally simple working of cosmic law which brings the spiritual man to birth, growth, and fulness of power, and prepares him for the splendid, toilsome further stages of his great journey home.

The Sutras are here brief to obscurity; only a few words, for example, are given to the great triune mystery and illusion of Time; a phrase or two indicates the sweep of some universal law. Yet it is hoped that, by keeping our eyes fixed on the spiritual man, remembering that he is the hero of the story, and that all that is written concerns him and his adventures, we may be able to find our way through this thicket of tangled words, and keep in our hands the clue to the mystery.

The last part of the last book needs little introduction. In a sense, it is the most important part of the whole treatise, since it unmasks the nature of the personality, that psychical 'mind,' which is the wakeful enemy of all who seek to tread the path. Even now, we can hear it whispering the doubt whether that can be a good path, which thus sets 'mind' at defiance.

If this, then, be the most vital and fundamental part of the teaching, should it not stand at the very beginning? It may seem so at first; but had it stood there, we should not have comprehended it. For he who would know the doctrine must lead the life, doing the will of his Father which is in Heaven.

Book IV

1. Psychic and spiritual powers may be inborn, or they may be gained by the use of drugs, or by incantations, or by fervour, or by Meditation.

Spiritual powers have been enumerated and described in the preceding sections. They are the normal powers of the spiritual man, the antetype, the divine edition, of the powers of the natural man. Through these powers, the spiritual man stands, sees, hears, speaks, in the spiritual world, as the physical man stands, sees, hears, speaks in the natural world.

There is a counterfeit presentment of the spiritual man, in the world of dreams, a shadow lord of shadows, who has his own dreamy powers of vision, of hearing, of movement; he has left the natural without reaching the spiritual. He has set forth from the shore, but has not gained the further verge of the river. He is borne along by the stream, with no foothold on either shore. Leaving the actual, he has fallen short of the real, caught in the limbo of vanities and delusions. The cause of this aberrant phantasm is always the worship of a false, vain self, the lord of dreams, within one's own breast. This is the psychic man, lord of delusive and bewildering psychic powers.

Spiritual powers, like intellectual or artistic gifts, may be inborn: the fruit, that is, of seeds planted and reared with toil in a former birth. So also the powers of the psychic man may be inborn, a delusive harvest from seeds of delusion.

Psychical powers may be gained by drugs, as poverty, shame, debasement may be gained by the self-same drugs. In their action, they are baneful, cutting the man off from consciousness of the restraining power of his divine nature, so that his forces break forth exuberant, like the laughter of drunkards, and he sees and hears things delusive. While sinking, he believes that he has risen; growing weaker, he thinks himself full of strength; beholding illusions, he takes them to be true. Such are the powers gained by drugs; they are wholly psychic, since the real powers, the spiritual, can never be so gained.

Incantations are affirmations of half-truths concerning spirit and matter, what is and what is not, which work upon the mind and slowly build up a wraith of powers and a delusive well-being. These, too, are of the psychic realm of dreams.

Lastly, there are the true powers of the spiritual man, built up and realized in Meditation, through reverent obedience to spiritual law, to the pure conditions of being, in the divine realm.

2. The transfer of powers from one venture to another comes through the flow of the natural creative forces.

Here, if we can perceive it, is the whole secret of spiritual birth, growth and life Spiritual being, like all being, is but an expression of the Self, of the inherent power and being of Atma. Inherent in the Self are consciousness and will, which have, as their lordly heritage, the wide sweep of the universe throughout eternity, for the Self is one with the Eternal. And the consciousness of the Self may make itself manifest as seeing, hearing, tasting, feeling, or whatsoever perceptive powers there may be, just as the white sunlight may divide into many-coloured rays. So may the will of the Self manifest itself in the uttering of words, or in handling, or in moving, and whatever powers of action there are throughout the seven worlds. Where the Self is, there will its powers be. It is but a question of the vesture through which these powers shall shine forth. And wherever the consciousness and desire of the ever-creative Self are fixed, there will a vesture be built up; where the heart is, there will the treasure be also.

Since through ages the desire of the Self has been toward the natural world, wherein the Self sought to mirror himself that he might know himself, therefore a vesture of natural elements came into being, through which blossomed forth the Self's powers of perceiving and of will: the power to see, to hear, to speak, to walk, to handle; and when the Self, thus come to self-consciousness, and, with it, to a knowledge of his imprisonment, shall set his desire on the divine and real world, and raise his consciousness thereto, the spiritual vesture shall be built up for him there, with its expression of his inherent powers. Nor will migration thither be difficult for the Self, since the divine is no strange or foreign land for him, but the house of his home, where he dwells from everlasting.

3. The apparent, immediate cause is not the true cause of the creative nature-powers; but, like the husbandman in his field, it takes obstacles away.

The husbandman tills his field, breaking up the clods of earth into fine mould, penetrable to air and rain; he sows his seed, carefully covering it, for fear of birds and the wind; he waters the seed-laden earth, turning the little rills from the irrigation tank now this way and that, removing obstacles from the channels, until the even How of water vitalizes the whole field. And so the plants germinate and grow, first the blade, then the ear, then the full corn in the ear. But it is not the husbandman who makes them grow. It is, first, the miraculous plasmic power in the grain of seed, which brings forth after its kind; then the alchemy of sunlight which, in presence of the green colouring matter of the leaves, gathers hydrogen from the water and carbon from the gases in the air, and mingles them in the hydro-carbons of plant growth; and, finally, the wholly occult vital powers of the plant itself, stored up through ages, and flowing down from the primal sources of life. The husbandman but removes the obstacles. He plants and waters, but God gives the increase.

So with the finer husbandman of diviner fields. He tills and sows, but the growth of the spiritual man comes through the surge and flow of divine, creative forces and powers. Here, again, God gives the increase. The divine Self puts forth, for the manifestation of its powers, a new and finer vesture, the body of the spiritual man.

4. Vestures of consciousness are built up in conformity with the Boston of the feeling of selfhood.

The Self, says a great Teacher, in turn attributes itself to three vestures: first, to the physical body, then to the finer body, and thirdly to the causal body. Finally it stands forth radiant, luminous, joyous, as the Self.

When the Self attributes itself to the physical body, there arise the states of bodily consciousness, built up about the physical self.

When the Self, breaking through this first illusion, begins to see and feel itself in the finer body, to find selfhood there, then the states of consciousness of the finer body come into being; or, to speak exactly, the finer body and its states of consciousness arise and grow together.

But the Self must not dwell permanently there. It must learn to find itself in the causal body, to build up the wide and luminous fields of consciousness that belong to that.

Nor must it dwell forever there, for there remains the fourth state, the divine, with its own splendour and everlastingness.

It is all a question of the states of consciousness; all a question of raising the sense of selfhood, until it dwells forever in the Eternal.

5. In the different fields of manifestation, the Consciousness, though one, is the elective cause of many states of consciousness.

Here is the splendid teaching of oneness that lies at the heart of the Eastern wisdom. Consciousness is ultimately One, everywhere and forever. The Eternal, the Father, is the One Self of All Beings. And so, in each individual who is but a facet of that Self, Consciousness is One. Whether it breaks through as the dull fire of physical life, or the murky flame of the psychic and passional, or the radiance of the spiritual man, or the full glory of the Divine, it is ever the Light, naught but the Light. The one Consciousness is the effective cause of all states of consciousness, on every plane.

6. Among states of consciousness, that which is born of Contemplation is free from the seed of future sorrow.

Where the consciousness breaks forth in the physical body, and the full play of bodily life begins, its progression carries with it inevitable limitations. Birth involves death. Meetings have their partings. Hunger alternates with satiety. Age follows on the heels of youth. So do the states of consciousness run along the circle of birth and death.

With the psychic, the alternation between prize and penalty is swifter. Hope has its shadow of fear, or it is no hope. Exclusive love is tortured by jealousy. Pleasure passes through deadness into pain. Pain's surcease brings pleasure back again. So here, too, the states of consciousness run their circle. In all psychic states there is egotism, which, indeed, is the very essence of the psychic; and where there is egotism there is ever the seed of future sorrow. Desire carries bondage in its womb.

But where the pure spiritual consciousness begins, free from self and stain, the ancient law of retaliation ceases; the penalty of sorrow lapses and is no more imposed. The soul now passes, no longer from sorrow to sorrow, but from glory to glory. Its growth and splendour have no limit. The good passes to better, best.

82

7. The works of followers after Union make neither for bright pleasure nor for dark pain The works of others make for pleasure or pain, or a mingling of these.

The man of desire wins from his works the reward of pleasure, or incurs the penalty of pain; or, as so often happens in life, his guerdon, like the passionate mood of the lover, is part pleasure and part pain. Works done with self-seeking bear within them the seeds of future sorrow; conversely, according to the proverb, present pain is future gain.

But, for him who has gone beyond desire, whose desire is set on the Eternal, neither pain to be avoided nor pleasure to be gained inspires his work. He fears no hell and desires no heaven. His one desire is, to know the will of the Father and finish His work. He comes directly in line with the divine Will, and works cleanly and immediately, without longing or fear. His heart dwells in the Eternal; all his desires are set on the Eternal.

8. From the force inherent in works comes the manifestation of those dynamic mind images which are conformable to the ripening out of each of these works.

We are now to consider the general mechanism of Karma, in order that we may pass on to the consideration of him who is free from Karma. Karma, indeed, is the concern of the personal man, of his bondage or freedom. It is the succession of the forces which built up the personal man, reproducing themselves in one personality after another.

Now let us take an imaginary case, to see how these forces may work out. Let us think of a man, with murderous intent in his heart, striking with a dagger at his enemy. He makes a red wound in his victim's breast; at the same instant he paints, in his own mind, a picture of that wound: a picture dynamic with all the fierce will-power he has put into his murderous blow. In other words he has made a deep wound in his own psychic body; and, when he comes to be born again, that body will become his outermost vesture, upon which, with its wound still there, bodily tissue will be built up. So the man will be born maimed, or with the predisposition to some mortal injury; he is unguarded at that point, and any trifling accidental blow will pierce the broken Joints of his psychic armour. Thus do the dynamic mind-images manifest themselves, coming to the surface, so that works done in the past may ripen and come to fruition.

9. Works separated by different nature, or place, or time, are brought together by the correspondence between memory and dynamic impression.

Just as, in the ripening out of mind-images into bodily conditions, the effect is brought about by the ray of creative force sent down by the Self, somewhat as the light of the magic lantern projects the details of a picture on the screen, revealing the hidden, and making secret things palpable and visible, so does this divine ray exercise a selective power on the dynamic mind-images, bringing together into one day of life the seeds gathered from many days. The memory constantly exemplifies this power; a passage of poetry will call up in the mind like passages of many poets, read at different times. So a prayer may call up many prayers.

In like manner, the same over-ruling selective power, which is a ray of the Higher Self, gathers together from different births and times and places those mind-images which are conformable, and may be grouped in the frame of a single life or a single event. Through this grouping, visible bodily conditions or outward circumstances are brought about, and by these the soul is taught and trained.

Just as the dynamic mind-images of desire ripen out in bodily conditions and circumstances, so the far more dynamic powers of aspiration, wherein the soul reaches toward the Eternal, have their fruition in a finer world, building the vesture of the spiritual man.

10. The series of dynamic mind-images is beginningless, because Desire is everlasting.

84

The whole series of dynamic mind-images, which make up the entire history of the personal man, is a part of the mechanism which the Self employs, to mirror itself in a reflection, to embody its powers in an outward form, to the end of self-expression, self-realization, self-knowledge. Therefore the initial impulse behind these dynamic mind-images comes from the Self and is the descending ray of the Self; so that it cannot be said that there is any first member of the series of images, from which the rest arose. The impulse is beginningless, since it comes from the Self, which is from everlasting. Desire is not to cease; it is to turn to the Eternal, and so become aspiration.

11. Since the dynamic mind-images are held together by impulses of desire, by the wish for personal reward, by the substratum of mental habit, by the support of outer things desired; therefore, when these cease, the self reproduction of dynamic mind-images ceases.

We are still concerned with the personal life in its bodily vesture, and with the process whereby the forces which have upheld it are gradually transferred to the life of the spiritual man, and build up for him his finer vesture in a finer world.

How is the current to be changed? How is the flow of self-reproductive mind-images, which have built the conditions of life after life in this world of bondage, to be checked, that the time of imprisonment may come to an end, the day of liberation dawn?

The answer is given in the Sutra just translated. The driving-force is withdrawn and directed to the upbuilding of the spiritual body.

When the building impulses and forces are withdrawn, the tendency to manifest a new psychical body, a new body of bondage, ceases with them.

12. The difference between that which is past and that which is not yet come, according to their natures, depends on the difference of phase of their properties.

Here we come to a high and difficult matter, which has always been held to be of great moment in the Eastern wisdom: the thought that the division of time into past, present and future is, in great measure, an illusion; that past, present, future all dwell together in the eternal Now.

The discernment of this truth has been held to be so necessarily a part of wisdom, that one of the names of the Enlightened is: 'he who has passed beyond the three times: past, present, future.'

So the Western Master said: 'Before Abraham was, I am'; and again, 'I am with you always, unto the end of the world'; using the eternal present for past and future alike. With the same purpose, the Master speaks of himself as 'the alpha and the omega, the beginning and the end, the first and the last.'

And a Master of our own days writes: 'I feel even irritated at having to use these three clumsy words—past, present, and future. Miserable concepts of the objective phases of the subjective whole, they are about as ill adapted for the purpose, as an axe for fine carving.'

In the eternal Now, both past and future are consummated.

Björklund, the Swedish philosopher, has well stated the same truth:

'Neither past nor future can exist to God; He lives undividedly, without limitations, and needs not, as man, to plot out his existence in a series of moments. Eternity then is not identical with unending time; it is a different form of existence, related to time as the perfect to the imperfect. Man as an entity for himself must have the natural limitations for the part. Conceived by God, man is eternal in the divine sense, but conceived by himself, man's eternal life is clothed in the limitations we call time. The eternal is a constant present without beginning or end, without past or future.'

13. These properties, whether manifest or latent, are of the nature of the Three Potencies.

The Three Potencies are the three manifested modifications of the one primal material, which stands opposite to perceiving consciousness. These Three Potencies are called Substance, Force, Darkness; or viewed rather for their moral colouring, Goodness, Passion, Inertness. Every material manifestation is a projection of substance into the empty space of darkness. Every mental state is either good, or passional, or inert. So, whether subjective or objective, latent or manifest, all things that present themselves to the perceiving consciousness are compounded of these three. This is a fundamental doctrine of the Sankhya system.

14. The external manifestation of an object takes place when the transformations ore in the same phase.

We should be inclined to express the same law by saying, for example, that a sound is audible, when it consists of vibrations within the compass of the auditory nerve; that an object is visible, when either directly or by reflection, it sends forth luminiferous vibrations within the compass of the retina and the optic nerve. Vibrations below or above that compass make no impression at all, and the object remains invisible; as, for example, a kettle of boiling water in a dark room, though the kettle is sending forth heat vibrations closely akin to light.

So, when the vibrations of the object and those of the perceptive power are in the same phase, the external manifestation of the object takes place.

There seems to be a further suggestion that the appearance of an object in the 'present,' or its remaining hid in the 'past,' or 'future,' is likewise a question of phase, and, just as the range of vibrations perceived might be increased by the development of finer senses, so the perception of things past, and things to come, may be easy from a higher point of view.

15. The paths of material things and of states of consciousness are distinct, as is manifest from the fact that the same object may produce different impressions in different minds.

Having shown that our bodily condition and circumstances depend on Karma, while Karma depends on perception and will, the sage recognizes the fact that from this may be drawn the false deduction that material things are in no wise different from states of mind. The same thought has occurred, and still occurs, to all philosophers; and, by various reasonings, they all come to the same wise conclusion; that the material world is not made by the mood of any human mind, but is rather the manifestation of the totality of invisible Being, whether we call this Mahat, with the ancients, or Ether, with the moderns.

16. Nor do material objects defend upon a single mind, for how could they remain objective to others, if that mind ceased to think of them?

This is but a further development of the thought of the preceding Sutra, carrying on the thought that, while the universe is spiritual, yet its material expression is ordered, consistent, ruled by law, not subject to the whims or affirmations of a single mind. Unwelcome material things may be escaped by spiritual growth, by rising to a realm above them, and not by denying their existence on their own plane. So that our system is neither materialistic, nor idealistic in the extreme sense, but rather intuitional and spiritual, holding that matter is the manifestation of spirit as a whole, a reflection or externalization of spirit, and, like spirit, everywhere obedient to law. The path of liberation is not through denial of matter but through denial of the wills of self, through obedience, and that aspiration which builds the vesture of the spiritual man.

17. An object is perceived, or not perceived, according as the mind is, or is not, tinged with the colour of the object.

The simplest manifestation of this is the matter of attention. Our minds apprehend what they wish to apprehend; all else passes unnoticed, or, on the other hand, we perceive what we resent, as, for example, the noise of a passing train; while others, used to the sound, do not notice it at all.

But the deeper meaning is, that out of the vast totality of objects ever present in the universe, the mind perceives only those which conform to the hue of its Karma. The rest remain unseen, even though close at hand.

This spiritual law has been well expressed by Emerson:

'Through solidest eternal things the man finds his road as if they did not subsist, and does not once suspect their being. As soon as he needs a new object, suddenly he beholds it, and no longer attempts to pass through it, but takes another way. When he has exhausted for the time the nourishment to be drawn from any one person or thing, that object is withdrawn from his observation, and though still in his immediate neighbourhood, he does not suspect its presence. Nothing is dead. Men feign themselves dead, and endure mock funerals and mournful obituaries, and there they stand looking out of the window, sound and well, in some new and strange disguise. Jesus is not dead, he is very well alive: nor John, nor Paul, nor Mahomet, nor Aristotle; at times we believe we have seen them all, and could easily tell the names under which they go.'

18. The movements of the psychic nature are perpetually objects of perception, since the Spiritual Man, who is the lord of them, remains unchanging.

Here is teaching of the utmost import, both for understanding and for practice.

To the psychic nature belong all the ebb and flow of emotion, all hoping and fearing, desire and hate: the things that make the multitude of men and women deem themselves happy or miserable. To it also belong the measuring and comparing, the doubt and questioning, which, for the same multitude, make up mental life. So that there results the emotion-soaked personality, with its dark and narrow view of life: the shivering, terror driven personality that is life itself for all but all of mankind.

Yet the personality is not the true man, not the living soul at all, but only a spectacle which the true man observes. Let us under stand this, therefore, and draw ourselves up inwardly to the height of the Spiritual Man, who, standing in the quiet light of the Eternal, looks down serene upon this turmoil of the outer life.

One first masters the personality, the 'mind,' by thus looking down on it from above, from within; by steadily watching its ebb and flow, as objective, outward, and therefore not the real Self. This standing back is the first step, detachment. The second, to maintain the vantage-ground thus gained, is recollection.

19. The Mind is not self-luminous, since it can be seen as an object.

This is a further step toward overthrowing the tyranny of the 'mind': the psychic nature of emotion and mental measuring. This psychic self, the personality, claims to be absolute, asserting that life is for it and through it; it seeks to impose on the whole being of man its narrow, materialistic, faithless view of life and the universe; it would clip the wings of the soaring Soul. But the Soul dethrones the tyrant, by perceiving and steadily affirming that the psychic self is no true self at all, not self-luminous, but only an object of observation, watched by the serene eyes of the Spiritual Man.

20. Nor could the Mind at the same time know itself and things external to it.

The truth is that the 'mind' knows neither external things nor itself. Its measuring and analyzing, its hoping and fearing, hating and desiring, never give it a true measure of life, nor any sense of real values. Ceaselessly active, it never really attains to knowledge; or, if we admit its knowledge, it ever falls short of wisdom, which comes only through intuition, the vision of the Spiritual Man.

Life cannot be known by the 'mind,' its secrets cannot be learned through the 'mind.' The proof is, the ceaseless strife and contradiction of opinion among those who trust in the mind. Much less can the 'mind' know itself, the more so, because it is pervaded by the illusion that it truly knows, truly is.

True knowledge of the 'mind' comes, first, when the Spiritual Man, arising, stands detached, regarding the 'mind' from above, with quiet eyes, and seeing it for the tangled web of psychic forces that it truly is. But the truth is divined long before it is clearly seen, and then begins the long battle of the 'mind,' against the Real, the 'mind' fighting doggedly, craftily, for its supremacy.

21. If the Mind be thought of as seen by another more inward Mind, then there would be an endless series of perceiving Minds, and a confusion of memories.

One of the expedients by which the 'mind' seeks to deny and thwart the Soul, when it feels that it is beginning to be circumvented and seen through, is to assert that this seeing is the work of a part of itself, one part observing the other, and thus leaving no need nor place for the Spiritual Man.

To this strategy the argument is opposed by our philosopher, that this would be no true solution, but only a postponement of the solution. For we should have to find yet another part of the mind to view the first observing part, and then another to observe this, and so on, endlessly.

The true solution is, that the Spiritual Man looks down upon the psychic nature, and observes it; when he views the psychic pictures gallery, this is 'memory,' which would be a hopeless, inextricable confusion, if we thought of one part of the 'mind,' with its memories, viewing another part, with memories of its own.

The solution of the mystery lies not in the 'mind' but beyond it, in the luminous life of the risen Lord, the Spiritual Man.

22. When the psychical nature takes on the form of the spiritual intelligence, by reflecting it, then the Self becomes conscious of its own spiritual intelligence.

We are considering a stage of spiritual life at which the psychical nature has been cleansed and purified. Formerly, it reflected in its plastic substance the images of the earthy; purified now, it reflects the image of the heavenly, giving the spiritual intelligence a visible form. The Self, beholding that visible form, in which its spiritual intelligence has, as it were, taken palpable shape, thereby reaches self-recognition, self-comprehension. The Self sees itself in this mirror, and thus becomes not only conscious, but self-conscious. This is, from one point of view, the purpose of the whole evolutionary process.

23. The psychic nature, taking on the colour of the Seer and of things seen, leads to the perception of all objects.

In the unregenerate man, the psychic nature is saturated with images of material things, of things seen, or heard, or tasted, or felt; and this web of dynamic images forms the ordinary material and driving power of life. The sensation of sweet things tasted clamours to be renewed, and drives the man into effort to obtain its renewal; so he adds image to image, each dynamic and importunate, piling up sin's intolerable burden.

Then comes regeneration, and the washing away of sin, through the fiery, creative power of the Soul, which burns out the stains of the psychic vesture, purifying it as gold is refined in the furnace. The suffering of regeneration springs from this indispensable purifying.

Then the psychic vesture begins to take on the colour of the Soul, no longer stained, but suffused with golden light; and the man red generate gleams with the radiance of eternity. Thus the

Spiritual Man puts on fair raiment; for of this cleansing it is said: Though your sins be as scarlet, they shall be white as snow; though they be as crimson, they shall be as wool.

24. The psychic nature, which has been printed with mind-images of innumerable material things, exists now for the Spiritual Man, building for him.

The 'mind,' once the tyrant, is now the slave, recognized as outward, separate, not Self, a well-trained instrument of the Spiritual Man.

For it is not ordained for the Spiritual Man that, finding his high realm, he shall enter altogether there, and pass out of the vision of mankind. It is true that he dwells in heaven, but he also dwells on earth. He has angels and archangels, the hosts of the just made perfect, for his familiar friends, but he has at the same time found a new kinship with the prone children of men, who stumble and sin in the dark. Finding sinlessness, he finds also that the world's sin and shame are his, not to share, but to atone; finding kinship with angels, he likewise finds his part in the toil of angels, the toil for the redemption of the world.

For this work, he, who now stands in the heavenly realm, needs his instrument on earth; and this instrument he finds, ready to his hand, and fitted and perfected by the very struggles he has waged against it, in the personality, the 'mind,' of the personal man. This once tyrant is now his servant and perfect ambassador, bearing witness, before men, of heavenly things and even in this present world doing the will and working the works of the Father.

25. For him who discerns between the Mind and the Spiritual Man, there comes perfect fruition of the longing after the real being of the Self.

How many times in the long struggle have the Soul's aspirations seemed but a hopeless, impossible dream, a madman's counsel of perfection. Yet every finest, most impossible aspiration shall be realized, and ten times more than realized, once the long, arduous fight against the 'mind,' and the mind's worldview is won. And then it will be seen that unfaith and despair were but weapons of the 'mind,' to daunt the Soul, and put off the day when the neck of the 'mind' shall be put under the foot of the Soul.

Have you aspired, well-nigh hopeless, after immortality? You shall be paid by entering the immortality of God.

Have you aspired, in misery and pain, after consoling, healing love? You shall be made a dispenser of the divine love of God Himself to weary souls.

Have you sought ardently, in your day of feebleness, after power? You shall wield power immortal, infinite, with God working the works of God.

Have you, in lonely darkness, longed for companionship and consolation? You shall have angels and archangels for your friends, and all the immortal hosts of the Dawn.

These are the fruits of victory. Therefore overcome. These are the prizes of regeneration. Therefore die to self, that you may rise again to God.

26. Thereafter, the whole personal being bends toward illumination, toward Eternal Life.

This is part of the secret of the Soul, that salvation means, not merely that a soul shall be cleansed and raised to heaven, but that the whole realm of the natural powers shall be redeemed, building up, even in this present world, the kingly figure of the Spiritual Man.

The traditions of the ages are full of his footsteps; majestic, uncomprehended shadows, myths, demi-gods, fill the memories of all the nobler peoples. But the time cometh, when he shall be known, no longer demi-god, nor myth, nor shadow, but the ever-present Redeemer, working amid men for the life and cleansing of all souls.

27. In the internals of the batik, other thoughts will arise, through the impressions of the dynamic mind-images.

The battle is long and arduous. Let there be no mistake as to that. Go not forth to this battle without counting the cost. Ages have gone to the strengthening of the foe. Ages of conflict must be spent, ere the foe, wholly conquered, becomes the servant, the Soul's minister to mankind.

And from these long past ages, in hours when the contest flags, will come new foes, mind-born children springing up to fight for mind, reinforcements coming from forgotten years, forgotten lives. For once this conflict is begun, it can be ended only by sweeping victory, and unconditional, unreserved surrender of the vanquished.

28. These are to be overcome as it was taught that hindrances should be overcome.

These new enemies and fears are to be overcome by ceaselessly renewing the fight, by a steadfast, dogged persistence, whether in victory or defeat, which shall put the stubbornness of the rocks to shame. For the Soul is older than all things, and invincible; it is of the very nature of the Soul to be unconquerable.

Therefore fight on, undaunted; knowing that the spiritual will, once awakened, shall, through the effort of the contest, come to its full strength; that ground gained can be held permanently; that great as is the dead-weight of the adversary, it is yet measurable, while the Warrior who fights for you, for whom you fight, is, in might, immeasurable, invincible, everlasting.

29. He who, after he has attained, is wholly free from self, reaches the essence of all that can be known, gathered together like a cloud. This is the true spiritual consciousness.

It has been said that, at the beginning of the way, we must kill out ambition, the great curse, the giant weed which grows as strongly in the heart of the devoted disciple as in the man of desire. The remedy is sacrifice of self, obedience, humility; that purity of heart which gives the vision of God. Thereafter, he who has attained is wrapt about with the essence of all that can be known, as with a cloud; he has that perfect illumination which is the true spiritual consciousness. Through obedience to the will of God, he comes into oneness of being with God; he is initiated into God's view of the universe, seeing all life as God sees it.

30. Thereon comes surcease from sorrow and the burden of toil.

Such a one, it is said, is free from the bond of Karma, from the burden of toil, from that debt to works which comes from works done in self-love and desire. Free from self-will, he is free from sorrow, too, for sorrow comes from the fight of self-will against the divine will, through the correcting stress of the divine will, which seeks to counteract the evil wrought by disobedience. When the conflict with the divine will ceases, then sorrow ceases, and he who has grown into obedience, thereby enters into joy.

31. When all veils are rent, all stains washed away, his knowledge becomes infinite; little remains for him to know.

The first veil is the delusion that thy soul is in some permanent way separate from the great Soul, the divine Eternal. When that veil is rent, thou shalt discern thy oneness with everlasting Life. The second veil is the delusion of enduring separateness from thy other selves, whereas in truth the soul that is in them is one with the soul that is in thee. The world's sin and shame are thy sin and shame: its joy also.

These veils rent, thou shalt enter into knowledge of divine things and human things. Little will remain unknown to thee.

32. Thereafter comes the completion of the series of transformations of the three nature potencies, since their purpose is attained.

It is a part of the beauty and wisdom of the great Indian teachings, the Vedanta and the Yoga alike, to hold that all life exists for the purposes of Soul, for the making of the spiritual man. They teach that all nature is an orderly process of evolution, leading up to this, designed for this end, existing only for this: to bring forth and perfect the Spiritual Man. He is the crown of evolution: at his coming, the goal of all development is attained.

33. The series of transformations is divided into moments. When the series is completed, time gives place to duration.

There are two kinds of eternity, says the commentary: the eternity of immortal life, which belongs to the Spirit, and the eternity of change, which inheres in Nature, in all that is not Spirit. While we are content to live in and for Nature, in the Circle of Necessity, Sansara, we doom ourselves to perpetual change. That which is born must die, and that which dies must be reborn. It is change evermore, a ceaseless series of transformations.

But the Spiritual Man enters a new order; for him, there is no longer eternal change, but eternal Being. He has entered into the joy of his Lord. This spiritual birth, which makes him heir of the Everlasting, sets a term to change; it is the culmination, the crowning transformation, of the whole realm of change.

34. Pure spiritual life is, therefore, the inverse resolution of the potencies of Nature, which have emptied themselves of their value for the Spiritual man; or it is the return of the power of pure Consciousness to its essential form.

Here we have a splendid generalization, in which our wise philosopher finally reconciles the naturalists and the idealists, expressing the crown and end of his teaching, first in the terms of the naturalist, and then in the terms of the idealist.

The birth and growth of the Spiritual Man, and his entry into his immortal heritage, may be regarded, says our philosopher, either as the culmination of the whole process of natural evolution and involution, where 'that which flowed from out the boundless deep, turns again home'; or it may be looked at, as the Vedantins look at it, as the restoration of pure spiritual Consciousness to its pristine and essential form. There is no discrepancy or conflict between these two views, which are but two accounts of the same thing. Therefore those who study the wise philosopher, be they naturalist or idealist, have no excuse to linger over dialetic subtleties or disputes. These things are lifted from their path, lest they should be tempted to delay over them, and they are left facing the path itself, stretching upward and onward from their feet to the everlasting hills, radiant with infinite Light.

THE BHAGAVAD GITA

Vyasa

Translated by Edwin Arnold.
Initially Published in 1885.

CHAPTER I: Of the Distress of Arjuna

Dhritirashtra. Ranged thus for battle on the sacred plain-
On Kurukshetra- say, Sanjaya! say
What wrought my people, and the Pandavas?
Sanjaya. When he beheld the host of Pandavas,
Raja Duryodhana to Drona drew,
And spake these words: "Ah, Guru! see this line,
How vast it is of Pandu fighting-men,
Embattled by the son of Drupada,
Thy scholar in the war! Therein stand ranked
Chiefs like Arjuna, like to Bhima chiefs,
Benders of bows; Virata, Yuyudhan,
Drupada, eminent upon his car,
Dhrishtaket, Chekitan, Kasi's stout lord,
Purujit, Kuntibhoj, and Saivya,
With Yudhamanyu, and Uttamauj
Subhadra's child; and Drupadi's;- all famed!
All mounted on their shining chariots!
On our side, too,- thou best of Brahmans! see
Excellent chiefs, commanders of my line,
Whose names I joy to count: thyself the first,
Then Bhishma, Karna, Kripa fierce in fight,
Vikarna, Aswatthaman; next to these
Strong Saumadatti, with full many more
Valiant and tried, ready this day to die
For me their king, each with his weapon grasped,
Each skilful in the field. Weakest- meseems-
Our battle shows where Bhishma holds command,
And Bhima, fronting him, something too strong!
Have care our captains nigh to Bhishma's ranks
Prepare what help they may! Now, blow my shell!"

Then, at the signal of the aged king,
With blare to wake the blood, rolling around
Like to a lion's roar, the trumpeter
Blew the great Conch; and, at the noise of it,
Trumpets and drums, cymbals and gongs and horns

100

Burst into sudden clamour; as the blasts
Of loosened tempest, such the tumult seemed!
Then might be seen, upon their car of gold
Yoked with white steeds, blowing their battle-shells,
Krishna the God, Arjuna at his side:
Krishna, with knotted locks, blew his great conch
Carved of the "Giant's bone;" Arjuna blew
Indra's loud gift; Bhima the terrible-
Wolf-bellied Bhima- blew a long reed-conch;
And Yudhisthira, Kunti's blameless son,
Winded a mighty shell, "Victory's Voice;"
And Nakula blew shrill upon his conch
Named the "Sweet-sounding," Sahadev on his
Called "Gem-bedecked," and Kasi's Prince on his.
Sikhandi on his car, Dhrishtadyumn,
Virata, Satyaki the Unsubdued,
Drupada, with his sons, (O Lord of Earth!)
Long-armed Subhadra's children, all blew loud,
So that the clangour shook their foemen's hearts,
With quaking earth and thundering heav'n.
Then 'twas-
Beholding Dhritirashtra's battle set,
Weapons unsheathing, bows drawn forth, the war
Instant to break- Arjun, whose ensign-badge
Was Hanuman the monkey, spake this thing
To Krishna the Divine, his charioteer:
"Drive, Dauntless One! to yonder open ground
Betwixt the armies; I would see more nigh
These who will fight with us, those we must slay
To-day, in war's arbitrament; for, sure,
On bloodshed all are bent who throng this plain,
Obeying Dhritirashtra's sinful son."

Thus, by Arjuna prayed, (O Bharata!)
Between the hosts that heavenly Charioteer
Drove the bright car, reining its milk-white steeds
Where Bhishma led, and Drona, and their Lords.
"See!" spake he to Arjuna, "where they stand,
Thy kindred of the Kurus:" and the Prince

Marked on each hand the kinsmen of his house,
Grandsires and sires, uncles and brothers and sons,
Cousins and sons-in-law and nephews, mixed
With friends and honoured elders; some this side,
Some that side ranged: and, seeing those opposed,
Such kith grown enemies- Arjuna's heart
Melted with pity, while he uttered this:
Arjuna. Krishna! as I behold, come here to shed
Their common blood, yon concourse of our kin,
My members fail, my tongue dries in my mouth,
A shudder thrills my body, and my hair
Bristles with horror; from my weak hand slips
Gandiv, the goodly bow; a fever burns
My skin to parching; hardly may I stand;
The life within me seems to swim and faint;
Nothing do I foresee save woe and wail!
It is not good, O Keshav! nought of good
Can spring from mutual slaughter! Lo, I hate
Triumph and domination, wealth and ease,
Thus sadly won! Aho! what victory
Can bring delight, Govinda! what rich spoils
Could profit; what rule recompense; what span
Of life itself seem sweet, bought with such blood?
Seeing that these stand here, ready to die,
For whose sake life was fair, and pleasure pleased,
And power grew precious:- grandsires, sires, and sons,
Brothers, and fathers-in-law, and sons-in-law,
Elders and friends! Shall I deal death on these
Even though they seek to slay us? Not one blow,
O Madhusudan! will I strike to gain
The rule of all Three Worlds; then, how much less
To seize an earthly kingdom! Killing these
Must breed but anguish, Krishna! If they be
Guilty, we shall grow guilty by their deaths;
Their sins will light on us, if we shall slay
Those sons of Dhritirashtra, and our kin;
What peace could come of that, O Madhava?
For if indeed, blinded by lust and wrath,
These cannot see, or will not see, the sin

Of kingly lines o'erthrown and kinsmen slain,
How should not we, who see, shun such a crime-
We who perceive the guilt and feel the shame-
O thou Delight of Men, Janardana?
By overthrow of houses perisheth
Their sweet continuous household piety,
And- rites neglected, piety extinct-
Enters impiety upon that home;
Its women grow unwomaned, whence there spring
Mad passions, and the mingling-up of castes,
Sending a Hell-ward road that family,
And whoso wrought its doom by wicked wrath.
Nay, and the souls of honoured ancestors
Fall from their place of peace, being bereft
Of funeral-cakes and the wan death-water.
So teach our holy hymns. Thus, if we slay
Kinsfolk and friends for love of earthly power,
Ahovat! what an evil fault it were!
Better I deem it, if my kinsmen strike,
To face them weaponless, and bare my breast
To shaft and spear, than answer blow with blow.

So speaking, in the face of those two hosts,
Arjuna sank upon his chariot-seat,
And let fall bow and arrows, sick at heart.

CHAPTER II: Of Doctrines

Sanjaya. Him, filled with such compassion and such grief,
With eyes tear-dimmed, despondent, in stern words
The Driver, Madhusudan, thus addressed:
Krishna. How hath this weakness taken thee?
Whence springs
The inglorious trouble, shameful to the brave,
Barring the path of virtue? Nay, Arjun!
Forbid thyself to feebleness! it mars
Thy warrior-name! cast off the coward-fit!
Wake! Be thyself! Arise, Scourge of thy Foes!

103

Arjuna. How can I, in the battle, shoot with shafts
On Bhishma, or on Drona- O thou Chief!-
Both worshipful, both honourable men?

Better to live on beggar's bread
With those we love alive,
Than taste their blood in rich feasts spread,
And guiltily survive!
Ah! were it worse- who knows?- to be
Victor or vanquished here,
When those confront us angrily
Whose death leaves living drear?
In pity lost, by doubtings tossed,
My thoughts- distracted- turn
To Thee, the Guide I reverence most,
That I may counsel learn:
I know not what would heal the grief
Burned into soul and sense,
If I were earth's unchallenged chief-
A god- and these gone thence!

Sanjaya. So spake Arjuna to the Lord of Hearts,
And sighing, "I will not fight!" held silence then.
To whom, with tender smile, (O Bharata!)
While the Prince wept despairing 'twixt those hosts,
Krishna made answer in divinest verse:
Krishna. Thou grievest where no grief should be! thou speak'st
Words lacking wisdom! for the wise in heart
Mourn not for those that live, nor those that die.
Nor I, nor thou, nor any one of these,
Ever was not, nor ever will not be,
For ever and for ever afterwards.
All, that doth live, lives always! To man's frame
As there come infancy and youth and age,
So come there raisings-up and layings-down
Of other and of other life-abodes,
Which the wise know, and fear not. This that irks-
Thy sense-life, thrilling to the elements-
Bringing thee heat and cold, sorrows and joys,

'Tis brief and mutable! Bear with it, Prince!
As the wise bear. The soul which is not moved,
The soul that with a strong and constant calm
Takes sorrow and takes joy indifferently,
Lives in the life undying! That which is
Can never cease to be; that which is not
Will not exist. To see this truth of both
Is theirs who part essence from accident,
Substance from shadow. Indestructible,
Learn thou! the Life is, spreading life through all;
It cannot anywhere, by any means,
Be anywise diminished, stayed, or changed.
But for these fleeting frames which it informs
With spirit deathless, endless, infinite,
They perish. Let them perish, Prince! and fight!
He who shall say, "Lo! I have slain a man!"
He who shall think, "Lo! I am slain!" those both
Know naught! Life cannot slay. Life is not slain!
Never the spirit was born; the spirit shall cease to be never;
Never was time it was not; End and Beginning are dreams!
Birthless and deathless and changeless remaineth the spirit for
ever;
Death hath not touched it at all, dead though the house of it
seems!
Who knoweth it exhaustless, self-sustained,
Immortal, indestructible,- shall such
Say, "I have killed a man, or caused to kill?"

Nay, but as when one layeth
His worn-out robes away,
And, taking new ones, sayeth,
"These will I wear to-day!"
So putteth by the spirit
Lightly its garb of flesh,
And passeth to inherit
A residence afresh.

I say to thee weapons reach not the Life;
Flame burns it not, waters cannot o'erwhelm,

Nor dry winds wither it. Impenetrable,
Unentered, unassailed, unharmed, untouched,
Immortal, all-arriving, stable, sure,
Invisible, ineffable, by word
And thought uncompassed, ever all itself,
Thus is the Soul declared! How wilt thou, then,-
Knowing it so,- grieve when thou shouldst not grieve?
How, if thou hearest that the man new-dead
Is, like the man new-born, still living man-
One same, existent Spirit- wilt thou weep?
The end of birth is death; the end of death
Is birth: this is ordained! and mournest thou,
Chief of the stalwart arm! for what befalls
Which could not otherwise befall? The birth
Of living things comes unperceived; the death
Comes unperceived; between them, beings perceive:
What is there sorrowful herein, dear Prince?

Wonderful, wistful, to contemplate!
Difficult, doubtful, to speak upon!
Strange and great for tongue to relate,
Mystical hearing for every one!
Nor wotteth man this, what a marvel it is,
When seeing, and saying, and hearing are done!

This Life within all living things, my Prince!
Hides beyond harm; scorn thou to suffer, then,
For that which cannot suffer. Do thy part!
Be mindful of thy name, and tremble not!
Nought better can betide a martial soul
Than lawful war; happy the warrior
To whom comes joy of battle- comes, as now,
Glorious and fair, unsought; opening for him
A gateway unto Heav'n. But, if thou shunn'st
This honourable field- a Kshattriya-
If, knowing thy duty and thy task, thou bidd'st
Duty and task go by- that shall be sin!
And those to come shall speak thee infamy
From age to age; but infamy is worse

For men of noble blood to bear than death!
The chiefs upon their battle-chariots
Will deem 'twas fear that drove thee from the fray.
Of those who held thee mighty-souled the scorn
Thou must abide, while all thine enemies
Will scatter bitter speech of thee, to mock
The valour which thou hadst; what fate could fall
More grievously than this? Either- being killed-
Thou wilt win Swarga's safety, or- alive
And victor- thou wilt reign an earthly king.
Therefore, arise, thou Son of Kunti! brace
Thine arm for conflict, nerve thy heart to meet-
As things alike to thee- pleasure or pain,
Profit or ruin, victory or defeat:
So minded, gird thee to the fight, for so
Thou shalt not sin!
                    Thus far I speak to thee
As from the "Sankhya"- unspiritually-
Hear now the deeper teaching of the Yog,
Which holding, understanding, thou shalt burst
Thy Karmabandh, the bondage of wrought deeds.
Here shall no end be hindered, no hope marred,
No loss be feared: faith- yea, a little faith-
Shall save thee from the anguish of thy dread.
Here, Glory of the Kurus! shines one rule-
One steadfast rule- while shifting souls have laws
Many and hard. Specious, but wrongful deem
The speech of those ill-taught ones who extol
The letter of their Vedas, saying, "This
Is all we have, or need;" being weak at heart
With wants, seekers of Heaven: which comes- they say-
As "fruit of good deeds done;" promising men
Much profit in new births for works of faith;
In various rites abounding; following whereon
Large merit shall accrue towards wealth and power;
Albeit, who wealth and power do most desire
Least fixity of soul have such, least hold
On heavenly meditation. Much these teach,
From Veds, concerning the "three qualities;"

But thou, be free of the "three qualities,"
Free of the "pairs of opposites," and free
From that sad righteousness which calculates;
Self-ruled, Arjuna! simple, satisfied.
Look! like as when a tank pours water forth
To suit all needs, so do these Brahmans draw
Text for all wants from tank of Holy Writ.
But thou, want not! ask not! Find full reward
Of doing right in right! Let right deeds be
Thy motive, not the fruit which comes from them.
And live in action! Labour! Make thine acts
Thy piety, casting all self aside,
Contemning gain and merit; equable
In good or evil: equability
Is Yog, is piety!
Yet, the right act
Is less, far less, than the right-thinking mind.
Seek refuge in thy soul; have there thy heaven!
Scorn them that follow virtue for her gifts!
The mind of pure devotion- even here-
Casts equally aside good deeds and bad,
Passing above them. Unto pure devotion
Devote thyself: with perfect meditation
Comes perfect act, and the righthearted rise-
More certainly because they seek no gain-
Forth from the bands of body, step by step,
To highest seats of bliss. When thy firm soul
Hath shaken off those tangled oracles
Which ignorantly guide, then shall it soar
To high neglect of what's denied or said,
This way or that way, in doctrinal writ.
Troubled no longer by the priestly lore,
Safe shall it live, and sure; steadfastly bent
On meditation. This is Yog- and Peace!
Arjuna. What is his mark who hath that steadfast heart,
Confirmed in holy meditation? How
Know we his speech, Kesava? Sits he, moves he
Like other men?
Krishna. When one, O Pritha's Son!-

Abandoning desires which shake the mind-
Finds in his soul full comfort for his soul,
He hath attained the Yog- that man is such!
In sorrows not dejected, and in joys
Not overjoyed; dwelling outside the stress
Of passion, fear, and anger; fixed in calms
Of lofty contemplation;- such an one
Is Muni, is the Sage, the true Recluse!
He who to none and nowhere overbound
By ties of flesh, takes evil things and good
Neither desponding nor exulting, such
Bears wisdom's plainest mark He who shall draw
As the wise tortoise draws its four feet safe
Under its shield, his five frail senses back
Under the spirit's buckler from the world
Which else assails them, such an one, my Prince!
Hath wisdom's mark! Things that solicit sense
Hold off from the self-governed; nay, it comes,
The appetites of him who lives beyond
Depart,- aroused no more. Yet may it chance,
O Son of Kunti that a governed mind
Shall some time feel the sense-storms sweep, and wrest
Strong self-control by the roots. Let him regain
His kingdom! let him conquer this, and sit
On Me intent. That man alone is wise
Who keeps the mastery of himself! If one
Ponders on objects of the sense, there springs
Attraction; from attraction grows desire,
Desire flames to fierce passion, passion breeds
Recklessness; then the memory- all betrayed-
Lets noble purpose go, and saps the mind,
Till purpose, mind, and man are all undone.
But, if one deals with objects of the sense
Not loving and not hating, making them
Serve his free soul, which rests serenely lord,
Lo! such a man comes to tranquillity;
And out of that tranquillity shall rise
The end and healing of his earthly pains,
Since the will governed sets the soul at peace.

The soul of the ungoverned is not his,
Nor hath he knowledge of himself; which lacked,
How grows serenity? and, wanting that,
Whence shall he hope for happiness?
The mind
That gives itself to follow shows of sense
Seeth its helm of wisdom rent away,
And, like a ship in waves of whirlwind, drives
To wreck and death. Only with him, great Prince!
Whose senses are not swayed by things of sense-
Only with him who holds his mastery,
Shows wisdom perfect. What is midnight-gloom
To unenlightened souls shines wakeful day
To his clear gaze; what seems as wakeful day
Is known for night, thick night of ignorance,
To his true-seeing eyes. Such is the Saint!
And like the ocean, day by day receiving
Floods from all lands, which never overflows;
Its boundary-line not leaping, and not leaving,
Fed by the rivers, but unswelled by those;-
So is the perfect one! to his soul's ocean
The world of sense pours streams of witchery,
They leave him as they find, without commotion,
Taking their tribute, but remaining sea.
Yea! whoso, shaking off the yoke of flesh
Lives lord, not servant, of his lusts; set free
From pride, from passion, from the sin of "Self,"
Toucheth tranquillity! O Pritha's Son!
That is the state of Brahm! There rests no dread
When that last step is reached! Live where he will,
Die when he may, such passeth from all 'plaining,
To blest Nirvana, with the Gods, attaining.

CHAPTER III: Of Virtue in Work

Arjuna. Thou whom all mortals praise, Janardana!
If meditation be a nobler thing
Than action, wherefore, then, great Kesava!

110

Dost thou impel me to this dreadful fight?
Now am I by thy doubtful speech disturbed!
Tell me one thing, and tell me certainly;
By what road shall I find the better end?
Krishna. I told thee, blameless Lord! there be paths
Shown to this world; two schools of wisdom. First
The Sankhya's, which doth save in way of works
Prescribed by reason; next, the Yog, which bids
Attain by meditation, spiritually:
Yet these are one! No man shall 'scape from act
By shunning action; nay, and none shall come
By mere renouncements unto perfectness.
Nay, and no jot of time, at any time,
Rests any actionless; his nature's law
Compels him, even unwilling, into act;
[For thought is act in fancy]. He who sits
Suppressing all the instruments of flesh,
Yet in his idle heart thinking on them,
Plays the inept and guilty hypocrite:
But he who, with strong body serving mind,
Gives up his mortal powers to worthy work,
Not seeking gain, Arjuna! such an one
Is honourable. Do thine allotted task!
Work is more excellent than idleness;
The body's life proceeds not, lacking work.
There is a task of holiness to do,
Unlike world-binding toil, which bindeth not
The faithful soul; such earthly duty do
Free from desire, and thou shalt well perform
Thy heavenly purpose. Spake Prajapati --
In the beginning, when all men were made,
And, with mankind, the sacrifice -- "Do this!
Work! sacrifice! Increase and multiply
With sacrifice! This shall be Kamaduk,
Your 'Cow of Plenty,' giving back her milk
Of all abundance. Worship the gods thereby;
The gods shall yield thee grace. Those meats ye
The gods will grant to Labour, when it pays
Tithes in the altar-flame. But if one eats

Fruits of the earth, rendering to kindly Heaven
No gift of toil, that thief steals from his world."

Who eat of food after their sacrifice
Are quit of fault, but they that spread a feast
All for themselves, eat sin and drink of sin.
By food the living live; food comes of rain,
And rain comes by the pious sacrifice,
And sacrifice is paid with tithes of toil;
Thus action is of Brahma, who is One,
The Only, All-pervading; at all times
Present in sacrifice. He that abstains
To help the rolling wheels of this great world,
Glutting his idle sense, lives a lost life,
Shameful and vain. Existing for himself,
Self-concentrated, serving self alone,
No part hath he in aught; nothing achieved,
Nought wrought or unwrought toucheth him; no hope
Of help for all the living things of earth
Depends from him. Therefore, thy task prescribed
With spirit unattached gladly perform,
Since in performance of plain duty man
Mounts to his highest bliss. By works alone
Janak and ancient saints reached blessedness!
Moreover, for the upholding of thy kind,
Action thou should'st embrace. What the wise choose
The unwise people take; what best men do
The multitude will follow. Look on me,
Thou Son of Pritha! in the three wide worlds
I am not bound to any toil, no height
Awaits to scale, no gift remains to gain,
Yet I act here! and, if I acted not --
Earnest and watchful -- those that look to me
For guidance, sinking back to sloth again
Because I slumbered, would decline from good,
And I should break earth's order and commit
Her offspring unto ruin, Bharata!
Even as the unknowing toil, wedded to sense,
So let the enlightened toil, sense-freed, but set

To bring the world deliverance, and its bliss;
Not sowing in those simple, busy hearts
Seed of despair. Yea! let each play his part
In all he finds to do, with unyoked soul.
All things are everywhere by Nature wrought
In interaction of the quahties.
The fool, cheated by self, thinks, "This I did"
And "That I wrought;" but -- ah, thou strong-armed Prince! --
A better-lessoned mind, knowing the play
Of visible things within the world of sense,
And how the qualities must qualify,
Standeth aloof even from his acts. Th' untaught
Live mixed with them, knowing not Nature's way,
Of highest aims unwitting, slow and dull.
Those make thou not to stumble, having the light;
But all thy dues discharging, for My sake,
With meditation centred inwardly,
Seeking no profit, satisfied, serene,
Heedless of issue -- fight! They who shall keep
My ordinance thus, the wise and willing hearts,
Have quittance from all issue of their acts;
But those who disregard My ordinance,
Thinking they know, know nought, and fall to loss,
Confused and foolish. 'Sooth, the instructed one
Doth of his kind, following what fits him most:
And lower creatures of their kind; in vain
Contending 'gainst the law. Needs must it be
The objects of the sense will stir the sense
To like and dislike, yet th' enlightened man
Yields not to these, knowing them enemies.
Finally, this is better, that one do
His own task as he may, even though he fail,
Than take tasks not his own, though they seem good.
To die performing duty is no ill;
But who seeks other roads shall wander still.
Arjuna. Yet tell me, Teacher! by what force doth man
Go to his ill, unwilling; as if one
Pushed him that evil path?
Krishna. Kama it is!

Passion it is! born of the Darknesses,
Which pusheth him. Mighty of appetite,
Sinful, and strong is this! -- man's enemy!
As smoke blots the white fire, as clinging rust
Mars the bright mirror, as the womb surrounds
The babe unborn, so is the world of things
Foiled, soiled, enclosed in this desire of flesh.
The wise fall, caught in it; the unresting foe
It is of wisdom, wearing countless forms,
Fair but deceitful, subtle as a flame.
Sense, mind, and reason -- these, O Kunti's Son!
Are booty for it; in its play with these
It maddens man, beguiling, blinding him.
Therefore, thou noblest child of Bharata!
Govern thy heart! Constrain th' entangled sense!
Resist the false, soft sinfulness which saps
Knowledge and judgment! Yea, the world is strong
But what discerns it stronger, and the mind
Strongest; and high o'er all the ruling Soul.
Wherefore, perceiving Him who reigns supreme,
Put forth full force of Soul in thy own soul!
Fight! vanquish foes and doubts, dear Hero! slay
What haunts thee in fond shapes, and would betray!

CHAPTER IV: Of the Religion of Knowledge

Krishna. This deathless Yoga, this deep union,
I taught Vivaswata, the Lord of Light;
Vivaswata to Manu gave it; he
To Ikshwaku; so passed it down the line
Of all my royal Rishis. Then, with years,
The truth grew dim and perished, noble Prince!
Now once again to thee it is declared-
This ancient lore, this mystery supreme-
Seeing I find thee votary and friend.
Arjuna. Thy birth, dear Lord, was in these later days
And bright Vivaswata's preceded time!
How shall I comprehend this thing thou sayest,

114

"From the beginning it was I who taught?"
Krishna. Manifold the renewals of my birth
Have been, Arjuna! and of thy births, too!
But mine I know, and thine thou knowest not,
O Slayer of thy Foes! Albeit I be
Unborn, undying, indestructible,
The Lord of all things living; not the less-
By Maya, by my magic which I stamp
On floating Nature-forms, the primal vast-
I come, and go, and come. When Righteousness
Declines, O Bharata! when Wickedness
Is strong, I rise, from age to age, and take
Visible shape, and move a man with men,
Succouring the good, thrusting the evil back,
And setting Virtue on her seat again.
Who knows the truth touching my births on earth
And my divine work, when he quits the flesh
Puts on its load no more, falls no more down
To earthly birth: to Me he comes, dear Prince!

Many there be who come! from fear set free,
From anger, from desire; keeping their hearts
Fixed upon me- my Faithful- purified
By sacred flame of Knowledge. Such as these
Mix with my being. Whoso worship me,
Them I exalt; but all men everywhere
Shall fall into my path; albeit, those souls
Which seek reward for works, make sacrifice
Now, to the lower gods. I say to thee
Here have they their reward. But I am He
Made the Four Castes, and portioned them a place
After their qualities and gifts. Yea, I
Created, the Reposeful; I that live
Immortally, made all those mortal births:
For works soil not my essence, being works
Wrought uninvolved. Who knows me acting thus
Unchained by action, action binds not him;
And, so perceiving, all those saints of old
Worked, seeking for deliverance. Work thou

As, in the days gone by, thy fathers did.
Thou sayst, perplexed, It hath been asked before
By singers and by sages, "What is act,
And what inaction?" I will teach thee this,
And, knowing, thou shalt learn which work doth save
Needs must one rightly meditate those three-
Doing,- not doing,- and undoing. Here
Thorny and dark the path is! He who sees
How action may be rest, rest action- he
Is wisest 'mid his kind; he hath the truth!
He doeth well, acting or resting. Freed
In all his works from prickings of desire,
Burned clean in act by the white fire of truth,
The wise call that man wise; and such an one,
Renouncing fruit of deeds, always content.
Always self-satisfying, if he works,
Doth nothing that shall stain his separate soul,
Which- quit of fear and hope- subduing self-
Rejecting outward impulse-yielding up
To body's need nothing save body, dwells
Sinless amid all sin, with equal calm
Taking what may befall, by grief unmoved,
Unmoved by joy, unenvyingly; the same
In good and evil fortunes; nowise bound
By bond of deeds. Nay, but of such an one,
Whose crave is gone, whose soul is liberate,
Whose heart is set on truth- of such an one
What work he does is work of sacrifice,
Which passeth purely into ash and smoke
Consumed upon the altar! All's then God!
The sacrifice is Brahm, the ghee and grain
Are Brahm, the fire is Brahm, the flesh it eats
Is Brahm, and unto Brahm attaineth he
Who, in such office, meditates on Brahm.
Some votaries there be who serve the gods
With flesh and altar-smoke; but other some
Who, lighting subtler fires, make purer rite
With will of worship. Of the which be they
Who, in white flame of continence, consume

Joys of the sense, delights of eye and ear,
Foregoing tender speech and sound of song:
And they who, kindling fires with torch of Truth,
Burn on a hidden altar-stone the bliss
Of youth and love, renouncing happiness:
And they who lay for offering there their wealth,
Their penance, meditation, piety,
Their steadfast reading of the scrolls, their lore
Painfully gained with long austerities:
And they who, making silent sacrifice,
Draw in their breath to feed the flame of thought,
And breathe it forth to waft the heart on high,
Governing the ventage of each entering air
Lest one sigh pass which helpeth not the soul:
And they who, day by day denying needs,
Lay life itself upon the altar-flame,
Burning the body wan. Lo! all these keep
The rite of offering, as if they slew
Victims; and all thereby efface much sin.
Yea! and who feed on the immortal food
Left of such sacrifice, to Brahma pass,
To The Unending. But for him that makes
No sacrifice, he hath nor part nor lot
Even in the present world. How should he share
Another, O thou Glory of thy Line?

In sight of Brahma all these offerings
Are spread and are accepted! Comprehend
That all proceed by act; for knowing this,
Thou shalt be quit of doubt. The sacrifice
Which Knowledge pays is better than great gifts
Offered by wealth, since gifts' worth- O my Prince!
Lies in the mind which gives, the will that serves:
And these are gained by reverence, by strong search,
By humble heed of those who see the Truth
And teach it. Knowing Truth, thy heart no more
Will ache with error, for the Truth shall show
All things subdued to thee, as thou to Me.
Moreover, Son of Pandu! wert thou worst

Of all wrong-doers, this fair ship of Truth
Should bear thee safe and dry across the sea
Of thy transgressions. As the kindled flame
Feeds on the fuel till it sinks to ash,
So unto ash, Arjuna! unto nought
The flame of Knowledge wastes works' dross away!
There is no purifier like thereto
In all this world, and he who seeketh it
Shall find it- being grown perfect- in himself.
Believing, he receives it when the soul
Masters itself, and cleaves to Truth, and comes-
Possessing knowledge- to the higher peace,
The uttermost repose. But those untaught,
And those without full faith, and those who fear
Are shent; no peace is here or other where,
No hope, nor happiness for whoso doubts.
He that, being self-contained, hath vanquished doubt,
Disparting self from service, soul from works,
Enlightened and emancipate, my Prince!
Works fetter him no more! Cut then atwain
With sword of wisdom, Son of Bharata!
This doubt that binds thy heart-beats! cleave the bond
Born of thy ignorance! Be bold and wise!
Give thyself to the field with me! Arise!

CHAPTER V: Of Religion by Renouncing Fruit of Works

Arjuna. Yet, Krishna at the one time thou dost laud
Surcease of works, and, at another time,
Service through work. Of these twain plainly tell
Which is the better way?
Krishna. To cease from works
Is well, and to do works in holiness
Is well; and both conduct to bliss supreme;
But of these twain the better way is his
Who working piously refraineth not.

That is the true Renouncer, firm and fixed,

Who- seeking nought, rejecting nought- dwells proof
Against the "opposites." O valiant Prince!
In doing, such breaks lightly from all deed:
'Tis the new scholar talks as they were two,
This Sankhya and this Yoga: wise men know
Who husbands one plucks golden fruit of both!
The region of high rest which Sankhyans reach
Yogins attain. Who sees these twain as one
Sees with clear eyes! Yet such abstraction, Chief!
Is hard to win without much holiness.
Whoso is fixed in holiness, self-ruled,
Pure-hearted, lord of senses and of self,
Lost in the common life of all which lives-
A "Yogayukt"- he is a Saint who wends
Straightway to Brahm. Such an one is not touched
By taint of deeds. "Nought of myself I do!"
Thus will he think- who holds the truth of truths-
In seeing, hearing, touching, smelling; when
He eats, or goes, or breathes; slumbers or talks,
Holds fast or loosens, opes his eyes or shuts;
Always assured "This is the sense-world plays
With senses." He that acts in thought of Brahm,
Detaching end from act, with act content,
The world of sense can no more stain his soul
Than waters mar th' enamelled lotus-leaf.
With life, with heart, with mind,- nay, with the help
Of all five senses- letting selfhood go-
Yogins toil ever towards their souls' release.
Such votaries, renouncing fruit of deeds,
Gain endless peace: the unvowed, the passion-bound,
Seeking a fruit from works, are fastened down.
The embodied sage, withdrawn within his soul,
At every act sits godlike in "the town
Which hath nine gateways," neither doing aught
Nor causing any deed. This world's Lord makes
Neither the work, nor passion for the work,
Nor lust for fruit of work; the man's own self
Pushes to these! The Master of this World
Takes on himself the good or evil deeds

Of no man- dwelling beyond! Mankind errs here
By folly, darkening knowledge. But, for whom
That darkness of the soul is chased by light,
Splendid and clear shines manifest the Truth
As if a Sun of Wisdom sprang to shed
Its beams of dawn. Him meditating still,
Him seeking, with Him blended, stayed on Him,
The souls illuminated take that road
Which hath no turning back- their sins flung off,
By strength of faith. [Who will may have this Light;
Who hath it sees.] To him who wisely sees,
The Brahman with his scrolls and sanctities,
The cow, the elephant, the unclean dog,
The Outcast gorging dog's meat, are all one.

The world is overcome- aye! even here!
By such as fix their faith on Unity.
The sinless Brahma dwells in Unity,
And they in Brahma. Be not over-glad
Attaining joy, and be not over-sad
Encountering grief, but, stayed on Brahma, still
Constant let each abide! The sage whose soul
Holds off from outer contacts, in himself
Finds bliss; to Brahma joined by piety,
His spirit tastes eternal peace. The joys
Springing from sense-life are but quickening wombs
Which breed sure griefs: those joys begin and end!
The wise mind takes no pleasure, Kunti's Son!
In such as those! But if a man shall learn,
Even while he lives and bears his body's chain,
To master lust and anger, he is blest!
He is the Yukta; he hath happiness,
Contentment, light, within: his life is merged
In Brahma's life; he doth Nirvana touch!
Thus go the Rishis unto rest, who dwell
With sins effaced, with doubts at end, with hearts
Governed and calm. Glad in all good they live,
Nigh to the peace of God; and all those live
Who pass their days exempt from greed and wrath,

Subduing self and senses, knowing the Soul!

The Saint who shuts outside his placid soul
All touch of sense, letting no contact through;
Whose quiet eyes gaze straight from fixed brows,
Whose outward breath and inward breath are drawn
Equal and slow through nostrils still and close;
That one- with organs, heart, and mind constrained,
Bent on deliverance, having put away
Passion, and fear, and rage;- hath even now,
Obtained deliverance, ever and ever freed.
Yea! for he knows Me Who am He that heeds
The sacrifice and worship, God revealed;
And He who heeds not, being Lord of Worlds,
Lover of all that lives, God unrevealed,
Wherein who will shall find surety and shield!

CHAPTER VI: Of Religion of Self-Restraint

Krishna. Therefore, who doeth work rightful to do,
Not seeking gain from work, that man, O Prince!
Is Sanyasi and Yogi- both in one
And he is neither who lights not the flame
Of sacrifice, nor setteth hand to task.

Regard as true Renouncer him that makes
Worship by work, for who renounceth not
Works not as Yogin. So is that well said:
"By works the votary doth rise to faith,
And saintship is the ceasing from all works;
Because the perfect Yogin acts- but acts
Unmoved by passions and unbound by deeds,
Setting result aside.
Let each man raise
The Self by Soul, not trample down his Self,
Since Soul that is Self's friend may grow Self's foe.
Soul is Self's friend when Self doth rule o'er Self,
But Self turns enemy if Soul's own self

Hates Self as not itself.
The sovereign soul
Of him who lives self-governed and at peace
Is centred in itself, taking alike
Pleasure and pain; heat, cold; glory and shame.
He is the Yogi, he is Yukta, glad
With joy of light and truth; dwelling apart
Upon a peak, with senses subjugate
Whereto the clod, the rock, the glistering gold
Show all as one. By this sign is he known
Being of equal grace to comrades, friends,
Chance-comers, strangers, lovers, enemies,
Aliens and kinsmen; loving all alike,
Evil or good.

Sequestered should he sit,
Steadfastly meditating, solitary,
His thoughts controlled, his passions laid away,
Quit of belongings. In a fair, still spot
Having his fixed abode,- not too much raised,
Nor yet too low,- let him abide, his goods
A cloth, a deerskin, and the Kusa-grass.
There, setting hard his mind upon The One,
Restraining heart and senses, silent, calm,
Let him accomplish Yoga, and achieve
Pureness of soul, holding immovable
Body and neck and head, his gaze absorbed
Upon his nose-end, rapt from all around,
Tranquil in spirit, free of fear, intent
Upon his Brahmacharya vow, devout,
Musing on Me, lost in the thought of Me.
That Yogin, so devoted, so controlled,
Comes to the peace beyond,- My peace, the peace
Of high Nirvana!

But for earthly needs
Religion is not his who too much fasts
Or too much feasts, nor his who sleeps away
An idle mind; nor his who wears to waste

His strength in vigils. Nay, Arjuna! I call
That the true piety which most removes
Earth-aches and ills, where one is moderate
In eating and in resting, and in sport;
Measured in wish and act; sleeping betimes,
Waking betimes for duty.

When the man,
So living, centres on his soul the thought
Straitly restrained- untouched internally
By stress of sense- then is he Yukta. See!
Steadfast a lamp burns sheltered from the wind;
Such is the likeness of the Yogi's mind
Shut from sense-storms and burning bright to Heaven.
When mind broods placid, soothed with holy wont;
When Self contemplates self, and in itself
Hath comfort; when it knows the nameless joy
Beyond all scope of sense, revealed to soul-
Only to soul! and, knowing, wavers not,
True to the farther Truth; when, holding this,
It deems no other treasure comparable,
But, harboured there, cannot be stirred or shook
By any gravest grief, call that state "peace,"
That happy severance Yoga; call that man
The perfect Yogin!

Steadfastly the will
Must toil thereto, till efforts end in ease,
And thought has passed from thinking. Shaking off
All longings bred by dreams of fame and gain,
Shutting the doorways of the senses close
With watchful ward; so, step by step, it comes
To gift of peace assured and heart assuaged,
When the mind dwells self-wrapped, and the soul broods
Cumberless. But, as often as the heart
Breaks- wild and wavering- from control, so oft
Let him re-curb it, let him rein it back
To the soul's governance; for perfect bliss
Grows only in the bosom tranquillised,

The spirit passionless, purged from offence,
Vowed to the Infinite. He who thus vows
His soul to the Supreme Soul, quitting sin,
Passes unhindered to the endless bliss
Of unity with Brahma. He so vowed,
So blended, sees the Life-Soul resident
In all things living, and all living things
In that Life-Soul contained. And whoso thus
Discerneth Me in all, and all in Me,
I never let him go; nor looseneth he
Hold upon Me; but, dwell he where he may,
Whate'er his life, in Me he dwells and lives,
Because he knows and worships Me, Who dwell
In all which lives, and cleaves to Me in all.
Arjuna! if a man sees everywhere-
Taught by his own similitude- one Life,
One Essence in the Evil and the Good,
Hold him a Yogi, yea! well perfected!

Arjuna. Slayer of Madhu! yet again, this Yog,
This Peace, derived from equanimity,
Made known by thee- I see no fixity
Therein, no rest, because the heart of men
Is unfixed, Krishna! rash, tumultuous,
Wilful and strong. It were all one, I think,
To hold the wayward wind, as tame man's heart.

Krishna. Hero long-armed! beyond denial, hard
Man's heart is to restrain, and wavering;
Yet may it grow restrained by habit, Prince!
By wont of self-command. This Yog, I say,
Cometh not lightly to th' ungoverned ones;
But he who will be master of himself
Shall win it, if he stoutly strive thereto.

Arjuna. And what road goeth he who, having faith,
Fails, Krishna! in the striving; falling back
From holiness, missing the perfect rule?
Is he not lost, straying from Brahma's light,
Like the vain cloud, which floats 'twixt earth and heaven
When lightning splits it, and it vanisheth?
Fain would I hear thee answer me herein,

Since, Krishna! none save thou can clear the doubt.
Krishna. He is not lost, thou Son of Pritha! No!
Nor earth, nor heaven is forfeit, even for him,
Because no heart that holds one right desire
Treadeth the road of loss! He who should fail,
Desiring righteousness, cometh at death
Unto the Region of the Just; dwells there
Measureless years, and being born anew,
Beginneth life again in some fair home
Amid the mild and happy. It may chance
He doth descend into a Yogin house
On Virtue's breast; but that is rare! Such birth
Is hard to be obtained on this earth, Chief!
So hath he back again what heights of heart
He did achieve, and so he strives anew
To perfectness, with better hope, dear Prince!
For by the old desire he is drawn on
Unwittingly; and only to desire
The purity of Yog is to pass
Beyond the Sabdabrahm, the spoken Ved.
But, being Yogi, striving strong and long,
Purged from transgressions, perfected by births
Following on births, he plants his feet at last
Upon the farther path. Such as one ranks
Above ascetics, higher than the wise,
Beyond achievers of vast deeds! Be thou
Yogi Arjuna! And of such believe,
Truest and best is he who worships Me
With inmost soul, stayed on My Mystery!

CHAPTER VII: Of Religion by Discernment

Krishna. Learn now, dear Prince! how, if thy soul be set
Ever on Me- still exercising Yog,
Still making Me thy Refuge- thou shalt come
Most surely unto perfect hold of Me.
I will declare to thee that utmost lore,
Whole and particular, which, when thou knowest,

Leaveth no more to know here in this world.

Of many thousand mortals, one, perchance,
Striveth for Truth; and of those few that strive-
Nay, and rise high- one only- here and there-
Knoweth Me, as I am, the very Truth.

Earth, water, flame, air, ether, life, and mind,
And individuality- those eight
Make up the showing of Me, Manifest.

These be my lower Nature; learn the higher,
Whereby, thou Valiant One! this Universe
Is, by its principle of life, produced;
Whereby the worlds of visible things are born
As from a Yoni. Know! I am that womb:
I make and I unmake this Universe:
Than me there is no other Master, Prince!
No other Maker! All these hang on me
As hangs a row of pearls upon its string.
I am the fresh taste of the water; I
The silver of the moon, the gold o' the sun,
The word of worship in the Veds, the thrill
That passeth in the ether, and the strength
Of man's shed seed. I am the good sweet smell
Of the moistened earth, I am the fire's red light,
The vital air moving in all which moves,
The holiness of hallowed souls, the root
Undying, whence hath sprung whatever is;
The wisdom of the wise, the intellect
Of the informed, the greatness of the great.
The splendour of the splendid. Kunti's Son!
These am I, free from passion and desire;
Yet am I right desire in all who yearn,
Chief of the Bharatas! for all those moods,
Soothfast, or passionate, or ignorant,
Which Nature frames, deduce from me; but all
Are merged in me- not I in them! The world-
Deceived by those three qualities of being-

Wotteth not Me Who am outside them all,
Above them all, Eternal! Hard it is
To pierce that veil divine of various shows
Which hideth Me; yet they who worship Me
Pierce it and pass beyond.

I am not known
To evil-doers, nor to foolish ones,
Nor to the base and churlish; nor to those
Whose mind is cheated by the show of things,
Nor those that take the way of Asuras.

Four sorts of mortals know me: he who weeps,
Arjuna! and the man who yearns to know;
And he who toils to help; and he who sits
Certain of me, enlightened.

Of these four,
O Prince of India! highest, nearest, best
That last is, the devout soul, wise, intent
Upon "The One." Dear, above all, am I
To him; and he is dearest unto me!
All four are good, and seek me; but mine own,
The true of heart, the faithful- stayed on me,
Taking me as their utmost, blessedness,
They are not "mine," but I- even I myself!
At end of many births to Me they come!
Yet hard the wise Mahatma is to find,
That man who sayeth, "All is Vasudev!"

There be those, too, whose knowledge, turned aside
By this desire or that, gives them to serve
Some lower gods, with various rites, constrained
By that which mouldeth them. Unto all such-
Worship what shrine they will, what shapes, in faith-
'Tis I who give them faith! I am content!
The heart thus asking favour from its God,
Darkened but ardent, hath the end it craves,
The lesser blessing- but 'tis I who give!

Yet soon is withered what small fruit they reap:
Those men of little minds, who worship so,
Go where they worship, passing with their gods.
But Mine come unto me! Blind are the eyes
Which deem th' Unmanifested manifest,
Not comprehending Me in my true Self!
Imperishable, viewless, undeclared,
Hidden behind my magic veil of shows,
I am not seen by all; I am not known-
Unborn and changeless- to the idle world.
But I, Arjuna! know all things which were,
And all which are, and all which are to be,
Albeit not one among them knoweth Me!

By passion for the "pairs of opposites,"
By those twain snares of Like and Dislike, Prince!
All creatures live bewildered, save some few
Who, quit of sins, holy in act, informed,
Freed from the "opposites," and fixed in faith,
Cleave unto Me.

Who cleave, who seek in Me
Refuge from birth and death, those have the Truth!
Those know Me BRAHMA: know Me Soul of Souls,
The ADHYATMAN: know KARMA, my work;
Know I am ADHIBHUTA, Lord of Life,
And ADHIDAIVA, Lord of all the Gods,
And ADHIYAJNA, Lord of Sacrifice;
Worship Me well, with hearts of love and faith,
And find and hold me in the hour of death.

CHAPTER VIII: Of Religion by Devotion to the One Supreme
God

Arjuna. Who is that BRAHMA? What that Soul of Souls,
The ADHYATMAN? What, Thou Best of All!
Thy work, the KARMA? Tell me what it is
Thou namest ADHIBHUTA? What again

Means ADHIDAIVA? Yea, and how it comes
Thou canst be ADHIYAJNA in thy flesh?
Slayer of Madhu! Further, make me know
How good men find thee in the hour of death?
Krishna. I BRAHMA am! the One Eternal GOD,
And ADHYATMAN is My Being's name,
The Soul of Souls! What goeth forth from Me,
Causing all life to live, is KARMA called:
And, Manifested in divided forms,
I am the ADHIBHUTA, Lord of Lives;
And ADHIDAIVA, Lord of all the Gods,
Because I am PURUSHA, who who begets.
And ADHIYAJNA, Lord of Sacrifice,
I- speaking with thee in this body here-
Am, thou embodied one! (for all the shrines
Flame unto Me!) And, at the hour of death,
He that hath meditated Me alone,
In putting off his flesh, comes forth to Me,
Enters into My Being- doubt thou not!
But, if he meditated otherwise
At hour of death, in putting off the flesh,
He goes to what he looked for, Kunti's Son!
Because the Soul is fashioned to its like.

Have Me, then, in thy heart always! and fight!
Thou too, when heart and mind are fixed on Me,
Shalt surely come to Me! All come who cleave
With never-wavering will of firmest faith,
Owning none other Gods: all come to Me,
The Uttermost, Purusha, Holiest!

Whoso hath known Me, Lord of sage and singer,
Ancient of days; of all the Three Worlds Stay,
Boundless,- but unto every atom Bringer
Of that which quickens it: whoso, I say,

Hath known My form, which passeth mortal knowing;
Seen my effulgence- which no eye hath seen-
Than the sun's burning gold more brightly glowing,

Dispersing darkness,- unto him hath been

Right life! And, in the hour when life is ending,
With mind set fast and trustful piety,
Drawing still breath beneath calm brows unbending,
In happy peace that faithful one doth die,-

In glad peace passeth to Purusha's heaven.
The place which they who read the Vedas name
AKSHARAM, "Ultimate;" whereto have striven
Saints and ascetics- their road is the same.

That way- the highest way- goes he who shuts
The gates of all his senses, locks desire
Safe in his heart, centres the vital airs
Upon his parting thought, steadfastly set;
And, murmuring OM, the sacred syllable-
Emblem of BRAHM- dies, meditating Me.

For who, none other Gods regarding, looks
Ever to Me, easily am I gained
By such a Yogi; and, attaining Me,
They fall not- those Mahatmas- back to birth,
To life, which is the place of pain, which ends,
But take the way of utmost blessedness.

The worlds, Arjuna!- even Brahma's world-
Roll back again from Death to Life's unrest;
But they, O Kunti's Son! that reach to Me,
Taste birth no more. If ye know Brahma's Day
Which is a thousand Yugas; if ye know
The thousand Yugas making Brahma's Night,
Then know ye Day and Night as He doth know!
When that vast Dawn doth break, th' Invisible
Is brought anew into the Visible;
When that deep Night doth darken, all which is
Fades back again to Him Who sent it forth;
Yea! this vast company of living things-
Again and yet again produced- expires

At Brahma's Nightfall; and, at Brahma's Dawn,
Riseth, without its will, to life new-born.
But- higher, deeper, innermost- abides
Another Life, not like the life of sense,
Escaping sight, unchanging. This endures
When all created things have passed away;
This is that Life named the Unmanifest,
The Infinite! the All! the Uttermost.
Thither arriving none return. That Life
Is Mine, and I am there! And, Prince! by faith
Which wanders not, there is a way to come
Thither. I, the PURUSHA, I Who spread
The Universe around me- in Whom dwell
All living Things- may so be reached and seen!

Richer than holy fruit on Vedas growing,
Greater than gifts, better than prayer or fast,
Such wisdom is! The Yogi, this way knowing,
Comes to the Utmost Perfect Peace at last.

CHAPTER IX: Of Religion by the Kingly Knowledge and the
Kingly Mystery

Krishna. Now will I open unto thee- whose heart
Rejects not- that last lore, deepest-concealed,
That farthest secret of My Heavens and Earths,
Which but to know shall set thee free from ills,-
A royal lore! a Kingly mystery!
Yea! for the soul such light as purgeth it
From every sin; a light of holiness
With inmost splendour shining; plain to see;
Easy to walk by, inexhaustible!

They that receive not this, failing in faith
To grasp the greater wisdom, reach not Me,
Destroyer of thy foes! They sink anew
Into the realm of Flesh, where all things change!

By Me the whole vast Universe of things
Is spread abroad;- by Me, the Unmanifest!
In Me are all existences contained;
Not I in them!
Yet they are not contained,
Those visible things! Receive and strive to embrace
The mystery majestical! My Being-
Creating all, sustaining all- still dwells
Outside of all!

See! as the shoreless airs
Move in the measureless space, but are not space,
[And space were space without the moving airs];
So all things are in Me, but are not I.

At closing of each Kalpa, Indian Prince!
All things which be back to My Being come:
At the beginning of each Kalpa, all
Issue new-born from Me.

By Energy
And help of Prakriti, my outer Self,
Again, and yet again, I make go forth
The realms of visible things- without their will-
All of them- by the power of Prakriti.

Yet these great makings, Prince! involve Me not
Enchain Me not ! I sit apart from them,
Other, and Higher, and Free; nowise attached!

Thus doth the stuff of worlds, moulded by Me,
Bring forth all that which is, moving or still,
Living or lifeless! Thus the worlds go on!

The minds untaught mistake Me, veiled in form;-
Naught see they of My secret Presence, nought
Of My hid Nature, ruling all which lives.
Vain hopes pursuing, vain deeds doing; fed
On vainest knowledge, senselessly they seek

An evil way, the way of brutes and fiends.
But My Mahatmas, those of noble soul
Who tread the path celestial, worship Me
With hearts unwandering,- knowing Me the Source,
Th' Eternal Source, of Life. Unendingly
They glorify Me; seek Me; keep their vows
Of reverence and love, with changeless faith
Adoring Me. Yea, and those too adore,
Who, offering sacrifice of wakened hearts,
Have sense of one pervading Spirit's stress,
One Force in every place, though manifold!
I am the Sacrifice! I am the Prayer!
I am the Funeral-Cake set for the dead!
I am the healing herb! I am the ghee,
The Mantra, and the flame, and that which burns!
I am- of all this boundless Universe-
The Father, Mother, Ancestor, and Guard!
The end of Learning! That which purifies
In lustral water! I am OM! I am
Rig-Veda, Sama-Veda, Yajur-Ved;
The Way, the Fosterer, the Lord, the Judge,
The Witness; the Abode, the Refuge-House,
The Friend, the Fountain and the Sea of Life
Which sends, and swallows up; Treasure of Worlds
And Treasure-Chamber! Seed and Seed-Sower,
Whence endless harvests spring! Sun's heat is mine;
Heaven's rain is mine to grant or to withhold;
Death am I, and Immortal Life I am,
Arjuna! SAT and ASAT, Visible Life,
And Life Invisible!
Yea! those who learn
The threefold Veds, who drink the Soma-wine,
Purge sins, pay sacrifice- from Me they earn
Passage to Swarga; where the meats divine

Of great gods feed them in high Indra's heaven.
Yet they, when that prodigious joy is o'er,
Paradise spent, and wage for merits given,
Come to the world of death and change once more.

They had their recompense! they stored their treasure,
Following the threefold Scripture and its writ;
Who seeketh such gaineth the fleeting pleasure
Of joy which comes and goes! I grant them it!

But to those blessed ones who worship Me,
Turning not otherwhere, with minds set fast,
I bring assurance of full bliss beyond.

Nay, and of hearts which follow other gods
In simple faith, their prayers arise to me,
O Kunti's Son! though they pray wrongfully;
For I am the Receiver and the Lord
Of every sacrifice, which these know not
Rightfully; so they fall to earth again!
Who follow gods go to their gods; who vow
Their souls to Pitris go to Pitris; minds
To evil Bhuts given o'er sink to the Bhuts;
And whoso loveth Me cometh to Me.
Whoso shall offer Me in faith and love
A leaf, a flower, a fruit, water poured forth,
That offering I accept, lovingly made
With pious will. Whate'er thou doest, Prince!
Eating or sacrificing, giving gifts,
Praying or fasting, let it all be done
For Me, as Mine. So shalt thou free thyself
From Karmabandh, the chain which holdeth men
To good and evil issue, so shalt come
Safe unto Me- when thou art quit of flesh-
By faith and abdication joined to Me!

I am alike for all! I know not hate,
I know not favour! What is made is Mine!
But them that worship Me with love, I love;
They are in Me, and I in them!

Nay, Prince!
If one of evil life turn in his thought

Straightly to Me, count him amidst the good;
He hath the high way chosen; he shall grow
Righteous ere long; he shall attain that peace
Which changes not. Thou Prince of India!
Be certain none can perish, trusting Me!
O Pritha's Son! whoso will turn to Me,
Though they be born from the very womb of Sin,
Woman or man; sprung of the Vaisya caste
Or lowly disregarded Sudra,- all
Plant foot upon the highest path; how then
The holy Brahmans and My Royal Saints?
Ah! ye who into this ill world are come-
Fleeting and false- set your faith fast on Me!
Fix heart and thought on Me! Adore Me! Bring
Offerings to Me! Make Me prostrations! Make
Me your supremest joy! and, undivided,
Unto My rest your spirits shall be guided.

CHAPTER X: Of Religion by the Heavenly Perfections

Krishna. Hear farther yet, thou Long-Armed Lord! these latest
words I say-
Uttered to bring thee bliss and peace, who lovest Me alway-
Not the great company of gods nor kingly Rishis know
My Nature, Who have made the gods and Rishis long ago;
He only knoweth- only he is free of sin, and wise,
Who seeth Me, Lord of the Worlds, with faith-enlightened eyes,
Unborn, undying, unbegun. Whatever Natures be
To mortal men distributed, those natures spring from Me!
Intellect, skill, enlightenment, endurance, self-control,
Truthfulness, equability, and grief or joy of soul,
And birth and death, and fearfulness, and fearlessness, and
shame,
And honour, and sweet harmlessness, and peace which is the
same
Whate'er befalls, and mirth, and tears, and piety and thrift,
And wish to give, and will to help,- all cometh of My gift!
The Seven Chief Saints, the Elders Four, the Lordly Manus set-

Sharing My work- to rule the worlds, these too did I beget;
And Rishis, Pitris, Manus, all, by one thought of My mind;
Thence did arise, to fill this world, the races of mankind;
Wherefrom who comprehends My Reign of mystic Majesty-
That truth of truths- is thenceforth linked in faultless faith to
Me:
Yea! knowing Me the source of all, by Me all creatures wrought,
The wise in spirit cleave to Me, into My Being brought;
Hearts fixed on Me; breaths breathed to Me; praising Me, each to
each,
So have they happiness and peace, with pious thought and
speech;
And unto these- thus serving well, thus loving ceaselessly-
I give a mind of perfect mood, whereby they draw to Me;
And, all for love of them, within their darkened souls I dwell,
And, with bright rays of wisdom's lamp, their ignorance dispel.
Arjuna. Yes! Thou art Parabrahm! The High Abode!
The Great Purification! Thou art God
Eternal, All-creating, Holy, First,
Without beginning! Lord of Lords and Gods!
Declared by all the Saints- by Narada,
Vyasa Asita, and Devalas;
And here Thyself declaring unto me!
What Thou hast said now know I to be truth,
O Kesava! that neither gods nor men
Nor demons comprehend Thy mystery
Made manifest, Divinest! Thou Thyself
Thyself alone dost know, Maker Supreme!
Master of all the living! Lord of Gods!
King of the Universe! To Thee alone
Belongs to tell the heavenly excellence
Of those perfections wherewith Thou dost fill
These worlds of Thine; Pervading, Immanent!
How shall I learn, Supremest Mystery!
To know Thee, though I muse continually?
Under what form of Thine unnumbered forms
Mayst Thou be grasped? Ah! yet again recount,
Clear and complete, Thy great appearances,
The secrets of Thy Majesty and Might,

Thou High Delight of Men! Never enough
Can mine ears drink the Amrit of such words!
Krishna. Hanta! So be it! Kuru Prince! I will to thee unfold
Some portions of My Majesty, whose powers are manifold!
I am the Spirit seated deep in every creature's heart;
From Me they come; by Me they live; at My word they depart!
Vishnu of the Adityas I am, those Lords of Light;
Maritchi of the Maruts, the Kings of Storm and Blight;
By day I gleam, the golden Sun of burning cloudless Noon;
By Night, amid the asterisms I glide, the dappled Moon!
Of Vedas I am Sama-Ved, of gods in Indra's Heaven
Vasava; of the faculties to living beings given
The mind which apprehends and thinks; of Rudras Sankara;
Of Yakshas and of Rakshasas, Vittesh; and Pavaka
Of Vasus, and of mountain-peaks Meru; Vrihaspati
Know Me 'mid planetary Powers; 'mid Warriors heavenly
Skanda; of all the water-floods the Sea which drinketh each,
And Bhrigu of the holy Saints, and OM of sacred speech;
Of prayers the prayer ye whisper; of hills Himila's snow,
And Aswattha, the fig-tree, of all the trees that grow;
Of the Devarshis, Narada; and Chitrarath of them
That sing in Heaven, and Kapila of Munis, and the gem
Of flying steeds, Uchchaisravas, from Amritwave which burst;
Of elephants Airavata; of males the Best and First;
Of weapons Heav'n's hot thunderbolt; of cows white Kamadhuk,
From whose great milky udder-teats all hearts' desires are strook;
Vasuki of the serpent-tribes, round Mandara entwined;
And thousand-fanged Ananta, on whose broad coils reclined
Leans Vishnu; and of water-things Varuna; Aryam
Of Pitris, and, of those that judge, Yama the Judge I am;
Of Daityas dread Prahlada; of what metes days and years,
Time's self I am; of woodland-beasts- buffaloes, deers, and
bears-
The lordly-painted tiger; of birds the vast Garud,
The whirlwind 'mid the winds; 'mid chiefs Rama with blood
imbrued,
Makar 'mid fishes of the sea, and Ganges 'mid the streams;
Yea! First, and Last, and Centre of all which is or seems
I am, Arjuna! Wisdom Supreme of what is wise,

Words on the uttering lips I am, and eyesight of the eyes.
And "A" of written characters, Dwandwa of knitted speech,
And Endless Life, and boundless Love, whose power
sustaineth each;
And bitter Death which seizes all, and joyous sudden Birth,
Which brings to light all beings that are to be on earth;
And of the viewless virtues, Fame, Fortune, Song am I,
And Memory, and Patience; and Craft, and Constancy:
Of Vedic hymns the Vrihatsam, of metres Gayatri,
Of months the Margasirsha, of all the seasons three
The flower-wreathed Spring; in dicer's-play the conquering
Double-Eight;
The splendour of the splendid, and the greatness of the great,
Victory I am, and Action! and the goodness of the good,
And Vasudev of Vrishni's race, and of this Pandu brood
Thyself!- Yea, my Arjuna! thyself; for thou art Mine!
Of poets Usana, of saints Vyasa, sage divine;
The policy of conquerors, the potency of kings,
The great unbroken silence in learning's secret things;
The lore of all the learned, the seed of all which springs.
Living or lifeless, still or stirred, whatever beings be,
None of them is in all the worlds, but it exists by Me!
Nor tongue can tell, Arjuna! nor end of telling come
Of these My boundless glories, whereof I teach thee some;
For wheresoe'er is wondrous work, and majesty, and might,
From Me hath all proceeded. Receive thou this aright!
Yet how shouldst thou receive, O Prince! the vastness of this
word?
I, who am all, and made it all, abide its separate Lord!

CHAPTER XI: Of the Manifesting of the One and Manifold

Arjuna. This, for my soul's peace, have I heard from Thee,
The unfolding of the Mystery Supreme
Named Adhyatman; comprehending which,
My darkness is dispelled; for now I know-
O Lotus-eyed!- whence is the birth of men,
And whence their death, and what the majesties

Of Thine immortal rule. Fain would I see,
As thou Thyself declar'st it, Sovereign Lord!
The likeness of that glory of Thy Form
Wholly revealed. O Thou Divinest One!
If this can be, if I may bear the sight,
Make Thyself visible, Lord of all prayers!
Show me Thy very self, the Eternal God!
Krishna. Gaze, then, thou Son of Pritha! I manifest for thee
Those hundred thousand thousand shapes that clothe my
Mystery:
I show thee all my semblances, infinite, rich, divine,
My changeful hues, my countless forms. See! in this face of
mine,
Adityas, Vasus, Rudras, Aswins, and Maruts; see
Wonders unnumbered, Indian Prince! revealed to none save thee.
Behold! this is the Universe!- Look! what is live and dead
I gather all in one- in Me! Gaze, as thy lips have said
On GOD, ETERNAL, VERY GOD! See ME! what thou prayest!

Thou canst not!- nor, with human eyes, Arjuna! ever mayest!
Therefore I give thee sense divine. Have other eyes, new light!
And, look! This is My glory, unveiled to mortal sight!
Sanjaya. Then, O King! to God, so saying,
Stood, to Pritha's Son displaying
All the splendour, wonder, dread
Of His vast Almighty-head.
Out of countless eyes beholding,
Out of countless mouths commanding,
Countless mystic forms enfolding
In one Form: supremely standing
Countless radiant glories wearing,
Countless heavenly weapons bearing,
Crowned with garlands of star-clusters,
Robed in garb of woven lustres,
Breathing from His perfect Presence
Breaths of every subtle essence
Of all heavenly odours; shedding
Blinding brilliance; overspreading-
Boundless, beautiful- all spaces

With His all-regarding faces;
So He showed! If there should rise
Suddenly within the skies
Sunburst of a thousand suns
Flooding earth with beams undeemed-of,
Then might be that Holy One's
Majesty and radiance dreamed of!

So did Pandu's Son behold
All this universe enfold
All its huge diversity
Into one vast shape, and be
Visible, and viewed, and blended
In one Body- subtle, splendid,
Nameless- th' All-comprehending
God of Gods, the Never-Ending
Deity!

But, sore amazed,
Thrilled, o'erfilled, dazzled, and dazed,
Arjuna knelt; and bowed his head,
And clasped his palms; and cried, and said:
Arjuna. Yea! I have seen! I see!
Lord! all is wrapped in Thee!
The gods are in Thy glorious frame! the creatures
Of earth, and heaven, and hell
In Thy Divine form dwell,
And in Thy countenance shine all the features

Of Brahma, sitting lone
Upon His lotus-throne;
Of saints and sages, and the serpent races
Ananta, Vasuki;
Yea! mightiest Lord! I see
Thy thousand thousand arms and breasts, and faces,

And eyes,- on every side
Perfect, diversified;
And nowhere end of Thee, nowhere beginning,

Nowhere a centre! Shifts-
Wherever soul's gaze lifts-
Thy central Self, all-wielding, and all-winning!

Infinite King! I see
The anadem on Thee,
The club, the shell, the discus; see Thee burning
In beams insufferable,
Lighting earth, heaven, and hell
With brilliance blazing, glowing, flashing; turning

Darkness to dazzling day,
Look I whichever way;
Ah, Lord! I worship Thee, the Undivided,
The Uttermost of thought,
The Treasure-Palace wrought
To hold the wealth of the worlds; the Shield provided

To shelter Virtue's laws;
The Fount whence Life's stream draws
All waters of all rivers of all being:
The One Unborn, Unending:
Unchanging and Unblending!
With might and majesty, past thought, past seeing!

Silver of moon and gold
Of sun are glories rolled
From Thy great eyes; Thy visage, beaming tender
Throughout the stars and skies,
Doth to warm life surprise
Thy Universe. The worlds are filled with wonder

Of Thy perfections! Space
Star-sprinkled, and void place
From pole to pole of the Blue, from bound to bound,
Hath Thee in every spot,
Thee, Thee!- Where Thou art not,
O Holy, Marvellous Form! is nowhere found!

O Mystic, Awful One!
At sight of Thee, made known,
The Three Worlds quake; the lower gods draw nigh Thee;
They fold their palms, and bow
Body, and breast, and brow,
And, whispering worship, laud and magnify Thee!

Rishis and Siddhas cry
"Hail! Highest Majesty!
From sage and singer breaks the hymn of glory
In dulcet harmony,
Sounding the praise of Thee;
While countless companies take up the story,

Rudras, who ride the storms,
Th' Adityas' shining forms,
Vasus and Sadhyas, Viswas, Ushmapas;
Maruts, and those great Twins
The heavenly, fair, Aswins,
Gandharvas, Rakshasas, Siddhas, and Asuras,-

These see Thee, and revere
In sudden-stricken fear;
Yea! the Worlds,- seeing Thee with form stupendous,
With faces manifold,
With eyes which all behold,
Unnumbered eyes, vast arms, members tremendous,

Flanks, lit with sun and star,
Feet planted near and far,
Tushes of terror, mouths wrathful and tender;-
The Three wide Worlds before Thee
Adore, as I adore Thee,
Quake, as I quake, to witness so much splendour!

I mark Thee strike the skies
With front, in wondrous wise
Huge, rainbow-painted, glittering; and thy mouth
Opened, and orbs which see

All things, whatever be
In all Thy worlds, east, west, and north and south.

O Eyes of God! O Head!
My strength of soul is fled,
Gone is heart's force, rebuked is mind's desire!
When I behold Thee so,
With awful brows a-glow,
With burning glance, and lips lighted by fire

Fierce as those flames which shall
Consume, at close of all,
Earth, Heaven! Ah me! I see no Earth and Heaven!
Thee, Lord of Lords! I see,
Thee only- only Thee!
Now let Thy mercy unto me be given,

Thou Refuge of the World!
Lo! to the cavern hurled
Of Thy wide-opened throat, and lips white-tushed,
I see our noblest ones,
Great Dhritarashtra's sons,
Bhishma, Drona, and Karna, caught and crushed!

The Kings and Chiefs drawn in,
That gaping gorge within;
The best of both these armies torn and riven!
Between Thy jaws they lie
Mangled full bloodily,
Ground into dust and death! Like streams down-driven

With helpless haste, which go
In headlong furious flow
Straight to the gulfing deeps of th' unfilled ocean,
So to that flaming cave
Those heroes great and brave
Pour, in unending streams, with helpless motion!

Like moths which in the night

Flutter towards a light,
Drawn to their fiery doom, flying and dying,
So to their death still throng,
Blind, dazzled, borne along
Ceaselessly, all those multitudes, wild flying!

Thou, that hast fashioned men,
Devourest them again,
One with another, great and small, alike!
The creatures whom Thou mak'st,
With flaming jaws Thou tak'st,
Lapping them up! Lord God! Thy terrors strike

From end to end of earth,
Filling life full, from birth
To death, with deadly, burning, lurid dread!
Ah, Vishnu! make me know
Why is Thy visage so?
Who art Thou, feasting thus upon Thy dead?

Who? awful Deity!
I bow myself to Thee,
Namostu Te, Devavara! Prasid!
O Mightiest Lord! rehearse
Why hast Thou face so fierce?
Whence doth this aspect horrible proceed?
Krishna. Thou seest Me as Time who kills,
Time who brings all to doom,
The Slayer Time, Ancient of Days, come hither to consume;
Excepting thee, of all these hosts of hostile chiefs arrayed,
There stands not one shall leave alive the battlefield! Dismayed
No longer be! Arise! obtain renown! destroy thy foes!
Fight for the kingdom waiting thee when thou hast vanquished
those.
By Me they fall- not thee! the stroke of death is dealt them now,
Even as they show thus gallantly; My instrument art thou!
Strike, strong-armed Prince, at Drona! at Bhishma strike! deal
death
On Karna, Jyadratha; stay all their warlike breath!

'Tis I who bid them perish! Thou wilt but slay the slain;
Fight! they must fall, and thou must live, victor upon this plain!
Sanjaya. Hearing mighty Keshav's word,
Trembling that helmed Lord
Clasped his lifted palms, and- praying
Grace of Krishna- stood there, saying,
With bowed brow and accents broken,
These words, timorously spoken:
Arjuna. Worthily, Lord of Might!
The whole world hath delight
In Thy surpassing power, obeying Thee;
The Rakshasas, in dread
At sight of Thee, are sped
To all four quarters; and the company

Of Siddhas sound Thy name.
How should they not proclaim
Thy Majesties, Divinest, Mightiest?
Thou Brahm, than Brahma greater!
Thou Infinite Creator!
Thou God of gods, Life's Dwelling-place and Rest.

Thou, of all souls the Soul!
The Comprehending Whole!
Of being formed, and formless being the Framer;
O Utmost One! O Lord!
Older than eld, Who stored
The worlds with wealth of life! O Treasure-Claimer,

Who wottest all, and art
Wisdom Thyself! O Part
In all, and All; for all from Thee have risen
Numberless now I see
The aspects are of Thee!
Vayu Thou art, and He who keeps the prison

Of Narak, Yama dark;
And Agni's shining spark;
Varuna's waves are Thy waves. Moon and starlight

145

Are Thine! Prajapati
Art Thou, and 'tis to Thee
They knelt in worshipping the old world's far light,

The first of mortal men.
Again, Thou God! again
A thousand thousand times be magnified!
Honour and worship be-
Glory and praise,- to Thee
Namo, Namaste, cried on every side;
Cried here, above, below,
Uttered when Thou dost go,
Uttered where Thou dost come! Namo! we call;
Namostu! God adored!
Namostu! Nameless Lord
Hail to Thee! Praise to Thee Thou One in all;

For Thou art All! Yea, Thou!
Ah! if in anger now
Thou shouldst remember I did think Thee Friend,
Speaking with easy speech,
As men use each to each;
Did call Thee "Krishna," "Prince," nor comprehend

Thy hidden majesty,
The might, the awe of Thee;
Did, in my heedlessness, or in my love,
On journey, or in jest,
Or when we lay at rest,
Sitting at council, straying in the grove,

Alone, or in the throng,
Do Thee, most Holy! wrong,
Be Thy grace granted for that witless sin
For Thou art, now I know,
Father of all below,
Of all above, of all the worlds within

Guru of Gurus; more

To reverence and adore
Than all which is adorable and high!
How, in the wide worlds three
Should any equal be?
Should any other share Thy Majesty?

Therefore, with body bent
And reverent intent,
I praise, and serve, and seek Thee, asking grace.
As father to a son,
As friend to friend, as one
Who loveth to his lover, turn Thy face

In gentleness on me!
Good is it I did see
This unknown marvel of Thy Form! But fear
Mingles with joy! Retake,
Dear Lord! for pity's sake
Thine earthly shape, which earthly eyes may bear!

Be merciful, and show
The visage that I know;
Let me regard Thee, as of yore, arrayed
With disc and forehead-gem,
With mace and anadem,
Thou that sustainest all things! Undismayed

Let me once more behold
The form I loved of old,
Thou of the thousand arms and countless eyes!
This frightened heart is fain
To see restored again
My Charioteer, in Krishna's kind disguise.

Krishna. Yea! thou hast seen, Arjuna! because I loved thee well,
The secret countenance of Me, revealed by mystic spell,
Shining, and wonderful, and majestic, manifold,
Which none save thou in all the years had favour to behold;
For not by Vedas cometh this, nor sacrifice, nor alms,

Nor works well-done, nor penance long, nor prayers, nor chanted
psalms,
That mortal eyes should bear to view the Immortal Soul unclad,
Prince of the Kurus! This was kept for thee alone! Be glad!
Let no more trouble shake thy heart, because thine eyes have
seen
My terror with My glory. As I before have been
So will I be again for thee; with lightened heart behold!
Once more I am thy Krishna, the form thou knew'st of old!
Sanjaya. These words to Arjuna spake
Vasudev, and straight did take
Back again the semblance dear
Of the well-loved charioteer;
Peace and joy it did restore
When the Prince beheld once more
Mighty BRAHMA'S form and face
Clothed in Krishna's gentle grace.
Arjuna. Now that I see come back, Janardana!
This friendly human frame, my mind can think
Calm thoughts once more; my heart beats still again!
Krishna. Yea! it was wonderful and terrible
To view me as thou didst, dear Prince! The gods
Dread and desire continually to view!
Yet not by Vedas, nor from sacrifice,
Nor penance, nor gift-giving, nor with prayer
Shall any so behold, as thou hast seen!
Only by fullest service, perfect faith,
And uttermost surrender am I known
And seen, and entered into, Indian Prince!
Who doeth all for Me; who findeth Me
In all; adoreth always; loveth all
Which I have made, and Me, for Love's sole end,
That man, Arjuna! unto Me doth wend.

CHAPTER XII: Of the Religion of Faith

Arjuna. Lord! of the men who serve Thee- true in heart-
As God revealed; and of the men who serve,

Worshipping Thee Unrevealed, Unbodied, Far,
Which take the better way of faith and life?
Krishna. Whoever serve Me- as I show Myself-
Constantly true, in full devotion fixed,
Those hold I very holy. But who serve-
Worshipping Me The One, The Invisible,
The Unrevealed, Unnamed, Unthinkable,
Uttermost, All-pervading, Highest, Sure-
Who thus adore Me, mastering their sense,
Of one set mind to all, glad in all good,
These blessed souls come unto Me.
Yet, hard
The travail is for such as bend their minds
To reach th' Unmanifest. That viewless path
Shall scarce be trod by man bearing the flesh!
But whereso any doeth all his deeds
Renouncing self for Me, full of Me, fixed
To serve only the Highest, night and day
Musing on Me- him will I swiftly lift
Forth from life's ocean of distress and death,
Whose soul clings fast to Me. Cling thou to Me!
Clasp Me with heart and mind! so shalt thou dwell
Surely with Me on high. But if thy thought
Droops from such height; if thou be'st weak to set
Body and soul upon Me constantly,
Despair not! give Me lower service! I seek
To reach Me, worshipping with steadfast will;
And, if thou canst not worship steadfastly,
Work for Me, toil in works pleasing to Me!
For he that laboureth right for love of Me
Shall finally attain! But, if in this
Thy faint heart fails, bring Me thy failure! find
Refuge in Me! let fruits of labour go,
Renouncing hope for Me, with lowliest heart,
So shalt thou come; for, though to know is more
Than diligence, yet worship better is
Than knowing, and renouncing better still.
Near to renunciation- very near-
Dwelleth Eternal Peace!

Who hateth nought
Of all which lives, living himself benign,
Compassionate, from arrogance exempt,
Exempt from love of self, unchangeable
By good or ill; patient, contented, firm
In faith, mastering himself, true to his word,
Seeking Me, heart and soul; vowed unto Me,-
That man I love! Who troubleth not his kind,
And is not troubled by them; clear of wrath,
Living too high for gladness, grief, or fear,
That man I love! Who, dwelling quiet-eyed,
Stainless, serene, well-balanced, unperplexed,
Working with Me, yet from all works detached,
That man I love! Who, fixed in faith on Me,
Dotes upon none, scorns none; rejoices not,
And grieves not, letting good or evil hap
Light when it will, and when it will depart,
That man I love! Who, unto friend and foe
Keeping an equal heart, with equal mind
Bears shame and glory; with an equal peace
Takes heat and cold, pleasure and pain; abides
Quit of desires, hears praise or calumny
In passionless restraint, unmoved by each;
Linked by no ties to earth, steadfast in Me,
That man I love! But most of all I love
Those happy ones to whom 'tis life to live
In single fervid faith and love unseeing,
Drinking the blessed Amrit of my Being!

CHAPTER XIII: Of Religion by Separation of Matter and Spirit

Arjuna. Now would I hear, O gracious Kesava!
Of Life which seems, and Soul beyond, which sees,
And what it is we know- or think to know.
Krishna. Yea! Son of Kunti! for this flesh ye see
Is Kshetra, is the field where Life disports;
And that which views and knows it is the Soul,

Kshetrajna. In all "fields," thou Indian prince!
I am Kshetrajna. I am what surveys!
Only that knowledge knows which knows the known
By the knower! What it is, that "field" of life,
What qualities it hath, and whence it is,
And why it changeth, and the faculty
That wotteth it, the mightiness of this,
And how it wotteth- hear these things from Me!

The elements, the conscious life, the mind,
The unseen vital force, the nine strange gates
Of the body, and the five domains of sense;
Desire, dislike, pleasure and pain, and thought
Deep-woven, and persistency of being;
These all are wrought on Matter by the Soul!

Humbleness, truthfulness, and harmlessness,
Patience and honour, reverence for the wise.
Purity, constancy, control of self,
Contempt of sense-delights, self-sacrifice,
Perception of the certitude of ill
In birth, death, age, disease, suffering, and sin;
Detachment, lightly holding unto home,
Children, and wife, and all that bindeth men;
An ever-tranquil heart in fortunes good
And fortunes evil, with a will set firm
To worship Me- Me only! ceasing not;
Loving all solitudes, and shunning noise
Of foolish crowds; endeavours resolute
To reach perception of the Utmost Soul,
And grace to understand what gain it were
So to attain,- this is true Wisdom, Prince!
And what is otherwise is ignorance!

Now will I speak of knowledge best to know-
That Truth which giveth man Amrit to drink,
The Truth of HIM, the Para-Brahm, the All,
The Uncreated; not Asat, nor Sat,
Not Form, nor the Unformed; yet both, and more;-

Whose hands are everywhere, and everywhere
Planted His feet, and everywhere His eyes
Beholding, and His ears in every place
Hearing, and all His faces everywhere
Enlightening and encompassing His worlds.
Glorified in the senses He hath given,
Yet beyond sense He is; sustaining all,
Yet dwells He unattached: of forms and modes
Master, yet neither form nor mode hath He;
He is within all beings- and without-
Motionless, yet still moving; not discerned
For subtlety of instant presence; close
To all, to each; yet measurelessly far!
Not manifold, and yet subsisting still
In all which lives; for ever to be known
As the Sustainer, yet, at the End of Times,
He maketh all to end- and re-creates.
The Light of Lights He is, in the heart of the Dark
Shining eternally. Wisdom He is
And Wisdom's way, and Guide of all the wise,
Planted in every heart.

So have I told
Of Life's stuff, and the moulding, and the lore
To comprehend. Whoso, adoring Me,
Perceiveth this, shall surely come to Me!

Know thou that Nature and the Spirit both
Have no beginning! Know that qualities
And changes of them are by Nature wrought;
That Nature puts to work the acting frame,
But Spirit doth inform it, and so cause
Feeling of pain and pleasure. Spirit, linked
To moulded matter, entereth into bond
With qualities by Nature framed, and, thus
Married to matter, breeds the birth again
In good or evil yonis.
Yet is this-
Yea! in its bodily prison!- Spirit pure,

Spirit supreme; surveying, governing,
Guarding, possessing; Lord and Master still
PURUSHA, Ultimate, One Soul with Me.

Whoso thus knows himself, and knows his soul
PURUSHA, working through the qualities
With Nature's modes, the light hath come for him!
Whatever flesh he bears, never again
Shall he take on its load. Some few there be
By meditation find the Soul in Self
Self-schooled; and some by long philosophy
And holy life reach thither; some by works:
Some, never so attaining, hear of light
From other lips, and seize, and cleave to it
Worshipping; yea! and those- to teaching true-
Overpass Death!
Wherever, Indian Prince!
Life is- of moving things, or things unmoved,
Plant or still seed- know, what is there hath grown
By bond of Matter and of Spirit: Know
He sees indeed who sees in all alike
The living, lordly Soul; the Soul Supreme,
Imperishable amid the Perishing:
For, whoso thus beholds, in every place,
In every form, the same, one, Living Life,
Doth no more wrongfulness unto himself,
But goes the highest road which brings to bliss.
Seeing, he sees, indeed, who sees that works
Are Nature's wont, for Soul to practise by
Acting, yet not the agent; sees the mass
Of separate living things- each of its kind-
Issue from One, and blend again to One:
Then hath he BRAHMA, he attains!
O Prince!
That Ultimate, High Spirit, Uncreate,
Unqualified, even when it entereth flesh
Taketh no stain of acts, worketh in nought!
Like to th' ethereal air, pervading all,
Which, for sheer subtlety, avoideth taint,

The subtle Soul sits everywhere, unstained:
Like to the light of the all-piercing sun
[Which is not changed by aught it shines upon,]
The Soul's light shineth pure in every place;
And they who, by such eye of wisdom, see
How Matter, and what deals with it, divide;
And how the Spirit and the flesh have strife,
Those wise ones go the way which leads to Life!

CHAPTER XIV: Of Religion by Separation from the Qualities

Krishna. Yet farther will I open unto thee
This wisdom of all wisdoms, uttermost,
The which possessing, all My saints have passed
To perfectness. On such high verities
Reliant, rising into fellowship
With Me, they are not born again at birth
Of Kalpas, nor at Pralyas suffer change!

This Universe the womb is where I plant
Seed of all lives! Thence, Prince of India, comes
Birth to all beings! Whoso, Kunti's Son!
Mothers each mortal form, Brahma conceives,
And I am He that fathers, sending seed!

Sattwan, Rajas, and Tamas, so are named
The qualities of Nature, "Soothfastness,"
"Passion," and "Ignorance." These three bind down
The changeless Spirit in the changeful flesh.
Whereof sweet "Soothfastness," by purity
Living unsullied and enlightened, binds
The sinless Soul to happiness and truth;
And Passion, being kin to appetite,
And breeding impulse and propensity,
Binds the embodied Soul, O Kunti's Son!
By tie of works. But Ignorance, begot
Of Darkness, blinding mortal men, binds down

154

Their souls to stupor, sloth, and drowsiness.
Yea, Prince of India! Soothfastness binds souls
In pleasant wise to flesh; and Passion binds
By toilsome strain; but Ignorance, which blots
The beams of wisdom, binds the soul to sloth.
Passion and Ignorance, once overcome,
Leave Soothfastness, O Bharata! Where this
With Ignorance are absent, Passion rules;
And Ignorance in hearts not good nor quick.
When at all gateways of the Body shines
The Lamp of Knowledge, then may one see well
Soothfastness settled in that city reigns;
Where longing is, and ardour, and unrest,
Impulse to strive and gain, and avarice,
Those spring from Passion- Prince!- engrained; and where
Darkness and dulness, sloth and stupor are,
'Tis Ignorance hath caused them, Kuru Chief!

Moreover, when a soul departeth, fixed
In Soothfastness, it goeth to the place-
Perfect and pure- of those that know all Truth.
If it departeth in set habitude
Of Impulse, it shall pass into the world
Of spirits tied to works; and, if it dies
In hardened Ignorance, that blinded soul
Is born anew in some unlighted womb.

The fruit of Soothfastness is true and sweet;
The fruit of lusts is pain and toil; the fruit
Of Ignorance is deeper darkness. Yea!
For Light brings light, and Passion ache to have;
And gloom, bewilderments, and ignorance
Grow forth from Ignorance. Those of the first
Rise ever higher; those of the second mode
Take a mid place; the darkened souls sink back
To lower deeps, loaded with witlessness!

When, watching life, the living man perceives
The only actors are the Qualities,

And knows what rules beyond the Qualities,
Then is he come nigh unto Me!
The Soul,
Thus passing forth from the Three Qualities-
Whereby arise all bodies- overcomes
Birth, Death, Sorrow, and Age; and drinketh deep
The undying wine of Amrit.
Arjuna. Oh, my Lord!
Which be the signs to know him that hath gone
Past the Three Modes? How liveth he? What way
Leadeth him safe beyond the threefold Modes?
Krishna. He who with equanimity surveys
Lustre of goodness, strife of passion, sloth
Of ignorance, not angry if they are,
Not wishful when they are not: he who sits
A sojourner and stranger in their midst
Unruffled, standing off, saying- serene-
When troubles break, "These be the Qualities!
He unto whom- self-centred- grief and joy
Sound as one word; to whose deep-seeing eyes
The clod, the marble, and the gold are one;
Whose equal heart holds the same gentleness
For lovely and unlovely things, firm-set,
Well-pleased in praise and dispraise; satisfied
With honour or dishonour; unto friends
And unto foes alike in tolerance;
Detached from undertakings,- he is named
Surmounter of the Qualities!

And such-
With single, fervent faith adoring Me,
Passing beyond the Qualities, conforms
To Brahma, and attains Me!

For I am
That whereof Brahma is the likeness! Mine
The Amrit is; and Immortality
Is mine; and mine perfect Felicity!

CHAPTER XV: Of Religion by Attaining the Supreme

Krishna. Men call the Aswattha,- the Banyan-tree,-
Which hath its boughs beneath, its roots above,-
The ever-holy tree. Yea! for its leaves
Are green and waving hymns which whisper Truth!
Who knows the Aswattha, knows Veds, and all.

Its branches shoot to heaven and sink to earth,
Even as the deeds of men, which take their birth
From qualities: its silver sprays and blooms,
And all the eager verdure of its girth,
Leap to quick life at kiss of sun and air,
As men's lives quicken to the temptings fair
Of wooing sense: its hanging rootlets seek
The soil beneath, helping to hold it there,

As actions wrought amid this world of men
Bind them by ever-tightening bonds again.
If ye knew well the teaching of the Tree,
What its shape saith; and whence it springs; and, then

How it must end, and all the ills of it,
The axe of sharp Detachment ye would whet,
And cleave the clinging snaky roots, and lay
This Aswattha of sense-life low,- to set

New growths upspringing to that happier sky,-
Which they who reach shall have no day to die,
Nor fade away, nor fall- to Him, I mean,
FATHER and FIRST, Who made the mystery

Of old Creation; for to Him come they
From passion and from dreams who break away;
Who part the bonds constraining them to flesh,
And,- Him, the Highest, worshipping alway-

No longer grow at mercy of what breeze
Of summer pleasure stirs the sleeping trees,

What blast of tempest tears them, bough and stem:
To the eternal world pass such as these!

Another Sun gleams there! another Moon!
Another Light,- not Dusk, nor Dawn, nor Noon-
Which they who once behold return no more;
They have attained My rest, life's Utmost boon!

When, in this world of manifested life,
The undying Spirit, setting forth from Me,
Taketh on form, it draweth to itself
From Being's storehouse,- which containeth all,-
Senses and intellect. The Sovereign Soul
Thus entering the flesh, or quitting it,
Gathers these up, as the wind gathers scents,
Blowing above the flower.-beds. Ear and Eye,
And Touch and Taste, and Smelling, these it takes,-
Yea, and a sentient mind;- linking itself
To sense-things so.
The unenlightened ones
Mark not that Spirit when he goes or comes,
Nor when he takes his pleasure in the form,
Conjoined with qualities; but those see plain
Who have the eyes to see. Holy souls see
Which strive thereto. Enlightened, they perceive
That Spirit in themselves; but foolish ones,
Even though they strive, discern not, having hearts
Unkindled, ill-informed!
Know, too, from Me
Shineth the gathered glory of the suns
Which lighten all the world: from Me the moons
Draw silvery beams, and fire fierce loveliness.
I penetrate the clay, and lend all shapes
Their living force; I glide into the plant-
Root, leaf, and bloom- to make the woodlands green
With springing sap. Becoming vital warmth,
I glow in glad, respiring frames, and pass,
With outward and with inward breath, to feed
The body by all meats.

For in this world
Being is twofold: the Divided, one;
The Undivided, one. All things that live
Are "the Divided." That which sits apart,
"The Undivided."
Higher still is He,
The Highest, holding all, whose Name is LORD,
The Eternal, Sovereign, First! Who fills all worlds,
Sustaining them. And- dwelling thus beyond
Divided Being and Undivided- I
Am called of men and Vedas, Life Supreme,
The PURUSHOTTAMA.
Who knows Me thus,
With mind unclouded, knoweth all, dear Prince!
And with his whole soul ever worshippeth Me.

Now is the sacred, secret Mystery
Declared to thee! Who comprehendeth this
Hath wisdom! He is quit of works in bliss!

CHAPTER XVI: Of the Separateness of the Divine and the
Undivine

Krishna. Fearlessness, singleness of soul, the wilL
Always to strive for wisdom; opened hand
And governed appetites; and piety,
And love of lonely study; humbleness,
Uprightness, heed to injure nought which lives,
Truthfulness, slowness unto wrath, a mind
That lightly letteth go what others prize;
And equanimity, and charity
Which spieth no man's faults; and tenderness
Towards all that suffer; a contented heart,
Fluttered by no desires; a bearing mild,
Modest, and grave, with manhood nobly mixed,
With patience, fortitude, and purity;
An unrevengeful spirit, never given

To rate itself too high;- such be the signs,
O Indian Prince! of him whose feet are set
On that fair path which leads to heavenly birth!

Deceitfulness, and arrogance, and pride,
Quickness to anger, harsh and evil speech,
And ignorance, to its own darkness blind,-
These be the signs, My Prince! of him whose birth
Is fated for the regions of the vile.

The Heavenly Birth brings to deliverance,
So should'st thou know! The birth with Asuras
Brings into bondage. Be thou joyous, Prince!
Whose lot is set apart for heavenly Birth.

Two stamps there are marked on all living men,
Divine and Undivine; I spake to thee
By what marks thou shouldst know the Heavenly Man,
Hear from me now of the Unheavenly!

They comprehend not, the Unheavenly,
How Souls go forth from Me; nor how they come
Back unto Me: nor is there Truth in these,
Nor purity, nor rule of Life. "This world
Hath not a Law, nor Order, nor a Lord,"
So say they: "nor hath risen up by Cause
Following on Cause, in perfect purposing,
But is none other than a House of Lust."
And, this thing thinking, all those ruined ones-
Of little wit, dark-minded- give themselves
To evil deeds, the curses of their kind.
Surrendered to desires insatiable,
Full of deceitfulness, folly, and pride,
In blindness cleaving to their errors, caught
Into the sinful course, they trust this lie
As it were true- this lie which leads to death-
Finding in Pleasure all the good which is,
And crying "Here it finisheth!"

Ensnared
In nooses of a hundred idle hopes,
Slaves to their passion and their wrath, they buy
Wealth with base deeds, to glut hot appetites;
"Thus much, to-day," they say, "we gained! thereby
Such and such wish of heart shall have its fill;
And this is ours! and th' other shall be ours!
To-day we slew a foe, and we will slay
Our other enemy to-morrow! Look!
Are we not lords? Make we not goodly cheer?
Is not our fortune famous, brave, and great?
Rich are we, proudly born! What other men
Live like to us? Kill, then, for sacrifice!
Cast largesse, and be merry!" So they speak
Darkened by ignorance; and so they fall-
Tossed to and fro with projects, tricked, and bound
In net of black delusion, lost in lusts-
Down to foul Naraka. Conceited, fond,
Stubborn and proud, dead-drunken with the wine
Of wealth, and reckless, all their offerings
Have but a show of reverence, being not made
In piety of ancient faith. Thus vowed
To self-hood, force, insolence, feasting, wrath,
These My blasphemers, in the forms they wear
And in the forms they breed, my foemen are,
Hateful and hating; cruel, evil, vile,
Lowest and least of men, whom I cast down
Again, and yet again, at end of lives,
Into some devilish womb, whence- birth by birth-
The devilish wombs re-spawn them, all beguiled;
And, till they find and worship Me, sweet Prince!
Tread they that Nether Road.

The Doors of Hell
Are threefold, whereby men to ruin pass,-
The door of Lust, the door of Wrath, the door
Of Avarice. Let a man shun those three!
He who shall turn aside from entering
All those three gates of Narak, wendeth straight

To find his peace, and comes to Swarga's gate.

CHAPTER XVII: Of Religion by the Threefold Kinds of Faith

Arjuna. If men forsake the holy ordinance,
Heedless of Shastras, yet keep faith at heart
And worship, what shall be the state of those,
Great Krishna! Sattwan, Rajas, Tamas? Say!
Krishna. Threefold the faith is of mankind, and springs
From those three qualities,- becoming "true,"
Or "passion-stained," or "dark," as thou shalt hear!

The faith of each believer, Indian Prince!
Conforms itself to what he truly is.
Where thou shalt see a worshipper, that one
To what he worships lives assimilate,
[Such as the shrine, so is the votary,]
The "soothfast" souls adore true gods; the souls
Obeying Rajas worship Rakshasas
Or Yakshas; and the men of Darkness pray
To Pretas and to Bhutas. Yea, and those
Who practise bitter penance, not enjoined
By rightful rule- penance which hath its root
In self-sufficient, proud hypocrisies-
Those men, passion-beset, violent, wild,
Torturing- the witless ones- My elements
Shut in fair company within their flesh,
(Nay, Me myself, present within the flesh!)
Know them to devils devoted, not to Heaven!
For like as foods are threefold for mankind
In nourishing, so is there threefold way
Of worship, abstinence, and almsgiving!
Hear this of Me! there is a food which brings
Force, substance, strength, and health, and joy to live,
Being well-seasoned, cordial, comforting,
The "Soothfast" meat. And there be foods which bring
Aches and unrests, and burning blood, and grief
Being too biting, heating, salt, and sharp,

And therefore craved by too strong appetite.
And there is foul food- kept from over-night,
Savourless, filthy, which the foul will eat,
A feast of rottenness, meet for the lips
Of such as love the "Darkness."

Thus with rites;-
A sacrifice not for rewardment made,
Offered in rightful wise, when he who vows
Sayeth, with heart devout, "This I should do!
Is "Soothfast" rite. But sacrifice for gain,
Offered for good repute, be sure that this,
O Best of Bharatas! is Rajas-rite,
With stamp of "passion." And a sacrifice
Offered against the laws, with no due dole
Of food-giving, with no accompaniment
Of hallowed hymn, nor largesse to the priests,
In faithless celebration, call it vile,
The deed of "Darkness!"- lost!
Worship of gods
Meriting worship; lowly reverence
Of Twice-borns, Teachers, Elders; Purity,
Rectitude, and the Brahmacharya's vow,
And not to injure any helpless thing,-
These make a true religiousness of Act.

Words causing no man woe, words ever true,
Gentle and pleasing words, and those ye say
In murmured reading of a Sacred Writ,-
These make the true religiousness of Speech.

Serenity of soul, benignity,
Sway of the silent Spirit, constant stress
To sanctify the Nature,- these things make
Good rite, and true religiousness of Mind.

Such threefold faith, in highest piety
Kept, with no hope of gain, by hearts devote
Is perfect work of Sattwan, true belief.

Religion shown in act of proud display
To win good entertainment, worship, fame,
Such- say I- is of Rajas, rash and vain.

Religion followed by a witless will
To torture self, or come at power to hurt
Another,- 'tis of Tamas, dark and ill.

The gift lovingly given, when one shall say
"Now must I gladly give!" when he who takes
Can render nothing back; made in due place,
Due time, and to a meet recipient,
Is gift of Sattwan, fair and profitable.

The gift selfishly given, where to receive
Is hoped again, or when some end is sought,
Or where the gift is proffered with a grudge,
This is of Rajas, stained with impulse, ill.

The gift churlishly flung, at evil time,
In wrongful place, to base recipient,
Made in disdain or harsh unkindliness,
Is gift of Tamas, dark; it doth not bless!

CHAPTER XVIII: Of Religion by Deliverance and Renunciation

Arjuna. Fain would I better know, Thou Glorious One!
The very truth- Heart's Lord!- of Sannyas,
Abstention; and Renunciation, Lord!
Tyaga; and what separates these twain!
Krishna. The poets rightly teach that Sannyas
Is the foregoing of all acts which spring
Out of desire; and their wisest say
Tyaga is renouncing fruit of acts.

There be among the saints some who have held
All action sinful, and to be renounced;

And some who answer, "Nay! the goodly acts-
As worship, penance, alms- must be performed!"
Hear now My sentence, Best of Bharatas!

'Tis well set forth, O Chaser of thy Foes!
Renunciation is of threefold form,
And Worship, Penance, Alms, not to be stayed;
Nay, to be gladly done; for all those three
Are purifying waters for true souls!

Yet must be practised even those high works
In yielding up attachment, and all fruit
Produced by works. This is My judgment, Prince!
This My insuperable and fixed decree!

Abstaining from a work by right prescribed
Never is meet! So to abstain doth spring
From "Darkness," and Delusion teacheth it.
Abstaining from a work grievous to flesh,
When one saith "'Tis unpleasing!" this is null!
Such an one acts from "passion;" nought of gain
Wins his Renunciation! But, Arjun!
Abstaining from attachment to the work,
Abstaining from rewardment in the work,
While yet one doeth it full faithfully,
Saying, "'Tis right to do!" that is "true" act
And abstinence! Who doeth duties so,
Unvexed if his work fail, if it succeed
Unflattered, in his own heart justified,
Quit of debates and doubts, his is "true" act:
For, being in the body, none may stand
Wholly aloof from act; yet, who abstains
From profit of his acts is abstinent.

The fruit of labours, in the fives to come,
Is threefold for all men,- Desirable,
And Undesirable, and mixed of both;
But no fruit is at all where no work was.

Hear from me, Long-armed Lord! the makings five
Which go to every act, in Sankhya taught
As necessary. First the force; and then
The agent; next, the various instruments;
Fourth, the especial effort; fifth, the God.
What work soever any mortal doth
Of body, mind, or speech, evil or good,
By these five doth he that. Which being thus,
Whoso, for lack of knowledge, seeth himself
As the sole actor, knoweth nought at all
And seeth nought. Therefore, I say, if one-
Holding aloof from self- with unstained mind
Should slay all yonder host, being bid to slay,
He doth not slay; he is not bound thereby!

Knowledge, the thing known, and the mind which knows,
These make the threefold starting-ground of act.
The act, the actor, and the instrument,
These make the threefold total of the deed.
But knowledge, agent, act, are differenced
By three dividing qualities. Hear now
Which be the qualities dividing them.

There is "true" Knowledge. Learn thou it is this:
To see one changeless Life in all the Lives,
And in the Separate, One Inseparable.
There is imperfect Knowledge: that which sees
The separate existences apart,
And, being separated, holds them real.
There is false Knowledge: that which blindly clings
To one as if 'twere all, seeking no Cause,
Deprived of light, narrow, and dull, and "dark."

There is "right" Action: that which- being enjoined-
Is wrought without attachment, passionlessly,
For duty, not for love, nor hate, nor gain.
There is "vain" Action: that which men pursue
Aching to satisfy desires, impelled
By sense of self, with all-absorbing stress:

This is of Rajas- passionate and vain.
There is "dark" Action: when one doth a thing
Heedless of issues, heedless of the hurt
Or wrong for others, heedless if he harm
His own soul- 'tis of Tamas, black and bad!

There is the "rightful" doer. He who acts
Free from self-seeking, humble, resolute,
Steadfast, in good or evil hap the same,
Content to do aright- he "truly" acts.
There is th' "impassioned" doer. He that works
From impulse, seeking profit, rude and bold
To overcome, unchastened; slave by turns
Of sorrow and of joy: of Rajas he!
And there be evil doers; loose of heart,
Low-minded, stubborn, fraudulent, remiss,
Dull, slow, despondent- children of the "dark."

Hear, too, of Intellect and Steadfastness
The threefold separation, Conqueror-Prince!
How these are set apart by Qualities.

Good is the Intellect which comprehends
The coming forth and going back of life,
What must be done, and what must not be done,
What should be feared, and what should not be feared,
What binds and what emancipates the soul:
That is of Sattwan, Prince! of "soothfastness."
Marred is the Intellect which, knowing right
And knowing wrong, and what is well to do
And what must not be done, yet understands
Nought with firm mind, nor as the calm truth is:
This is of Rajas, Prince! and "passionate!"
Evil is Intellect which, wrapped in gloom,
Looks upon wrong as right, and sees all things
Contrariwise of Truth. O Pritha's Son!
That is of Tamas, "dark" and desperate!

Good is the steadfastness whereby a man

Masters his beats of heart, his very breath
Of life, the action of his senses; fixed
In never-shaken faith and piety:
That is of Sattwan, Prince! "soothfast" and fair!
Stained is the steadfastness whereby a man
Holds to his duty, purpose, effort, end,
For life's sake, and the love of goods to gain,
Arjuna! 'tis of Rajas, passion-stamped!
Sad is the steadfastness wherewith the fool
Cleaves to his sloth, his sorrow, and his fears,
His folly and despair. This- Pritha's Son!-
Is born of Tamas, "dark" and miserable!

Hear further, Chief of Bharatas! from Me
The threefold kinds of Pleasure which there be.

Good Pleasure is the pleasure that endures,
Banishing pain for aye; bitter at first
As poison to the soul, but afterward
Sweet as the taste of Amrit. Drink of that!
It springeth in the Spirit's deep content.
And painful Pleasure springeth from the bond
Between the senses and the sense-world. Sweet
As Amrit is its first taste, but its last
Bitter as poison. 'Tis of Rajas, Prince!
And foul and "dark" the Pleasure is which springs
From sloth and sin and foolishness; at first
And at the last, and all the way of life
The soul bewildering. 'Tis of Tamas, Prince!

For nothing lives on earth, nor 'midst the gods
In utmost heaven, but hath its being bound
With these three Qualities, by Nature framed.

The work of Brahmans, Kshatriyas, Vaisyas,
And Sudras, O thou Slayer of thy Foes!
Is fixed by reason of the Qualities
Planted in each:
A Brahman's virtues, Prince

Born of his nature, are serenity,
Self-mastery, religion, purity,
Patience, uprightness, learning, and to know
The truth of things which be. A Kshatriya's pride,
Born of his nature, lives in valour, fire,
Constancy, skilfulness, spirit in fight,
And open-handedness and noble mien,
As of a lord of men. A Vaisya's task,
Born with his nature, is to till the ground,
Tend cattle, venture trade. A Sudra's state,
Suiting his nature, is to minister.

Whoso performeth- diligent, content-
The work allotted him, whate'er it be,
Lays hold of perfectness! Hear how a man
Findeth perfection, being so content:
He findeth it through worship- wrought by work-
Of HIM that is the Source of all which lives,
Of HIM by Whom the universe was stretched.

Better thine own work is, though done with fault,
Than doing others' work, ev'n excellently.
He shall not fall in sin who fronts the task
Set him by Nature's hand! Let no man leave
His natural duty, Prince! though it bear blame!
For every work hath blame, as every flame
Is wrapped in smoke! Only that man attains
Perfect surcease of work whose work was wrought
With mind unfettered, soul wholly subdued,
Desires for ever dead, results renounced.

Learn from me, Son of Kunti! also this,
How one, attaining perfect peace, attains
BRAHM, the supreme, the highest height of all!

Devoted- with a heart grown pure, restrained
In lordly self-control, forgoing wiles
Of song and senses, freed from love and hate,
Dwelling 'mid solitudes, in diet spare,

169

With body, speech, and will tamed to obey,
Ever to holy meditation vowed,
From passions liberate, quit of the Self,
Of arrogance, impatience, anger, pride;
Freed from surroundings, quiet, lacking nought-
Such an one grows to oneness with the BRAHM;
Such an one, growing one with BRAHM, serene,
Sorrows no more, desires no more; his soul,
Equally loving all that lives, loves well
Me, Who have made them, and attains to Me.
By this same love and worship doth he know
Me as I am, how high and wonderful,
And knowing, straightway enters into Me.
And whatsoever deeds he doeth- fixed
In Me, as in his refuge- he hath won
For ever and for ever by My grace
Th' Eternal Rest! So win thou! In thy thoughts
Do all thou dost for Me! Renounce for Me!
Sacrifice heart and mind and will to Me!
Live in the faith of Me! In faith of Me
All dangers thou shalt vanquish, by My grace;
But, trusting to thyself and heeding not,
Thou can'st but perish! If this day thou say'st,
Relying on thyself, "I will not fight!"
Vain will the purpose prove! thy qualities
Would spur thee to the war. What thou dost shun,
Misled by fair illusions, thou wouldst seek
Against thy will, when the task comes to thee
Waking the promptings in thy nature set.
There lives a Master in the hearts of men
Maketh their deeds, by subtle pulling-strings,
Dance to what tune HE will. With all thy soul
Trust Him, and take Him for thy succour, Prince!
So- only so, Arjuna!- shalt thou gain-
By grace of Him- the uttermost repose,
The Eternal Place!
Thus hath been opened thee
This Truth of Truths, the Mystery more hid
Than any secret mystery. Meditate!

And- as thou wilt- then act!

Nay! but once more
Take My last word, My utmost meaning have!
Precious thou art to Me; right well-beloved!
Listen! tell thee for thy comfort this.
Give Me thy heart! adore Me! serve Me! cling
In faith and love and reverence to Me!
So shalt thou come to Me! I promise true,
For thou art sweet to Me!
And let go those-
Rites and writ duties! Fly to Me alone!
Make Me thy single refuge! will free
Thy soul from all its sins! Be of good cheer!

[Hide, the holy Krishna saith,
This from him that hath no faith,
Him that worships not, nor seeks
Wisdom's teaching when she speaks:
Hide it from all men who mock;
But, wherever, 'mid the flock
Of My lovers, one shall teach
This divinest, wisest, speech-
Teaching in the faith to bring
Truth to them, and offering
Of all honour unto Me-
Unto Brahma cometh he!
Nay, and nowhere shall ye find
Any man of all mankind
Doing dearer deed for Me;
Nor shall any dearer be
In My earth. Yea, furthermore,
Whoso reads this converse o'er,
Held by Us upon the plain,
Pondering piously and fain,
He hath paid Me sacrifice!
(Krishna speaketh in this wise!)
Yea, and whoso, full of faith,
Heareth wisely what it saith,

Heareth meekly,- when he dies,
Surely shall his spirit rise
To those regions where the Blest,
Free of flesh, in joyance rest.]

Hath this been heard by thee, O Indian Prince!
With mind intent? hath all the ignorance-
Which bred thy trouble- vanished, My Arjun?
Arjuna. Trouble and ignorance are gone! the Light
Hath come unto me, by Thy favour, Lord!
Now am I fixed! my doubt is fled away!
According to Thy word, so will I do!

Sanjaya. Thus gathered I the gracious speech of Krishna, O my
King!
Thus have I told, with heart a-thrill, this wise and wondrous
thing
By great Vyasa's learning writ, how Krishna's self made known
The Yoga, being Yoga's Lord. So is the high truth shown!
And aye, when I remember, O Lord my King, again
Arjuna and the God in talk, and all this holy strain,
Great is my gladness: when I muse that splendour, passing
speech,
Of Hari, visible and plain, there is no tongue to reach
My marvel and my love and bliss. O Archer-Prince! all hail!
O Krishna, Lord of Yoga! surely there shall not fail
Blessing, and victory, and power, for Thy most mighty sake,
Where this song comes of Arjun, and how with God he spake.

THE END.

THE SCIENCE OF BREATH

By: YOGI RAMACHARAKA

Previously titled: *The Hindu-Yogi Science of Breath* By: Yogi Ramacharaka aka William Walker Atkinson (1862-1932). Initially Published in 1904.

CHAPTER I - SALAAM.

The Western student is apt to be somewhat confused in his ideas regarding the Yogis and their philosophy and practice. Travelers to India have written great tales about the hordes of fakirs, mendicants and mountebanks who infest the great roads of India and the streets of its cities, and who impudently claim the title "Yogi." The Western student is scarcely to be blamed for thinking of the typical Yogi as an emaciated, fanatical, dirty, ignorant Hindu, who either sits in a fixed posture until his body becomes ossified, or else holds his arm up in the air until it becomes stiff and withered and forever after remains in that position, or perhaps clenches his fist and holds it tight until his fingernails grow through the palms of his hands. That these people exist is true, but their claim to the title "Yogi" seems as absurd to the true Yogi as does the claim to the title "Doctor" on the part of the man who pares one's corns seem to the eminent surgeon, or as does the title of "Professor," as assumed by the street corner vendor of worm medicine, seem to the President of Harvard or Yale.

There have been for ages past in India and other Oriental countries men who devoted their time and attention to the development of Man, physically, mentally and spiritually. The experience of generations of earnest seekers has been handed down for centuries from teacher to pupil, and gradually a definite Yogi science was built up. To these investigations and teachings was finally applied the term "Yogi," from the Sanskrit word "Yug," meaning "to join." From the same source comes the English word "yoke," with a similar meaning. Its use in connection with these teachings is difficult to trace, different authorities giving different explanations, but probably the most ingenious is that which holds that it is intended as the Hindu equivalent for the idea conveyed by the English phrase, "getting into harness," or "yoking up," as the Yogi undoubtedly "gets into harness" in his work of controlling the body and mind by the Will.

Yoga is divided into several branches, ranging from that which teaches the control of the body, to that which teaches the attainment of the highest spiritual development. In the work we will not go into the higher phases of the subject, except when the "Science of Breath" touches upon the same. The "Science of Breath" touches Yoga at many points, and although chiefly concerned with the development and control of the physical, has also its psychic side, and even enters the field of spiritual development.

In India there are great schools of Yoga, comprising thousands of the leading minds of that great country. The Yoga philosophy is the rule of life for many people. The pure Yogi teachings, however, are given only to the few, the masses being satisfied with the crumbs which fall from the tables of the educated classes, the Oriental custom in this respect being opposed to that of the Western world. But Western ideas are beginning to have their effect even in the Orient, and teachings which were once given only to the few are now freely offered to any who are ready to receive them. The East and the West are growing closer together, and both are profiting by the close contact, each influencing the other.

The Hindu Yogis have always paid great attention to the Science of Breath, for reasons which will be apparent to the student who reads this book. Many Western writers have touched upon this phase of the Yogi teachings, but we believe that it has been reserved for the writer of this work to give to the Western student, in concise form and simple language, the underlying principles of the Yogi Science of Breath, together with many of the favorite Yogi breathing exercises and methods. We have given the Western idea as well as the Oriental, showing how one dovetails into the other. We have used the ordinary English terms, almost entirely, avoiding the Sanskrit terms, so confusing to the average Western reader.

The first part of the book is devoted to the physical phase of the Science of Breath; then the psychic and mental sides are considered, and finally the spiritual side is touched upon.

We may be pardoned if we express ourselves as pleased with our success in condensing so much Yogi lore into so few pages, and by the use of words and terms which may be understood by anyone. Our only fear is that its very simplicity may cause some to pass it by as unworthy of attention, while they pass on their way searching for something "deep," mysterious and non-understandable. However, the Western mind is eminently practical, and we know that it is only a question of a short time before it will recognize the practicability of this work.

We greet our students, with our most profound salaam, and bid them be seated for their first lessons in the Yogi Science of Breath.

CHAPTER II - "BREATH IS LIFE"

Life is absolutely dependent upon the act of breathing. "Breath is Life."

Differ as they may upon details of theory and terminology, the Oriental and the Occidental agree upon these fundamental principles.

To breathe is to live, and without breath there is no life. Not only are the higher animals dependent upon breath for life and health, but even the lower forms of animal life must breathe to live, and plant life is likewise dependent upon the air for continued existence.

The infant draws in a long, deep breath, retains it for a moment to extract from it its life-giving properties, and then exhales it in a long wail, and lo! its life upon earth has begun. The old man gives a faint gasp, ceases to breathe, and life is over. From the first faint breath of the infant to the last gasp of the dying man, it is one long story of continued breathing. Life is but a series of breaths.

Breathing may be considered the most important of all of the functions of the body, for, indeed, all the other functions depend upon it. Man may exist some time without eating; a shorter time without drinking; but without breathing his existence may be measured by a few minutes.

And not only is Man dependent upon Breath for life, but he is largely dependent upon correct habits of breathing for continued vitality and freedom from disease. An intelligent control of our breathing power will lengthen our days upon earth by giving us increased vitality and powers of resistance, and, on the other hand, unintelligent and careless breathing will tend to shorten our days, by decreasing our vitality and laying us open to disease.

Man in his normal state had no need of instruction in breathing. Like the lower animal and the child, he breathed naturally and properly, as nature intended him to do, but civilization has changed him in this and other respects. He has contracted improper methods and attitudes of walking, standing and sitting, which have robbed him of his birthright of natural and correct breathing. He has paid a high price for civilization. The savage, to-day, breathes naturally, unless he has been contaminated by the habits of civilized man.

The percentage of civilized men who breathe correctly is quite small, and the result is shown in contracted chests and stooping shoulders, and the terrible increase in diseases of the respiratory organs, including that dread monster, Consumption, "the white scourge." Eminent authorities have stated that one generation of correct breathers would regenerate the race, and disease would be so rare as to be looked upon as a curiosity. Whether looked at from the standpoint of the Oriental or Occidental, the connection between correct breathing and health is readily seen and explained.

The Occidental teachings show that the physical health depends very materially upon correct breathing. The Oriental teachers not only admit that their Occidental brothers are right, but say that in addition to the physical benefit derived from correct habits of breathing, Man's mental power, happiness, self-control, clear-sightedness, morals, and even his spiritual growth may be increased by an understanding of the "Science of Breath." Whole schools of Oriental Philosophy have been founded upon this science, and this knowledge when grasped by the Western races, and by them put to the practical use which is their strong point, will work wonders among them. The theory of the East, wedded to the practice of the West, will produce worthy offspring.

This work will take up the Yogi "Science of Breath," which includes not only all that is known to the Western physiologist and hygienist, but the occult side of the subject as well. It not only points out the way to physical health along the lines of what

Western scientists have termed "deep breathing," etc., but also goes into the less known phases of the subject, and shows how the Hindu Yogi controls his body, increasing his mental capacity, and develops the spiritual side of his nature by the "Science of Breath."

The Yogi practices exercises by which he attains control of his body, and is enabled to send to any organ or part an increased flow of vital force or "Prana," thereby strengthening and invigorating the part or organ. He knows all that his Western scientific brother knows about the physiological effect of correct breathing, but he also knows that the air contains more than oxygen and hydrogen and nitrogen, and that something more is accomplished than the mere oxygenating of the blood. He knows something about "Prana," of which his Western brother is ignorant, and he is fully aware of the nature and manner of handling that great principle of energy, and is fully informed as to its effect upon the human body and mind. He knows that by rhythmical breathing one may bring himself into harmonious vibration with nature, and aid in the unfoldment of his latent powers. He knows that by controlled breathing he may not only cure disease in himself and others, but also practically do away with fear and worry and the baser emotions.

To teach these things is the object of this work. We will give in a few chapters concise explanations and instructions, which might be extended into volumes. We hope to awaken the minds of the Western world to the value of the Yogi "Science of Breath."

CHAPTER III - THE EXOTERIC THEORY OF BREATH I

In this chapter we will give you briefly the theories of the Western scientific world regarding the functions of the respiratory organs, and the part in the human economy played by the breath. In subsequent chapters we will give the additional theories and ascertained facts of the Oriental school of thought and research. The Oriental accepts the theories and facts of his Western brothers (which have been known to him for centuries) and adds thereto much that the latter do not now accept, but

178

which they will in due time "discover" and which, after renaming, they will present to the world as a great truth.

Before taking up the Western idea, it will perhaps be better to give a hasty general idea of the Organs of Respiration.

The Organs of Respiration consist of the lungs and the air passages leading to them. The lungs are two in number, and occupy the pleural chamber of the thorax, one en each side of the median line, being separated from each other by the heart, the greater blood vessels and the larger air tubes. Each lung is free in all directions, except at the root, which consists chiefly of the bronchi, arteries and veins connecting the lungs with the trachea and heart. The lungs are spongy and porous, and their tissues are very elastic. They are covered with a delicately constructed but strong sac, known as the pleural sac, one wall of which closely adheres to the lung, and the other to the inner wall of the chest, and which secretes a fluid which allows the inner surfaces of the walls to glide easily upon each other in the act of breathing.

The Air Passages consist of the interior of the nose, pharynx, larynx, windpipe or trachea, and the bronchial tubes. When we breathe, we draw in the air through the nose, in which it is warmed by contact with the mucous membrane, which is richly supplied with blood, and after it has passed through the pharynx and larynx it passes into the trachea or windpipe, which subdivides into numerous tubes called the bronchial tubes (bronchia), which in turn subdivide into and terminate in minute subdivisions in all the small air spaces in the lungs, of which the lungs contain millions. A writer has stated that if the air cells of the lungs were spread out over an unbroken surface, they would cover an area of fourteen thousand square feet.

The air is drawn into the lungs by the action of the diaphragm, a great, strong, flat, sheet-like muscle, stretched across the chest, separating the chest-box from the abdomen. The diaphragm's action is almost as automatic as that of the heart, although it may be transformed into a semi-voluntary muscle by an effort of the will. When it expands, it increases the size of the chest and lungs, and the air rushes into the vacuum thus created. When it relaxes the chest and lungs contract and the air is expelled from the lungs.

Now, before considering what happens to the air in the lungs, let us look a little into the matter of the circulation of the blood. The blood, as you know, is driven by the heart, through the arteries, into the capillaries, thus reaching every part of the body, which it vitalizes, nourishes and strengthens. It then returns by means of the capillaries by another route, the veins, to the heart, from whence it is drawn to the lungs.

The blood starts on its arterial journey, bright red and rich, laden with life-giving qualities and properties. It returns by the venous route, poor, blue and dull, being laden down with the waste matter of the system. It goes out like a fresh stream from the mountains; it returns as a stream of sewer water. This foul stream goes to the right auricle of the heart. When this auricle becomes filled, it contracts and forces the stream of blood through an opening in the right ventricle of the heart, which in turn sends it on to the lungs, where it is distributed by millions of hair-like blood vessels to the air cells of the lungs, of which we have spoken. Now, let us take up the story of the lungs at this point. The foul stream of blood is now distributed among the millions of tiny air cells in the lungs. A breath of air is inhaled and the oxygen of the air comes in contact with the impure blood through the thin walls of the hair-like blood vessels of the lungs, which walls are thick enough to hold the blood, but thin enough to admit the oxygen to penetrate them. When the oxygen comes in contact with the blood, a form of combustion takes place, and the blood takes up oxygen and releases carbonic acid gas generated from the waste products and poisonous matter which has been gathered up by the blood from all parts of the system. The blood thus purified and oxygenated is carried back to the heart, again rich, red and bright, and laden with life-giving properties and qualities. Upon reaching the left auricle of the heart, it is forced into the left ventricle, from whence it is again forced out through the arteries on its mission of life to all parts of the system. It is estimated that in a single day of twenty-four hours, 35,000 pints of blood traverse the capillaries of the lungs, the blood corpuscles passing in single file and being exposed to the oxygen of the air on both of their surfaces. When one considers the minute details of the process alluded to, he is lost in wonder and admiration at Nature's infinite care and intelligence.

It will be seen that unless fresh air in sufficient quantities reaches the lungs, the foul stream of venous blood cannot be purified, and consequently not only is the body thus robbed of nourishment, but the waste products which should have been destroyed are returned to the circulation and poison the system, and death ensues. Impure air acts in the same way, only in a lessened degree. It will also be seen that if one does not breathe in a sufficient quantity of air, the work of the blood cannot go on properly, and the result is that the body is insufficiently nourished and disease ensues, or a state of imperfect health is experienced. The blood of one who breathes improperly is, of course, of a bluish, dark color, lacking the rich redness of pure arterial blood. This often shows itself in a poor complexion. Proper breathing, and a consequent good circulation, results in a clear, bright complexion.

A little reflection will show the vital importance of correct breathing. If the blood is not fully purified by the regenerative process of the lungs, it returns to the arteries in an abnormal state, insufficiently purified and imperfectly cleansed of the impurities which it took up on its return journey. These impurities if returned to the system will certainly manifest in some form of disease, either in a form of blood disease or some disease resulting from impaired functioning of some insufficiently nourished organ or tissue.

The blood, when properly exposed to the air in the lungs, not only has its impurities consumed, and parts with its noxious carbonic acid gas, but it also takes up and absorbs a certain quantity of oxygen which it carries to all parts of the body, where it is needed in order that Nature may perform her processes properly. When the oxygen comes in contact with the blood, it unites with the hemoglobin of the blood and is carried to every cell, tissue, muscle and organ, which it invigorates and strengthens, replacing the worn out cells and tissue by new materials which Nature converts to her use. Arterial blood, properly exposed to the air, contains about 25 per cent of free oxygen.

Not only is every part vitalized by the oxygen, but the act of digestion depends materially upon a certain amount of oxygenation of the food, and this can be accomplished only by the oxygen in the blood coming in contact with the food and producing a certain form of combustion. It is therefore necessary that a proper supply of oxygen be taken through the lungs. This accounts for the fact that weak lungs and poor digestion are so often found together. To grasp the full significance of this statement, one must remember that the entire body receives nourishment from the food assimilated, and that imperfect assimilation always means an imperfectly nourished body. Even the lungs themselves depend upon the same source for nourishment, and if through imperfect breathing the assimilation becomes imperfect, and the lungs in turn become weakened, they are rendered still less able to perform their work properly, and so in turn the body becomes further weakened. Every particle of food and drink must be oxygenated before it can yield us the proper nourishment, and before the waste products of the system can be reduced to the proper condition to be eliminated from the system. Lack of sufficient oxygen means Imperfect nutrition, Imperfect elimination and imperfect health. Verily, "breath is life."

The combustion arising from the change in the waste products generates heat and equalizes the temperature of the body. Good breathers are not apt to "take cold," and they generally have plenty of good warm blood which enables them to resist the changes in the outer temperature.

In addition to the above-mentioned important processes the act of breathing gives exercise to the internal organs and muscles, which feature is generally overlooked by the Western writers on the subject, but which the Yogis fully appreciate.

In imperfect or shallow breathing, only a portion of the lung cells are brought into play, and a great portion of the lung capacity is lost, the system suffering in proportion to the amount of under-oxygenation. The lower animals, in their native state, breathe naturally, and primitive man undoubtedly did the same. The abnormal manner of living adopted by civilized man—the shadow that follows upon civilization—has robbed us of our natural habit of breathing, and the race has greatly suffered thereby. Man's only physical salvation is to "get back to Nature."

CHAPTER IV - THE ESOTERIC THEORY OF BREATH II

The Science of Breath, like many other teachings, has its esoteric or inner phase, as well as its exoteric or external. The physiological phase may be termed the outer or exoteric side of the subject, and the phase which we will now consider may be termed its esoteric or inner side. Occultists, in all ages and lands, have always taught, usually secretly to a few followers, that there was to be found in the air a substance or principle from which all activity, vitality and life was derived. They differed in their terms and names for this force, as well as in the details of the theory, but the main principle is to be found in all occult teachings and philosophies, and has for centuries formed a portion of the teachings of the Oriental Yogis.

In order to avoid misconceptions arising from the various theories regarding this great principle, which theories are usually attached to some name given the principle, we, in this work, will speak of the principle as "Prana," this word being the Sanskrit term meaning "Absolute Energy." Many occult authorities teach that the principle which the Hindus term "Prana" is the universal principle of energy or force, and that all energy or force is derived from that principle, or, rather, is a particular form of manifestation of that principle. These theories do not concern us in the consideration of the subject matter of this work, and we will therefore confine ourselves to an understanding of Prana as the principle of energy exhibited in all living things, which distinguishes them from a lifeless thing. We may consider it as the active principle of life—Vital Force, if you please. It is found in all forms of life, from the amoeba to man—from the most elementary form of plant life to the highest form of animal life. Prana is all pervading. It is found in all things having life, and as the occult philosophy teaches that life is in all things—in every atom—the apparent lifelessness of some things being only a lesser degree of manifestation, we may understand their teachings that Prana is everywhere, in everything. Prana must not be confounded with the Ego—that bit of Divine Spirit in every soul, around which clusters matter and energy. Prana is merely a form of energy used by the Ego in its material manifestation. When the Ego leaves the body, the Prana, being no longer under its control, responds only to the orders of the individual atoms, or groups of atoms, forming the body, and as the body disintegrates and is resolved to its original elements, each atom takes with it sufficient Prana to enable it to form new combinations, the unused Prana returning to the great universal storehouse from which it came. With the Ego in control, cohesion exists and the atoms are held together by the Will of the Ego.

Prana is the name by which we designate a universal principle, which principle is the essence of all motion, force or energy, whether manifested in gravitation, electricity, the revolution of the planets, and all forms of life, from the highest to the lowest. It may be called the soul of Force and Energy in all their forms, and that principle which, operating in a certain way, causes that form of activity which accompanies Life.

This great principle is in all forms of matter, and yet it is not matter. It is in the air, but it is not the air nor one of its chemical constituents. Animal and plant life breathe it in with the air, and yet if the air contained it not they would die even though they might be filled with air. It is taken up by the system along with the oxygen, and yet is not the oxygen. The Hebrew writer of the book of Genesis knew the difference between the atmospheric air and the mysterious and potent principle contained within it. He speaks of neshemet ruach chayim, which, translated, means "the breath of the spirit of life." In the Hebrew neshemet means the ordinary breath of atmospheric air, and chayim means life or lives, while the word ruach means the "spirit of life," which occultists claim is the same principle which we speak of as Prana.

Prana is in the atmospheric air, but it is also elsewhere, and it penetrates where the air cannot reach. The oxygen in the air plays an important part in sustaining animal life, and the carbon plays a similar part with plant life, but Prana has its own distinct part to play in the manifestation of life, aside from the physiological functions.

We are constantly inhaling the air charged with Prana, and are as constantly extracting the latter from the air and appropriating it to our uses. Prana is found in its freest state in the atmospheric air, which when fresh is fairly charged with it, and we draw it to us more easily from the air than from any other source. In ordinary breathing we absorb and extract a normal supply of Prana, but by controlled and regulated breathing (generally known as Yogi breathing) we are enabled to extract a greater supply, which is stored away in the brain and nerve centers, to be used when necessary. We may store away Prana, just as the storage battery stores away electricity. The many powers attributed to advanced occultists is due largely to their knowledge of this fact and their intelligent use of this stored-up energy. The Yogis know that by certain forms of breathing they establish certain relations with the supply of Prana and may draw on the same for what they require. Not only do they strengthen all parts of their body in this way, but the brain itself may receive increased energy from the same source, and latent faculties be developed and psychic powers attained. One who has mastered the science of storing away Prana, either consciously or unconsciously, often radiates vitality and strength which is felt by those coming in contact with him, and such a person may impart this strength to others, and give them increased vitality and health. What is called "magnetic healing" is performed in this way, although many practitioners are not aware of the source of their power.

Western scientists have been dimly aware of this great principle with which the air is charged, but finding that they could find no chemical trace of it, or make it register in any of their instruments, they have generally treated the Oriental theory with disdain. They could not explain this principle, and so denied it. They seem, however, to recognize that the air in certain places possesses a greater amount of "something" and sick people are directed by their physicians to seek such places in hopes of regaining, lost health.

The oxygen in the air is appropriated by the blood and is made use of by the circulatory system. The Prana in the air is appropriated by the nervous system, and is used in its work. And as the oxygenated blood is carried to all parts of the system, building up and replenishing, so is the Prana carried to all parts of the nervous system, adding strength and vitality. If we think of Prana as being the active principle of what we call "vitality," we will be able to form a much clearer idea of what an important part it plays in our lives. Just as is the oxygen in the blood used up by the wants of the system, so the supply of Prana taken up by the nervous system is exhausted by our thinking, willing, acting, etc., and in consequence constant replenishing is necessary. Every thought, every act, every effort of the will, every motion of a muscle, uses up a certain amount of what we call nerve force, which is really a form of Prana. To move a muscle the brain sends out an impulse over the nerves, and the muscle contracts, and so much Prana is expended. When it is remembered that the greater portion of Prana acquired by man comes to him from the air inhaled, the importance of proper breathing is readily understood.

CHAPTER V THE NERVOUS SYSTEM.

It will be noticed that the Western scientific theories regarding the breath confine themselves to the effects of the absorption of oxygen, and its use through the circulatory system, while the Yogi theory also takes into consideration the absorption of Prana, and its manifestation through the channels of the Nervous System. Before proceeding further, it may be as well to take a hasty glance at the Nervous System.
The Nervous System of man is divided into two great systems, viz., the Cerebro-Spinal System and the Sympathetic System. The Cerebro-Spinal System consists of all that part of the Nervous System contained within the cranial cavity and the spinal canal, viz., the brain and the spinal cord, together with the nerves which branch off from the same. This system presides over the functions of animal life known as volition, sensation, etc. The Sympathetic System includes all that part of the Nervous System located principally in the thoracic, abdominal

and pelvic cavities, and which is distributed to the internal organs. It has control over the involuntary processes, such as growth, nutrition, etc.

The Cerebro-Spinal System attends to all the seeing, hearing, tasting, smelling, feeling, etc. It sets things in motion; it is used by the Ego to think—to manifest consciousness. It is the instrument with which the Ego communicates with the outside world. This system may be likened to a telephone system, with the brain as the central office, and the spinal column and nerves as cable and wires respectively.

The brain is a great mass of nerve tissue, and consists of three parts, viz., the Cerebrum or brain proper, which occupies the upper, front, middle and back portion of the skull; the Cerebellum, or "little brain," which fills the lower and back portion of the skull; and the Medulla Oblongata, which Is the broadened commencement of the spinal cord, lying before and in front of the Cerebellum.

The Cerebrum is the organ of that part of the mind which manifests itself in intellectual action. The Cerebellum regulates the movements of the voluntary muscles. The Medulla Oblongata is the upper enlarged end of the spinal cord, and from it and the Cerebrum branch forth the Cranial Nerves which reach to various parts of the head, to the organs of special sense, and to some of the thoracic and abdominal organs, and to the organs of respiration.

The Spinal Cord, or spinal marrow, fills the spinal canal in the vertebral column, or "backbone." It is a long mass of nerve tissue, branching off at the several vertebrae to nerves communicating with all parts of the body. The Spinal Cord is like a large telephone cable, and the emerging nerves are like the private wires connecting therewith.

The Sympathetic Nervous System consists of a double chain of Ganglia on the side of the Spinal column, and scattered ganglia in the head, neck, chest and abdomen. (A ganglion is a mass of nervous matter including nerve cells.) These ganglia are connected with each other by filaments, and are also connected with the Cerebro-Spinal System by motor and sensory nerves. From these ganglia numerous fibers branch out to the organs of the body, blood vessels, etc. At various points, the nerves meet together and form what are known as plexuses. The Sympathetic System practically controls the involuntary processes, such as circulation, respiration and digestion.

The power or force transmitted from the brain to all parts of the body by means of the nerves, is known to Western science as "nerve force," although the Yogi knows it to be a manifestation of Prana. In character and rapidity it resembles the electric current. It will be seen that without this "nerve force" the heart cannot beat; the blood cannot circulate; the lungs cannot breathe; the various organs cannot function; in fact the machinery of the body comes to a stop without it. Nay more, even the brain cannot think without Prana be present. When these facts are considered, the importance of the absorption of Prana must be evident to all, and the Science of Breath assumes an importance even greater than that accorded it by Western science.

The Yogi teachings go further than does Western science, in one important feature of the Nervous System. We allude to what Western science terms the "Solar Plexus," and which it considers as merely one of a series of certain matted nets of sympathetic nerves with their ganglia found in various parts of the body. Yogi science teaches that this Solar Plexus is really a most important part of the Nervous System, and that it is a form of brain, playing one of the principal parts in the human economy. Western science seems to be moving gradually towards a recognition of this fact which has been known to the Yogis of the East for centuries, and some recent Western writers have termed the Solar Plexus the "Abdominal Brain." The Solar Plexus is situated in the Epigastric region, just back of the "pit of the stomach" on either side of the spinal column. It is composed of white and gray brain matter, similar to that composing the other brains of man. It has control of the main internal organs of man, and plays a much more important part than is generally recognized. We will not go into the Yogi theory regarding the Solar Plexus, further than to say that they know it as the great central store-house of Prana. Men have been known to be instantly killed by a severe blow over the Solar Plexus, and prize fighters recognize its vulnerability and frequently temporarily paralyze their opponents by a blow over this region.

The name "Solar" is well bestowed on this "brain," as it radiates strength and energy to all parts of the body, even the upper brains depending largely upon it as a storehouse of Prana. Sooner or later Western science will fully recognize the real function of the Solar Plexus, and will accord to it a far more important place then it now occupies in their text-books and teachings.

CHAPTER VI - NOSTRIL-BREATHING VS. MOUTH-BREATHING.

One of the first lessons in the Yogi Science of Breath, is to learn how to breathe through the nostrils, and to overcome the common practice of mouth-breathing.

The breathing mechanism of Man is so constructed that he may breathe either through the mouth or nasal tubes, but it is a matter of vital importance to him which method he follows, as one brings health and strength and the other disease and weakness. It should not be necessary to state to the student that the proper method of breathing is to take the breath through the nostrils, but alas, the ignorance among civilized people regarding this simple matter is astounding. We find people in all walks of life habitually breathing through their mouths, and allowing their children to follow their horrible and disgusting example.

Many of the diseases to which civilized man is subject are undoubtedly caused by this common habit of mouth-breathing. Children permitted to breathe in this way grow up with impaired vitality and weakened constitutions, and in manhood and womanhood break down and become chronic invalids. The mother of the savage race does better, being evidently guided by her intuition. She seems to instinctively recognize that the nostrils are the proper channels for the conveyer of air to the lungs, and she trains her infant to close its little lips and breathe through the nose. She tips its head forward when it is asleep, which attitude closes the lips and makes nostril-breathing imperative. If our civilized mothers were to adopt the same plan, it would work a great good for the race.

Many contagious diseases are contracted by the disgusting habit of mouth-breathing, and many cases of cold and catarrhal affections are also attributable to the same cause. Many persons who, for the sake of appearances, keep their mouth closed during the day, persist in mouth-breathing at night and often contract disease in this way.

Carefully conducted scientific experiments have shown that soldiers and sailors who sleep with their mouths open are much more liable to contract contagious diseases than those who breathe properly through the nostrils. An instance is related in which small-pox became epidemic on a man-of-war in foreign parts, and every death which resulted was that of some sailor or marine who was a mouth-breather, not a single nostril-breather succumbing.

The organs of respiration have their only protective apparatus, filter, or dust-catcher, in the nostrils. When the breath is taken through the mouth, there is nothing from mouth to lungs to strain the air, or to catch the dust and other foreign matter in the air. From mouth to lungs the dirt or impure substance has a clear track, and the entire respiratory system is unprotected. And, moreover, such incorrect breathing admits cold air to the organs, thereby injuring them. Inflammation of the respiratory organs often results from the inhalation of cold air through the mouth. The man who breathes through the mouth at night, always awakens with a parched feeling in the mouth and a dryness in the throat. He is violating one of nature's laws, and is sowing the seeds of disease.

Once more, remember that the mouth affords no protection to the respiratory organs, and cold air, dust and impurities and germs readily enter by that door. On the other hand, the nostrils and nasal passages show evidence of the careful design of nature in this respect. The nostrils are two narrow, tortuous channels, containing numerous bristly hairs which serve the purpose of a filter or sieve to strain the air of its impurities, etc., which are expelled when the breath is exhaled. Not only do the nostrils serve this important purpose, but they also perform an important function in warming the air inhaled. The long narrow winding nostrils are filled with warm mucous membrane, which coming in contact with the inhaled air warms it so that it can do no damage to the delicate organs of the throat, or to the lungs.

No animal, excepting man, sleeps with the mouth open or breathes through the mouth, and in fact it is believed that it is only civilized man who so perverts nature's functions, as the savage and barbarian races almost invariably breathe correctly. It is probable that this unnatural habit among civilized men has been acquired through unnatural methods of living, enervating luxuries and excessive warmth.

The refining, filtering and straining apparatus of the nostrils renders the air fit to reach the delicate organs of the throat and the lungs, and the air is not fit to so reach these organs until it has passed through nature's refining process. The impurities which are stopped and retained by the sieves and mucous membrane of the nostrils, are thrown out again by the expelled breath, in exhalation, and in case they have accumulated too rapidly or have managed to escape through the sieves and have penetrated forbidden regions, nature protects us by producing a sneeze which violently ejects the intruder.

The air, when it enters the lungs is as different from the outside air, as is distilled water different from the water of the cistern. The intricate purifying organization of the nostrils, arresting and holding the impure particles in the air, is as important as is the action of the mouth in stopping cherry-stones and fish-bones and preventing them from being carried on to the stomach. Man should no more breathe through his mouth than he would attempt to take food through his nose.

Another feature of mouth-breathing is that the nasal passages, being thus comparatively unused, consequently fail to keep themselves clean and clear, and become clogged up and unclean, and are apt to contract local diseases. Like abandoned roads that soon become filled with weeds and rubbish, unused nostrils become filled with impurities and foul matter.

One who habitually breathes through the nostrils is not likely to be troubled with clogged or stuffy nostrils, but for the benefit of those who have been more or less addicted to the unnatural mouth-breathing, and who wish to acquire the natural and rational method, it may perhaps be well to add a few words regarding the way to keep their nostrils clean and free from impurities.

A favorite Oriental method is to snuff a little water up the nostrils allowing it to run down the passage into the throat, from thence it may be ejected through the mouth. Some Hindu yogis immerse the face in a bowl of water, and by a sort of suction draw in quite a quantity of water, but this latter method requires considerable practice, and the first mentioned method is equally efficacious, and much more easily performed.

Another good plan is to open the window and breathe freely, closing one nostril with the finger or thumb, sniffing up the air through the open nostril. Then repeat the process on the other nostril. Repeat several times, changing nostrils. This method will usually clear the nostrils of obstructions.

In case the trouble is caused by catarrh it is well to apply a little Vaseline or camphor ice or similar preparation. Or sniff up a little witch-hazel extract once in a while, and you will notice a marked improvement. A little care and attention will result in the nostrils becoming clean and remaining so.

We have given considerable space to this subject of nostril-breathing, not only because of its great importance in its reference to health, but because nostril-breathing is a prerequisite to the practice of the breathing exercises to be given later in this book, and because nostril-breathing is one of the basic principles underlying the Yogi Science of Breath.

We urge upon the student the necessity of acquiring this method of breathing if he has it not, and caution him against dismissing this phase of the subject as unimportant.

CHAPTER VII - FOUR METHODS OF RESPIRATION.

In the consideration of the question of respiration, we must begin by considering the mechanical arrangements whereby the respiratory movements are effected. The mechanics of respiration manifest through (1) the elastic movements of the lungs, and (2) the activities of the sides and bottom of the thoracic cavity in which the lungs are contained. The thorax is that portion of the trunk between the neck and the abdomen, the cavity of which (known as the thoracic cavity) is occupied mainly by the lungs and heart. It is bounded by the spinal column, the ribs with their cartilages, the breastbone, and below by the diaphragm. It is generally spoken of as "the chest." It has been compared to a completely shut, conical box, the small end of which is turned upward, the back of the box being formed by the spinal column, the front by the breastbone and the sides by the ribs.

The ribs are twenty-four in number, twelve on each side, and emerge from each side of the spinal column. The upper seven pair are known as "true ribs," being fastened to the breastbone direct, while the lower five pairs are called (false ribs) or "floating ribs," because they are not so fastened, the upper two of them being fastened by cartilage to the other ribs, the remainder having no cartilages, their forward ends being free.

The ribs are moved in respiration by two superficial muscular layers, known as the intercostal muscles. The diaphragm, the muscular partition before alluded to, separates the chest box from the abdominal cavity.

In the act of inhalation the muscles expand the lungs so that a vacuum is created and the air rushes in in accordance with the well-known law of physics. Everything depends upon the muscles concerned in the process of respiration, which we may as, for convenience, term the "respiratory muscles." Without the aid of these muscles the lungs cannot expand, and upon the proper use and control of these muscles the Science of Breath largely depends. The proper control of these muscles will result in the ability to attain the maximum degree of lung expansion, and the greatest amount of the life giving properties of the air into the system.

The Yogis classify Respiration into four general methods, viz:
(1) High Breathing.
(2) Mid Breathing.
(3) Low Breathing.
(4) Yogi Complete Breathing.

We will give a general idea of the first three methods, and a more extended treatment of the fourth method, upon which the Yogi Science of Breath is largely based.

(1) HIGH BREATHING.

This form of breathing is known to the Western world as Clavicular Breathing, or Collarbone Breathing. One breathing in this way elevates the ribs and raises the collarbone and shoulders, at the same time drawing in the abdomen and pushing its contents up against the diaphragm, which in turn is raised. The upper part of the chest and lungs, which is the smallest, is used, and consequently but a minimum amount of air enters the lungs. In addition to this, the diaphragm being raised, there can be no expansion in that direction. A study of the anatomy of the chest will convince any student that in this way a maximum amount of effort is used to obtain a minimum amount of benefit. High Breathing is probably the worst form of breathing known to man and requires the greatest expenditure of energy with the smallest amount of benefit. It is an energy-wasting, poor-returns plan. It is quite common among the Western races, many women being addicted to it, and even singers, clergymen, lawyers and others, who should know better, using it ignorantly.

Many diseases of the vocal organs and organs of respiration may be directly traced to this barbarous method of breathing, and the straining of delicate organs caused by this method, often results in the harsh, disagreeable voices heard on all sides. Many persons who breathe In this way become addicted to the disgusting practice of "mouth-breathing" described in a preceding chapter.

If the student has any doubts about what has been said regarding this form of breathing, let him try the experiment of expelling all the air from his lungs, then standing erect, with hands at sides, let him raise the shoulders and collar-bone and inhale. He will find that the amount of air inhaled far below normal. Then let him inhale a full breath, after dropping the shoulders and collar-bone, and he will receive an object lesson in breathing which he will be apt to remember much longer than he would any words, printed or spoken.

(2) MID BREATHING.

This method of respiration is known to Western students as Rib Breathing, or Inter-Costal Breathing, and while less objectionable than High Breathing, is far inferior to either Low Breathing or to the Yogi Complete Breath. In Mid Breathing the

194

diaphragm is pushed upward, and the abdomen drawn in. The ribs are raised somewhat, and the chest is partially expanded. It is quite common among men who have made no study of the subject. As there are two better methods known, we give it only passing notice, and that principally to call your attention to its short-comings.

(3) LOW BREATHING.

This form of respiration is far better than either of the two preceding forms: and of recent years many Western writers have extolled its merits, and have exploited it under the names of "Abdominal Breathing," "Deep Breathing," "Diaphragmatic Breathing," etc., etc., and much good has been accomplished by the attention of the public having been directed to the subject, and many having been Induced to substitute it for the interior and injurious methods above alluded to. Many "systems" of breathing have been built around Low Breathing, and students have paid high prices to learn the new (?) systems. But, as we have said, much good has resulted, and after all the students who paid high prices to learn revamped old systems undoubtedly got their money's worth if they were Induced to discard the old methods of High Breathing and Low Breathing.

Although many Western authorities write and speak of this method as the best known form of breathing, the Yogis know it to be but a part of a system which they have used for centuries and which they know as "The Complete Breath." It must be admitted, however, that one must be acquainted with the principles of Low Breathing before he can grasp the idea of Complete Breathing.

Let us again consider the diaphragm. What is it? We have seen that it is the great partition muscle, which separates the chest and its contents from the abdomen and its contents. When at rest it presents a concave surface to the abdomen. That is, the diaphragm as viewed from the abdomen would seem like the sky as viewed from the earth—the interior of an arched surface. Consequently the side of the diaphragm toward the chest organs is like a protruding rounded surface—like a hill. When the diaphragm is brought into use the hill formation is lowered and the diaphragm presses upon the abdominal organs and forces out the abdomen.

195

In Low Breathing, the lungs are given freer play than in the methods already mentioned, and consequently more air is inhaled. This fact has led the majority of Western writers to speak and write of Low Breathing (which they call Abdominal Breathing) as the highest and best method known to science. But the Oriental Yogi has long known of a better method, and some few Western writers have also recognized this fact. The trouble with all methods of breathing, other than "Yogi Complete Breathing" is that in none of these methods do the lungs become filled with air—at the best only a portion of the lung space is filled, even in Low Breathing. High Breathing fills only the upper portion of the lungs. Mid Breathing fills only the middle and a portion of the upper parts. Low Breathing fills only the lower and middle parts. It is evident that any method that fills the entire lung space must be far preferable to those filling only certain parts Any method which will fill the entire lung space must be the greatest value to Man in the way of allowing him to absorb the greatest quantity of oxygen and to store away the greatest amount of Prana. The Complete Breath is known to the Yogis to be the best method of respiration known to science.

THE YOGI COMPLETE BREATH.

Yogi Complete Breathing includes all the good points of High Breathing, Mid Breathing and Low Breathing, with the objectionable features of each eliminated. It brings into play the entire respiratory apparatus, every part of the lungs, every air-cell, and every respiratory muscle. The entire respiratory organism responds to this method of breathing, and the maximum amount of benefit is derived from the minimum expenditure of energy. The chest cavity is increased to its normal limits in all directions and every part of the machinery performs its natural work and functions.

One of the most important features of this method of breathing is the fact that the respiratory muscles are fully called into play, whereas in the other forms of breathing only a portion of these muscles are so used. In Complete Breathing, among other muscles, those controlling the ribs are actively used, which increases the space in which the lungs may expand, and also gives the proper support to the organs when needed, Nature availing herself of the perfection of the principle of leverage in

196

this process. Certain muscles hold the lower ribs firmly in position, while other muscles bend them outward.

Then again, in this method, the diaphragm is under perfect control and is able to perform its functions properly, and in such manner as to yield the maximum degree of service.

In the rib-action, above alluded to, the lower ribs are controlled by the diaphragm which draws them slightly downward, while other muscles hold them in place and the intercostal muscles force them outward, which combined action increases the mid-chest cavity to its maximum. In addition to this muscular action, the upper ribs are also lifted and forced outward by the intercostal muscles, which increases the capacity of the upper chest to its fullest extent.

If you have studied the special features of the four given methods of breathing, you will at once see that the Complete Breath comprises all the advantageous features of the three other methods, plus the reciprocal advantages accruing from the combined action of the high-chest, mid-chest, and diaphragmatic regions, and the normal rhythm thus obtained.

In our next chapter, we will take up the Complete Breath in practice, and will give full directions for the acquirement of this superior method of breathing, with exercises, etc.

CHAPTER VIII - HOW TO ACQUIRE THE YOGI COMPLETE BREATH.

The Yogi Complete Breath is the fundamental breath of the entire Yogi Science of Breath, and the student must fully acquaint himself with it, and master it perfectly before he can hope to obtain results from the other forms of breath-mentioned and given in this book. He should not be content with half-learning it, but should go to work in earnest until it becomes his natural method of breathing. This will require work, time and patience, but without these things nothing is ever accomplished. There is no royal road to the Science of Breath, and the student must be prepared to practice and study in earnest if he expect to receive results. The results obtained by a complete mastery of the Science of Breath are great, and no one who has attained them would willingly go back to the old methods, and he will tell his friends that he considers himself amply repaid for all his work. We say these things now, that you may fully understand the necessity and importance of mastering this fundamental method of Yogi Breathing, instead of passing it by and trying some of the attractive looking variations given later on in this book. Again, we say to you: Start right, and right results will follow; but neglect your foundations and your entire building will topple over sooner or later.

Perhaps the better way to teach you how to develop the Yogi Complete Breath, would be to give you simple directions regarding the breath itself, and then follow up the same with general remarks concerning it, and then later on giving exercises for developing the chest, muscles and lungs which have been allowed to remain in an undeveloped condition by imperfect methods of breathing. Right here we wish to say that this Complete Breath is not a forced or abnormal thing, but on the contrary is a going back to first principles—a return to Nature. The healthy adult savage and the healthy infant of civilization both breathe in this manner, but civilized man has adopted unnatural methods of living, clothing, etc., and has lost his birthright. And we wish to remind the reader that the Complete Breath does not necessarily call for the complete filling of the lungs at every inhalation. One may inhale the average amount of air, using the Complete Breathing Method and distributing the air inhaled, be the quantity large or small, to all parts of the lungs. But one should inhale a series of full Complete Breaths several times a day, whenever opportunity offers, in order to keep the system in good order and condition.

The following simple exercise will give you a clear idea of what the

Complete Breath is:

(1) Stand or sit erect. Breathing through the nostrils, inhale steadily, first filling the lower part of the lungs, which is accomplished by bringing into play the diaphragm, which descending exerts a gentle pressure on the abdominal organs, pushing forward the front walls of the abdomen. Then fill the

middle part of the lungs, pushing out the lower ribs, breast-bone and chest. Then fill the higher portion of the lungs, protruding the upper chest, thus lifting the chest, including the upper six or seven pairs of ribs. In the final movement, the lower part of the abdomen will be slightly drawn in, which movement gives the lungs a support and also helps to fill the highest part of the lungs. At first reading it may appear that this breath consists of three distinct movements. This, however, is not the correct idea. The inhalation is continuous, the entire chest cavity from the lowered diaphragm to the highest point of the chest in the region of the collar-bone, being expanded with a uniform movement. Avoid a jerky series of inhalations, and strive to attain a steady continuous action. Practice will soon overcome the tendency to divide the inhalation into three movements, and will result in a uniform continuous breath. You will be able to complete the inhalation in a couple of seconds after a little practice.

(2) Retain the breath a few seconds.

(3) Exhale quite slowly, holding the chest in a firm position, and having the abdomen in a little and lifting it upward slowly as the air leaves the lungs. When the air is entirely exhaled, relax the chest and abdomen. A little practice will render this part of the exercise easy, and the movement once acquired will be afterwards performed almost automatically.

It will be seen that by this method of breathing all parts of the respiratory apparatus is brought into action, and all parts of the lungs, including the most remote air cells, are exercised. The chest cavity is expanded in all directions. You will also notice that the Complete Breath is really a combination of Low, Mid and High Breaths, succeeding each other rapidly in the order given, in such a manner as to form one uniform, continuous, complete breath.

You will find it quite a help to you if you will practice this breath before a large mirror, placing the hands lightly over the abdomen so that you may feel the movements. At the end of the inhalation, it is well to occasionally slightly elevate the shoulders, thus raising the collarbone and allowing the air to pass freely into the small upper lobe of the right lung, which place is sometimes the breeding place of tuberculosis.

At the beginning of practice, you may have more or less trouble in acquiring the Complete Breath, but a little practice will make perfect, and when you have once acquired it you will never willingly return to the old methods.

CHAPTER IX - PHYSIOLOGICAL EFFECT OF THE COMPLETE BREATH.

Scarcely too much can be said of the advantages attending the practice of the Complete Breath. And yet the student who has carefully read the foregoing pages should scarcely need to have pointed out to him such advantages.

The practice of the Complete Breath will make any man or woman immune to Consumption and other pulmonary troubles, and will do away with all liability to contract "colds," as well as bronchial and similar weaknesses. Consumption is due principally to lowered vitality attributable to an insufficient amount of air being inhaled. The impairment of vitality renders the system open to attacks from disease germs. Imperfect breathing allows a considerable part of the lungs to remain inactive, and such portions offer an inviting field for bacilli, which invading the weakened tissue soon produce havoc. Good healthy lung tissue will resist the germs, and the only way to have good healthy lung tissue is to use the lungs properly. Consumptives are nearly all narrow-chested. What does this mean? Simply that these people were addicted to improper habits of breathing, and consequently their chests failed to develop and expand. The man who practices the Complete Breath will have a full broad chest, end the narrow-chested man may develop his chest to normal proportions if he will but adopt this mode of breathing. Such people must develop their chest cavities if they value their lives. Colds may often be prevented by practicing a little vigorous Complete Breathing whenever you feel that you are being unduly exposed. When chilled, breathe vigorously a few minutes, and you will feel a glow all over your body. Most colds can be cured by Complete Breathing and partial fasting for a day.

The quality of the blood depends largely upon its proper oxygenation in the lungs, and if it is under-oxygenated it becomes poor in quality and laden with all sorts of impurities, and the system suffers from lack of nourishment, and often becomes actually poisoned by the waste products remaining uneliminated in the blood. As the entire body, every organ and every part, is dependent upon the blood for nourishment, impure blood must have a serious effect upon the entire system. The remedy is plain—practice the Yogi Complete Breath.

The stomach and other organs of nutrition suffer much from improper breathing. Not only are they ill nourished by reason of the lack of oxygen, but as the food must absorb oxygen from the blood and become oxygenated before it can be digested and assimilated, it is readily seen how digestion and assimilation is impaired by incorrect breathing. And when assimilation is not normal, the system receives less and less nourishment, the appetite fails, bodily vigor decreases, and energy diminishes, and the man withers and declines. All from the lack of proper breathing.

Even the nervous system suffers from improper breathing, inasmuch as the brain, the spinal cord, the nerve centers, and the nerves themselves, when improperly nourished by means of the blood, become poor and inefficient instruments for generating, storing and transmitting the nerve currents. And improperly nourished they will become if sufficient oxygen is not absorbed through the lungs. There is another aspect of the case whereby the nerve currents themselves, or rather the force from which the nerve currents spring, becomes lessened from want of proper breathing, but this belongs to another phase of the subject which is treated of in other chapters of this book, and our purpose here is to direct your attention to the fact that the mechanism of the nervous system is rendered inefficient as an instrument for conveying nerve force, as the indirect result of a lack of proper breathing.

The effect of the reproductive organs upon the general health is too well known to be discussed at length here, but we may be permitted to say that with the reproductive organs in a weakened condition the entire system feels the reflex action and suffers sympathetically. The Complete Breath produces a rhythm which is Nature's own plan for keeping this important part of the system in normal condition, and, from the first, it will be noticed that the reproductive functions are strengthened and vitalized, thus, by sympathetic reflex action, giving tone to the whole system. By this, we do not mean that the lower sex impulses will be aroused; far from it. The Yogis are advocates of continence and chastity, and have learned to control the animal passions.

But sexual control does not mean sexual weakness, and the Yogi teachings are that the man or woman whose reproductive organism is normal and healthy, will have a stronger will with which to control himself or herself. The Yogi believes that much of the perversion of this wonderful part of the system comes from a lack of normal health, and results from a morbid rather than a normal condition of these organs. A little careful consideration of this question will prove that the Yogi teachings are right. This is not the place to discuss the subject fully, but the Yogis know that sex-energy may be conserved and used for the development of the body and mind of the individual, instead of being dissipated in unnatural excesses as is the wont of so many uninformed people. By special request we will give in this book one of the favorite Yogi exercises for this purpose. But whether or not the student wishes to adopt the Yogi theories of continence and clean-living, he or she will find that the Complete Breath will do more to restore health to this part of the system than anything else ever tried. Remember, now, we mean normal health, not undue development. The sensualist will find that normal means a lessening of desire rather than an increase; the weakened man or woman will find a toning up and a relief from the weakness which has heretofore depressed him or her. We do not wish to be misunderstood or misquoted on this subject. The Yogis' ideal is a body strong in all its parts, under the control of a masterful and developed Will, animated by high ideals.

In the practice of the Complete Breath, during inhalation, the diaphragm contracts and exerts a gentle pressure upon the liver, stomach and other organs, which in connection with the rhythm of the lungs acts as a gentle massage of these organs and stimulates their actions, and encourages normal functioning. Each inhalation aids in this internal exercise, and assists in causing a normal circulation to the organs of nutrition and elimination. In High or Mid Breathing the organs lose the benefit accruing from this internal massage.

The Western world is paying much attention to Physical Culture just now, which is a good thing. But in their enthusiasm they must not forget that the exercise of the external muscles is not everything. The internal organs also need exercise, and Nature's plan for this exercise is proper breathing. The diaphragm is Nature's principal instrument for this internal exercise. Its motion vibrates the important organs of nutrition and elimination, and massages and kneads them at each inhalation and exhalation, forcing blood into them, and then squeezing it out, and imparting a general tone to the organs. Any organ or part of the body which is not exercised gradually atrophies and refuses to function properly, and lack of the internal exercise afforded by the diaphragmatic action leads to diseased organs. The Complete Breath gives the proper motion to the diaphragm, as well as exercising the middle and upper chest. It is indeed "complete" in its action.

From the standpoint of Western physiology alone, without reference to the Oriental philosophies and science, this Yogi system of Complete Breathing is of vital importance to every man, woman and child who wishes to acquire health and keep it. Its very simplicity keeps thousands from seriously considering it, while they spend fortunes in seeking health through complicated and expensive "systems." Health knocks at their door and they answer not. Verily the stone which the builders reject is the real cornerstone of the Temple of Health.

CHAPTER X - A FEW BITS OF YOGI LORE.

We give below three forms of breath, quite popular among the Yogis. The first is the well-known Yogi Cleansing Breath, to which is attributed much of the great lung endurance found among the Yogis. They usually finish up a breathing exercise with this Cleansing Breath, and we have followed this plan in this book. We also give the Yogi Nerve Vitalizing Exercise, which has been handed down among them for ages, and which has never been improved on by Western teachers of Physical Culture, although some of them have "borrowed" it from teachers of Yoga. We also give the Yogi Vocal Breath, which accounts largely for the melodious, vibrant voices of the better class of the Oriental Yogis. We feel that if this book contained nothing more than these three exercises, it would be invaluable to the Western student. Take these exercises as a gift from your Eastern brothers and put them into practice.

THE YOGI CLEANSING BREATH.

The Yogis have a favorite form of breathing which they practice when they feel the necessity of ventilating and cleansing the lungs. They conclude many of their other breathing exercises with this breath, and we have followed this practice in this book. This Cleansing Breath ventilates and cleanses the lungs, stimulates the cells and gives a general tone to the respiratory organs, and is conducive to their general healthy condition. Besides this effect, it is found to greatly refresh the entire system. Speakers, singers, etc., will find this breath especially restful, after having tired the respiratory organs.

(1) Inhale a complete breath.

(2) Retain the air a few seconds.

(3) Pucker up the lips as if for a whistle (but do not swell out the cheeks), then exhale a little air through the opening, with considerable vigor. Then stop for a moment, retaining the air, and then exhale a little more air. Repeat until the air is completely exhaled. Remember that considerable vigor is to be used in exhaling the air through the opening in the lips.

This breath will be found quite refreshing when one is tired and generally "used up." A trial will convince the student of its merits. This exercise should be practiced until it can be performed naturally and easily, as it is used to finish up a number of other exercises given in this book, and it should be thoroughly understood.

THE YOGI NERVE VITALIZING BREATH.

This is an exercise well known to the Yogis, who consider it one of the strongest nerve stimulants and invigorants known to man. Its purpose is to stimulate the Nervous System, develop nerve force, energy and vitality. This exercise brings a stimulating pressure to bear on important nerve centers, which in turn stimulate and energize the entire nervous system, and send an increased flow of nerve force to all parts of the body.

(1) Stand erect.

(2) Inhale a Complete Breath, and retain same.

(3) Extend the arms straight in front of you, letting them be somewhat limp and relaxed, with only sufficient nerve force to hold them out.

(4) Slowly draw the hands back toward the shoulders, gradually contracting the muscles and putting force into them, so that when they reach the shoulders the fists will be so tightly clenched that a tremulous motion is felt.

(5) Then, keeping the muscles tense, push the fists slowly out, and then draw them back rapidly (still tense) several times.

(6) Exhale vigorously through the mouth.

(7) Practice the Cleansing Breath.

The efficiency of this exercise depends greatly upon the speed of the drawing back of the fists, and the tension of the muscles, and, of course, upon the full lungs. This exercise must be tried to be appreciated. It is without equal as a "bracer," as our Western friends put it.

THE YOGI VOCAL BREATH.

The Yogis have a form of breathing to develop the voice. They are noted for their wonderful voices, which are strong, smooth and clear, and have a wonderful trumpet-like carrying power. They have practiced this particular form of breathing exercise which has resulted in rendering their voices soft, beautiful and flexible, imparting to it that indescribable, peculiar floating quality, combined with great power. The exercise given below will in time impart the above-mentioned qualities, or the Yogi

Voice, to the student who practices it faithfully. It is to be understood, of course, that this form of breath is to be used only as an occasional exercise, and not as a regular form of breathing.

(1) Inhale a Complete Breath very slowly, but steadily, through the nostrils, taking as much time as possible in the inhalation.

(2) Retain for a few seconds.

(3) Expel the air vigorously in one great breath, through the wide opened mouth.

(4) Rest the lungs by the Cleansing Breath.

Without going deeply into the Yogi theories of sound-production in speaking and singing, we wish to say that experience has taught them that the timbre, quality and power of a voice depends not alone upon the vocal organs in the throat, but that the facial muscles, etc., have much to do with the matter. Some men with large chests produce but a poor tone, while others with comparatively small chests produce tones of amazing strength and quality. Here is an interesting experiment worth trying: Stand before a glass and pucker up your mouth and whistle, and note the shape of your mouth and the general expression of your face. Then sing or speak as you do naturally, and see the difference. Then start to whistle again for a few seconds, and then, *without changing the position of your lips or face*, sing a few notes and notice what a vibrant, resonant, clear and beautiful tone is produced.

CHAPTER XI - THE SEVEN YOGI DEVELOPING EXERCISES.

The following are the seven favorite exercises of the Yogis for developing the lungs, muscles, ligaments, air cells, etc. They are quite simple but marvelously effective. Do not let the simplicity of these exercises make you lose interest, for they are the result of careful experiments and practice on the part of the Yogis, and are the essence of numerous intricate and complicated exercises, the non-essential portions being eliminated and the essential features retained.

(1) THE RETAINED BREATH.

This is a very important exercise which tends to strengthen and develop the respiratory muscles as well as the lungs, and its frequent practice will also tend to expand the chest. The Yogis have found that an occasional holding of the breath, after the lungs have been filled with the Complete Breath, is very beneficial, not only to the respiratory organs but to the organs of nutrition, the nervous system and the blood itself. They have found that an occasional holding of the breath tends to purify the air which has remained in the lungs from former inhalations, and to more fully oxygenate the blood. They also know that the breath so retained gathers up all the waste matter, and when the breath is expelled it carries with it the effete matter of the system, and cleanses the lungs just as a purgative does the bowels. The Yogis recommend this exercise for various disorders of the stomach, liver and blood, and also find that it frequently relieves bad breath, which often arises from poorly ventilated lungs. We recommend students to pay considerable attention to this exercise, as it has great merits. The following directions will give you a clear idea of the exercise:

(1) Stand erect.

(2) Inhale a Complete Breath.

(3) Retain the air as long as you can comfortably.

(4) Exhale vigorously through the open mouth.

(5) Practice the Cleansing Breath.

At first you will be able to retain the breath only a short time, but a little practice will also show a great improvement. Time yourself with a watch if you wish to note your progress.

(2) LUNG CELL STIMULATION.

This exercise is designed to stimulate the air cells in the lungs, but beginners must not overdo it, and in no case should it be indulged in too vigorously. Some may find a slight dizziness resulting from the first few trials, in which case let them walk around a little and discontinue the exercise for a while.

(1) Stand erect, with hands at sides.

(2) Breathe in very slowly and gradually.

(3) While inhaling, gently tap the chest with the finger tips, constantly changing position.

(4) When the lungs are filled, retain the breath and pat the chest with the palms of the hands.

(5) Practice the Cleansing Breath.

This exercise is very bracing and stimulating to the whole body, and is a well-known Yogi practice. Many of the air cells of the lungs become inactive by reason of incomplete breathing, and often become almost atrophied. One who has practiced imperfect breathing for years will find it not so easy to stimulate all these ill-used air cells into activity all at once by the Complete Breath, but this exercise will do much toward bringing about the desired result, and is worth study and practice.

(3) RIB STRETCHING.

We have explained that the ribs are fastened by cartilages, which admit of considerable expansion. In proper breathing, the ribs play an important part, and it is well to occasionally give them a little special exercise in order to preserve their elasticity. Standing or sitting in unnatural positions, to which many of the Western people are addicted, is apt to render the ribs more or less stiff and inelastic, and this exercise will do much to overcome same.

(1) Stand erect.

(2) Place the hands one on each side of the body, as high up under the armpits as convenient, the thumbs reaching toward the back, the palms on the side of the chest and the fingers to the front over the breast.

(3) Inhale a Complete Breath.

(4) Retain the air for a short time.

(5) Then gently squeeze the sides, at the same time slowly exhaling.

(6) Practice the cleansing breath.

Use moderation in this exercise and do not overdo it

(4) CHEST EXPANSION.

The chest is quite apt to be contracted from bending over one's work, etc. This exercise is very good for the purpose of restoring natural conditions and gaining chest expansion.

(1) Stand erect.

(2) Inhale a Complete Breath.

(3) Retain the air.

(4) Extend both arms forward and bring the two clenched fists together on a level with the shoulder.

(5) Then swing back the fists vigorously until the arms stand out straight sideways from the shoulders.

(6) Then bring back to Position 4, and swing to Position 5. Repeat several times.

(7) Exhale vigorously through the opened mouth.

(8) Practice the Cleansing Breath.

Use moderation and do not overdo this exercise.

(5) WALKING EXERCISE.

(1) Walk with head up, chin drawn slightly in, shoulders back, and with measured tread.

(2) Inhale a Complete Breath, counting (mentally) 1, 2, 3, 4, 5, 6, 7, 8, one count to each step, making the inhalation extend over the eight counts.

(3) Exhale slowly through the nostrils, counting as before—1, 2, 3, 4, 5, 6, 7, 8—one count to a step.

(4) Rest between breaths, continuing walking and counting, I, 2, 3, 4, 5, 8, 7, 8, one count to a step.

(5) Repeat until you begin to feel tired. Then rest for a while, and resume at pleasure. Repeat several times a day.

Some Yogis vary this exercise by retaining the breath during a 1, 2, 3, 4, count, and then exhale in an eight-step count. Practice whichever plan seems most agreeable to you.

(6) MORNING EXERCISE.

(1) Stand erect in a military attitude, head up, eyes front, shoulders back, knees stiff, hands at sides.

(2) Raise body slowly on toes, inhaling a Complete Breath, steadily and slowly.

(3) Retain the breath for a few seconds, maintaining the same position.

(4) Slowly sink to first position, at the same time slowly exhaling the air through the nostrils.

(5) Practice Cleansing Breath.

(6) Repeat several times, varying by using right leg alone, then left leg alone.

(7) STIMULATING CIRCULATION.

(1) Stand erect.

(2) Inhale a Complete Breath and retain.

(3) Bend forward slightly and grasp a stick or cane steadily and firmly, and gradually exerting your entire strength upon the grasp.

(4) Relax the grasp, return to first position, and slowly exhale.

(5) Repeat several times.

(6) Finish with the Cleansing Breath.

This exercise may be performed without the use of a stick or cane, by grasping an imaginary cane, using the will to exert the pressure. The exercise is a favorite Yogi plan of stimulating the circulation by driving the arterial blood to the extremities, and drawing back the venous blood to the heart and lungs that it may take up the oxygen which has been inhaled with the air. In cases of poor circulation there is not enough blood in the lungs to absorb the increased amount of oxygen inhaled, and the system does not get the full benefit of the improved breathing.

In such cases, particularly, it is well to practice this exercise, occasionally with the regular Complete Breathing exercise.

CHAPTER XII - SEVEN MINOR YOGI EXERCISES.

This chapter is composed of seven minor Yogi Breathing Exercises, bearing no special names, but each distinct and separate from the others and having a different purpose in view. Each student will find several of these exercises best adapted to the special requirements of his particular case. Although we have styled these exercises "minor exercises," they are quite valuable and useful, or they would not appear in this book. They give one a condensed course in "Physical Culture" and "Lung Development," and might readily be "padded out" and elaborated into a small book on these subjects. They have, of course, an additional value, as Yogi Breathing forms a part of each exercise. Do not pass them by because they are marked "minor." Some one or more of these exercises may be just what you need. Try them and decide for yourself.

EXERCISE I.

(1) Stand erect with hands at sides.

(2) Inhale Complete Breath.

(3) Raise the arms slowly, keeping them rigid until the hands touch overhead.

(4) Retain the breath a few minutes with hands over head.

(5) Lower hands slowly to sides, exhaling slowly at same time.

(6) Practice Cleansing Breath.

EXERCISE II.

(1) Stand erect, with arms straight In front of you.

(2) Inhale Complete Breath and retain.

(3) Swing arms back as far as they will go; then back to first position; then repeat several times, returning the breath all the while.

(4) Exhale vigorously through mouth.

(5) Practice Cleansing Breath.

EXERCISE III.

(1) Stand erect with arms straight In front of you,

(2) Inhale Complete Breath.

(3) Swing arms around in a circle, backward, a few times. Then reverse a few times, retaining the breath all the while. You may vary this by rotating them alternately like the sails of a windmill.

(4) Exhale the breath vigorously through the mouth.

(5) Practice Cleansing Breath.

EXERCISE IV.

(1) Lie on the floor with your face downward and palms of hands flat upon the floor by your sides.

(2) Inhale Complete Breath and retain.

(3) Stiffen the body and raise yourself up by the strength of your arms until you rest on your hands and toes

(4) Then lower yourself to original position. Repeat several times.

(5) Exhale vigorously through your mouth.

(6) Practice Cleansing Breath.

EXERCISE V.

(1) Stand erect with your palms against the wall.

(2) Inhale Complete Breath and retain.

(3) Lower the chest to the wall, resting your weight on your hands.

(4) Then raise yourself back with the arm muscles alone, keeping the body stiff.

(5) Exhale vigorously through the mouth.

(6) Practice Cleansing Breath.

EXERCISE VI.

(1) Stand erect with arms "akimbo," that is, with hands resting around the waist and elbows standing out.

(2) Inhale Complete Breath and retain.

(3) Keep legs and hips stiff and bend well forward, as If bowing, at the same time exhaling slowly.

(4) Return to first position and take another Complete Breath.

(5) Then bend backward, exhaling slowly.

(6) Return to first position and take a Complete Breath.

(7) Then bend sideways, exhaling slowly. (Vary by bending to right and then to left.)

(8) Practice Cleansing Breath.

EXERCISE VII.

(1) Stand erect, or sit erect, with straight spinal column.

(2) Inhale a Complete Breath, but instead of inhaling in a continuous steady stream, take a series of short, quick "sniffs," as if you were smelling aromatic salts or ammonia and did not wish to get too strong a "whiff." Do not exhale any of these little breaths, but add one to the other until the entire lung space Is filled.

(3) Retain for a few seconds.

(4) Exhale through the nostrils in a long, restful, sighing breath.

(5) Practice Cleansing Breath.

CHAPTER XIII - VIBRATION AND YOGI RHYTHMIC BREATHING

All is in vibration. From the tiniest atom to the greatest sun, everything is in a state of vibration. There is nothing in absolute rest in nature. A single atom deprived of vibration would wreck the universe. In incessant vibration the universal work is performed. Matter is being constantly played upon by energy and countless forms and numberless varieties result, and yet even the forms and varieties are not permanent. They begin to change the moment they are created, and from them are born innumerable forms, which in turn change and give rise to newer forms, and so on and on, in infinite succession. Nothing is permanent in the world of forms, and yet the great Reality is unchangeable. Forms are but appearances—they come, they go, but the Reality is eternal and unchangeable.

The atoms of the human body are in constant vibration. Unceasing changes are occurring. In a few months there is almost a complete change in the matter composing the body, and scarcely a single atom now composing your body will be found in It a few months hence. Vibration, constant vibration. Change, constant change.

In all vibration is to be found a certain rhythm. Rhythm pervades the universe. The swing of the planets around the sun; the rise and fall of the sea; the beating of the heart; the ebb and flow of the tide; all follow rhythmic laws. The rays of the sun reach us; the rain descends upon us, in obedience to the same law. All growth is but an exhibition of this law. All motion is a manifestation of the law of rhythm.

Our bodies are as much subject to rhythmic laws as is the planet in its revolution around the sun. Much of the esoteric side of the Yogi Science of Breath is based upon this known principle of nature. By falling in with the rhythm of the body, the Yogi manages to absorb a great amount of Prana, which he disposes of to bring about results desired by him. We will speak of this at greater length later on.

The body which you occupy is like a small inlet running in to the land from the sea. Although apparently subject only to its own laws, it is really subject to the ebb and flow of the tides of the ocean. The great sea of life is swelling and receding, rising and falling, and we are responding to its vibrations and rhythm. In a normal condition we receive the vibration and rhythm of the great ocean of life, and respond to it, but at times the mouth of the inlet seems choked up with debris, and we fail to receive the impulse from Mother Ocean, and inharmony manifests within us. You have heard how a note on a violin, if sounded repeatedly and in rhythm, will start into motion vibrations which will in time destroy a bridge. The same result is true when a regiment of soldiers crosses a bridge, the order being always given to "break step" on such an occasion, lest the vibration bring down both bridge and regiment. These manifestations of the effect of rhythmic motion will give you an idea of the effect on the body of rhythmic breathing. The whole system catches the vibration and becomes in harmony with the will, which causes the rhythmic motion of the lungs, and while in such complete harmony will respond readily to orders from the will. With the body thus attuned, the Yogi finds no difficulty in increasing the circulation in any part of the body by an order from the will, and in the same way he can direct an increased current of nerve force to any part or organ, strengthening and stimulating it.

In the same way the Yogi by rhythmic breathing "catches the swing," as it were, and is able to absorb and control a greatly increased amount of Prana, which is then at the disposal of his will. He can and does use it as a vehicle for sending forth thoughts to others and for attracting to him all those whose thoughts are keyed in the same vibration. The phenomena of telepathy, thought transference, mental healing, mesmerism, etc., which subjects are creating such an interest in the Western world at the present time, but which have been known to the Yogis for centuries, can be greatly increased and augmented If the person sending forth the thoughts will do so after rhythmic breathing. Rhythmic breathing will increase the value of mental healing, magnetic healing, etc., several hundred per cent.

In rhythmic breathing the main thing to be acquired is the mental idea of rhythm. To those who know anything of music, the idea of measured counting is familiar. To others, the rhythmic step of the soldier: "Left, right; left, right; left, right; one, two, three, four; one, two, three, four," will convey the idea.

The Yogi bases his rhythmic time upon a unit corresponding with the beat of his heart. The heart beat varies in different persons, but the heart beat unit of each person is the proper rhythmic standard for that particular individual in his rhythmic breathing. Ascertain your normal heart beat by placing your fingers over your pulse, and then count: "1, 2, 3, 4, 5, 6; 1, 2, 3, 4, 5, 6," etc., until the rhythm becomes firmly fixed in your mind. A little practice will fix the rhythm, so that you will be able to easily reproduce it. The beginner usually inhales in about six pulse units, but he will be able to greatly increase this by practice.

The Yogi rule for rhythmic breathing is that the units of inhalation and exhalation should be the same, while the units for retention and between breaths should be one-half the number of those of inhalation and exhalation.

The following exercise in Rhythmic Breathing should be thoroughly mastered, as it forms the basis of numerous other exercises, to which reference will be made later.

(1) Sit erect, in an easy posture, being sure to hold the chest, neck and head as nearly in a straight line as possible, with shoulders slightly thrown back and hands resting easily on the lap. In this position the weight of the body is largely supported by the ribs and the position may be easily maintained. The Yogi has found that one cannot get the best effect of rhythmic breathing with the chest drawn in and the abdomen protruding.

(2) Inhale slowly a Complete Breath, counting six pulse units.

(3) Retain, counting three pulse units.

(4) Exhale slowly through the nostrils, counting six pulse units.

(5) Count three pulse beats between breaths.

(6) Repeat a number of times, but avoid fatiguing yourself at the start.

(7) When you are ready to close the exercise, practice the cleansing breath, which will rest you and cleanse the lungs.

After a little practice you will be able to increase the duration of the inhalations and exhalations, until about fifteen pulse units are consumed. In this increase, remember that the units for retention and between breaths is one-half the units for inhalation and exhalation.

Do not overdo yourself in your effort to increase the duration of the breath, but pay as much attention as possible to acquiring the "rhythm," as that is more important than the length of the breath. Practice and try until you get the measured "swing" of the movement, and until you can almost "feel" the rhythm of the vibratory motion throughout your whole body. It will require a little practice and perseverance, but your pleasure at your improvement will make the task an easy one. The Yogi is a most patient and persevering man, and his great attainments are due largely to the possession of these qualities.

CHAPTER XIV - PHENOMENA OF YOGI PSYCHIC BREATHING.

With the exception of the instructions in the Yogi Rhythmic Breathing, the majority of the exercises heretofore given in this book relate to the physical plane of effort, which, while highly important in itself, is also regarded by the Yogis as in the nature of affording a substantial basis for efforts on the psychic and spiritual plane. Do not, however, discard or think lightly of the physical phase of the subject, for remember that it needs a sound body to support a sound mind, and also that the body is the temple of the Ego, the lamp in which burns the light of the Spirit. Everything is good in its place, and everything has its place. The developed man is the "all-around man," who recognizes body, mind and spirit and renders to each its due. Neglect of either is a mistake which must be rectified sooner or later; a debt which must be repaid with interest.

We will now take up the Psychic phase of the Yogi Science of Breath in the shape of a series of exercises, each exercise carrying with it its explanation.

You will notice that in each exercise rhythmic breathing is accompanied with the instructions to "carry the thought" of certain desired results. This mental attitude gives the Will a cleared track upon which to exercise its force. We cannot, in this work, go into the subject of the power of the Will, and must assume that you have some knowledge of the subject. If you have no acquaintance with the subject, you will find that the actual practice of the exercises themselves will give you a much clearer knowledge than any amount of theoretical teaching, for as the old Hindu proverb says, "He who tastes a grain of mustard seed knows more of its flavor than he who sees an elephant load of it."

(1) GENERAL DIRECTIONS FOR YOGI PSYCHIC BREATHING.

The basis of all Yogi Psychic Breathing is the Yogi Rhythmic Breath, instruction regarding which we gave in our last chapter. In the following exercises, in order to avoid useless repetition, we will say merely, "Breathe Rhythmically," and then give the instruction for the exercise of the psychic force, or directed Will power working in connection with the rhythmic breath vibrations. After a little practice you will find that you will not need to count after the first rhythmic breath, as the mind will grasp the idea of time and rhythm and you will be able to breathe rhythmically at pleasure, almost automatically. This will leave the mind clear for the sending of the psychic vibrations under the direction of the Will. (See the following first exercise for directions in using the Will.)

(2) PRANA DISTRIBUTING.

Lying flat on the floor or bed, completely relaxed, with hands resting lightly over the Solar Plexus (over the pit of the stomach, where the ribs begin to separate), breathe rhythmically. After the rhythm is fully established *will* that each inhalation will draw in an increased supply of Prana or vital energy from the Universal supply, which will be taken up by the nervous system and stored in the Solar Plexus. At each exhalation will that the Prana or vital energy is being distributed all over the body, to every organ and part; to every muscle, cell and atom; to nerve, artery and vein; from the top of your head to the soles of your feet; invigorating, strengthening and stimulating every nerve; recharging every nerve center; sending energy, force and strength all over the system. While exercising the will, try to form a mental picture of the inrushing Prana, coming in through the lungs and being taken up at once by the Solar Plexus, then

219

with the exhaling effort, being sent to all parts of the system, down to the finger tips and down to the toes. It is not necessary to use the Will with an effort. Simply commanding that which you wish to produce and then making the mental picture of it is all that is necessary. Calm command with the mental picture is far better than forcible willing, which only dissipates force needlessly. The above exercise is most helpful and greatly refreshes and strengthens the nervous system and produces a restful feeling all over the body. It is especially beneficial In cases where one is tired or feels a lack of energy.

(3) INHIBITING PAIN.

Lying down or sitting erect, breath rhythmically, holding the thought that you are inhaling Prana. Then when you exhale, send the Prana to the painful part to re-establish the circulation and nerve current. Then inhale more Prana for the purpose of driving out the painful condition; then exhale, holding the thought that you are driving out the pain. Alternate the two above mental commands, and with one exhalation stimulate the part and with the next drive out the pain. Keep this up for seven breaths, then practice the Cleansing Breath and rest a while. Then try it again until relief comes, which will be before long. Many pains will be found to be relieved before the seven breaths are finished. If the hand is placed over the painful part, you may get quicker results. Send the current of Prana down the arm and into the painful part.

(4) DIRECTING THE CIRCULATION.

Lying down or sitting erect, breathe rhythmically, and with the exhalations direct the circulation to any part you wish, which may be suffering from imperfect circulation. This is effective in cases of cold feet or in cases of headache, the blood being sent downward in both cases, in the first case warming the feet, and in the latter, relieving the brain from too great pressure. In the case of headache, try the Pain Inhibiting first, then follow with sending the blood downward. You will often feel a warm feeling in the legs as the circulation moves downward. The circulation is largely under the control of the will and rhythmic breathing renders the task easier.

(5) SELF-HEALING.

Lying in a relaxed condition, breathe rhythmically, and command that a good supply of Prana be inhaled. With the exhalation, send the Prana to the affected part for the purpose of stimulating it. Vary this occasionally by exhaling, with the mental command that the diseased condition be forced out and disappear. Use the hands in this exercise, passing them down the body from the head to the affected part. In using the hands in healing yourself or others always hold the mental image that the Prana is flowing down the arm and through the finger tips into the body, thus reaching the affected part and healing it. Of course we can give only general directions in this book without taking up the several forms of disease in detail, but a little practice of the above exercise, varying it slightly to fit the conditions of the case, will produce wonderful results. Some Yogis follow the plan of placing both hands on the affected part, and then breathing rhythmically, holding the mental image that they are fairly pumping Prana into the diseased organ and part, stimulating it and driving out diseased conditions, as pumping into a pail of dirty water will drive out the latter and fill the bucket with fresh water. This last plan is very effective if the mental image of the pump is clearly held, the inhalation representing the lifting of the pump handle and the exhalation the actual pumping.

(6) HEALING OTHERS.

We cannot take up the question of the psychic treatment of disease by Prana in detail in this book, as such would be foreign to its purpose. But we can and will give you simple, plain instructions whereby you may be enabled to do much good in relieving others. The main principle to remember is that by rhythmic breathing and controlled thought you are enabled to absorb a considerable amount of Prana, and are also able to pass it into the body of another person, stimulating weakened parts and organs and imparting health and driving out diseased conditions. You must first learn to form such a clear mental image of the desired condition that you will be able to actually feel the influx of Prana, and the force running down your arms and out of your fingertips into the body of the patient. Breathe rhythmically a few times until the rhythm is fairly established, then place your bands upon the affected part of the body of the patient, letting them rest lightly over the part. Then follow the "pumping" process described to the preceding exercise (Self-

221

Healing) and fill the patient full of Prana until the diseased condition is driven out. Every once in a while raise the hands and "flick" the fingers as if you were throwing off the diseased condition. It is well to do this occasionally and also to wash the hands after treatment, as otherwise you may take on a trace of the diseased condition of the patient. Also practice the Cleansing Breath several times after the treatment. During the treatment let the Prana pour into the patient in one continuous stream, allowing yourself to be merely the pumping machinery connecting the patient with the universal supply of Prana, and allowing it to flow freely through you. You need not work the hands vigorously, but simply enough that the Prana freely reaches the affected parts. The rhythmic breathing must be practiced frequently during the treatment, so as to keep the rhythm normal and to afford the Prana a free passage. It is better to place the hands on the bare skin, but where this is not advisable or possible place them over the clothing. Vary above method occasionally during the treatment by stroking the body gently and softly with the finger tips, the fingers being kept slightly separated. This is very soothing to the patient. In cases of long standing you may find it helpful to give the mental command in words, such as "get out, get out," or "be strong, be strong," as the case may be, the words helping you to exercise the will more forcibly and to the point. Vary these instructions to suit the needs of the case, and use your own judgment and inventive faculty. We have given you the general principles and you can apply them in hundreds of different ways. The above apparently simple instruction, if carefully studied and applied, will enable one to accomplish all that the leading "magnetic healers" are able to, although their "systems" are more or less cumbersome and complicated. They are using Prana ignorantly and calling it "magnetism." If they would combine rhythmic breathing with their "magnetic" treatment they would double their efficiency.

(7) DISTANT HEALING.

Prana colored by the thought of the sender may be projected to persons at a distance, who are willing to receive it, and healing work done in this way. This is the secret of the "absent healing," of which the Western world has heard so much of late years. The thought of the healer sends forth and colors the Prana of the sender, and it flashes across space and finds lodgment in the psychic mechanism of the patient. It is unseen, and like the Marconi waves, it passes through intervening obstacles and seeks the person attuned to receive it. In order to treat persons at a distance, you must form a mental image of them until you can feel yourself to be in rapport with them. This is a psychic process dependent upon the mental imagery of the healer. You can feel the sense of rapport when it is established, it manifesting in a sense of nearness. That is about as plain as we can describe it. It may be acquired by a little practice, and some will get it at the first trial. When rapport is established, say mentally to the distant patient, "I am sending you a supply of vital force or power, which will invigorate you and heal you." Then picture the Prana as leaving your mind with each exhalation of rhythmic breath, and traveling across space instantaneously and reaching the patient and healing him. It is not necessary to fix certain hours for treatment, although you may do so if you wish. The receptive condition of the patient, as he is expecting and opening himself up to your psychic force, attunes him to receive your vibrations whenever you may send them. If you agree upon hours, let him place himself in a relaxed attitude and receptive condition. The above is the great underlying principle of the "absent treatment" of the Western world. You may do these things as well as the most noted healers, with a little practice.

CHAPTER XV - MORE PHENOMENA OF YOGI PSYCHIC BREATHING.

(1) THOUGHT PROJECTION.

Thoughts may be projected by following the last mentioned method (Distant Healing) and others will feel the effect of thought so sent forth, it being remembered always that no evil thought can ever injure another person whose thoughts are good. Good thoughts are always positive to bad ones, and bad ones always negative to good ones. One can, however, excite the interest and attention of another by sending him thought waves in this way, charging the Prana with the message he wishes to convey. If you desire another's love and sympathy, and possess love and sympathy for him, you can send him thoughts of this kind with effect, providing your motives are pure. Never, however, attempt to influence another to his hurt, or from impure or selfish motives, as such thoughts only recoil upon the sender with redoubled force, and injure him, while the innocent party is not affected. Psychic force when legitimately used is all right, but beware of "black magic" or improper and unholy uses of it, as such attempts are like playing with a dynamo, and the person attempting such things will be surely punished by the result of the act itself. However, no person of impure motives ever acquires a great degree of psychic power, and a pure heart and mind is an invulnerable shield against improper psychic power. Keep yourself pure and nothing can hurt you.

(2) FORMING AN AURA.

If you are ever in the company of persons of a low order of mind, and you feel the depressing influence of their thought, breathe rhythmically a few times, thus generating an additional supply of Prana, and then by means of the mental image method surround yourself with an egg-shaped thought aura, which will protect you from the gross thought and disturbing influences of others.

(3) RECHARGING YOURSELF.

If you feel that your vital energy is at a low ebb, and that you need to store up a new supply quickly, the best plan is to place the feet close together (side by side, of course) and to lock the fingers of both hands in any way that seems the most comfortable. This closes the circuit, as it were, and prevents any escape of Prana through the extremities. Then breathe rhythmically a few times, and you will feel the effect of the recharging.

(4) RECHARGING OTHERS.

If some friend is deficient in vitality you may aid him by sitting in front of him, your toes touching his, and his hands in yours. Then both breathe rhythmically, you forming the mental image of sending Prana into his system, and he holding the mental image of receiving the Prana. Persons of weak vitality or passive will should be careful with whom they try this experiment, as the Prana of a person of evil desires will be colored with the thoughts of that person, and may give him a temporary influence over the weaker person. The latter, however, may easily remove such influence by closing the circuit (as before mentioned) and breathing a few rhythmic breaths, closing with the Cleansing Breath.

(5) CHARGING WATER.

Water may be charged with Prana, by breathing rhythmically, and holding the glass of water by the bottom, in the left hand, and then gathering the fingers of the right hand together and shaking them gently over the water, as if you were shaking drops of water off of your fingertips into the glass. The mental image of the Prana being passed into the water must also be held. Water thus charged is found stimulating to weak or sick persons, particularly if a healing thought accompanies the mental image of the transfer of the Prana. The caution given in the last exercise applies also to this one, although the danger exists only in a greatly lessened degree.

(6) ACQUIRING MENTAL QUALITIES.

Not only can the body be controlled by the mind under direction of the will, but the mind itself can be trained and cultivated by the exercise of the controlling will. This, which the Western world knows as "Mental Science," etc., has proved to the West portions of that truth which the Yogi has known for ages. The mere calm demand of the Will will accomplish wonders in this direction, but if the mental exercise is accompanied by rhythmic breathing, the effect is greatly increased. Desirable qualities may be acquired by holding the proper mental image of what is desired during rhythmic breathing. Poise and Self Control, desirable qualities; increased power, etc., may be acquired in this way. Undesirable qualities may be eliminated by cultivating the opposite qualities. Any or all the "Mental Science" exercises, "treatments" and "affirmations" may be used with the Yogi Rhythmic Breath. The following is a good general exercise for the acquirement and development of desirable mental qualities: Lie in a passive attitude, or sit erect. Picture to yourself the qualities you desire to cultivate, seeing yourself as possessed of the qualities, and demanding that your mind develop the quality. Breathe rhythmically, holding the mental picture firmly. Carry the mental picture with you as much as possible, and endeavor to live up to the ideal you have set up in your mind. You will find yourself gradually growing up to your ideal. The rhythm of the breathing assists the mind in forming new combinations, and the student who has followed the Western system will find the Yogi Rhythmic a wonderful ally in his "Mental Science" works.

(7) ACQUIRING PHYSICAL QUALITIES.

Physical qualities may be acquired by the same methods as above mentioned in connection with mental qualities. We do not mean, of course, that short men can be made tall, or that amputated limbs may be replaced, or similar miracles. But the expression of the countenance may be changed; courage and general physical characteristics improved by the control of the Will, accompanied by rhythmic breathing. As a man thinks so does he look, act, walk, sit, etc. Improved thinking will mean improved looks and actions. To develop any part of the body, direct the attention to it, while breathing rhythmically, holding the mental picture that you are sending an increased amount of Prana, or nerve force, to the part, and thus increasing its vitality and developing it. This plan applies equally well to any part of the body which you wish to develop. Many Western athletes use a modification of this plan in their exercises. The student who has followed our instructions so far will readily understand haw to apply the Yogi principles in the above work. The general rule of exercise is the same as in the preceding exercise (acquiring Mental Qualities). We have touched upon the subject of the cure of physical ailments in preceding pages.

(8) CONTROLLING THE EMOTIONS.

The undesirable emotions, such as Fear, Worry, Anxiety, Hate, Anger, Jealousy, Envy, Melancholy, Excitement, Grief, etc., are amenable to the control of the Will, and the Will is enabled to operate more easily in such cases if rhythmic breathing is practiced while the student is "willing." The following exercise has been found most effective by the Yogi students, although the advanced Yogi has but little need of it, as he has long since gotten rid of these undesirable mental qualities by growing spiritually beyond them. The Yogi student, however, finds the exercise a great help to him while he is growing.

Breathe rhythmically, concentrating the attention upon the Solar Plexus, and sending to it the mental command "Get Out." Send the mental command firmly, just as you begin to exhale, and form the mental picture of the undesirable emotions being carried away with the exhaled breath. Repeat seven times, and finish with the Cleansing Breath, and then see how good you feel. The mental command must be given "in earnest," as trifling will not do the work.

(9) TRANSMUTATION OF THE REPRODUCTIVE ENERGY.

The Yogis possess great knowledge regarding the use and abuse of the reproductive principle in both sexes. Some hints of this esoteric knowledge have filtered out and have been used by Western writers on the subject, and much good has been accomplished in this way. In this little book we cannot do more than touch upon the subject, and omitting all except a bare mention of theory, we will give a practical breathing exercise whereby the student will be enabled to transmute the reproductive energy into vitality for the entire system, instead of dissipating and wasting it in lustful indulgences in or out of the marriage relations. The reproductive energy is creative energy, and may be taken up by the system and transmuted into strength and vitality, thus serving the purpose of regeneration instead of generation. If the young men of the Western world understood these underlying principles they would be saved much misery and unhappiness in after years, and would be stronger mentally, morally and physically.

This transmutation of the reproductive energy gives great vitality to those practicing it. They will be filled with great vital force, which will radiate from them and will manifest in what has been called "personal magnetism." The energy thus transmuted may be turned into new channels and used to great advantage. Nature has condensed one of its most powerful manifestations of Prana into reproductive energy, as its purpose is to create. The greatest amount of vital force is concentrated in the smallest area. The reproductive organism is the most powerful storage battery in animal life, and its force can be drawn upward and used, as well as expended in the ordinary functions of reproduction, or wasted in riotous lust. The majority of our students know something of the theories of regeneration; and we can do little more than to state the above facts, without attempting to prove them.

The Yogi exercise for transmuting reproductive energy is simple. It is coupled with rhythmic breathing, and can be easily performed. It may be practiced at any time, but is specially recommended when one feels the instinct most strongly, at which time the reproductive energy is manifesting and may be most easily transmuted for regenerative purposes. The exercise is as follows: Keep the mind fixed on the idea of Energy, and away from ordinary sexual thoughts or imaginings. If these thoughts come into the mind do not be discouraged, but regard them as manifestations of a force which you intend using for the purposes of strengthening the body and mind. Lie passively or sit erect, and fix your mind on the idea of drawing the reproductive energy upward to the Solar Plexus, where it will be transmuted and stored away as a reserve force of vital energy. Then breathe rhythmically, forming the mental image of drawing up the reproductive energy with each inhalation. With each inhalation make a command of the Will that the energy be drawn upward from the reproductive organization to the Solar Plexus. If the rhythm is fairly established and the mental image is clear, you will be conscious of the upward passage of the energy, and will feel its stimulating effect. If you desire an increase in mental force, you may draw it up to the brain instead of to the Solar Plexus, by giving the mental command and holding the mental image of the transmission to the brain. The man or woman doing metal creative work, or bodily creative work, will be able to use this creative energy in their work by following the above exercise, drawing up the energy with the inhalation and sending it forth with the exhalation. In this last form of exercise, only such portions as are needed in the work will pass into the work being done, the balance remaining stored up in the Solar Plexus. You will understand, of course, that it is not the reproductive fluids which are drawn up and used, but the etheripranic energy (Subtle Energy) which animates the latter, the soul of the reproductive organism, as it were. It is usual to allow the head to bend forward easily and naturally during the transmuting exercise.

(10) BRAIN STIMULATING.

The Yogis have found the following exercise most useful in stimulating the action of the brain for the purpose of producing clear thinking and reasoning. It has a wonderful effect in clearing the brain and nervous system, and those engaged in mental work will find it most useful to them, both in the direction of enabling them to do better work and also as a means of refreshing the mind and clearing it after arduous mental labor.

Sit in an erect posture, keeping the spinal column straight, and the eyes well to the front, letting the hands rest on the upper part of the legs. Breathe rhythmically, but instead of breathing through both nostrils as in the ordinary exercises, press the left nostril close with the thumb, and inhale through the right nostril. Then remove the thumb, and close the right nostril with the finger, and then exhale through the left nostril. Then, without changing the fingers, inhale through the left nostril, and changing fingers, exhale through the right. Then inhale through right and exhale through left, and so on, alternating nostrils as above mentioned, closing the unused nostril with the thumb or forefinger. This is one of the oldest forms of Yogi breathing, and is quite important and valuable, and is well worthy of acquirement. But it is quite amusing to the Yogis to know that to the Western world this method is often held out as being the "whole secret" of Yogi Breathing. To the minds of many Western readers, "Yogi Breathing" suggests nothing more than a picture of a Hindu, sitting erect, and alternating nostrils in the act of breathing. "Only this and nothing more." We trust that this little work will open the eyes of the Western world to the great possibilities of Yogi Breathing, and the numerous methods whereby it may be employed.

(11) THE GRAND YOGI PSYCHIC BREATH.

The Yogis have a favorite form of psychic breathing which they practice occasionally, to which has been given a Sanskrit term of which the above is a general equivalent. We have given it last, as it requires practice on the part of the student in the line of rhythmic breathing and mental imagery, which he has now acquired by means of the preceding exercises. The general principles of the Grand Breath may be summed up in the old Hindu saying: "Blessed is the Yogi who can breathe through his bones." This exercise will fill the entire system with Prana, and the student will emerge from it with every bone, muscle, nerve, cell, tissue, organ and part energized and attuned by the Prana and the rhythm of the breath. It is a general housecleaning of the system, and he who practices it carefully will feel as if he had been given a new body, freshly created, from the crown of his head to the tips of his toes. We will let the exercise speak for itself.

(1) Lie in a relaxed position, at perfect ease.

(2) Breathe rhythmically until the rhythm is perfectly established.

(3) Then, inhaling and exhaling, form the mental image of the breath being drawn up through the bones of the legs, and then forced out through them; then through the bones of the arms; then through the top of the skull; then through the stomach; then through the reproductive region; then as if it were traveling upward and downward along the spinal column; and then as if the breath were being inhaled and exhaled through every pore of the skin, the whole body being filled with Prana and life.

(4) Then (breathing rhythmically) send the current of Prana to the Seven Vital Centers, in turn, as follows, using the mental picture as in previous exercises:

(a) To the forehead.

(b) To the back of the head.

(c) To the base of the brain.

(d) To the Solar Plexus.

(e) To the Sacral Region (lower part of the spine).

(f) To the region of the navel.

(g) To the reproductive region.

Finish by sweeping the current of Prana, to and fro from head to feet several times.

(5) Finish with Cleansing Breath.

CHAPTER XVI - YOGI SPIRITUAL BREATHING.

The Yogis not only bring about desired mental qualities and properties by will-power coupled with rhythmic breathing, but they also develop spiritual faculties, or rather aid in their unfoldment, in the same way. The Oriental philosophies teach that man has many faculties which are at present in a dormant state, but which will become unfolded as the race progresses. They also teach that man, by the proper effort of the will, aided by favorable conditions, may aid in the unfoldment of these spiritual faculties, and develop them much sooner than in the ordinary process of evolution. In other words, one may even now develop spiritual powers of consciousness which will not become the common property of the race until after long ages of gradual development under the law of evolution. In all of the exercises directed toward this end, rhythmic breathing plays an important part. There is of course no mystic property in the breath itself which produces such wonderful results, but the rhythm produced by the Yogi breath is such as to bring the whole system, including the brain, under perfect control, and in perfect harmony, and by this means, the most perfect condition is obtained for the unfoldment of these latent faculties.

In this work we cannot go deeply into the philosophy of the East regarding spiritual development, because this subject would require volumes to cover it, and then again the subject is too abstruse to interest the average reader. There are also other reasons, well known to occultists, why this knowledge should not be spread broadcast at this time. Rest assured, dear student, that when the time comes for you to take the next step, the way will be opened out before you. "When the chela (student) is ready, the guru (master) appears." In this chapter we will give you directions for the development of two phases of spiritual consciousness, i.e., (1) the consciousness of the identity of the Soul, and (2) the consciousness of the connection of the Soul with the Universal Life. Both of the exercises given below are simple, and consist of mental images firmly held, accompanied with rhythmic breathing. The student must not expect too much at the start, but must make haste slowly, and be content to develop as does the flower, from seed to blossom.

SOUL CONSCIOUSNESS.

The real Self is not the body or even the mind of man. These things are but a part of his personality, the lesser self. The real Self is the Ego, whose manifestation is in individuality. The real Self is independent of the body, which it inhabits, and is even independent of the mechanism of the mind, which it uses as an instrument. The real Self is a drop from the Divine Ocean, and is eternal and indestructible. It cannot die or be annihilated, and no matter what becomes of the body, the real Self still exists. It is the Soul. Do not think of your Soul as a thing apart from you, for YOU are the Soul, and the body is the unreal and transitory part of you which is changing in material every day, and which you will some day discard. You may develop the faculties so that they will be conscious of the reality of the Soul, and its independence of the body. The Yogi plan for such development is by meditation upon the real Self or Soul, accompanied by rhythmic breathing. The following exercise is the simplest form.

EXERCISE.—Place your body in a relaxed, reclining position. Breathe rhythmically, and meditate upon the real Self, thinking of yourself as an entity independent of the body, although inhabiting it and being able to leave it at will. Think of yourself, not as the body, but as a spirit, and of your body as but a shell, useful and comfortable, but not a part of the real You. Think of yourself as an independent being, using the body only as a convenience. While meditating, ignore the body entirely, and you will find that you will often become almost entirely unconscious of it, and will seem to be out of the body to which you may return when you are through with the exercise.

This is the gist of the Yogi meditative breathing methods, and if persisted in will give one a wonderful sense of the reality of the Soul, and will make him seem almost independent of the body. The sense of immortality will often come with this increased consciousness, and the person will begin to show signs of spiritual development which will be noticeable to himself and others. But he must not allow himself to live too much in the

232

upper regions, or to despise his body, for he is here on this plane for a purpose, and he must not neglect his opportunity to gain the experiences necessary to round him out, nor must he fail to respect his body, which is the Temple of the Spirit.

THE UNIVERSAL CONSCIOUSNESS.

The Spirit in man, which is the highest manifestation of his Soul, is a drop in the ocean of Spirit, apparently separate and distinct, but yet really in touch with the ocean itself, and with every other drop in it. As man unfolds in spiritual consciousness he becomes more and more aware of his relation to the Universal Spirit, or Universal Mind as some term it. He feels at times as if he were almost at-one-ment with it, and then again he loses the sense of contact and relationship. The Yogis seek to attain this state of Universal Consciousness by meditation and rhythmic breathing, and many have thus attained the highest degree of spiritual attainment possible to man in this stage of his existence. The student of this work will not need the higher instruction regarding adeptship at this time, as he has much to do and accomplish before he reaches that stage, but it may be well to initiate him into the elementary stages of the Yogi exercises for developing Universal Consciousness, and if he is in earnest he will discover means and methods whereby he may progress. The way is always opened to him who is ready to tread the path. The following exercise will be found to do much toward developing the Universal Consciousness in those who faithfully practice it.

EXERCISE.—Place your body in a reclining, relaxed position. Breathe rhythmically, and meditate upon your relationship with the Universal Mind of which you are but an atom. Think of yourself as being in touch with All, and at-one-ment with All. See All as One, and your Soul as a part of that One. Feel that you are receiving the vibrations from the great Universal Mind, and are partaking of its power and strength and wisdom. The two following lines of meditation may be followed.

(a) With each inhalation, think of yourself as drawing in to yourself the strength and power of the Universal Mind. When exhaling think of yourself as passing out to others that same power, at the same time being filled with love for every living thing, and desiring that it be a partaker of the same blessings

233

which you are now receiving. Let the Universal Power circulate through you.

(b) Place your mind in a reverential state, and meditate upon the grandeur of the Universal Mind, and open yourself to the inflow of the Divine Wisdom, which will fill you with illuminating wisdom, and then let the same flow out from you to your brothers and sisters whom you love and would help.

This exercise leaves with those who have practiced it a new-found sense of strength, power and wisdom, and a feeling of spiritual exaltation and bliss. It must be practiced only in a serious, reverential mood, and must not be approached triflingly or lightly.

GENERAL DIRECTIONS.

The exercises given in this chapter require the proper mental attitude and conditions, and the trifler and person of a non-serious nature, or one without a sense of spirituality and reverence, had better pass them by, as no results will be obtained by such persons, and besides it is a willful trifling with things of a high order, which course never benefits those who pursue it. These exercises are for the few who can understand them, and the others will feel no attraction to try them.

During meditation let the mind dwell upon the ideas given in the exercise, until it becomes clear to the mind, and gradually manifests in real consciousness within you. The mind will gradually become passive and at rest, and the mental image will manifest clearly. Do not indulge in these exercises too often, and do not allow the blissful state produced to render you dissatisfied with the affairs of everyday life, as the latter are useful and necessary for you, and you must never shirk a lesson, however disagreeable to you it may be. Let the joy arising from the unfolding consciousness buoy you up and nerve you for the trials of life, and not make you dissatisfied and disgusted. All is good, and everything has its place. Many of the students who practice these exercises will in time wish to know more. Rest assured that when the time comes we will see that you do not seek in vain. Go on in courage and confidence, keeping your face toward the East, from whence comes the rising Sun.

Peace be unto you, and unto all men.

AUM.

LESSONS IN MINDFULNESS

12 Lessons in Yogic Wisdom

By: Yogi Ramacharaka aka William Walker Atkinson (1862-1932). Previously titled: *A series of Lessons in Raja Yoga* Published in 1904

THE FIRST LESSON - The One

The Yogi Philosophy may be divided into several great branches, or fields. What is known as "Hatha Yoga" deals with the physical body and its control; its welfare; its health; its preservation; its laws, etc. What is known as "Raja Yoga" deals with the Mind; its control; its development; its unfoldment, etc. What is known as "Bhakti Yoga" deals with the Love of the Absolute—God. What is known as "Gnani Yoga" deals with the scientific and intellectual knowing of the great questions regarding Life and what lies back of Life—the Riddle of the Universe.

Each branch of Yoga is but a path leading toward the one end—unfoldment, development, and growth. He who wishes first to develop, control and strengthen his physical body so as to render it a fit instrument of the Higher Self, follows the path of "Hatha Yoga." He who would develop his will-power and mental faculties, unfolding the inner senses, and latent powers, follows the path of "Raja Yoga." He who wishes to develop by "knowing"—by studying the fundamental principles, and the wonderful truths underlying Life, follows the path of "Gnani Yoga." And he who wishes to grow into a union with the One Life by the influence of Love, he follows the path of "Bhakti Yoga."

But it must not be supposed that the student must ally himself to only a single one of these paths to power. In fact, very few do. The majority prefer to gain a rounded knowledge, and acquaint themselves with the principles of the several branches, learning something of each, giving preference of course to those branches that appeal to them more strongly, this attraction being the indication of *need*, or requirement, and, therefore, being the hand pointing out the path.

It is well for everyone to know something of "Hatha Yoga," in order that the body may be purified, strengthened, and kept in health in order to become a more fitting instrument of the Higher Self. It is well that each one should know something of "Raja Yoga," that he may understand the training and control of the mind, and the use of the Will. It is well that everyone should learn the wisdom of "Gnani Yoga," that he may realize the wonderful truths underlying life—the science of Being. And, most assuredly everyone should know something of Bhakti Yogi, that he may understand the great teachings regarding the Love underlying all life.

We have written a work on "Hatha Yoga," and a course on "Raja Yoga" which is now in book form. We have told you something regarding "Gnani Yoga" in our Fourteen Lessons, and also in our Advanced Course. We have written something regarding "Bhakti Yoga" in our Advanced Course, and, we hope, have taught it also all through our other lessons, for we fail to see how one can teach or study any of the branches of Yoga without being filled with a sense of Love and Union with the Source of all Life. To know the Giver of Life, is to love him, and the more we know of him, the more love will we manifest.

In this course of lessons, of which this is the first, we shall take up the subject of "Gnani Yoga"—the Yoga of Wisdom, and will endeavor to make plain some of its most important and highest teachings. And, we trust that in so doing, we shall be able to awaken in you a still higher realization of your relationship with the One, and a corresponding Love for that in which you live, and move and have your being. We ask for your loving sympathy and cooperation in our task.

Let us begin by a consideration of what has been called the "Questions of Questions"—the question: "What is Reality?" To understand the question we have but to take a look around us and view the visible world. We see great masses of something that science has called "matter." We see in operation a wonderful something called "force" or "energy" in its countless forms of manifestations. We see things that we call "forms of life," varying in manifestation from the tiny speck of slime that we call the Moneron, up to that form that we call Man.

But study this world of manifestations by means of science and research—and such study is of greatest value—still we must find ourselves brought to a point where we cannot progress further. Matter melts into mystery—Force resolves itself into something else—the secret of living-forms subtly elude us—and mind is seen as but the manifestation of something even finer. But in losing these things of appearance and manifestation, we find ourselves brought up face to face with a Something Else that we see must underlie all these varying forms, shapes and manifestations. And that Something Else, we call Reality, because it is Real, Permanent, Enduring. And although men may differ, dispute, wrangle, and quarrel about this Reality, still there is one point upon which they must agree, and that is that *Reality is One*—that underlying all forms and manifestations there must be a *One* Reality from which all things flow. And this inquiry into this One Reality is indeed the Question of Questions of the Universe.

The highest reason of Man—as well as his deepest intuition—has always recognized that this Reality or Underlying Being must be but ONE, of which all Nature is but varying degrees of manifestation, emanation, or expression. All have recognized that Life is a stream flowing from One great fount, the nature and name of which is unknown—some have said unknowable. Differ as men do about theories regarding the nature of this one, they all agree that it can be but One. It is only when men begin to name and analyze this One, that confusion results.

Let us see what men have thought and said about this One—it *may* help us to understand the nature of the problem.

The materialist claims that this one is a something called Matter—self-existent—eternal—infinite—containing within itself the potentiality of Matter, Energy and Mind. Another school, closely allied to the materialists, claim that this One is a something called Energy, of which Matter and Mind are but modes of motion. The Idealists claim that the One is a something called Mind, and that Matter and Force are but ideas in that One Mind. Theologians claim that this One is a something called a personal God, to whom they attribute certain qualities, characteristics, etc., the same varying with their creeds and dogmas. The Naturistic school claims that this One is a something called Nature, which is constantly manifesting itself in countless forms. The occultists, in their varying schools, Oriental and Occidental, have taught that the One was a Being whose Life constituted the life of all living forms.

All philosophies, all science, all religions, inform us that this world of shapes, forms and names is but a phenomenal or shadow world—a show-world—back of which rests Reality, called by some name of the teacher. But remember this, *all philosophy that counts* is based upon some form of monism—Oneness—whether the concept be a known or unknown god; an unknown or unknowable principle; a substance; an Energy, or Spirit. There is but One—there can be but One—such is the inevitable conclusion of the highest human reason, intuition or faith.

And, likewise, the same reason informs us that this One Life must permeate all apparent forms of life, and that all apparent material forms, forces, energies, and principles must be emanations from that One, and, consequently "of" it. It may be objected to, that the creeds teaching a personal god do not so hold, for they teach that their God is the creator of the Universe, which he has set aside from himself as a workman sets aside his workmanship. But this objection avails naught, for where could such a creator obtain the material for his universe, except from himself; and where the energy, except from the same source; and where the Life, unless from his One Life. So in the end, it is seen that there must be but One—not two, even if we prefer the terms God *and* his Universe, for even in this case the Universe must have proceeded from God, and can only live, and move and act, and think, by virtue of his Essence permeating it.

In passing by the conceptions of the various thinkers, we are struck by the fact that the various schools seem to manifest a one-sidedness in their theories, seeing only that which fits in with their theories, and ignoring the rest. The Materialist talks about Infinite and Eternal Matter, although the latest scientific investigations have shown us Matter fading into Nothingness—the Eternal Atom being split into countless particles called Corpuscles or Electrons, which at the last seem to be nothing but a unit of Electricity, tied up in a "knot in the Ether"—although just what the Ether is, Science does not dare to guess. And Energy, also seems to be unthinkable except as operating through matter, and always seems to be acting under the operation of Laws—and Laws without a Law giver, and a Law giver without mind or something higher than Mind, is unthinkable. And Mind, as we know it, seems to be bound up with matter and energy in a wonderful combination, and is seen to be subject to laws outside of itself, and to be varying, inconstant, and changeable, which attributes cannot be conceived of as belonging to the Absolute. Mind as we know it, as well as Matter and Energy, is held by the highest occult teachers to be but an appearance and a relativity of something far more fundamental and enduring, and we are compelled to fall back upon that old term which wise men have used in order to describe that Something Else that lies back of, and under, Matter, Energy and Mind—and that word is "Spirit."

We cannot tell just what is meant by the word "Spirit," for we have nothing with which to describe it. But we can think of it as meaning the "essence" of Life and Being—the Reality underlying Universal Life.

Of course no name can be given to this One, that will fitly describe it. But we have used the term "The Absolute" in our previous lessons, and consider it advisable to continue its use, although the student may substitute any other name that appeals to him more strongly. We do not use the word God (except occasionally in order to bring out a shade of meaning) not because we object to it, but because by doing so we would run the risk of identifying The Absolute with some idea of a personal god with certain theological attributes. Nor does the word "Principle" appeal to us, for it seems to imply a cold, unfeeling, abstract thing, while we conceive the Absolute Spirit or Being to be a warm, vital, living, acting, feeling Reality. We do not use the word Nature, which many prefer, because of its materialistic meaning to the minds of many, although the word is very dear to us when referring to the outward manifestation of the Absolute Life.

Of the real nature of The Absolute, of course, we can know practically nothing, because it transcends all human experience and Man has nothing with which he can measure the Infinite. Spinoza was right when he said that "to define God is to deny him," for any attempt to define, is, of course an attempt to limit or make finite the Infinite. To define a thing is to identify it with something else—and where is the something else with which to identify the Infinite? The Absolute cannot be described in terms of the Relative. It is not Something, although it contains within itself the reality underlying Everything. It cannot be said to have the qualities of any of its apparently separated parts, for it is the ALL. It is all that really IS.

It is beyond Matter, Force, or Mind as we know it, and yet these things emanate from it, and must be within its nature. For what is in the manifested must be in the manifestor—no stream can rise higher than its source—the effect cannot be greater than the cause—you cannot get something out of nothing.

But it is hard for the human mind to take hold of That which is beyond its experience—many philosophers consider it impossible—and so we must think of the Absolute in the concepts and terms of its highest manifestation. We find Mind higher in the scale than Matter or Energy, and so we are justified in using the terms of Mind in speaking of the Absolute, rather than the terms of Matter or Energy—so let us try to think of an Infinite Mind, whose powers and capacities are raised to an infinite degree—a Mind of which Herbert Spencer said that it was "a mode of being as much transcending intelligence and will, as these transcend mere mechanical motion."

While it is true (as all occultists know) that the best information regarding the Absolute come from regions of the Self higher than Intellect, yet we are in duty bound to examine the reports of the Intellect concerning its information regarding the One. The Intellect has been developed in us for use—for the purpose of examining, considering, thinking—and it behooves us to employ it. By turning it to this purpose, we not only strengthen and unfold it, but we also get certain information that can reach us by no other channel. And moreover, by such use of the Intellect we are able to discover many fallacies and errors that have crept into our minds from the opinions and dogmas of others—as Kant said: "The chief, and perhaps the only, use of a philosophy of pure reason is a negative one. It is not an organon for extending, but a discipline for limiting! Instead of discovering truth, its modest function is to guard against error." Let us then listen to the report of the Intellect, as well as of the higher fields of mentation.

One of the first reports of the Intellect, concerning the Absolute, is that it must have existed forever, and must continue to exist forever. There is no escape from this conclusion, whether one view the matter from the viewpoint of the materialist, philosopher, occultist, or theologian. The Absolute could not have sprung from Nothing, and there was no other cause outside of itself from which it could have emanated. And there can be no cause outside of itself which can terminate its being. And we cannot conceive of Infinite Life, or Absolute Life, dying. So the Absolute must be Eternal—such is the report of the Intellect. This idea of the Eternal is practically unthinkable to the human mind, although it is forced to believe that it must be a quality of the Absolute. The trouble arises from the fact that the Intellect is compelled to see everything through the veil of Time, and Cause and Effect. Now, Cause and Effect, and Time, are merely phenomena or appearances of the relative world, and have no place in the Absolute and Real. Let us see if we can understand this.

Reflection will show you that the only reason that you are unable to think of or picture a Causeless Cause, is because everything that you have experienced in this relative world of the senses has had a cause—something from which it sprung. You have seen Cause and Effect in full operation all about you, and quite naturally your Intellect has taken it for granted that there can be nothing uncaused—nothing without a preceding cause. And the Intellect is perfectly right, so far as Things are concerned, for all Things are relative and are therefore caused. But back of the caused things must lie THAT which is the Great Causer of Things, and which, not being a Thing itself, cannot have been caused—cannot be the effect of a cause. Your minds reel when you try to form a mental image of That which has had no cause, because you have had no experience in the sense world of such a thing, and there fail to form the image. It is out of your experience, and you cannot form the mental picture. But yet your mind is compelled to believe that there must have been an Original One, that can have had no cause. This is a hard task for the Intellect, but in time it comes to see just where the trouble lies, and ceases to interpose objections to the voice of the higher regions of the self.

And, the Intellect experiences a similar difficulty when it tries to think of an Eternal—a That which is above and outside of Time. We see Time in operation everywhere, and take it for granted that Time is a reality—an actual thing. But this is a mistake of the senses. There is no such thing as Time, in reality. Time exists solely in our minds. It is merely a form of perception by which we express our consciousness of the Change in Things.

We cannot think of Time except in connection with a succession of changes of things in our consciousness—either things of the outer world, or the passing of thought-things through our mind. A day is merely the consciousness of the passing of the sun—an hour or minute merely the subdivision of the day, or else the consciousness of the movement of the hands of the clock—merely the consciousness of the movement of Things—the symbols of changes in Things. In a world without changes in Things, there would be no such thing as Time. Time is but a mental invention. Such is the report of the Intellect.

And, besides the conclusions of pure abstract reasoning about Time, we may see many instances of the relativity of Time in our everyday experiences. We all know that when we are interested Time seems to pass rapidly, and when we are bored it drags along in a shameful manner. We know that when we are happy, Time develops the speed of a meteor, while when we are unhappy it crawls like a tortoise. When we are interested or happy our attention is largely diverted from the changes occurring in things—because we do not notice the Things so closely. And while we are miserable or bored, we notice the details in Things, and their changes, until the length of time seems interminable. A tiny insect mite may, and does, live a lifetime of birth, growth, marriage, reproduction, old age, and death, in a few minutes, and no doubt its life seems as full as does that of the elephant with his hundred years. Why? *Because so many things haze happened!* When we are conscious of many things happening, we get the impression and sensation of the length of time. The greater the consciousness of things, the greater the sensation of Time. When we are so interested in talking to a loved one that we forget all that is occurring about us, then the hours fly by unheeded, while the same hours seem like days to one in the same place who is not interested or occupied with some task.

Men have nodded, and in the second before awakening they have dreamed of events that seemed to have required the passage of years. Many of you have had experiences of this kind, and many such cases have been recorded by science. On the other hand, one may fall asleep and remain unconscious, but without dreams, for hours, and upon awakening will insist that he has merely nodded. Time belongs to the relative mind, and has no place in the Eternal or Absolute.

Next, the Intellect informs us that it must think of the Absolute as Infinite in Space—present everywhere—Omnipresent. It cannot be limited, for there is nothing outside of itself to limit it. There is no such place as Nowhere. Every place is in the Everywhere. And Everywhere is filled with the All—the Infinite Reality—the Absolute.

And, just as was the case with the idea of Time, we find it most difficult—if not indeed impossible—to form an idea of an Omnipresent—of That which occupies Infinite Space. This because everything that our minds have experienced has had dimensions and limits. The secret lies in the fact that Space, like Time, has no real existence outside of our perception of consciousness of the relative position of Things—material objects. We see this thing here, and that thing there. Between them is Nothingness. We take another object, say a yard-stick, and measure off this Nothingness between the two objects, and we call this measure of Nothingness by the term Distance. And yet we cannot have measured Nothingness—that is impossible. What have we really done? Simply this, determined how many lengths of yard-stick could be laid between the other two objects. We call this process measuring Space, but Space is Nothing, and we have merely determined the relative position of objects. To "measure Space" we must have three Things or objects, *i.e.*, (1) The object from which we start the measure; (2) The object with which we measure; and (3) The object with which we end our measurement. We are unable to conceive of Infinite Space, because we lack the third object in the measuring process—the ending object. We may use ourselves as a starting point, and the mental yard-stick is always at hand, but where is the object at the other side of Infinity of Space by which the measurement may be ended? It is not there, and we cannot think of the end without it. Let us start with ourselves, and try to imagine a million million miles, and then multiply them by another million million miles, a million million times. What have we done? Simply extended our mental yard-stick a certain number of times to an imaginary point in the Nothingness that we call Space. So far so good, but the mind intuitively recognizes that beyond that imaginary point at the end of the last yard-stick, there is a capacity for an infinite extension of yard-sticks—an infinite capacity for such extension. Extension of what? Space? No! Yard-sticks! Objects! Things! Without material objects Space is unthinkable. It has no existence outside of our consciousness of Things. There is no such thing as Real Space. Space is merely an infinite capacity for extending objects. Space itself is merely a name for Nothingness. If you can form an idea of an object swept out of existence, and nothing to take its place, that Nothing would be called Space, the term implying the possibility of placing something there without displacing anything else.

Size, of course, is but another form of speaking of Distance. And in this connection let us not forget that just as one may think of Space being infinite in the direction of largeness, so may we think of it as being infinite in the sense of smallness. No matter how small may be an object thought of, we are still able to think of it as being capable of subdivision, and so on infinitely. There is no limit in this direction either. As Jakob has said: "The conception of the infinitely minute is as little capable of being grasped by us, as is that of the infinitely great. Despite this, the admission of the reality of the infinitude, both in the direction of greatness and of minuteness, is inevitable."

And, as Radenhausen has said: "The idea of Space is only an unavoidable illusion of our Consciousness, or of our finite nature, and does not exist outside of ourselves; the universe is infinitely small and infinitely great."

The telescope has opened to us ideas of magnificent vastness and greatness, and the perfected microscope has opened to us a world of magnificent smallness and minuteness. The latter has shown us that a drop of water is a world of minute living forms who live, eat, fight, reproduce, and die. The mind is capable of imagining a universe occupying no more space than one million-millionth of the tiniest speck visible under the strongest microscope—and then imagining such a universe containing millions of suns and worlds similar to our own, and inhabited by living forms akin to ours—living, thinking men and women, identical in every respect to ourselves. Indeed, as some philosophers have said, if our Universe were suddenly reduced to such a size—the relative proportions of everything being preserved, of course—then we would not be conscious of any change, and life would go on the same, and we would be of the same importance to ourselves and to the Absolute as we are this moment. And the same would be true were the Universe suddenly enlarged a million-million times. These changes would make no difference in reality. Compared with each other, the tiniest speck and the largest sun are practically the same size when viewed from the Absolute.

We have dwelt upon these things so that you would be able to better realize the relativity of Space and Time, and perceive that they are merely symbols of Things used by the mind in dealing with finite objects, and have no place in reality. When this is realized, then the idea of Infinity in Time and Space is more readily grasped.

As Radenhausen says: "Beyond the range of human reason there is neither Space nor Time; they are arbitrary conceptions of man, at which he has arrived by the comparison and arrangement of different impressions which he has received from the outside world. The conception of Space arises from the sequence of the various forms which fill Space, by which the external world appears to the individual man. The conception of Time arises from the sequence of the various forms which change in space (motion), by which the external world acts on the individual man, and so on. But externally to ourselves, the distinction between repletion of Space and mutation of Space does not exist, for each is in constant transmutation, whatever is is filling and changing at the same time—nothing is at a standstill," and to quote Ruckert: "The world has neither beginning nor end, in space nor in time. Everywhere is center and turning-point, and in a moment is eternity."

Next, the Intellect informs us that we must think of the Absolute as containing within Itself all the Power there is, because there can be no other source or reservoir of Power, and there can be no Power outside of the All-Power. There can be no Power outside of the Absolute to limit, confine, or conflict with It. Any laws of the Universe must have been imposed by It, for there is no other law-giver, and every manifestation of Energy, Force, or Power, perceived or evident in Nature must be a part of the Power of the Absolute working along lines laid down by it. In the Third Lesson, which will be entitled The Will-to-Live, we shall see this Power manifesting along the lines of Life as we know it.

Next, the Intellect informs us that it is compelled to think of the Absolute as containing within Itself all possible Knowledge or Wisdom, because there can be no Knowledge or Wisdom outside of It, and therefore all the Wisdom and Knowledge possible must be within It. We see Mind, Wisdom, and Knowledge manifested by relative forms of Life, and such must emanate from the Absolute in accordance with certain laws laid down by It, for otherwise there would be no such wisdom, etc., for there is nowhere outside of the All from whence it could come. The effect cannot be greater than the cause. If there is anything unknown to the Absolute, then it will never be known to finite minds. So, therefore, ALL KNOWLEDGE that Is, Has Been, or Can Be, must be NOW vested in the One—the Absolute.

This does not mean that the Absolute *thinks*, in any such sense as does Man. The Absolute must Know, without Thinking. It does not have to gather Knowledge by the process of Thinking, as does Man—such an Idea would be ridiculous, for from whence could the Knowledge come outside of itself. When man thinks he draws to himself Knowledge from the Universal source by the action of the Mind, but the Absolute has only itself to draw on. So we cannot imagine the Absolute compelled to Think as we do.

But, lest we be misunderstood regarding this phase of the subject, we may say here that the highest occult teachings inform us that the Absolute *does* manifest a quality somewhat akin to what we would call constructive thought, and that such "thoughts" manifest into objectivity and manifestation, and become Creation. Created Things, according to the Occult teachings are "Thoughts of God." Do not let this idea disturb you, and cause you to feel that you are nothing, because you have been called into being by a Thought of the Infinite One. Even a Thought of that One would be intensely real in the relative world—actually Real to all except the Absolute itself—and even the Absolute knows that the *Real* part of its Creations must be a part of itself manifested through its thought, for the

Thought of the Infinite must be Real, and a part of Itself, for it cannot be anything else, and to call it Nothing is merely to juggle with words. The faintest Thought of the Infinite One would be far more real than anything man could create—as solid as the mountain—as hard as steel—as durable as the diamond—for, verily, even these are emanations of the Mind of the Infinite, and are things of but a day, while the higher Thoughts—the soul of Man—contains within itself a spark from the Divine Flame itself—the Spirit of the Infinite. But these things will appear in their own place, as we proceed with this series. We have merely given you a little food for thought at this point, in connection with the Mind of the Absolute.

So you see, good friends and students, that the Intellect in its highest efforts, informs us that it finds itself compelled to report that the One—the Absolute—That which it is compelled to admit really exists—must be a One possessed of a nature so far transcending human experience that the human mind finds itself without the proper concepts, symbols, and words with which to think of It. But none the less, the Intellect finds itself bound by its own laws to postulate the existence of such an One.

It is the veriest folly to try to think of the One as It is "in Itself"—for we have nothing but human attributes with which to measure it, and It so far transcends such measurements that the mental yard-sticks run out into infinity and are lost sight of. The highest minds of the race inform us that the most exalted efforts of their reason compels them to report that the One—in Itself— cannot be spoken of as possessing attributes or qualities capable of being expressed in human words employed to describe the Things of the relative world—and all of our words are such. All of our words originate from such ideas, and all of our ideas arise from our experience, directly or indirectly. So we are not equipped with words with which to think of or speak of that which transcends experience, although our Intellect informs us that Reality lies back of our experience.

Philosophy finds itself unable to do anything better than to bring us face to face with high paradoxes. Science in its pursuit of Truth finds it cunningly avoiding it, and ever escaping its net. And we believe that the Absolute purposely causes this to be, that in the end Man may be compelled to look for the Spirit within himself—the only place where he can come in touch with it. This, we think, is the answer to the Riddle of the Sphinx— "Look Within for that which Thou needest."

But while the Spirit may be discerned only by looking within ourselves, we find that once the mind realizes that the Absolute Is, it will be able to see countless evidences of its action and presence by observing manifested Life without. All Life is filled with the Life Power and Will of the Absolute.

To us Life is but One—the Universe is a living Unity, throbbing, thrilling and pulsating with the Will-to-Live of the Absolute. Back of all apparent shapes, forms, names, forces, elements, principles and substances, there is but One—One Life, present everywhere, and manifesting in an infinitude of shapes, forms, and forces All individual lives are but centers of consciousness in the One Life underlying, depending upon it for degree of unfoldment, expression and manifestation.

This may sound like Pantheism to some, but it is very different from the Pantheism of the schools and cults. Pantheism is defined as "the doctrine that God consists in the combined forces and laws manifested in the existing Universe," or that "the Universe taken or conceived as a whole is God." These definitions do not fit the conception of the Absolute, of the Yogi Philosophy—they seem to breathe but a refined materialism. The Absolute is not "the combined forces and laws manifested in the universe," nor "the universe conceived as a whole." Instead, the Universe, its forces and laws, even conceived as a whole, have no existence in themselves, but are mere manifestations of the Absolute. Surely this is different from Pantheism.

We teach that the Absolute is immanent in, and abiding in all forms of Life in the Universe, as well as in its forces and laws— all being but manifestations of the Will of the One. And we teach that this One is superior to all forms of manifestations, and that Its existence and being does not depend upon the manifestations, which are but effects of the Cause.

The Pantheistic Universe—God is but a thing of phenomenal appearance, but the Absolute is the very Spirit of Life—a Living, Existing Reality, and would be so even if every manifestation were withdrawn from appearance and expression—drawn back into the source from which it emanated. The Absolute is more than Mountain or Ocean—Electricity or Gravitation—Monad or Man—It is SPIRIT—LIFE—BEING—REALITY—the ONE THAT IS. Omnipotent, Omnipresent; Omniscient; Eternal; Infinite; Absolute; these are Man's greatest words, and yet they but feebly portray a shadow thrown by the One Itself.

The Absolute is not a far-away Being directing our affairs at long range—not an absentee Deity—but an Immanent Life in and about us all—manifesting in us and creating us into individual centers of consciousness, in pursuance with some great law of being.

And, more than this, the Absolute instead of being an indifferent and unmoved spectator to its own creation, is a thriving, longing, active, suffering, rejoicing, feeling Spirit, partaking of the feelings of its manifestations, rather than callously witnessing them. It lives in us—with us—through us. Back of all the pain in the world may be found a great feeling and suffering love. The pain of the world is not punishment or evidence of divine wrath, but the incidents of the working out of some cosmic plan, in which the Absolute is the Actor, through the forms of Its manifestations.

The message of the Absolute to some of the Illumined has been, "All is being done in the best and only possible way—I am doing the best I can—all is well—and in the end will so appear."

The Absolute is no personal Deity—yet in itself it contains all that goes to make up all personality and all human relations. Father, Mother, Child, Friend, is in It. All forms of human love and craving for sympathy, understanding and companionship may find refuge in loving the Absolute.

The Absolute is constantly in evidence in our lives, and yet we have been seeking it here and there in the outer world, asking it to show itself and prove Its existence. Well may it say to us: "Hast thou been so long time with me, and hast thou not known me?" This is the great tragedy of Life, that the Spirit comes to us—Its own—and we know It not. We fail to hear Its words: "Oh, ye who mourn, I suffer with you and through you. Yea, it is I who grieve in you. Your pain is mine—to the last pang. I suffer all pain through you—and yet I rejoice beyond you, for I know that through you, and with you, I shall conquer."

And this is a faint idea of what we believe the Absolute to be. In the following lessons we shall see it in operation in all forms of life, and in ourselves. We shall get close to the workings of Its mighty Will—close to Its Heart of Love.

Carry with you the Central Thought of the Lesson: CENTRAL THOUGHT. There is but One Life in the Universe. And underlying that One Life—Its Real Self—Its Essence—Its Spirit—is The Absolute, living, feeling, suffering, rejoicing, longing, striving, in and through us. The Absolute is all that really Is, and all the visible Universe and forms of Life is Its expression, through Its Will. We lack words adequate to describe the nature of the Absolute, but we will use two words describing its inmost nature as best we see it. These two words are LIFE and LOVE, the one describing the outer, the other the inner nature. Let us manifest both Life and Love as a token of our origin and inner nature. Peace be with you.

THE SECOND LESSON - Omnipresent Life

In our First Lesson of this series, we brought out the idea that the human mind was compelled to report the fact that it could not think of The Absolute except as possessing the quality of Omnipresence—Present-Everywhere. And, likewise, the human mind is compelled to think that all there IS must be The Absolute, or *of* the Absolute. And if a thing is *of* the Absolute, then the Absolute must be *in* it, in some way—must be the *essence* of it. Granting this, we must then think that everything must be filled with the essence of Life, for Life must be one of the qualities of the Absolute, or rather what we call Life must be the outward expression of the essential Being of the Absolute. And if this be so, then it would follow that *everything in the Universe must be Alive*. The mind cannot escape this conclusion. And if the facts do not bear out this conclusion then we must be forced to admit that the entire basic theory of the Absolute and its emanations must fall, and be considered as an error. No chain is stronger than its weakest link, and if this link be too weak to bear the weight of the facts of the universe, then must the chain be discarded as imperfect and useless, and another substituted. This fact is not generally mentioned by those speaking and writing of All being One, or an emanation of the One, but it must be considered and met. If there is a single thing in the Universe that is "dead"—non-living—lifeless—then the theory must fall. If a thing is non-living, then the essence of the Absolute cannot be in it—it must be alien and foreign to the Absolute, and in that case the Absolute cannot be Absolute for there is something outside of itself. And so it becomes of the greatest importance to examine into the evidences of the presence of Life in all things, organic or inorganic. The evidence is at hand—let us examine it.

The ancient occultists of all peoples always taught that the Universe was Alive—that there was Life in everything—that there was nothing dead in Nature—that Death meant simply a change in form in the material of the dead bodies. They taught that Life, in varying degrees of manifestation and expression, was present in everything and object, even down to the hardest mineral form, and the atoms composing that form.

Modern Science is now rapidly advancing to the same position, and each months investigations and discoveries serve only to emphasize the teachings.

Burbank, that wonderful moulder of plant life, has well expressed this thought, when he says: "All my investigations have led me away from the idea of a dead material universe tossed about by various forces, to that of a universe which is absolutely all force, life, soul, thought, or whatever name we may choose to call it. Every atom, molecule, plant, animal or planet, is only an aggregation of organized unit forces, held in place by stronger forces, thus holding them for a time latent, though teeming with inconceivable power. All life on our planet is, so to speak, just on the outer fringe of this infinite ocean of force. The universe is not half dead, but all alive."

Science today is gazing upon a living universe. She has not yet realized the full significance of what she has discovered, and her hands are raised as if to shade her eyes from the unaccustomed glare that is bursting upon her. From the dark cavern of universal dead matter, she has stepped out into the glare of the noon-day sun of a Universe All-Alive even to its smallest and apparently most inert particle.

Beginning at Man, the highest form of Life known to us, we may pass rapidly down the scale of animal life, seeing life in full operation at each descending step. Passing from the animal to the vegetable kingdom, we still see Life in full operation, although in lessened degrees of expression. We shall not stop here to review the many manifestations of Life among the forms of plant-life, for we shall have occasion to mention them in our next lesson, but it must be apparent to all that Life is constantly manifesting in the sprouting of seeds; the putting forth of stalk, leaves, blossoms, fruit, etc., and in the enormous manifestation of force and energy in such growth and development. One may see the life force in the plant pressing forth for expression and manifestation, from the first sprouting of the seed, until the last vital action on the part of the mature plant or tree.

Besides the vital action observable in the growth and development of plants, we know, of course, that plants sicken and die, and manifest all other attributes of living forms. There is no room for argument about the presence of life in the plant kingdom.

But there are other forms of life far below the scale of the plants. There is the world of the bacteria, microbes, infusoria—the groups of cells with a common life—the single cell creatures, down to the Monera, the creatures lower than the single cells— the Things of the slime of the ocean bed.

These tiny Things—living Things—present to the sight merely a tiny speck of jelly, without organs of any kind. And yet they exercise all the functions of life—movement, nutrition, reproduction, sensation, and dissolution. Some of these elementary forms are all stomach, that is they are all one organ capable of performing all the functions necessary for the life of the animal. The creature has no mouth, but when it wishes to devour an object it simply envelopes it—wraps itself around it like a bit of glue around a gnat, and then absorbs the substance of its prey through its whole body.

Scientists have turned some of these tiny creatures inside out, and yet they have gone on with their life functions undisturbed and untroubled. They have cut them up into still tinier bits, and yet each bit lived on as a separate animal, performing all of its functions undisturbed. They are all the same all over, and all the way through. They reproduce themselves by growing to a certain size, and then separating into two, and so on. The rapidity of the increase is most remarkable.

Haekel says of the Monera: "The Monera are the simplest permanent cytods. Their entire body consists of merely soft, structureless plasm. However thoroughly we may examine them with the help of the most delicate reagents and the strongest optical instruments, we yet find that all the parts are completely homogeneous. These Monera are therefore, in the strictest sense of the word, 'organisms without organs,' or even in a strict philosophical sense they might not even be called organisms, since they possess no organs and since they are not composed of various particles. They can only be called organisms in so far as they are capable of exercising the organic phenomena of life, of nutrition, reproduction, sensation and movement."

Verworn records an interesting instance of life and mind among the *Rhizopods*, a very low form of living thing. He relates that the *Difflugia ampula*, a creature occupying a tiny shell formed of minute particles of sand, has a long projection of its substance, like a feeler or tendril, with which it searches on the bottom of the sea for sandy material with which to build the shell or outer covering for its offspring, which are born by division from the parent body. It grasps the particle of sand by the feeler, and passes it into its body by enclosing it. Verworn removed the sand from the bottom of the tank, replacing it by very minute particles of highly colored glass. Shortly afterward he noticed a collection of these particles of glass in the body of the creature, and a little later he saw a tiny speck of protoplasm emitted from the parent by separation. At the same time he noticed that the bits of glass collected by the mother creature were passed out and placed around the body of the new creature, and cemented together by a substance secreted by the body of the parent, thus forming a shell and covering for the offspring. This proceeding showed the presence of a mental something sufficient to cause the creature to prepare a shell for the offspring previous to its birth—or rather to gather the material for such shell, to be afterward used; to distinguish the proper material; to mould it into shape, and cement it. The scientist reported that a creature always gathered just exactly enough sand for its purpose—never too little, and never an excess. And this in a creature that is little more than a tiny drop of glue!

We may consider the life actions of the Moneron a little further, for it is the lowest form of so-called "living matter"—the point at which living forms pass off into non-living forms (so-called). This tiny speck of glue—an organism without organs—is endowed with the faculty called sensation. It draws away from that which is likely to injure it, and toward that which it desires—all in response to an elementary sensation. It has the instinct of self-preservation and self-protection. It seeks and finds its prey, and then eats, digests and assimilates it. It is able to move about by "false-feet," or bits of its body which it pushes forth at will from any part of its substance. It reproduces itself, as we have seen, by separation and self-division.

The life of the bacteria and germs—the yeasty forms of life—are familiar to many of us. And yet there are forms of life still below these. The line between living forms and non-living forms is being set back further and further by science. Living creatures are now known that resemble the non-living so closely that the line cannot be definitely drawn.

Living creatures are known that are capable of being dried and laid away for several years, and then may be revived by the application of moisture. They resemble dust, but are full of life and function. Certain forms of bacilli are known to Science that have been subjected to degrees of heat and cold that are but terms to any but the scientific mind.

Low forms of life called Diatoms or "living crystals" are known. They are tiny geometrical forms. They are composed of a tiny drop of plasm, resembling glue, covered by a thin shell of siliceous or sandy material. They are visible only through the microscope, and are so small that thousands of them might be gathered together on the head of a pin. They are so like chemical crystals that it requires a shrewd and careful observer to distinguish them. And yet they are alive, and perform all the functions of life.

Leaving these creatures, we enter the kingdom of the crystals, in our search for life. Yes, the crystals manifest life, as strange as this statement may appear to those who have not followed the march of Science. The crystals are born, grow, live, and may be killed by chemicals or electricity. Science has added a new department called "Plasmology," the purpose of which is the study of crystal life. Some investigators have progressed so far as to claim that they have discovered signs of rudimentary sex functioning among crystals. At any rate, crystals are born and grow like living things. As a recent scientific writer has said: "Crystallization, as we are to learn now, is not a mere mechanical grouping of dead atoms. It is a birth."

The crystal forms from the mother liquor, and its body is built up systematically, regularly, and according to a well defined plan or pattern, just as are the body and bones of the animal form, and the wood and bark of the tree. There is life at work in the growth of the crystal. And not only does the crystal grow, but it also reproduces itself by separation or splitting-off, just as is the case with the lower forms of life, just mentioned.

The principal point of difference between the growth and development of the crystals and that of the lower forms of life referred to is that the crystal takes its nourishment from the outside, and builds up from its outer surface, while the Monera absorbs its nourishment from within, and grows outwardly from within. If the crystal had a soft center, and took its nourishment in that way, it would be almost identical with the Diatom, or, if the Diatom grew from the outside, it would be but a crystal. A very fine dividing line.

Crystals, like living forms, may be sterilized and rendered incapable of reproduction by chemical process, or electrical discharges. They may also be "killed" and future growth prevented in this manner. Surely this looks like "Life," does it not?

To realize the importance of this idea of life among the crystals, we must remember that our hardest rocks and metals are composed of crystals, and that the dirt and earth upon which we grow and live are but crumbled rock and miniature crystals. Therefore the very dust under our feet is alive. *There is nothing dead.* There is no transformation of "dead matter" into live plant matter, and then into live animal matter. The chemicals are alive, and from chemical to man's body there is but a continuous change of shape and form of living matter. Any man's body, decomposing, is again resolved into chemicals, and the chain begins over again. Merely changes in living forms—that's all, so far as the bodies are concerned.

Nature furnishes us with many examples of this presence of life in the inorganic world. We have but to look around to see the truth of the statement that All is Alive. There is that which is known as the "fatigue of elasticity" in metals. Razors get tired, and require a rest. Tuning forks lose their powers of vibration, to a degree, and have to be given a vacation. 'Machinery in mills and manufactories needs an occasional day off. Metals are subject to disease and infection, and have been poisoned and restored by antidotes. Window glass, especially stained glass, is subject to a disease spreading from pane to pane.

Men accustomed to handling and using tools and machinery naturally drop into the habit of speaking of these things as if they were alive. They seem to recognize the presence of "feeling" in tools or machine, and to perceive in each a sort of "character" or personality, which must be respected, humored, or coaxed in order to get the best results.

Perhaps the most valuable testimony along these lines, and which goes very far toward proving the centuries-old theories of the Yogis regarding Omnipresent Life, comes from Prof. J. Chunder Bose, of the Calcutta University, a Hindu educated in the English Universities, under the best teachers, and who is now a leading scientific authority in the western world, tie has given to the world some very valuable scientific information along these lines in his book entitled "*Response in the Living and Non-living*," which has caused the widest comment and created the greatest interest among the highest scientific authorities. His experiments along the lines of the gathering of evidence of life in the inorganic forms have revolutionized the theories of modern science, and have done much to further the idea that life is present everywhere, and that there is no such thing as dead matter.

He bases his work upon the theory that the best and only true test for the presence of life in matter is the response of matter to external stimulus. Proceeding from this fundamental theory he has proven by in-numerable experiments that so-called inorganic matter, minerals, metals, etc., give a response to such stimulus, which response is similar, if not identical, to the response of the matter composing the bodies of plants, animals, men.

He devised delicate apparatus for the measurement of the response to the outside stimulus, the degree, and other evidence being recorded in traces on a revolving cylinder. The tracings or curves obtained from tin and other metals, when compared with those obtained from living muscle, were found to be identical.

He used a galvanometer, a very delicate and accurate scientific instrument, in his experiments. This instrument is so finely adjusted that the faintest current will cause a deflection of the registering needle, which is delicately swung on a tiny pivot. If the galvanometer be attached to a human nerve, and the end of the nerve be irritated, the needle will register.

Prof. Bose found that when he attached the galvanometer to bars of various metals they gave a similar response when struck or twisted. The greater the irritation applied to the metal, the greater the response registered by the instrument. The analogy between the response of the metal and that of the living muscle was startling. For instance, just as in the case of the living animal muscle or nerve matter, the response becomes fatigued, so in the case of the metal the curve registered by the needle became fainter and still fainter, as the bar became more and more fatigued by the continued irritation. And again, just after such fatigue the muscle would become rested, and would again respond actively, so would the metal when given a chance to recuperate.

Tetanus due to shocks constantly repeated, was caused and recovered. Metals recorded evidences of fatigue. Drugs caused identical effects on metals and animals—some exciting; some depressing; some killing. Some poisonous chemicals killed pieces of metal, rendering them immobile and therefore incapable of registering records on the apparatus. In some cases antidotes were promptly administered, and saved the life of the metal.

Prof. Bose also conducted experiments on plants in the same way. Pieces of vegetable matter were found to be capable of stimulation, fatigue, excitement, depression, poison. Mrs. Annie Besant, who witnessed some of these experiments in Calcutta, has written as follows regarding the experiments on plant life: "There is something rather pathetic in seeing the way in which the tiny spot of light which records the pulses in the plant, travels in ever weaker and weaker curves, when the plant is under the influence of poison, then falls into a final despairing straight line, and—stops. One feels as though a murder has been committed—as indeed it has."

In one of Prof. Bose's public experiments he clearly demonstrated that a bar of iron was fully as sensitive as the human body, and that it could be irritated and stimulated in the same way, and finally could be poisoned and killed. "Among such phenomena," he asks, "how can we draw the line of demarkation, and say, 'Here the physical ends, and there the physiological begins'? No such barrier exists." According to his theory, which agrees with the oldest occult theories, by the way, life is present in every object and form of Nature, and all forms respond to external stimulus, which response is a proof of the presence of life in the form.

Prof. Bose's great book is full of the most startling results of experiments. He proves that the metals manifest something like sleep; can be killed; exhibit torpor and sluggishness; get tired or lazy; wake up; can be roused into activity; may be stimulated, strengthened, weakened; suffer from extreme cold and heat; may be drugged or intoxicated, the different metals manifesting a different response to certain drugs, just as different men and animals manifest a varying degree of similar resistance. The response of a piece of steel subjected to the influence of a chemical poison shows a gradual fluttering and weakening until it finally dies away, just as animal matter does when similarly poisoned. When revived in time by an antidote, the recovery was similarly gradual in both metal and muscle. A remarkable fact is noted by the scientist when he tells us that the very poisons that kill the metals are themselves alive and may be killed, drugged, stimulated, etc., showing the same response as in the case of the metals, proving the existence in them of the same life that is in the metals and animal matter that they influence.

Of course when these metals are "killed" there is merely a killing of the metal as metal—the atoms and principles of which the metal is composed remaining fully alive and active, just as is the case with the atom of the human body after the soul passes out—the body is as much alive after death as during the life of the person, the activity of the parts being along the lines of dissolution instead of construction in that case.

We hear much of the claims of scientists who announce that they are on the eve of "*creating* life" from non-living matter. This is all nonsense—life can come only from life. Life from non-life is an absurdity. And all Life comes from the One Life underlying All. But it is true that Science has done, is doing, and will do, something very much like "creating life," but of course this is merely changing the form of Life into other forms—the lesser form into the higher—just as one produces a plant from a seed, or a fruit from a plant. The Life is always there, and responds to the proper stimulus and conditions.

A number of scientists are working on the problem of generating living forms from inorganic matter. The old idea of "spontaneous generation," for many years relegated to the scrap-pile of Science, is again coming to the front. Although the theory of Evolution compels its adherents to accept the idea that at one time in the past living forms sprung from the non-living (so-called), yet it has been generally believed that the conditions which brought about this stage of evolution has forever passed. But the indications now all point to the other view that this stage of evolution is, and always has been, in operation, and that new forms of life are constantly evolving from the inorganic forms. "Creation," so-called (although the word is an absurdity from the Yogi point of view), is constantly being performed.

Dr. Charlton Bastian, of London, Eng., has long been a prominent advocate of this theory of continuous spontaneous generation. Laughed down and considered defeated by the leading scientific minds of a generation ago, he still pluckily kept at work, and his recent books were like bombshells in the orthodox scientific camp. He has taken more than five thousand photo-micrographs, all showing most startling facts in connection with the origin of living forms from the inorganic. He claims that the microscope reveals the development in a previously clear liquid of very minute black spots, which gradually enlarge and transform into bacteria—living forms of a very low order. Prof. Burke, of Cambridge, Eng., has demonstrated that he may produce in sterilized boullion, subjected to the action of sterilized radium chloride, minute living bodies which manifest growth and subdivision. Science is being gradually forced to the conclusion that living forms are still arising in the world by natural processes, which is not at all remarkable when one remembers that natural law is uniform and continuous. These recent discoveries go to swell the already large list of modern scientific ideas which correspond with the centuries-old Yogi teachings. When the Occult explanation that there is Life in everything, *inorganic as well as organic*, and that evolution is constant, is heard, then may we see that these experiments simply prove that the forms of life may be changed and developed—not that Life may be "created."

The chemical and mineral world furnish us with many instances of the growth and development of forms closely resembling the forms of the vegetable world. What is known as "metallic vegetation," as shown in the "lead tree," gives us an interesting example of this phenomenon. The experiment is performed by placing in a wide-necked bottle a clear acidulated solution of acetate of lead. The bottle is corked, a piece of copper wire being fastened to the cork, from which wire is suspended a piece of zinc, the latter hanging as nearly as possible in the center of the lead solution. When the bottle is corked the copper wire immediately begins to surround itself with a growth of metallic lead resembling fine moss. From this moss spring branches and limbs, which in turn manifest a growth similar to foliage, until at last a miniature bush or tree is formed. Similar "metallic vegetation" may be produced by other metallic solutions.

All of you have noticed how crystals of frost form on window panes in shapes of leaves, branches, foliage, flowers, blossoms, etc. Saltpeter when subjected to the effect of polarized light assumes forms closely resembling the forms of the orchid. Nature is full of these resemblances.

A German scientist recently performed a remarkable experiment with certain metallic salts. He subjected the salts to the action of a galvanic current, when to his surprise the particles of the salts grouped themselves around the negative pole of the battery, and then grew into a shape closely resembling a miniature mushroom, with tiny stem and umbrella top. These metallic mushrooms at first presented a transparent appearance, but gradually developed color, the top of the umbrella being a bright red, with a faint rose shade on the under surface. The stems showed a pale straw color. This was most interesting, but the important fact of the experiment consists in the discovery that these mushrooms have fine veins or tubes running along the stems, through which the nourishment, or additional material for growth, is transported, so that the growth is actually from the inside, just as is the case with fungus life. To all intents and purposes, these inorganic metallic growths were low forms of vegetable his.

But the search for Life does not end with the forms of the mineral world as we know them. Science has separated the material forms into smaller forms, and again still smaller. And if there is Life in the form composed of countless particles, then must there be Life in the particles themselves. For Life cannot come from non-Life, and if there be not Life in the particles, the theory of Omnipresent Life must fan. So we must look beyond the form and shape of the mineral—mist separate it into its constituent parts, and then examine the parts for indications of Life.

Science teaches us that all forms of matter are compiled of minute particles called molecules. A molecule is the smallest particle of matter that is possible, unless the chemical atoms composing the matter fly apart and the matter be resolved into its original elements. For instance, let us take the familiar instance of a drop of water. Let us divide and subdivide the drop, until at last we get to the smallest possible particle of water. That smallest possible particle would be a "molecule" of water. We cannot subdivide this molecule without causing its atoms of hydrogen and oxygen to fly apart—and then there would be no *water* at all. Well, these molecules manifest a something called Attraction for each other. They attract other molecules of the same kind, and are likewise attracted. The operation of this law of attraction results in the formation of masses of matter, whether those masses be mountains of solid rock, or a drop of water, or a volume of gas. All masses of matter are composed of aggregations of molecules, held together by the law of attraction. This law of attraction is called Cohesion. This Cohesive Attraction is not a mere mechanical force, as many suppose, but is an exhibition of Life action, manifesting in the presence of the molecule of a "like" or "love" for the similar molecule. And when the Life energies begin to manifest on a certain plane, and proceed to mould the molecules into crystals, so that we may see the actual process under way, we begin to realize very clearly that there is "something at work" in this building up.

But wonderful as this may seem to those unfamiliar with the idea, the manifestation of Life among the atoms is still more so. The atom, you will remember, is the chemical unit which, uniting with other atoms, makes up the molecule. For instance, if we take two atoms of the gas called hydrogen and one atom of the gas called oxygen, and place them near each other, they will

264

at once rush toward each other and form a partnership, which is called a molecule of water. And so it is with all atoms—they are continually forming partnerships, or dissolving them. Marriage and divorce is a part of the life of the atoms. These evidences of attraction and repulsion among the atoms are receiving much attention from careful thinkers, and some of the most advanced minds of the age see in this phenomena the corroboration of the old Yogi idea that there is Life and vital action in the smallest particles of matter.

The atoms manifest vital characteristics in their attractions and repulsions. They move along the lines of their attractions and form marriages, and thus combining they form the substances with which we are familiar. When they combine, remember, they do not lose their individuality and melt into a permanent substance, but merely unite and yet remain distinct. If the combination be destroyed by chemical action, electrical discharge, etc., the atoms fly apart, and again live their own separate lives, until they come in contact with other atoms with which they have affinities, and form a new union or partnership. In many chemical changes the atoms divorce themselves, each forsaking its mate or mates, and seeking some newer affinity in the shape of a more congenial atom. The atoms manifest a fickleness and will always desert a lesser attraction for a greater one. This is no mere bit of imagery, or scientific poetry. It is a scientific statement of the action of atoms along the lines of vital manifestation.

The great German scientist, Haekel, has said: "I cannot imagine the simplest chemical and physical processes without attributing the movement of the material particles to unconscious sensation. The idea of Chemical Affinity consists in the fact that the various chemical elements perceive differences in the qualities of other elements, and experience pleasure or revulsion at contact with them, and execute their respective movements on this ground." He also says: "We may ascribe the feeling of pleasure or pain (satisfaction or dissatisfaction) to all atoms, and thereby ascribe the elective affinities of chemistry to the attraction between living atoms and repulsion between hating atoms." He also says that "the sensations in animal and plant life are connected by a long series of evolutionary stages with the simpler forms of sensation that we find in the inorganic elements, and that reveal themselves in chemical affinity." Naegli says: "If the molecules possess something that is related, however distantly, to sensation, it must be comfortable for them to be able to follow their attractions and repulsions, and uncomfortable for them when they are forced to do otherwise." We might fill page after page with quotations from eminent thinkers going to prove the correctness of the old Yogi teachings that Life is Omnipresent. Modern Science is rapidly advancing to this position, leaving behind her the old idea of "dead matter." Even the new theories of the electron—the little particles of electrical energy which are now believed to constitute the base of the atom—does not change this idea, for the electrons manifest attraction, and response thereto, and form themselves into groups composing the atom. And even if we pass beyond matter into the mystical Ether which Science assumes to be the material base of things, we must believe that there is life there too, and that as Prof. Dolbear says: "The Ether has besides the function of energy and motion, other inherent properties, out of which could emerge, under proper circumstances, other phenomena, such as life, mind, or whatever may be in the substratum," and, that as Prof. Cope has hinted, that the basis of Life lies back of the atoms and may be found in the Universal Ether.

Some scientists go even further, and assert that not only is Life present in everything, but that Mind is present where Life is. Verily, the dreams of the Yogi fathers are coming true, and from the ranks of the materialists are coming the material proofs of the spiritual teachings. Listen to these words from Dr. Saleeby, in his recent valuable scientific work, "*Evolution, the Master Key.*" He says:

"Life is potential in matter; life-energy is not a thing unique and created at a particular time in the past. If evolution be true, living matter has been evolved by natural processes from matter which is, apparently, not alive. But if life is potential in matter, it is a thousand times more evident that Mind is potential in Life. The evolutionist is impelled to believe that Mind is potential in matter. (I adopt that form of words for the moment, but not without future criticism.) The microscopic cell, a minute speck of matter that is to become man, has in it the promise and the germ of mind. May we not then draw the inference that the elements of mind are present in those chemical elements—carbon, oxygen, hydrogen, nitrogen, sulphur, phosphorus, sodium, potassium, chlorine—that are found in the cell. Not only must we do so, but we must go further, since we know that each of these elements, and every other, is built up out of one invariable unit, the electron, and we must therefore assert that Mind is potential in the unit of Matter—the electron itself... It is to assert the sublime truth first perceived by Spinoza, that Mind and Matter are the warp and woof of what Goethe called 'the living garment of God.' Both are complementary expressions of the Unknowable Reality which underlies both."

There is no such thing as non-vital attraction or repulsion. All inclinations for or against another object, or thing, is an evidence of Life. Each thing has sufficient life energy to enable it to carry on its work. And as each form advances by evolution into a higher form, it is able to have more of the Life energy manifest through it. As its material machinery is built up, it becomes able to manifest a greater and higher degree of Life. It is not that one thing has a low life, or another a high life—this cannot be, for there is but One Life. It is like the current of electricity that is able to run the most delicate machinery or manifest a light in the incandescent lamp. Give it the organ or machinery of manifestation, and it manifests—give it a low form, and it will manifest a low degree—give it a high form, and it will manifest a high degree. The same steam power runs the clumsy engine, or the perfect apparatus which drives the most delicate mechanism. And so it is with the One Life—its manifestations may seem low and clumsy, or high and perfect—but it all depends upon the material or mental machinery through which it works. There is but One Life, manifesting in countless forms and shapes, and degrees. One Life underlying All—in All.

From the highest forms of Life down through the animal, vegetable and mineral kingdoms, we see Life everywhere present—Death an illusion. Back of all visible forms of material life there is still the beginnings of manifested life pressing forward for expression and manifestation. And underneath all is the Spirit of Life—longing, striving, feeling, acting.

In the mountain and the ocean—the flower and the tree—the sunset—the dawn—the suns—the stars—all is Life—manifestations of the One Life. Everything is Alive, quick with living force, power, action; thrilling with vitality; throbbing with feeling; filled with activity. All is from the One Life—and all that is from the One Life is Alive. There is no dead substance in the Universe—there can be none—for Life cannot Die. All is Alive. And Life is in All.

Carry with you this Central Thought of the Lesson:

CENTRAL THOUGHT: *There is but One Life, and its manifestations comprise all the forms and shapes of the Universe. From Life comes but Life—and Life can come only from Life. Therefore we have the right to expect that all manifestations of the One Life should be Alive. And we are not mocked in such belief. Not only do the highest Occult Teachings inform us that Everything is Alive, but Modern Science has proven to us that Life is present everywhere—even in that which was formerly considered dead matter. It now sees that even the atom, and what lies back of the atom, is charged with Life Energy and Action. Forms and shapes may change, and do change—but Life remains eternal and infinite. It cannot Die—for it is LIFE.*

Peace be with thee.

THE THIRD LESSON - The Creative Will

In our first lesson of this series, we stated that among the other qualities and attributes that we were compelled, by the laws of our reason, to think that the Absolute possessed, was that of Omnipotence or All-Power. In other words we are compelled to think of the One as being the source and fount of all the Power there is, ever has been, or ever can be in the Universe. Not only, as is generally supposed, that the Power of the One is greater than any other Power,—but more than this, that there can be no other power, and that, therefore, each and every, any and all manifestations or forms of Power, Force or Energy must be a part of the great one Energy which emanates from the One. There is no escape from this conclusion, as startling as it may appear to the mind unaccustomed to it. If there is any power not from and of the One, from whence comes such power, for there is nothing else outside of the One? Who or what exists outside of the One that can manifest even the faintest degree of power of any kind? All power must come from the Absolute, and must in its nature be but one.

Modern Science has recognized this truth, and one of its fundamental principles is the Unity of Energy—the theory that all forms of Energy are, at the last, One. Science holds that all forms of Energy are interchangeable, and from this idea comes the theory of the Conservation of Energy or Correlation of Force. Science teaches that every manifestation of energy, power, or force, from the operation of the law of gravitation, up to the highest form of mental force is but the operation of the One Energy of the Universe.

Just what this Energy is, in its inner nature, Science does not know. It has many theories, but does not advance any of them as a law. It speaks of the Infinite and Eternal Energy from which all things proceed, but pronounces its nature to be unknowable. But some of the latter-day scientists are veering around to the teachings of the occultists, and are now hinting that it is something more than a mere mechanical energy. They are speaking of it in terms of mind. Wundt, the German scientist, whose school of thought is called voluntarism, considers the motive-force of Energy to be something that may be called Will. Crusius, as far back as 1744 said: "Will is the dominating force of the world." And Schopenhauer based his fascinating but gloomy philosophy and metaphysics upon the underlying principle of an active form of energy which he called the Will-to-Live, which he considered to be the Thing-in-Itself, or the Absolute. Balzac, the novelist, considered a something akin to Will, to be the moving force of the Universe. Bulwer advanced a similar theory, and made mention of it in several of his novels This idea of an active, creative Will, at work in the Universe, building up; tearing down; replacing; repairing; changing— always at work—ever active—has been entertained by numerous philosophers and thinkers, under different names and styles. Some, like Schopenhauer have thought of this Will as the final thing—that which took the place of God—the First Cause. But others have seen in this Will an active living principle emanating from the Absolute or God, and working in accordance with the laws impressed by Him upon it. In various forms, this latter idea is seen all through the history of philosophical thought. Cudsworth, the English philosopher, evolved the idea of a something called the "Plastic Nature," which so closely approaches the Yogi idea of the Creative Will, that we feel justified in quoting a passage from his book. He says:

"It seems not so agreeable to reason that Nature, as a distinct thing from the Deity, should be quite superseded or made to signify nothing, God Himself doing all things immediately and miraculously; from whence it would follow also that they are all done either forcibly and violently, or else artificially only, and none of them by any inward principle of their own.

"This opinion is further confuted by that slow and gradual process that in the generation of things, which would seem to be but a vain and idle pomp or a trifling formality if the moving power were omnipotent; as also by those errors and bungles which are committed where the matter is inept and contumacious; which argue that the moving power be not irresistible, and that Nature is such a thing as is not altogether incapable (as well as human art) of being sometimes frustrated and disappointed by the indisposition of matter. Whereas an omnipotent moving power, as it could dispatch its work in a moment, so would it always do it infallibly and irresistibly, no ineptitude and stubbornness of matter being ever able to hinder such a one, or make him bungle or fumble in anything. "Wherefore, since neither all things are produced fortuitously, or by the unguided mechanism of matter, nor God himself may be reasonably thought to do all things immediately and miraculously, it may well be concluded that there is a Plastic Nature under him, which, as an inferior and subordinate instrument, doth drudgingly execute that part of his providence which consists in the regular and orderly motion of matter; yet so as there is also besides this a higher providence to be acknowledged, which, presiding over it, doth often supply the defects of it, and sometimes overrules it, forasmuch as the Plastic Nature cannot act electively nor with discretion."

The Yogi Philosophy teaches of the existence of a Universal Creative Will, emanating from the Absolute—infilled with the power of the Absolute and acting under established natural laws, which performs the active work of creation in the world, similar to that performed by "Cudsworth's Plastic Nature," just mentioned. This Creative Will is not Schopenhauer's Will-to-Live. It is not a Thing-in-itself, but a vehicle or instrument of the Absolute. It is an emanation of the mind of the Absolute—a manifestation in action of its Will—a mental product rather than a physical, and, of course, saturated with the life-energy of its projector.

This Creative Will is not a mere blind, mechanical energy or force—it is far more than this. We can explain it only by referring you to the manifestation of the Will in yourself. You wish to move your arm, and it moves. The immediate force may seem to be a mechanical force, but what is back of that force—what is the essence of the force? The Will! All manifestations of energy—all the causes of motion—all forces—are forms of the action of the Will of the One—the Creative Will—acting under natural laws established by the One, ever moving, acting, forcing, urging, driving, leading. We do not mean that every little act is a thought of the moment on the part of the Absolute, and a reaching out of the Will in obedience to that thought. On the contrary, we mean that the One set the Will into operation as a whole, conceiving of laws and limitations in its action, the Will constantly operating in obedience to that conception, the results manifesting in what we call natural law; natural forces, etc. Besides this, the Absolute is believed to manifest its Will specially upon occasions; and moreover permits its Will to be applied and used by the individual wills of individual Egos, under the general Law and laws, and plan of the One.

But you must not suppose that the Will is manifested only in the form of mechanical forces, cohesion, chemical attraction, electricity, gravitation, etc.

It does more than this. It is in full operation in all forms of life, and living things. It is present everywhere. Back of all forms of movement and action, we find a moving cause—usually a *Pressure*. This is true of that which we have been calling mechanical forces, and of all forms of that which we call Life Energy. Now, note this, this great Pressure that you will observe in all Life Action, is the Creative Will—the Will Principle of the One—bending toward the carrying out of the Great Plan of Life. Look where we will, on living forms, and we may begin to recognize the presence of a certain creative energy at work— building up; moulding, directing; tearing down; replacing, etc.— always active in its efforts to create, preserve and conserve life. This visible creative energy is what the Yogi Philosophy calls "the Creative Will," and which forms the subject of this lesson. The Creative Will is that striving, longing, pressing forward, unfolding, progressing evolutionary effort, that all thoughtful people see in operation in all forms of life—throughout all Nature. From the lowest to the highest forms of life, the Effort, Energy, Pressure, may be recognized in action, creating, preserving, nourishing, and improving its forms. It is that Something that we recognize when we speak of "Nature's Forces" at work in plant growth and animal functioning. If you will but keep the word and idea—"NATURE"—before you, you will be able to more clearly form the mental concept of the Creative Will. The Creative Will is that which you have been calling "Nature at Work" in the growth of the plant; the sprouting of the seed; the curling and reaching of the tendril; the fertilization of the blossoms, etc. You have seen this Will at work, if you have watched growing things.

272

We call this energy "the Creative Will," because it is the objective manifestation of the Creative Energy of the Absolute—Its visible Will manifested in the direction of physical life. It is as much Will in action, as the Will that causes your arm to move in response to its power. It is no mere chance thing, or mechanical law—it is life action in operation.

This Creative Will not only causes movement in completed life, but all movement and action in life independent of the personal will of its individual forms. All the phenomena of the so-called Unconscious belong to it. It causes the body to grow; attends to the details of nourishment, assimilation, digestion, elimination, and all of the rest. It builds up bodies, organs, and parts, and keeps them in operation and function.

The Creative Will is directed to the outward expression of Life—to the objectification of Life. You may call this energy the "Universal Life Energy" if you wish, but, to those who know it, it is a Will—an active, living Will, in full operation and power, pressing forward toward the manifestation of objective life.

The Creative Will seems to be filled with a strong Desire to manifest. It longs to express itself, and to give birth to forms of activity. Desire lies under and in all forms of its manifestations. The ever present Desire of the Creative Will causes lower forms to be succeeded by higher forms—and is the moving cause of evolution—it is the Evolutionary Urge itself, which ever cries to its manifestations, "Move on; move upward."

In the Hindu classic, the "Mahabarata," Brahma created the most beautiful female being ever known, and called her Tillotama. He presented her in turn to all the gods, in order to witness their wonder and admiration. Siva's desire to behold her was so great that it developed in him four faces, in succession, as she made the tour of the assembly; and Indra's longing was so intense that his body became all eyes. In this myth may be seen exemplified the effect of Desire and Will in the forms of life, function and shape—all following Desire and Need, as in the case of the long neck of the giraffe which enables him to reach for the high branches of the trees in his native land; and in the long neck and high legs of the fisher birds, the crane, stork, ibis, etc.

The Creative Will finds within itself a desire to create suns, and they are formed. It desired planets to revolve around the suns, and they were thrown off in obedience to the law. It desired plant life, and plant life appeared, working from higher to lower form. Then came animal life, from nomad to man. Some of the animal forms yielded to the desire to fly, and wings appeared gradually, and we called it bird-life. Some felt a desire to burrow in the ground, and lo! came the moles, gophers, etc. It wanted a thinking creature, and Man with his wonderful brain was evolved. Evolution is more than a mere survival of the fittest; natural selection, etc. Although it uses these laws as tools and instruments, still back of them is that insistent urge—that ever-impelling desire—that ever-active Creative Will. Lamark was nearer right than Darwin when he claimed that Desire was back of it all, and preceded function and form. Desire wanted form and function, and produced them by the activity of the Creative Will.

This Creative Will acts like a living force—and so it is indeed—but it does not act as a reasoning, intellectual Something, in one sense—instead it manifests rather the "feeling," wanting, longing, instinctive phase of mind, akin to those "feelings" and resulting actions that we find within our natures. The Will acts on the Instinctive Plane.

Evolution shows us Life constantly pressing forward toward higher and still higher forms of expression. The urge is constantly upward and onward. It is true that some species sink out of sight their work in the world having been done, but they are succeeded by other species more in harmony with their environment and the needs of their times. Some races of men decay, but others build on their foundations, and reach still greater heights.

The Creative Will is something different from Reason or Intellect. But it underlies these. In the lower forms of life, in which mind is in but small evidence, the Will is in active operation, manifesting in Instinct and Automatic Life Action, so called. It does not depend upon brains for manifestation—for these lowly forms of life have no brains—but is in operation through every part of the body of the living thing.

Evidences of the existence of the Creative Will acting independently of the brains of animal and plant life may be had in overwhelming quantity if we will but examine the life action in the lower forms of life.

The testimony of the investigators along the lines of the Evolutionary school of thought, show us that the Life Principle was in active operation in lowly animal and plant life millions of years before brains capable of manifesting Thought were produced. Haekel informs us that during more than half of the enormous time that has elapsed since organic life first became evident, no animal sufficiently advanced to have a brain was in existence. Brains were evolved according to the law of desire or necessity, in accordance with the Great Plan, but they were not needed for carrying on the wonderful work of the creation and preservation of the living forms. And they are not today. The tiny infant, and the senseless idiot are not able to think intelligently, but still their life functions go on regularly and according to law, in spite of the absence of thinking brains. And the life work of the plants, and of the lowly forms of animal life, is carried on likewise. This wonderful thing that we call Instinct is but another name for the manifestation of the Creative Will which flows from the One Life, or the Absolute.

Even as far down the scale of life as the Monera, we may see the Creative Will in action. The Monera are but tiny bits of slimy, jelly-like substances—mere specks of glue without organs of any kind, and yet they exercise the organic phenomena of life, such as nutrition, reproduction, sensation and movement, all of which are usually associated with an organized structure. These creatures are incapable of thought in themselves, and the phenomenon is due to the action of the Will through them. This Instinctive impulse and action is seen everywhere, manifesting upon Higher and still higher lines, as higher forms of organisms are built up.

Scientists have used the term, "Appetency," defining it as, "the instinctive tendency of living organisms to perform certain actions; the tendency of an unorganized body to seek that which satisfies the wants of its organism." Now what is this tendency? It cannot be an effort of reason, for the low form of life has nothing with which to reason. And it is impossible to think of "purposive tendency" without assuming the existence of mental power of some kind. And where can such a power be located if not in the form itself? When we consider that the Will is acting in and through all forms of Life, from highest to lowest—from Moneron to Man—we can at once recognize the source of the power and activity. It is the Great Life Principle—the Creative Will, manifesting itself.

We can perhaps better form an idea of the Creative Will, by reference to its outward and visible forms of activity. We cannot see the Will itself—the Pressure and the Urge—but we can see its action through living forms. Just as we cannot see a man behind a curtain, and yet may practically see him by watching the movements of his form as he presses up against the curtain, so may we see the Will by watching it as it presses up against the living curtain of the forms of life. There was a play presented on the American stage a few years ago, in which one of the scenes pictured the place of departed spirits according to the Japanese belief. The audience could not see the actors representing the spirits, but they could see their movements as they pressed up close to a thin silky curtain stretched across the stage, and their motions as they moved to and fro behind the curtain were plainly recognized. The deception was perfect, and the effect was startling. One almost believed that he saw the forms of formless creatures. And this is what we may do in viewing the operation of the Creative Will—we may take a look at the moving form of the Will behind the curtain of the forms of the manifestation of life. We may see it pressing and urging here, and bending there—building up here, and changing there—always acting, always moving, striving, doing, in response to that insatiable urge and craving, and longing of its inner desire. Let us take a few peeps at the Will moving behind the curtain!

Commencing with the cases of the forming of the crystals, as spoken of in our last lesson, we may pass on to plant life. But before doing so, it may be well for us to take a parting look at the Will manifesting crystal forms. One of the latest scientific works makes mention of the experiments of a scientist who has been devoting much attention to the formation of crystals, and reports that he has noticed that certain crystals of organic compounds, instead of being built up symmetrically, as is usual with crystals, were "enation-morphic," that is, opposed to each other, in rights and lefts, like hands or gloves, or shoes, etc. These crystals are never found alone, but always form in pairs. Can you not see the Will behind the curtain here?

Let us look for the Will in plant-life. Passing rapidly over the wonderful evidences in the cases of the fertilization of plants by insects, the plant shaping its blossom so as to admit the entrance of the particular insect that acts as the carrier of its pollen, think for a moment how the distribution of the seed is provided for. Fruit trees and plants surround the seed with a sweet covering, that it may be eaten by insect and animal, and the seed distributed. Others have a hard covering to protect the seed or nut from the winter frosts, but which covering rots with the spring rains and allows the germ to sprout. Others surround the seed with a fleecy substance, so that the wind may carry it here and there and give it a chance to find a home where it is not so crowded. Another tree has a little pop-gun arrangement, by means of which it pops its seed to a distance of several feet. Other plants have seeds that are covered with a burr or "sticky" bristles, which enables them to attach themselves to the wool of sheep and other animals, and thus be carried about and finally dropped in some spot far away from the parent plant, and thus the scattering of the species be accomplished. Some plants show the most wonderful plans and arrangements for this scattering of the seed in new homes where there is a better opportunity for growth and development, the arrangements for this purpose displaying something very much akin to what we would call "ingenuity" if it were the work of a reasoning mind. There are plants called cockle-burs whose seed-pods are provided with stickers in every direction, so that anything brushing against them is sure to pick them up. At the end of each sticker is a very tiny hook, and these hooks fasten themselves tightly into anything that brushes against it, animal wool, hair, or clothing, etc. Some of these seeds have been known to have been carried to other quarters of the globe in wool, etc., there to find new homes and a wider field.

Other plants, like the thistle, provide their seed with downy wings, by which the wind carries them afar to other fields. Other seeds have a faculty of tumbling and rolling along the ground to great distances, owing to their peculiar shape and formation. The maple provides its seed with a peculiar arrangement something like a propeller screw, which when the wind strikes the trees and looses the seed, whirls the latter through the air to a distance of a hundred yards or more. Other seeds are provided with floating apparatus, which enables them to travel many miles by stream or river, or rain washes. Some of these not only float, but actually swim, having spider-like filaments, which wriggle like legs, and actually propel the tiny seed along to its new home. A recent writer says of these seeds that "so curiously lifelike are their movements that it is almost impossible to believe that these tiny objects, making good progress through the water, are really seeds, and not insects."

The leaves of the Venus' Fly-trap fold upon each other and enclose the insect which is attracted by the sweet juice on the leaf, three extremely sensitive bristles or hairs giving the plant notice that the insect is touching them. A recent writer gives the following description of a peculiar plant. He says: "On the shores of Lake Nicaragua is to be found an uncanny product of the vegetable kingdom known among the natives by the expressive name of 'the Devil's Noose.' Dunstan, the naturalist, discovered it long ago while wandering on the shores of the lake. Attracted by the cries of pain and terror from his dog, he found the animal held by black sticky bands which had chafed the skin to bleeding point. These bands were branches of a newly-discovered carnivorous plant which had been aptly named the 'land octopus.' The branches are flexible, black, polished and without leaves, and secrete a viscid fluid."

You have seen flowers that closed when you touched them. You remember the Golden Poppy that closes when the sun goes down. Another plant, a variety of orchid, has a long, slender, flat stem, or tube, about one-eighth of an inch thick, with an opening at the extreme end, and a series of fine tubes where it joins the plant. Ordinarily this tube remains coiled up into a spiral, but when the plant needs water (it usually grows upon the trunks of trees overhanging swampy places) it slowly uncoils the little tube and bends it over until it dips into the water, when it proceeds to suck up the water until it is filled, when it slowly coils around and discharges the water directly upon the plant, or its roots. Then it repeats the process until the plant is satisfied. When the water is absent from under the plant the tube moves this way and that way until it finds what it wants—just like the trunk of an elephant. If one touches the tube or trunk of the plant while it is extended for water, it shows a great sensitiveness and rapidly coils itself up. Now what causes this life action? The plant has no brains, and cannot have reasoned out this process, nor even have acted upon them by reasoning processes. It has nothing to think with to such a high degree. It is the Will behind the curtain, moving this way and that way, and doing things. There was once a French scientist named Duhamel. He planted some beans in a cylinder—something like a long tomato can lying on its side. He waited until the beans began to sprout, and send forth roots downward, and shoots upward, according to nature's invariable rule. Then he moved the cylinder a little—rolled it over an inch or two. The next day he rolled it over a little more. And so on each day, rolling it over a little each time. Well, after a time Duhamel shook the dirt and growing beans out of the cylinder, and what did he find? This, that the beans in their endeavor to grow their roots downward had kept on bending each day downward; and in their endeavor to send shoots upward, had kept on bending upward a little each day, until at last there had been formed two complete spirals—the one spiral being the roots ever turning downward, and the other the shoots ever bending upward. How did the plant know direction? What was the moving power. The Creative Will behind the curtain again, you see!

Potatoes in dark cellars have sent out roots or sprouts twenty and thirty feet to reach light. Plants will send out roots many feet to reach water. They know where the water and light are, and where to reach them. The tendrils of a plant know where the stake or cord is, and they reach out for it and twine themselves around it. Unwind them, and the next day they are found again twined around it. Move the stake or cord, and the tendril moves after it. The insect-eating plants are able to distinguish between nitrogenous and non-nitrogenous food, accepting the one and rejecting the other. They recognize that cheese has the same nourishing properties as the insect, and they accept it, although it is far different in feeling, taste, appearance and every other characteristic from their accustomed food.

Case after case might be mentioned and cited to show the operation of the Will in plant-life. But wonderful as are many of these cases, the mere action of the Will as shown in the *growing* of the plant is just as wonderful. Just imagine a tiny seed, and see it sprout and draw to itself the nourishment from water, air, light and soil, then upward until it becomes a great tree with bark, limbs, branches, leaves, blossoms, fruit and all. Think of this miracle, and consider what must be the power and nature of that Will that causes it.

The growing plant manifests sufficient strength to crack great stones, and lift great slabs of pavement, as may be noticed by examining the sidewalks of suburban towns and parks. An English paper prints a report of four enormous mushrooms having lifted a huge slab of paving stone in a crowded street overnight. Think of this exhibition of Energy and Power. This wonderful faculty of exerting force and motion and energy is fundamental in the Will, for indeed every physical change and growth is the result of motion, and motion arises only from force and pressure. Whose force, energy, power and motion? The Will's!

On all sides of us we may see this constant and steady urge and pressure behind living forces, and inorganic forms as well— always a manifestation of Energy and Power. And all this Power is in the Will—and the Will is but the manifestation of the All-Power—the Absolute. Remember this.

And this power manifests itself not only in the matter of growth and ordinary movements, but also in some other ways that seem quite mysterious to even modern Science. How is it that certain birds are able to fly directly against a strong wind, without visible movement of their wings? How do the buzzards float in the air, and make speed without a motion of the wing? What is the explanation of the movements of certain microscopic creatures who lack organs of movement? Listen to this instance related by the scientist Benet. He states that the Polycystids have a most peculiar manner of moving—a sort of sliding motion, to the right or left, upward, backward, sideways, stopping and starting, fast or slow, as it wills. It has no locomotive organs, and no movement can be seen to take place in the body from within or without. It simply slides. How?

Passing on to the higher animal life—how do eggs grow into chickens? What is the power in the germ of the egg? Can the germ think, and plan, and move, and grow into a chicken? Or is the Will at work there? And what is true in this case, is true of the birth and growth of all animal life—all animal life develops from a single germ cell. How, and Why?

There is a mental energy resident in the germ cell—of this there can be no doubt. And that mental energy is the Creative Will ever manifesting. Listen to these words from Huxley, the eminent scientist. He says:

"The student of Nature wonders the more and is astonished the less, the more conversant he becomes with her operations; but of all the perennial miracles she offers to his inspection, perhaps the most worthy of his admiration is the development of a plant or of an animal from its embryo. Examine the recently laid egg of some common animal, such as a salamander or a newt. It is a minute spheroid in which the best microscope will reveal nothing but a structureless sac, enclosing a glairy fluid, holding granules in suspension. But strange possibilities lie dormant in that semi-fluid globule. Let a moderate supply of warmth reach its watery cradle, and the plastic matter undergoes changes so rapid, and so purposelike in their succession, that one can only compare them to those operated by a skilled modeller upon a formless lump of clay. As with an invisible trowel, the mass is divided and subdivided into smaller and smaller portions, until it is reduced to an aggregation of granules not too large to build withal the finest fabrics of the nascent organism. And, then, it is as if a delicate finger traced out the line to be occupied by the spinal column, and moulded the contour of the body; pinching up the head at one end, the tail at the other, and fashioning flank and limb into due salamanderine proportions, in so artistic a way that, after watching the process hour by hour, one is almost involuntarily possessed by the notion that some more subtle aid to vision than the achromatic lens would show the hidden artist, with his plan before him, striving with skilful manipulation to perfect his work.

"As life advances and the young amphibian ranges the waters, the terror of his insect contemporaries, not only are the nutritious particles supplied by its prey (by the addition of which to its frame growth takes place) laid down, each in its proper spot, and in due proportion to the rest, as to reproduce the form, the color, and the size, characteristic of the parental stock; but even the wonderful powers of reproducing lost parts possessed by these animals are controlled by the same governing tendency. Cut off the legs, the tail, the jaws, separately or all together, and as Spallanzani showed long ago, these parts not only grow again, but the new limb is formed on the same type as those which were lost. The new jaw, or leg, is a newt's, and never by any accident more like that of a frog's."

In this passage from Huxley one may see the actual working of the Creative Will of the Universe,—moving behind the curtain— and a very thin curtain at that. And this wonderful work is going on all around us, all the time. Miracles are being accomplished every second—they are so common that we fail to regard them. And in our bodies is the Will at work? Most certainly. What built you up from single cell to maturity? Did you do it with your intellect? Has not every bit of it been done without your conscious knowledge? It is only when things go wrong, owing to the violation of some law, that you become aware of your internal organs. And, yet, stomach and liver, and heart and the rest have been performing their work steadily—working away day and night, building up, repairing, nourishing, growing you into a man or woman, and keeping you sound and strong. Are you doing this with your reason or with your personal will? No, it is the great Creative Will of the Universe, Universe,—the expression of the purpose and power of the One, working in and through you. It is the One Life manifesting in you through its Creative Will.

And not only is this all. The Creative Will is all around us in every force, energy and principle. The force that we call mental power is the principle of the Will directed by our individual minds. In this statement we have a hint of the great mystery of Mental Force and Power, and the so-called Psychic Phenomena. It also gives us a key to Mental Healing. This is not the place to go into detail regarding these phases—but think over it a bit. This Will Power of the Universe, in all of its forms and phases, from Electricity to Thought-power, is always at the disposal of Man, within limits, and subject always to the laws of the

Creative Will of the Universe. Those who acquire an understanding of the laws of any force may use it. And any force may be used or misused.

And the nearer in understanding and consciousness that we get to the One Life and Power, the greater will be our possible power, for we are thus getting closer and closer to the source of All Power. In these lessons we hope to be able to tell you how you may come into closer touch with this One Life of which you and all living things are but forms, shapes and channels of expression, under the operation of the Creative Will.

We trust that this lesson may have brought to your minds the realization of the Oneness of All—the fact that we are all parts of the one encircling unity, the heart-throbs and pulsations of which are to be felt even to the outer edge of the circle of life—in Man, in Monad, in Crystal, in Atom. Try to feel that inner essence of Creative Will that is within yourselves, and endeavor to realize your complete inner unity in it, with all other forms of life. Try to realize, as some recent writer has expressed it, "that all the living world is but mankind in the making, and that we are but part of the All." And also remember that splendid vistas of future unfoldment spread themselves out before the gaze of the awakened soul, until the mind fails to grasp the wondrous sight. We will now close this lesson by calling your attention to its CENTRAL THOUGHT.

There is but One Power in the Universe—One Energy—One Force. And that Power, Energy and Force is a manifestation of the One Life. There can be no other Power, for there is none other than the One from whom Power may come. And there can be no manifestation of Power that is not the Power of the One, for no other Power can be in existence. The Power of the One is visible in its manifestations to us in the natural laws and forces of Nature—which we call the Creative Will. This Creative Will is the inner moving power, urge and pressure behind all forms and shapes of Life. In atom, and molecule; in monad, in cell, in plant, in fish, in animal, in man,—the Life Principle or Creative Will is constantly in action, creating, preserving, and carrying on life in its functions. We may call this Instinct or Nature, but it is the Creative Will in action. This Will is back of all Power, Energy, or Force—be it physical, mechanical or mental force.

And all Force that we use, consciously or unconsciously, comes from the One Great Source of Power. If we could but see clearly, we would know that back of us is the Power of the Universe, awaiting our intelligent uses, under the control of the Will of the All. There is nothing to be afraid of, for we are manifestations of the One Life, from which all Power proceeds, and the Real Self is above the effect, for it is part of the Cause. But over and above—under and behind—all forms of Being, Matter, Energy, Force and Power, is the ABSOLUTE—ever Calm; ever Peaceful; ever Content. In knowing this it becomes us to manifest that spirit of absolute Trust, Faith and Confidence in the Goodness and Ultimate Justice of That which is the only Reality there is.

Peace be with you.

THE FOURTH LESSON - The Unity of Life

In our First Lesson of this series we spoke of the One Reality underlying all Life. This One Reality was stated to be higher than mind or matter, the nearest term that can be applied to it being "Spirit." We told you that it was impossible to explain just what "Spirit" is, for we have nothing else with which to compare or describe it, and it can be expressed only in its own terms, and not in the terms applicable to its emanations or manifestations. But, as we said in our First Lesson, we may think of "Spirit" as meaning the "essence" of Life and Being—the Reality underlying Universal Life, and from which the latter emanates. In the Second Lesson we stated that this "Spirit," which we called "The Absolute," expressed itself in the Universal Life, which Universal Life manifested itself in countless forms of life and activity. In the same lesson we showed you that the Universe is alive—that there is not a single dead thing in it—that there can be no such thing as a dead object in the Universe, else the theory and truth of the One underlying Life must fall and be rejected. In that lesson we also showed you that even in the world of inorganic things there was ever manifest life—in every atom and particle of inorganic matter there is the universal life energy manifesting itself, and in constant activity.

In the Third Lesson, we went still further into this phase of the general subject, and showed you that the Creative Will—that active principle of the Universal Life—was ever at work, building up new forms, shapes and combinations, and then tearing them down for the purpose of rebuilding the material into new forms, shapes, and combinations. The Creative Will is ever at work in its threefold function of creating, preserving and destroying forms—the change, however, being merely in the shape and form or combination, the real substance remaining unchanged in its inner aspect, notwithstanding the countless apparent changes in its objective forms. Like the great ocean the depths of which remain calm and undisturbed, and the real nature of which is unchanged in spite of the waves, and billows of surface manifestation, so does the great ocean of the Universal Life remain unchanged and unaltered in spite of the constant play of the Creative Will upon the surface. In the same lesson we gave you many examples of the Will in action—of its wondrous workings in the various forms of life and activity—all of which went to show you that the One Power was at work everywhere and at all times.

In our next lesson—the Fifth Lesson—we shall endeavor to make plain to you the highest teachings of the Yogi Philosophy regarding the One Reality and the Many Manifestations—the One and the Many—how the One apparently becomes Many—that great question and problem which lies at the bottom of the well of truth. In that lesson we shall present for your consideration some fundamental and startling truths, but before we reach that point in our teachings, we must fasten upon your mind the basic truth that all the various manifestations of Life that we see on all hands in the Universe are but forms of manifestation of One Universal Life which is itself an emanation of the Absolute.

Speaking generally, we would say to you that the emanation of the Absolute is in the form of a grand manifestation of One Universal Life, in which the various apparent separate forms of Life are but centers of Energy or Consciousness, the separation being more apparent than real, there being a bond of unity and connection underlying all the apparently separated forms. Unless the student gets this idea firmly fixed in his mind and consciousness, he will find it difficult to grasp the higher truths of the Yogi Philosophy. That all Life is One, at the last,—that all forms of manifestation of Life are in harmonious Unity, underlying—is one of the great basic truths of the Yogi Teaching, and all the students of that philosophy must make this basic truth their own before they may progress further. This grasping of the truth is more than a mere matter of intellectual conception, for the intellect reports that all forms of Life are separate and distinct from each other, and that there can be no unity amidst such diversity. But from the higher parts of the mind comes the message of an underlying Unity, in spite of all apparent diversity, and if one will meditate upon this idea he will soon begin to realize the truth, and will *feel* that he, himself, is but a center of consciousness in a great ocean of Life—that he and all other centers are connected by countless spiritual and mental filaments—and that all emerge from the One. He will find that the illusion of separateness is but "a working fiction of the Universe," as one writer has so aptly described it—and that All is One, at the last, and underlying all is One.

Some of our students may feel that we are taking too long a path to lead up to the great basic truths of our philosophy, but we who have traveled The Path, and know its rocky places and its sharp turns, feel justified in insisting that the student be led to the truth gradually and surely, instead of attempting to make short cuts across dangerous ravines and canyons. We must insist upon presenting our teachings in our own way—for this way has been tested and found good. We know that every student will come to realize that our plan is a wise one, and that he will thank us for giving him this gradual and easy approach to the wondrous and awful truth which is before us. By this gradual process, the mind becomes accustomed to the line of thought and the underlying principles, and also gradually discards wornout mental sheaths which have served their purposes, and which must be discarded because they begin to weigh heavily upon the mind as it reaches the higher altitudes of The Path of Attainment. Therefore, we must ask you to consider with us, in this lesson, some further teachings regarding the Unity of Life.

All the schools of the higher Oriental thought, as well as many of the great philosophical minds of the Western world, have agreed upon the conception of the Unity of Life—the Oneness of All Life. The Western thinkers, and many of the Eastern philosophers arrived at this conclusion by means of their Intellectual powers, greatly heightened and stimulated by concentration and meditation, which latter process liberated the faculties of the Spiritual Mind so that it passed down knowledge to the Intellect, which then seized upon the higher knowledge which it found within itself, and amplified and theorized upon the same. But among the Eastern Masters there are other sources of information open, and from these sources come the same report—the Oneness and Unity of Universal Life. These higher sources of information to which we have alluded, consist of the knowledge coming from those Beings who have passed on to higher planes of Life than ours, and whose awakened spiritual faculties and senses enable them to see things quite plainly which are quite dark to us. And from these sources, also, comes the message of the Oneness of Life—of the existence of a wonderful Universal Life including all forms of life as we know it, and many forms and phases unknown to us—many centers in the great Ocean of Life. No matter how high the source of inquiry, the answer is the same—"All Life is One." And this One Life includes Beings as much higher than ourselves, as we are higher than the creatures in the slime of the ocean-bed. Included in it are beings who would seem as archangels or gods to us, and they inform that beyond them are still higher and more radiant creatures, and so on to infinity of infinities. And yet all are but centers of Being in the One Life—all but a part of the great Universal Life, which itself is but an emanation of The Absolute. The mind of man shrinks back appalled from the contemplation of such wonders, and yet there are men who dare to attempt to speak authoritatively of the attributes and qualities of "God," as if He, the Absolute, were but a magnified man. Verily, indeed, "fools rush in where angels fear to tread," as the poet hath said. Those who will read our next lesson and thus gain an idea of the sublime conception of the Absolute held by the Yogi teachers may shudder at the presumption of those mortals who dare to think of the Absolute as possessing "attributes" and "qualities" like unto the meanest of things in this his emanated Universe. But even these spiritual infants are doing well—that is, they are beginning to *think*, and when man begins to *think* and *question*, he begins to progress. It is not the fact of these people's immature ideas that has caused these remarks on our part, but rather their tendency to set up their puny conceptions as the absolute truth, and then insisting upon forcing these views upon the outer world of men, whom they consider "poor ignorant heathen." Permit each man to think according to his light—and help him by offering to share with him the best that you possess—but do not attempt to force upon him your own views as absolute truth to be swallowed by him under threat of damnation or eternal punishment. Who are you that dares to speak of punishment and damnation, when the smell of the smoke of the hell of materialism is still upon your robes. When you realize just what spiritual infants you still are—the best of you—you will blush at these things. Hold fast to the best that you know—be generous to others who seem to wish to share

288

your knowledge—but give without blame or feeling of superiority—for those whom you teach today may be your teachers tomorrow—there are many surprises of this kind along The Path. Be brave and confident, but when you begin to feel puffed up by your acquirement of some new bit of knowledge, let your prayer—*our* prayer, for we too are infants—be, "Lord, be merciful unto me, a fool!"

The above words are for us, the students of the Yogi Philosophy—the teachers of the same—for human nature is the same in spite of names, and we must avoid the "vanity of vanities"—Spiritual Pride and Arrogance—that fault which has sent many a soul tumbling headlong from a high position on The Path, and compelled it to again begin the journey, chastened and bruised. The fall of Lucifer has many correspondences upon the occult plane, and is, indeed, in itself an allegorical illustration of just this law. Remember, always, that you are but a Centre in the Ocean of Life, and that all others are Centres in the same ocean, and that underlying both and all of you is the same calm bed of Life and Knowledge, the property of all. The highest and the lowest are part of the same One Life—each of you has the same life blood flowing through your veins—you are connected with every other form of life, high or low, with invisible bonds, and none is separate from another. We are speaking, of course, to the personalities of the various students who are reading these words. The Real Self of each is above the need of such advice and caution, and those who are able to reach the Real Self in consciousness have no need for these words, for they have outlived this stage of error. To many, the consciousness of the One Life—the Universal Life—in which all are centres of consciousness and being—has come gradually as a final step of a long series of thought and reasoning, aided by flashes of truth from the higher regions of the mind. To others it has come as a great illumination, or flash of Truth, in which all things are seen in their proper relations and positions to each other, and all as phases of being in the One. The term "Cosmic Consciousness," which has been used in the previous series of these lessons, and by other writers, means this sudden flash of "knowing" in which all the illusionary dividing lines between persons and things are broken down and the Universal Life is seen to be actually existent as One Life. To those who have reached this consciousness by either route just mentioned—or by other routes—there is no sense of loss of individuality or power or strength. On the contrary there is always a new sense of increased power and strength and knowing—instead of losing Individuality, there is a sense of having found it. One feels that he has the whole Universe at his back, or within him, rather than that he has lost his identity in the great Ocean of Life.

While we are speaking of this phase of the subject, we should like to ask you if you have ever investigated and inquired into the real meaning of the much-used word "Individuality?" Have you ever looked up its origin and real meaning, as given by the standard authorities? We are sure that many of you have no real idea of the actual meaning of the term, as strange as this statement may appear to you at first glance. Stop now, and define the word to yourself, as you have been accustomed to think of it. Ninety-five people of a hundred will tell you that it means something like "a strong personality." Let us see about this.

Webster defines the word "Individual" as follows: "Not divided, or not to be divided; existing as one distinct being or object; single; one." The same authority informs us that the word arises from the Latin word *individuus*, meaning "indivisible; not divisible." Does not this help you to gain a clearer idea of the Individuality that knows itself to be a Centre of Consciousness in the One Life, rather than a separate, puny, insignificant thing apart from all other centres or forms of Life, or the source of Life? We think it will help to clear your mind of some of the fog that has not as yet lifted itself.

And while we are on the subject of definitions, let us take a little look at the word "Personality," that is generally believed to be a synonym of "Individuality," and is often so used. Webster tells us that the word "Person" originated from the Latin word *persona*, meaning "a mask used by actors," which word in turn arose from two other words, *per*, meaning "through," and *sonare*, meaning "to sound," the two combined words meaning "to sound through." The same authority informs us that the archaic meaning of the word was "a character or part, as in a play; an assumed character." If you will think of Personality as "a mask used by an actor," or as "a part in a play," or as something used to "sound through" or to speak through, by the real Individual behind the mask of Personality, then perhaps you will see a little further into the Mystery of Personality and Individuality.

Oh, dear students, be not deceived by the mask of Personality which you may happen to be wearing at this moment, or by the masks which are worn by those around you. Realize that back of your mask is the great Individual—the Indivisible—the Universal Life, in which you are a centre of consciousness and activity. This does not wipe out your identity—instead it gives you a greater and grander identity. Instead of your sinking into a Nirvana of extinction of consciousness, your consciousness so enlarges as you unfold, that you will in the end feel your identity to be the identity of the Universe. Instead of your gaining Nothingness, you gain Allness. All spiritual growth and unfoldment gives you a constantly increasing sense of relationship with, and agreement with, the All. You grow into Allness as you unfold. Be not deceived by this chatter about Nothingness, and loss of Individuality, in the Oriental thought, although some of the presentations of its teachings may so seem to mean at first reading. Remember always that Personality is the mask, and Individuality the Real One.

You have often heard persons, claiming to be acquainted with the teachings of Theosophy and other expositions of the Oriental Wisdom Religion (including our own presentation), asserting that the Oriental mind was ever bent upon attaining a final stage of Nothingness or Extinction in Nirvana. In addition to what we have said, and to what we shall say on this subject, let us quote from the inspired writer of the "*Secret Doctrine*" (a standard Theosophical work) when she says, in that work on page 286, Vol. I: "Is this annihilation, as some think? ... To see in Nirvana annihilation, amounts to saying of a man plunged in a sound, dreamless sleep—one that leaves no impression on the physical memory and brain, because the sleeper's Higher Self is in its original state of absolute consciousness during these hours—that he too is annihilated. The latter simile answers only to one side of the question—the most material; since reabsorption is by no means such a dreamless sleep, but, on the contrary, absolute existence, an unconditional unity, or a state, to describe which human language is absolutely and hopelessly inadequate... Nor is the individuality—nor even the essence of the personality, if any be left behind—lost because re-absorbed." As J. Wm. Lloyd says, in connection with the above quotation, "This seems conclusive proof that Theosophy does not regard Nirvana as annihilation, but as an infinite enlargement of consciousness." And we would add that this is true not only as regards the Nirvana of the Theosophist, but also of the consciousness of the Unity of Life—the Universal Life. This too is not annihilation of individual consciousness, but an "infinite enlargement of consciousness" as this Western writer Lloyd has so well expressed it.

The very consciousness of Life that every man feels within him, comes not from something belonging exclusively to himself as a separate or personal thing. On the contrary, it belongs to his Individuality, not to his Personality, and is a phase of his consciousness or "awareness" of his relation to the One Universal Life which underlies his existence, and in which he is a center of consciousness. Do you grasp this idea? If not, meditate and concentrate upon it, for it is important. You must learn to *feel* the Life within you, and to know that it is the Life of the great Ocean of Universal Life upon the bosom of which you are borne as a centre of consciousness and energy. In this thought there is Power, Strength, Calm, Peace, and Wisdom. Acquire it, if you are wise. It is indeed a Gift from the Gods.

In this lesson we are not attempting to build up your idea of the Unity of Life by a series of arguments taken from a world of phenomena in which separateness and non-Unity is apparent. No such arguments would suffice, for it would be like trying to prove the existence and laws of color to a man born blind, by arguments taken from his world of darkness. On the contrary we are appealing to that region of the mind in which is stored the capacity for intuitively apprehending truth. We are endeavoring to speak in tones which will awaken a similar vibration in that part of your mentality, and if these vibrations be started into being, then will you be able to *feel* and *know* the truth, and then will your Intellect eagerly seize upon the new idea that it finds within itself, and will proceed to apply the same to the various problems that have been bothering you in the past.

This consciousness of Unity must come from the higher regions of the mind, for the Intellect alone knows it not,—it is out of its field. Just as one may not know that the earth is round by means of his senses which report quite the contrary, but may and does know this truth by abstract reasoning and higher intellectual effort; so may one know the truth that All Life is indeed One, at the last, and underlying, by the higher faculties of the mind, although his senses and ordinary intellectual processes fail to so inform him. The senses cannot inform man that the earth is round, *because they cannot see it as a whole, but only in part*— while the higher reasoning faculties are able to visualize the earth as a whole, and know it must be round. And the Intellect, in its ordinary field can see only separateness, and cannot report Oneness, but the Higher Mind sees Life as a Whole, and knows it to be One. And it is the Higher Mind that we are trying to bring into the field of consciousness in the appeal to you in this lesson. We trust that we may be successful—in fact we *know* that we shall be so, in many cases, for we know that the field is ready for the sowing of the seed—and that the call has been heard, and the message passed on to us to answer the call—else these words would not have been written.

The consciousness of the Unity of Life is something that must be experienced before the truth may be realized. It is not necessary for one to wait until he acquire full Cosmic Consciousness before he may realize, at least partially, the Oneness of All Life, for he may unfold gradually into the Cosmic Knowing, experiencing at each stage a fuller conception of the underlying Unity of Life, in which he is a centre of consciousness and manifestation. But there must be at least a partial unfoldment before one is able to *feel* the sense of Unity. To those who have not unfolded sufficiently to gain at least a glimmering of the truth, everything appears separate from every other thing, and there is no Unity of All. It is as if every leaf on a mighty tree were to consider itself a being separate and distinct from everything else in the world, failing to perceive its connection with the branch or limb, and tree, and its unity in being with every other leaf on the tree. After a bit the unfolding consciousness of the leaf enables it to perceive the stem that connects it with the twig. Then it begins to realize certain relationships, and feels its vital connection with the twig and the few other leaves attached to the same twig. Later on, it unfolds sufficiently to perceive that certain other leaf-bearing twigs are connected with the same branch, and it learns to feel its relationship with all twigs and leaves springing from that branch. Then again, a little later on, it begins to realize that other branches spring from the same limb as its branch, and the sense of relationship and dawning Unity begins to widen still further. And so it goes on, until at last, the tiny leaflet realizes that the life of the tree is the life of all of its parts—limbs, branches, twigs, leaves, blossoms, fruit, seed, etc., and that it, itself, is but a centre of expression in the One Life of the tree. Does the leaf feel less important and real from this discovery? We should say assuredly not, for it must feel that behind its tiny form and limited strength is the strength and vitality of the entire organism of the tree. It must know that the tree is ever at work extracting nourishment from the earth, air, and water, and transmitting that nourishment to its every part, including our little friend the leaflet. It knows that the sap will rise in the Spring to renew the manifestations of life, and it knows that although its leafy form may wither and die, still the essence of its life—its real Life—does not die but remains ever active and strong awaiting its chance for future expression and re-embodiment. Of course this figure of the leaf and the tree fails us if we attempt to carry it very far, but it will give us at least a partial idea of the relationship between the life of the person, and the One Life. Some of the Oriental teachers have illustrated this idea to their students by various familiar examples and figures of speech. Some bid the student hold up his hand, and then point out to him that each finger is apparently separate and distinct if one does not look down to where it joins the hand. Each finger, if it had consciousness, might well argue that it was a separate individual, having no relationship with any other finger. It might prove this to its own satisfaction, and to that of its listeners, by showing that it could move itself without stirring the other fingers. And so long as its consciousness was confined to its upper two joints it would remain under the illusion of separateness. But when its consciousness at last permeated the depths of its being, it would find that it emerged from the same hand from which also sprung the other fingers, and that its real life and power was vested in the hand rather than in itself, and that although apparently separate and independent, it was really but a part of the hand. And when its consciousness, through the consciousness of the hand, broadened and widened, it would perceive its relationship with, and interdependence with, the whole body, and would also recognize the power of the brain, and its mighty Will.

Another favorite illustration of the Eastern teachers is the stream of water flowing over a rocky bed. They point to the stream before it comes to a rocky place, and show the *chela* (student) that it is One. Then they will move a little way down the stream and show him how the rocks and stones divide the stream into countless little streams, each of which might imagine itself a separate and distinct stream, until later on it again joins the main united stream, and finds that it was but a form of expression of the One.

Another illustration that is frequently used by the teachers, is that which bids the student consider himself as a minute cell, or "little-life" as the Hindus call it, in a body. It may be a cell in the blood performing the office of a carrier or messenger, or it may be a working cell in one of the organs of the body; or it may be a thinking cell in the brain. At any rate, the cell manifests capacity for thought, action and memory—and a number of secondary attributes quite wonderful in the way. (See "*Hatha Yoga*," Chapter XVIII.) Each cell might well consider itself as a separate individual—in a certain sense it *does*. It has a certain degree of something akin to consciousness, enabling it to perform its work correctly and properly, and is called upon at times to manifest something like judgment. It may well be excused for thinking of itself as a "person" having a separate life. The analogy between its illusions and that of the man when seen by a Master, is very close. But we know that the life of the cell is merely a centre of expression of the life of the body—that its consciousness is merely a part of the consciousness of the mind animating the body. The cell will die and apparently perish, but the *essence* of it will remain in the life of the person whose body it occupied, and nothing really dies or perishes. Would the cell feel any less real if it knew that behind its Personality as a cell, there was the Individuality of the Man—that its Real Self was the Man, not the cell? Of course, even this figure of speech can be carried only so far, and then must stop, for the personality of the man, when it is dissolved, leaves behind it an essence which is called Character, which becomes the property of the Ego and which accompanies it into after life according to the Law of Karma, of which we shall speak in future lessons. But back even of these attributes of Personality, is the Ego which exists in spite of Personality, and lives on and on throughout many Personalities, and yet learning the lessons of each, until at last it rises above Personality and enters into higher sphere of Knowing and Being.

Still another favorite illustration of the Hindu teachers is that of the sun beating down upon the ocean and causing a portion of the water to rise in the form of vapor. This vapor forms clouds which spread all over the earth, and which eventually condense in the form of rain drops, dew, etc. This rain and dew form streams, rivers, etc., and sooner or later every drop finds its way back to Mother Ocean which is its Real Self. Separate though the dewdrop be, yet it is a part of the Ocean, no matter how far distant it may be, and the attraction of the Ocean will surely, and without fail, draw it back to its bosom. And the dewdrop, if it could know the truth, would be so much happier and stronger, and braver if it could know that it was superior to accident, time and space, and that it could not escape its own good, and that nothing could prevent its final triumph and victory when at last "the dewdrop glides into the shining sea." How cheerfully it could have met its many changes of form. and the incidents of its journey, if it could have gotten rid of the illusion of separateness, and knew that instead of being a tiny insignificant dewdrop it was a part of the Mighty Ocean—in fact that its Real Self was that Ocean itself—and that the Ocean was continually drawing it toward it, and that the many changes, up and down, were in response to that mighty power of attraction which was slowly but irresistibly drawing it back Home to Rest, Peace, and Power.

As valuable as are all these illustrations, examples, and figures of speech, still all must of necessity fall short of the truth in the case of the Soul of Man—that wondrous something which has been built up by the Absolute after aeons and aeons of time, and which is destined to play an important part in the great Cosmic Drama which it has pleased the Absolute to think into existence. Drawing its Life from the Universal Life, it has the roots of its being still further back in the Absolute itself, as we shall see in the next lesson. Great and wonderful is it all, and our minds are but illy fitted to receive the truth, and must be gradually accustomed to the glare of the Sun. But it will come to all—none can escape his glorious destiny.

The Oriental writings are full of allusions to the underlying Oneness, in fact the entire Oriental philosophies rest upon it. You may find it everywhere if you will but look for it. The experience of Cosmic Consciousness, which is naught but a sudden or gradual "awareness" of the underlying Unity of Life, is evidenced everywhere in the *Upanishads*, that wonderful series of teachings in the Hindu classics. Every writer in the collection gives his evidence regarding this awareness of Unity and Oneness, and the experiences and mental characteristics arising from the same. The following quotations will give an idea of the prevalence of this thought:

"He that beholds all beings in the Self, and the Self in all things, he never turns away from it."

"When to a man who understands, the Self has become all things, what sorrow, what trouble, can there be to him who once beheld that unity."

The Hindu father explains to his son that the One Life is in all forms and shapes, points out object after object, saying to the boy: "*Tat tuam asi*, Thou art that; That thou art."

And the Mystics have added their testimony to that of others who have experienced this consciousness. Plotinus said:

"Knowledge has three degrees: opinion, science, and illumination. The last is absolute knowledge founded upon the identity of the knowing mind with the known object."

And Eckhardt, the German mystic, has told his pupils that: "God is the soul of all things. He is the light that shines in us when the veil is rent."

And Tennyson, in his wonderful verse describing the temporary lifting of the veil for him, has described a phase of Cosmic Consciousness in the following words:

"For knowledge is the swallow on the lake
That sees and stirs the surface-shadow there,
But never yet hath dippt into the abysm,
The Abysm of all Abysms, beneath, within
The blue of sky and sea, the green of earth,
And in the million-millionth of a grain
Which cleft and cleft again for evermore
And ever vanishing, never vanishes. . .
And more, my son, for more than once when I
Sat all alone, revolving in myself
That word which is the symbol of myself,
The mortal symbol of the Self was loosed,
And past into the Nameless, as a cloud
Melts into Heaven. I touched my limbs, the limbs
Were strange, not mine—and yet no shadow of doubt,
But utter clearness, and through loss of Self
The gain of such large life as matched with ours
Were Sun to spark, unshadowable in words,
Themselves but shadows of a shadow-world."

And not only among the mystics and poets is this universal truth
experienced and expressed, but among the great philosophers of
all ages may we find this teaching of the Unity of Life originally
voiced in the*Upanishads*. The Grecian thinkers have expressed
the thought; the Chinese philosophers have added their
testimony; the modern philosophers, Spinoza, Berkeley, Kant,
Hegel, Schopenhauer, Hartman, Ferrier, Royce, although
differing widely in their theories, all have expressed as a
fundamental truth the Unity of Life—a One Life underlying. The
basic teachings of the Vedas are receiving confirmation at the
hands of Modern Science, which while calling itself Rationalistic
and inclining to a Materialistic conception of the Universe, still
finds itself compelled to say, "At the last, All is One."

And in nearly every human soul there is a secret chamber in
which the text of this knowledge lies hidden, and in the rare
moments in which the chamber door is opened in response to
poetry, music, art, deep religious feeling, or those unaccountable
waves of uplift that come to all, the truth is recognized for the
moment and the soul feels at peace and is content in the feeling
that it is at harmony with the All. The sense of Beauty, however

expressed, when keenly experienced, has a tendency to lift us out of our consciousness of separateness into another plane of mind in which the keynote is Unity. The higher the human feeling, the nearer is the conscious realization of the underlying Unity. This realization of the Unity of Life—the Oneness of Life—the Great Life—even when but faintly experienced, renders Life quite a different thing to the person. He feels no longer that he is a mere "part" of something that may be destroyed—or that he is a tiny personal something, separate from and opposed to all the rest of the Universe—but that he is, instead, a Unit of Expression—a Centre of Consciousness—in the Great One Life. He realizes that he has the Power, and Strength, and Life, and Wisdom of the Whole back of him, upon which he may learn to draw as he unfolds. He realizes that he is at Home, and that he cannot be thrust out, for there is no outside of the All. He feels within himself the certainty of infinite Life and being, for his Life is the all Life, and that cannot die. The petty cares, and worries, and griefs, and pains of everyday personal life are seen for what they are, and they cease to threaten and dominate him as of old. He sees the things of personality as merely the costume and trappings of the part in the play of life that he is acting out, and he knows that when he discards them he will still be "I." When one really feels the consciousness of the One Life underlying, he acquires a confident trust and faith, and a new sense of freedom and strength comes to him, for is he not indeed delivered from the bondage of fear that has haunted him in his world of separateness. He feels within him the spiritual pulse of the Universal Life, and at once he thrills with a sense of new-found power and being. He becomes reconciled with Life in all its phases, for he knows these things as but temporary phases in the working out of some great Universal plan, instead of things permanent and fixed and beyond remedy. He begins to feel the assurance of Ultimate Justice and God, and the old ideas of Injustice and Evil begin to fade from him. He who enters into the consciousness of the Universal Life, indeed enters into a present realization of the Life Everlasting. All fear of being "lost" or "eternally damned" fades away, and one instinctively realizes that he is "saved" because he is of the One Life and cannot be lost. All the fear of being lost arises from the sense of illusion of separateness or apartness from the One Life. Once the consciousness of Unity is gained, fear drops from the soul like a wornout garment.

When the idea and consciousness of the Unity takes possession of one, he feels a new sense of cheerfulness and optimism entirely different from any other feeling that he has ever experienced. He loses that distrust and hardness which seems to cling to so many in this age who have arrived at the Intellectual stage of development, and have been unable to progress further. A new sense of peace and harmony comes to one, and illuminates his entire character and life. The bitterness engendered by the illusion of separateness is neutralized by the sweetness of the sense of Unity. When one enters into this consciousness he finds that he has the key to many a riddle of life that has heretofore perplexed him. Many dark corners are illuminated—many hard sayings are made clear. Paradoxes become understandable truths, and the pairs of opposites that dwell in all advanced intellectual conceptions, seem to bend around their ends and form themselves into a circle.

To the one who understands the Unity, all Nature seems akin and friendly. There is no sense of antagonism or opposition— everything is seen to fit into its place, and work out its appointed task in the Universal plan. All Nature is seen to be friendly, when properly understood, and Man regains that sense of harmonious environment and at-home-ness that he lost when he entered the stage of self-consciousness. The lower animal and the children feel this Unity, in their poor imperfect way, but Man lost this Paradise when he discovered Good and Evil. But Paradise Lost becomes Paradise Regained when Man enters into this new stage of consciousness. But unlike the animal or child, which instinctively feels the Unity, the awakened soul of man possesses the Unity consciousness, coupled with intelligent comprehension, and unfolding spiritual power. He has found that which he lost, together with the accumulated interest of the ages. This new kingdom of Consciousness is before the race. All must enter into it in time—all will enter into it—many are entering into it now, by gradual stages. This dawning sense of Unity is that which is causing the spiritual unrest which is now agitating the world, and Which in time will bring the race to a realization

300

of the Fatherhood of God and the Brotherhood of Man, and his kinship to Every Living Thing. We are entering into this new cycle of human unfoldment, and the greatest changes are before the race. Ye who read these words are in the foremost ranks of the new dispensation, else you would not be interested in this subject. You are the leaven which is designed to lighten the heavy mass of the world-mind. Play well your parts. You are not alone. Mighty forces and great Intelligences are behind you in the work. Be worthy of them. Peace be with you.

Carry with you the Central Thought of this lesson:

CENTRAL THOUGHT. *There is but One Life—a Universal Life—in the world. This One Life is an emanation from the Absolute. It infills all forms, shapes and manifestations of Life, and is the Real Life that each imagines to be his personal property. There is but One—and you are centres of consciousness and expression in that One. There is a Unity and Harmony which becomes apparent to those who enter into the consciousness of the One Life. There is Peace and Calm in the thought. There is Strength and Power in the knowledge. Enter ye into your Kingdom of Power—possess yourselves of your Birthright of Knowledge. In the very center of your being you will find a holy of holies in which dwells the Consciousness of the One Life, underlying. Enter into the Silence of the Shrine within.*

THE FIFTH LESSON - The One and the Many

As we have stated in previous Lessons, all philosophies which thinkers have considered worthy of respect, find their final expression of Truth in the fundamental thought that there is but *One Reality*, underlying all the manifold manifestations of shape and form. It is true that the philosophers have differed widely in their conception of that One, but, nevertheless, they have all agreed upon the logical necessity of the fundamental conception that there is, at least, but One Reality, underlying All. Even the Materialists have conceded this conclusion, and they speak and think of a something called "Matter," as the One— holding that, inherent in Matter, is the potentiality of all Life. The school of Energists, holding that Matter in itself is non-existent, and that it is merely a mode of manifestation of a something called "Energy," asserts that this something called Energy is One, fundamental, real, and self-sufficient.

The various forms of Western religious thought, which hold to the various conceptions of a Personal Deity, also hold to a Oneness, inasmuch as they teach that in the beginning there was God, only, and that all the Universe has been *created* by Him. They do not go into details regarding this creation, and, unlike the Oriental teachers, they fail to distinguish between the conception of the *creation of shape and form*, on the one hand; and the *creation of the substance of these shapes and forms*, on the other hand. But, even accepting the premises of these people who hold to the Personal Deity conception, it will be seen that the Reason requires the acceptance of one or two ideas, *viz.*, (1) That the Deity created the substance of these shapes and forms from *Nothing*; or else (2) that he created them out of *his own substance*—out of Himself, in fact. Let us consider, briefly, these two conceptions.

In the first conception, *i.e.*, Creation from Nothing, we are brought face to face with an impregnable obstacle, inasmuch as the human reason positively refuses to think of Anything coming from Nothing. While it is perfectly true that the finite human mind cannot undertake to limit the powers of the Infinite; or to insist that the possibilities of the Divine Power must be measured and limited by the finite power of Man—still it must hearken to the report of its own highest faculties, and say "I cannot Think it," or else blindly accept the teachings of other finite minds which are equally unable to "Think it," and which have no superior sources of information. The Infinite Power has endowed us with reasoning faculties, and evidently expects us to use them to their full capacity—else the gift were a mockery. And in the absence of information from higher sources than the Reason, we must use the Reason in thinking of this matter, or else refuse to think of it at all.

In view of the above thought, let us then consider the report of the Reason, regarding this matter, And then, after having done so, let us apply the test of this report of the Reason, to the highest teaching of the Yogi Philosophy, and see how the latter stands the test. And, after having done this, we will apply the test of the Higher Consciousness to the same teachings. Remember this always, that while there is knowledge that transcends Reason—that is knowledge that comes from the Higher Regions of the Mind—still even such information of the Spiritual Mind *does not run contrary to Reason*, although it goes beyond it. There is harmony between the Spiritual Mind and the Highest Reason. Returning to the consideration of the matter of Creation of Substance from Nothing, we again assert that *the Reason is unable to think of the creation of Something from Nothing*. It finds the statement unthinkable, and contrary to all the laws of thought. It is true that the Reason is compelled to accept as a final truth, many things that it cannot *understand* by reason of its finitude—but this is not one of them. There is no logical necessity for the Reason to accept any such conception as this—there is no warrant in the Reason for any such theory, idea or conclusion. Let us stop here, for a moment, and examine into this difference—it may help us to think clearer, hereafter.

We find it impossible to *understand* the fact of the Infinite Being having always existed—and Being without Cause. We find it impossible to conceive of the nature of an Eternal, Causeless, and Infinite Being—to conceive the *nature of*, such a Being, remember.

But, while this is so, still our Reason, by its own laws, compels us to think that there *must be* such a Being, so long as we think at

303

all. For, if we think at all, we *must* think of there being a Fundamental Reality—and we *must* think of that Reality as being without Cause (because there can be no Cause for the First Cause); and we *must* think of that Reality as being Eternal (because It could not have sprung into Being from Nothing, and therefore must have always been); and we *must* think of that Reality as Infinite (because there is nothing outside of Itself to limit It). Think over this statement for a moment—until you grasp it fully.

But there is no such necessity, or compulsion, in the case of the question of Creation from Nothingness. On the contrary, the necessity and compulsion is all the other way. Not only is the Reason unable to *think of* Creation from Nothing—not only does all its laws forbid it to hold such a conception—but, more than this, it finds within itself a conception, full-grown and potent, which contradicts this idea. It finds within itself the strong certainty that *Whatever Really Is has Always Been*, and that all transient and finite shapes, forms, and manifestations, *must* proceed from that which is Real, Infinite, Causeless, and Infinite—and moreover *must be composed of the substance of that Reality*, for there is nothing else Real from which they could have been composed; and their composition from Nothing is unthinkable, for Nothing is Nothing, and always will be Nothing. "Nothing" is merely a name of denial of existence—an absolute denial of substantiality of any degree, kind or form—an absolute denial of Reality. And from such could come only Nothing—from Nothing, Nothing comes. Therefore, finding within itself the positive report that All, and Anything There Is, must be composed of the Substance of the Reality, the Reason is compelled to think that the Universe is composed of the Substance of the One Reality—whether we call that One Reality, by the name of The Absolute; or whether we call it God. *We must believe that from this Absolute-God all things in the Universe have flown out, or been emanated, rather than created—begotten, rather than "made."*

This does not mean the Pantheistic idea that the Universe *is* God—but rather that God, while existing separate and apart from His Universe, in his Essence, and Being, is nevertheless *in* His Universe, and His Universe *in* Him. And this, no matter what conception of God or Deity is had—or whether one thinks of The Absolute as Principle. The Truth is the same— Truth no matter by what names it is called, or by what misconception it is surrounded. The Truth is that *One is in All, and All is in One*—such is the report of the highest Reason of Man—such is the report of the Illumined—such is the Highest Teachings that have come down to the race from the great souls that have trodden The Path of Attainment.

And now let us submit the Yogi Philosophy to these conceptions, and reports of the Reason. And let us discover just what more the Yogi Philosophy has to say concerning the *nature of* the Substance of the Divine, which infills all Life—and how it solves the Riddle of the Sphinx, concerning the One in All; and All in One. We hope to show you that the Riddle is capable of solution, and that the old Yogi teachers have long ago grasped that for which the human mind has ever sought. This phase of the Teachings is the highest, and it is usually hinted at, rather than expressed, in the writings on the subject—owing to danger of confusion and misconception. But in these Lessons we shall speak the Truth plainly, and without fear—for such is the Message which has been given us to deliver to our students—and we will perform the Right action, leaving the Result, or Fruits of the Action, where it belongs, according to the higher teachings found in the "*Bhagavad Gita*," and in the Higher Teachings of the Yogi Philosophy.

The fundamental Truth embedded in the Wisdom-Philosophies of the East—the Higher Yogi Teachings—is the impregnable doctrine of the One Self in the many selves—the many selves in the One Self. This fundamental Truth underlies all the Oriental Philosophies which are esoteric in their nature.

Notwithstanding the crude and often repulsive conceptions and practices of the masses of the people who represent the exoteric, or popular, phase of the teachings (and these two phases are to be found in *all* regions) still there is always this Inner Doctrine of the One Self, to be found to those who look for it.

Not only is this true among the Hindus; but even among the Mahommedans, of all countries, there is an Inner Circle of Mystics, known as the *Sufis*, holding to this Truth. And the inner teachings of the philosophies of all ages and races, have held likewise. And the highest thought of the philosophers of the Western races, has found refuge in this idea of the Over-soul, or Universal Self. But, it is only among the Yogis that we find an attempt made to explain the real nature of the manifestation of the One in Many—the holding of the Many forms in the One Self.

Before proceeding to the consideration of *how* the One becomes as Many, as expounded by the Higher Yogi Teachings, it becomes necessary to speak of a matter upon which there has been much confusion and misunderstanding, not only on the part of the students of various Oriental Philosophies, but also upon the part of some of the teachers themselves. We allude to the connection between THE ONE—THE ABSOLUTE—in Its ESSENCE—and that which has been called the One Life; the Universal Life, etc.

Many writers have spoken of the Universal Life, and The One, as being identical—but such is a grievous error, finding no warrant in the Highest Yogi Teachings. It is true that all living forms dwell in, and are infilled with the Universal Life—that All Life is One. We have taught this truth, and it is indeed Truth, without qualification. But there is still a Higher Truth—the Highest Truth, in fact—and that is, that even this Universal Life is not the One, but, instead, is in itself a manifestation of, and emanation from, THE ONE. There is a great difference here—- see that you perceive and understand it, before proceeding further.

THE ONE—THE ABSOLUTE—according to the Highest Teachings, is Pure Spirit, and not Life, Mind, or Being as we understand them in our finite and mortal expressions. But, still all Life, Mind, and Being, as we understand them, spring from, flow from, and emanate from, the One—and more than this, may be spoken of as *reflections* of the Life, Mind, and Being of The One, if we may be permitted to apply the names of finite manifestations to the Infinite Reality.

So, the Highest Teaching is that the Universal Life infilling all living things, is not, in itself, the Being and Life of THE ONE— but is rather a great fundamental emanation of The One, the manner and nature of which will be spoken of as we proceed. Remember this, please.

Leading up to the Supreme Idea of the One in All—All in One—let us examine into the report of the Reason upon the *nature of* the Substance—the Divine Substance—from which all living forms are shaped; and from which all that we know as Finite Mind is likewise composed. *How can these imperfect and finite forms be composed of a Divine and Perfect Substance?* This is the question that must occur to the minds of those who are capable of deep thought on the subject—and it is a question that must be answered. And it can be answered—and *is* answered in the Higher Yogi Philosophy. Let us examine the reports of the Reason, a little further—then shall we be ready for the Teachings.

Of what can the Substance of the Infinite be composed? Can it be Matter? Yes, if you are satisfied with the reasoning of the Materialists, and cannot see further into the Truth! These teach that Matter is God, and that God is Matter. But if you be among those who reject the Materialistic teachings, you will not be satisfied with this answer. Even if you incline toward a Non-mental Infinite, still if you are familiar with the results of modern scientific investigation, and know that Science has seen Matter resolve itself into something like Electric Energy, you will know that the Truth must lie behind and beyond Matter.

Then is it Pure Energy? you may ask. Pure Energy? what's that? Can you think of Energy apart from material manifestation? Have you ever known of such a thing? Do you not know that even the Electron Theory, which is attracting the attention of advanced Modern Science, and which holds that all things are composed of minute particles of Electric Energy, called Electrons, from which the Atoms are built—do you not know that even this theory recognizes the necessity of a "something like Matter, only infinitely finer," which they call the Ether, to enfold the Electric Energy as a unit—to give it a *body*, as it were? And can you escape from the fact that the most advanced scientific minds find confronting them—*the fact that in all Energy, and governing its actions, there 'is manifested "something like Mind"*?

And does not all this teach thinkers that just as Energy creates from itself, that which is called Matter, and then uses it as a vehicle of expression and action—so does this "Something like

Mind" create from itself that which we call Energy, and proceeds to use it, with its accompanying phase of Matter, for its expression? Does not all advanced research show us that in all Matter and Energy there are evidences of the operation of this "Something like Mind"? And if this be so, are we not justified as regarding Matter and Energy as mere Effects—and to look to this "Something like Mind" as the more fundamental Substance? We think so—and Science is beginning to think so, too. And soon will Science be regarding with the most profound respect, the Metaphysical axiom that "All is Mind."

You will see by reference to our "*Advanced Course in Yogi Philosophy, etc.*," the general Yogi teachings regarding the Emanation of the One, known respectively as Mind, Energy, and Matter. You will see that the Yogis teach that Mind, Energy, and Matter comprise a threefold emanation of the Absolute. You will also see that it is taught that Mind was the Parent-Emanation— the Universal Mind; and that the Universal Energy was the Second-Emanation (proceeding from Mind); and that the Universal Matter was the Third Emanation (proceeding from Energy) In the same book you will find that the Teaching is that above Matter, Energy, and Mind, is the Essence of the Absolute, which is called Spirit—the nature of which is non-understandable to the mind of Man, the highest conception of which is the highest manifestation of itself—Mind. But as we cannot comprehend spirit otherwise, we are justified in thinking of it as Something like Infinite Mind—Something as much higher than Finite Mind as that is higher than mere energy.

Now, then—we have seen the folly of thinking of the Divine Substance as Matter or Energy. And we have come to know it as Spirit, something like Mind, only infinitely higher, but which still may be thought of in terms of Infinite Mind, for we can have no higher terms in our thinking operations. So we may then assume that this Divine Nature or substance is SPIRIT, which we will think of as Infinite Mind, for want of a better form of conception.

We have seen the folly of thinking of the Divine Essential Substance as the Body of God. We have likewise seen the folly of thinking of it as the Vital Energy of God. And we have found

308

that we could not escape thinking of it as the Spirit, or infinite Mind of God. Beyond this we cannot think intelligently.

But do you not see that all this exercise of the Reason has brought us to the point where we must think that this Divine Substance, which the Absolute-God uses in the manifestation of Universal Life; the Universe; and all the forms, and shapes, and manifestations of life and things in the Universe—this Divine Substance which must be *in* All Things—and *in which* All Things must rest, even as the bubble rests on the Ocean—that this can be nothing less than Spirit, and that this Spirit can be thought of only as Infinite Mind?

And, if this be so, then indeed must *All be Mind, and Mind be All*—meaning, of course, the Infinite Mind, not the finite manifestation that we *call* Mind.

Then, if this reasoning has been correct, then must we think that All Life—all the Universe—Everything except the Absolute itself—*must be held in the Infinite Mind of the Absolute*!

And, so, by the exercise of our Reason—by listening to, and examining its reports, we have been brought face to face—eye to eye—heart to heart—with the Teaching of the Illumined Ones, which has come down to us as the Highest Teaching of the Yogi Philosophy! For this, indeed, is the highest conception of Truth in the Yogi Teachings—this, that ALL MANIFESTATIONS AND EMANATIONS OF THE ABSOLUTE ARE MENTAL CREATIONS OF THE ABSOLUTE—THOUGHT-FORMS HELD IN THE INFINITE MIND—THE INFINITE SPIRIT IN THEM—AND THEY IN THE INFINITE SPIRIT. _And that the only Real Thing about Man is THE SPIRIT involved in the Thought-Form, the rest is mere Personality, which changes and ceases to be. The Spirit in the Soul of Man, is the SOUL OF THE SOUL, which is never born; never changeth; never dieth— this is The Real Self of *Man, in which, indeed, he is "One with the Father."*

This is the point where the Reasoning Mind of Man has come to a sense of Agreement with the Highest Yogi Teachings. Let us now pass on to the Teachings themselves—let us listen to The Message of Truth.

In this consideration of the Highest Yogi Philosophy, and its teaching, we would again say to our students, that which we said to them in *"The Advanced Course"*—that we do not attempt to teach the "why" of the Manifestation of The Absolute, but rest content with delivering the Message of the Yogi Sages, which deals with the "how." As we stated in the lessons referred to, we incline to that school of the Higher Teachings, which holds that the "Why" of the Infinite Manifestation must, of necessity, rest with the Infinite alone, and that the finite mind cannot hope to answer the question. We hold that in all the Universal Mind, or in any of its Mind Manifestations, there is to be found no answer to this question! Wrapped in the Essence of the Absolute Spirit, alone, is this Final Answer!

The Sages, and Masters, from their high spiritual points of observation, possess many truths regarding the "how" side of the question that would appear almost like Infinite Wisdom itself, compared with our puny knowledge. But even these great souls report that they do not possess the answer to the Final Question—the "Why" of the Infinite Manifestation. And so we may be excused from attempting to answer it—and without shame or sense of shortcoming do we still say, to this question, "We do not know!"

In order that the Final Question may be fully understood let us consider it for a moment. We find the Question arising from the following condition:

The human Reason is compelled to admit that there is an Infinite, Eternal, Causeless REALITY underlying all forms of manifestation in the phenomenal world. It is likewise compelled to admit that this REALITY must comprise All that Really Is— and that there can be nothing Real outside of Itself. Arising from this is the Truth, that all forms of phenomenal manifestation, must emanate *from* the One Reality, for there is nothing else Real from which they could emanate. And the twin-Truth that these forms of manifestation, must also be *in* the Being of the One Reality, for there is nowhere outside of the All wherein they might find a place. So this One Reality is seen to be "That from which All Things flow"; and "That in which All Things live, and move and have their being."

Therefore All Things *emanate from*, and are *contained in* the One Reality. We shall consider "just how" later on, but the question which confronts us, and which has been called the

"Final Question"—and that which we pronounce unanswerable—is this: "Why has the Infinite manifested and emanated Finite forms of being?" You will see the nature of the question when you stop to consider: (1) The Infinite cannot have Desire, for that is a Finite quality; (2) It cannot lack anything, for that would take away from its Infinity; (3) and even if it did lack anything, from whence could it expect to acquire it; for there is nothing outside of itself—if It lacks anything, it must continue to always lack it, for there is no outside source from which It could obtain anything which it does not already possess. And Desire would be, of course, a *wanting* for something which it lacked— so It could not Desire unless it Lacked—and it would know that Desire would be hopeless, even if indeed it did Lack.

So you see that if we regard the Infinite Reality as Perfect, we must drop all ideas of It Desiring or Lacking—and of it Growing or Improving—or of it obtaining more Power, or Knowledge. These ideas are ridiculous, for an Absolute, Infinite Reality, must possess All-Knowledge; All-Power; All-Presence, else it is not Absolute and Infinite. And, if It does not possess these attributes of Being, then It can never hope to acquire them, for there is Nowhere from whence they could be acquired—there is no Source outside of the All-Source. A Finite Thing, may lack, and desire, and improve and develop, for there is the Universal Source from which it may draw. But the Infinite has no Universal Source, for it is Its own Source. Do you see the nature of the Final Question? If not we will again state it—it is this: "Why should the Infinite Reality, which possesses all that may be possessed, and which in itself is the only Source of Things— WHY should It Desire to manifest a Universe from and within Itself?"

A little consideration will show you that there is no intelligent answer to the "Why," either in your own minds, or in the writings and teachings of the greatest minds. The matter is important, to those who are confronted every day with some of the many attempts to answer this Final Question—it is well that our students inform them regarding the futility of such questioning. And with this end in view, we shall herein give a few of the wise "guesses" at the answer, and our reasons for considering them inadequate. We ask the student to consider carefully these remarks, for by so doing he will post himself, and will be saved much tedious and perplexing wandering along the dangerous places in the Swamp of Metaphysics, following the will-o'-the-wisp of Finite Mind masquerading as the Infinite Wisdom! Beware of the False Lights! They lead to the quagmire and quicksands of thought!

Let us now consider some of these "guesses" at the answer to the Final Question. Some thinkers have held that the Absolute was bound by a Divine Necessity to manifest itself as Many. The answer to this is that the Absolute could not be *bound* by anything, inner or outer, else it would not be Absolute and Infinite, but would be Relative and Finite. Another set of thinkers have held that the Absolute found within itself a Desire to Manifest as Many. From whence could come such an action-causing Desire? The Absolute could lack nothing, and there would be nothing for it to desire to gain, other than that which It already possessed. One does not desire things one already has, but only what he lacks.

Another school would tell us that the Infinite wished to *Express* itself in the phenomenal world. Why? Such a phenomenal world could only be reflection of Its power, witnessed only by Itself, and could contain nothing that was not already contained in the All. To what end would such a wish tend? What would be accomplished or gained? The Infinite All could not become anything more than It already was—so why the wish for expression? Some say that the whole phenomenal world is but *Maya*, or Illusion, and does not exist at all. Then who else than the Infinite caused the Illusion, and why the necessity? This answer only removes the question back one point, and does not really answer it. Some would say that the Universe is the "dream of the Infinite." Can we conceive the Infinite Being as exercising the finite faculty of "dreaming"—is not this childish?

Others would have us believe that the Absolute is indulging in a "game" or "play," when he makes Universes, and those inhabiting them. Can anyone really believe this of The Absolute—playing like a child, with men and women, worlds and suns, as Its blocks and tin-soldiers? Why should the Infinite

312

"play"?—does It need amusement and "fun" like a child? Poor Man, with his attempts to read the Riddle of the Infinite!

We know of teachers who gravely instruct their pupils in the idea that the Absolute and Infinite One manifests Universes and Universal Life, and all that flows from them, because It wishes to "gain experience" through objective existence. This idea, in many forms has been so frequently advanced that it is worth while to consider its absurdity. In the first place, what "experience" could be gained by the Absolute and Infinite One? What could It expect to gain and learn, that it did not already know and possess? One can gain experience only from others, and outside things—not from oneself entirely separated from the outside world of things. And there would be no "outside" for the Infinite. These people would have us believe that The Absolute emanated a Universe from Itself—which could contain nothing except that which was obtained from Itself—and then proceeded to gain experience from it. Having no "outside" from which it could obtain experiences and sentences and sensations, it proceeded to make (from Itself) an imitation one—that is what this answer amounts to. Can you accept it?

The whole trouble in all of these answers, or attempted answers, is that the answerer first conceives of the Absolute-Infinite Being, as a Relative-Finite Man, and then proceeds to explain what this Big Man would do. This is but an exaggerated form of anthropomorphism—the conception of God as a Man raised to great proportions. It is but an extension of the idea which gave birth to the savage conceptions of Deity as a cruel chief or mighty warrior, with human passions, hates, and revenge; love, passions, and desires.

Arising from the same cause, and akin to the theories advanced above are similar ones, which hold that the Absolute cannot dwell alone, but must forever bring forth souls from Itself—this was the idea of *Plotinus*, the Greek philosopher. Others have thought that the Infinite was possessed of such a consuming love, that It manifested objects upon which it could bestow Its affections. Others have thought that It was lonesome, and desired companionship. Some have spoken of the Absolute as "sacrificing" itself, in becoming Many, instead of remaining One. Others have taught that the Infinite somehow has become entangled in Its Manifestations, and had lost the knowledge of Its Oneness—hence their teachings of "I Am God." Others, holding to a similar idea, tell us that the Infinite is deliberately "masquerading" as the Many, in order to fool and mystify Itself—a show of Itself; by Itself, and for Itself! Is not this Speculative Metaphysics run wild? Can one in calm thought so regard the Infinite and Absolute Being—All-Wise—Causeless— All-Powerful—All-Present—All-Possessing— Lacking Nothing—Perfect One—as acting and performing thus, and from these motives? Is not this as childish as the childishness of the savage, and barbarians, in their Mumbo-Jumbo conceptions? Let us leave this phase of the subject.

The Higher Yogi Teachings hold to no such ideas or theories. It holds that the Answer to the Secret is vested in the Infinite alone, and that finite "guesses" regarding the "Why" are futile and pitiful. It holds that while one should use the Reason to the full, still there are phases of Being that can be considered only in Love, Faith, and Confidence in THAT from which All Things flow, and in which we live and move and have our being. It recognizes that the things of the Spirit, are known by the Mind. It explores the regions of the Universal Mind to its utmost limits, fearlessly—but it pauses before the Closed Door of The Spirit, reverently and lovingly.

But, remember this—that while the Higher Yogi Teachings contain no "guess," or speculative theory, regarding the "Why" of the Divine Manifestation, still they do not deny the existence of a "Why". In fact, they expressly hold that the Absolute Manifestation of the Many is in pursuance of some wondrous Divine Plan, and that the Unfoldment of the Plan proceeds along well-established and orderly lines, and according to Law. They trust in the Wisdom and Love of the Absolute Being, and manifest a perfect Confidence, Trust and Peaceful Patience in the Ultimate Justice, and Final Victory of the Divine Plan. No doubt disturbs this idea—it pays no attention to the apparent contradictions in the finite phenomenal world, but sees that all things are proceeding toward some far-away goal, and that "All is Well with the Universe".

But they do not think for a moment, or teach in the slightest degree, that all this Unfoldment, and Plan of the Universe, has

for its object any advantage, benefit or gain to the Absolute—
such a thought would be *folly*, for the Absolute is already
Perfect, and Its Perfection cannot be added to, or taken away
from. But they do positively teach that there is a great beneficial
purpose in all the Plan, accruing in the end to the developed
souls that have evolved through the workings of the plan. These
souls do not possess the qualities of the Infinite—they are Finite,
and thus are capable of receiving benefits; of growing,
developing, unfolding, attaining. And, therefore, the Yogis teach
that this building up of Great Souls seems to be the idea of the
Infinite, so far as may be gained from an observation of the
Workings of the Plan. The Absolute cannot *need these* Great
Souls for Its own pleasure, and therefore their building-up must
be for their own advantage, happiness and benefit.

The Yogis teach, on this subject, that there can be only ONE
Real Perfect Being—Perfect without experience—Perfect from
the Beginning—but only ONE! In other words, they teach that
there can be no such thing as Absolute Perfection, outside of the
Absolute Itself—and that not even the Absolute Being can create
another Absolute Being, for in that case there would be no
Absolute Being at all, but only *two Relative Beings*.

Think over this for a moment, and you will see its truth. The
ABSOLUTE must always be "the One without a Second", as the
Yogis express it—there cannot be *two* Perfect ones. And so, all
Finite Beings, being Finite, must work their way up toward the
plane of Perfection by The Path of Life, with all of its lessons,
tasks, cares, pains, and strivings. This is the only way open to
them—and even the Absolute cannot have it otherwise, and still
be the Absolute. There is a fine point here—the Absolute is All-
Powerful, but even that All-Power is not sufficient to enable It to
destroy Its Absolute Being. And so, you who have wondered,
perhaps you may now understand our words in the First Lesson
of this series, in which we said that the message of the Absolute
to some of the Illumined has been: "All is being done in the best
and only possible way—I am doing the best I can—all is well—
and in the end will so appear."

And, as we also said in that First Lesson: "The Absolute, instead
of being an indifferent and unmoved spectator to its own
creation, is a striving, longing, active, suffering, rejoicing,

315

feeling Spirit, partaking of the feelings of Its manifestations, rather than callously witnessing them. It lives in us—with us—through us. Back of all the pain in the world, may be found a great feeling and suffering love." And in this thought there is comfort to the doubting soul—peace to the troubled mind.

In the Sixth Lesson, we shall proceed to deliver to you the further

Message of Truth, concerning "how" the One Absolute manifests Its

Mental Images as Universe; Universal Life; and Forms and Shapes; and

Individualities, and Personalities. We had hoped to include the whole

Message in this Fifth Lesson, but now find that we have merely laid the

steps by which the student may reach the Essential Truth.

But, lest the student may be left in an uncertain state of mind, awaiting the conclusion of the consideration of the subject—and lest he may think that we intend teaching him that the Universe, and all in it, including himself are "Dreams," because we have said that All Things are Thought-Forms in the Mind of the Absolute—lest this misunderstanding may arise, we wish to add a few parting words to what we have said.

We wish to impress upon the mind of the student that though all Things are but Thought-Forms in the Mind of the Absolute Being, and that while it is true that the entire Universe of Universes is simply a Thought-Form held in the Mind of the Absolute—still this fact does not mean that all Things are "illusions" or "dreams." Remember this, now and forever, O Student—that that which is held in the Absolute Mind as a Thought-Form IS, and is all there IS, outside of the Absolute Itself. When the Absolute forms a Thought-Form, It forms it out of Its own mental substance—when the Absolute "holds anything in Its Mind," It holds it in Itself—for the Absolute is ALL-MIND.

The Absolute is not a material Being, from which Material Beings are created. It is a Spiritual Being—a Being whose Substance is akin to that which we call "Mind," only raised to Infinity and Absolute Perfection and Power. And this is the only way it can "create"—by creating a Thought-Form in Its Mental, or Spiritual Substance. The faintest "Thought" of the Absolute is more real and durable than anything that man can create—in fact, man can "create" nothing, for all the hard and real material he uses in his "creations," such as steel, diamonds, granite, are but some of the minor Forms, "thought" into being by the Absolute.

And also remember this, that the Absolute cannot "think" of anything, without putting Itself in that thing, as its Essence. Just as a man's Mental Images are not only *in* his mind, *but his mind is in them, also*.

Why, you doubting and timorous ones, does not even the finite "thinking" of Man manifest itself in physical and material changes of form and shape?—does not a man's every thought actually "create" physical forms and shapes, in his brain-cells and physical tissue? You who are reading these words— yea, *while* you are reading these words—are "creating" changes of form and shape in your brain-cells, and physical organism. Your mind is constantly at work, also, in building up your physical body, along the lines of the Instinctive Mind (see previous series of lessons)—you are mentally creating in a miniature universe, every moment of your life. And yet, the idea of the Absolute "creating" a Universe by pure Thought, in Its own Mind, and thereafter causing the work of the Universe to proceed according to Law, by simply "Willing" it so, causes you to wonder, and perhaps to doubt.

O, ye of little faith, you would deny to the Absolute even the power you possess yourself. You plan things in your mind every day, and then proceed to cause them to appear in material manifestation, and yet you doubt the ability of the Absolute to do likewise. Why even the poets, or writers of fiction, create characters in their minds—and these seem so real, that even you imagine them to be actual entities, and you weep over their pains, and smile at their joys—and yet all this is on the finite plane. Why, even the "imaginations" of your petty finite, undeveloped minds, have sufficient power to make your physical bodies sick, or well, or even to cause you to "die," from some imagined ailment. And yet you doubt the power of the Absolute, to "think" things into being! You tiny students in the great

Kindergarten of Life—you must learn better lessons from your little blocks and games. And you *will*—this is the Law.

And you who are filled with the sense of your smallness, and "unreality"—know you that so long as you are "held in the Mind of God," then so long are you "remembered" by Him. And so long as you are remembered by Him, no real harm can befall you, and your Reality is second only to His own. Even though you pass out of your mortal frame—doth he remember you in His Mind, and keeping you there, he holds you safe and unharmed. The greatest satisfaction that can come to one, is to be able to fully realize that he, or she, is held firmly IN THE MIND OF THE INFINITE BEING. To such comes the knowledge that in THAT LIFE there can be NO DEATH.

Peace be with you in this Realization. May you make it your own!

THE SIXTH LESSON - Within the Mind of the ONE

In our last lesson we gave you the Inner Teachings of the Yogi Philosophy, relating to the real nature of the Universe, and all that is therein contained. We trust that you have pondered well and carefully the statements contained in that lesson, for in them is to be found the essence of the highest Yogi teachings. While we have endeavored to present these high truths to you in the simplest possible form, yet unless your minds have been trained to grasp the thought, you may have trouble in fully assimilating the essence of the teachings. But, be not discouraged, for your mind will gradually unfold like the flower, and the Sun of Truth will reach into its inmost recesses. Do not be troubled if your comprehension seems dull, or your progress slow, for all things will come to you in time. You cannot escape the Truth, nor can the Truth escape you. And it will not come to you one moment sooner than you are ready to receive it, nor will it be delayed one moment in its coming, when you are ready for it. Such is the Law, and none can escape it, nor alter it, nor modify it. All is Well, and All is Under the Law—nothing ever "happens."

To many, the thought that the Universe and all that is therein contained, are simply "Thought Forms" in the Infinite Mind—Mental Creations of the Absolute, may seem startling, and a sense of unreality may pervade one. This is inevitable, but the reaction will come. To some who have grasped this mighty truth there has come a feeling that "All is Nothing," which idea is embodied in their teachings and writings. But this is merely the Negative Phase of the Truth—there is a Positive Phase which comes as one advances.

The Negative Phase shows us that all that we have considered as real and permanent—the foundations of the Universe itself—is but a mental image in the mind of the Absolute, and therefore lacks the fundamental reality that we had previously associated with it. And realizing this, we are at first apt to feel that, indeed "all is nothing," and to fall into a state of apathy, and lack of desire to play our part in the world. But, then, happily the reaction sets in, sooner or later, and we begin to see the Positive Phase of the Truth. This Positive Phase shows us that while all the forms, shapes, and phenomena of the Universe are but parts

319

of a great show-world, still the *essence of* all must be Reality, itself, else there would not be even the "appearance" of a Universe. Before a thing can be a Mental Image, there must be a Mind to hold that Mental Image, and a BEING to possess that Mind. And, the very essence of that BEING must pervade and be immanent in every Image in that Mind. Just as *You* are really in your Mental Images, as well as they in You, so must the Absolute be *in* Its Mental Images, or Creations, or Thought Forms, as truly as they are in the Mind of the Absolute. Do you see this plainly? Think well over it—ponder it well—for in it lies the Truth.

And so, this Positive Phase of the Truth, is far from depressing—it is the most stimulating conception one can hold, if he but grasps it in its entirety and fulness. Even if it be true that all these shapes, and forms, and appearances, and phenomena, and personalities, be but illusion as compared to the inner Reality—what of it? Are you not then assured that the Spirit within Yourself is the Spirit of the Absolute—that the Reality within You is the Reality of the Absolute—that you ARE, because the Absolute IS, and cannot be otherwise? Does not the Peace, and Calm, and Security, and Bliss that comes to you with this Realization, far more than counterbalance the petty nothings that you have discarded? We think that there can be but one answer to this, when you have fully Realized the Truth.

What gives you the greatest Satisfaction and Content in Life? Let us see. Well, there is the Satisfaction of Immortality. The human mind instinctively craves this. Well, what that even the highest finite conceptions of Future Life have given you, can compare with the assurance of Actual Being, in and of the Absolute? What are your petty conceptions of "heavens," "paradises," "happy-hunting-grounds," "divine regions of the blessed," and the other ideas of the various religious sects, when compared with the conceptions of your Infinite and Eternal Existence in Spirit—your relation with The One—that conception of Infinite Wisdom, Being, and Bliss? When you grasp this truth, you will see that you are "in Eternity right Now," and are Immortal even this moment, as you have always been.

Now, what we have said above is not intended to deny the "heaven-worlds," or planes. On the contrary, you will find much in the teachings regarding these, which the Yogis enter into with much detail. But, we mean that back of all the "heavens" and "celestial planes," there is a still higher state of being being—the "Absolute Being." Even the "heavens," and "heaven-worlds," and regions of the *Devas*, or Archangels, are but relative states—there is a state higher than even these exalted relative states, and that is the State of the Conscious Unity and Identity with the One. When one enters into that State, he becomes more than Man—more than gods—he is then "in the bosom of the Father." And now, before proceeding to a consideration of the phenomenal manifestation of the Absolute—the evolving of the Universe in the Infinite Mind—we will again call your attention to the fact that underlies all the Universe of forms, shapes and appearances, and that is, as we stated in our last lesson:

All Manifestations and Emanations of the Absolute are Mental Creations of the Absolute—Thought-Forms held in the Infinite Mind—the Infinite Spirit in them—and they in the Infinite Spirit. And, the only Real Thing about Man is the Spirit involved in the Thought-Form—the rest is mere Personality, which changes and ceases to be. The Spirit in the Soul of Man, is the Soul of the Soul, which is never born; never changeth; never dieth—this is The Real Self of Man, in which, indeed, he is "One with the Father."

And, now let us consider the Yogi Teachings regarding the creation of the Universe, and the evolution of the living forms thereon. We shall endeavor to give you the story as plainly as may be, holding fast to the main thought, and avoiding the side-paths of details, etc., so far as is possible.

In the first place, we must imagine ourselves back to the beginning of a "Day of Brahm,"—the first dawn of that Day, which is breaking from the darkness of a "Night of Brahm." Before we proceed further, we must tell you something about these "Days and Nights of Brahm," of which you have seen much mention in the Oriental writings.

The Yogi Teachings contain much regarding the "Days and Nights of Brahm;" the "In-breathing and Out-breathing of the Creative Principle;" the periods of "*Manvantara*," and the periods of "*Pralaya*." This thought runs through all the Oriental thought, although in different forms, and with various interpretations. The thought refers to the occult truth that there is in Cosmic Nature alternate periods of Activity and Inactivity—Days and Nights—In-breathings and Out-breathings—Wakefulness and Sleep. This fundamental law manifests in all Nature, from Universes to Atoms. Let us see it now in its application to Universes.

At this point we would call the attention of the student that in many of the presentations of the Hindu Teachings the writers speak as if the Absolute, *Itself*, were subject to this law of Rhythm, and had Its Periods of Rest and Work, like Its manifestations. This is incorrect. The highest teachings do not so hold, although at first glance it would so appear. The teaching really is that while the Creative Principle manifests this rhythm, still even this principle, great though it be, is a manifestation of the Absolute, and not the Absolute itself. The highest Hindu teachings are firm and unmistakable about this point.

And, another point, in which there is much mistaken teaching. In the periods of Creative Inactivity in a Universe it must not be supposed that there is no Activity anywhere. On the contrary, there is never a cessation of Activity on the part of the Absolute. While it is Creative Night in one Universe, or System of Universes, there is intense activity of Mid-Day in others. When we say "The Universe" we mean the Universe of Solar Systems—millions of such systems—that compose the particular universe of which we have any knowledge. The highest teachings tell us that this Universe is but one of a System of Universes, millions in number—and that this System is but one, in a higher System, and so on and on, to infinity. As one Hindu Sage hath said: "Well do we know that the Absolute is constantly creating Universes in Its Infinite Mind—and constantly destroying them—and, though millions upon millions of aeons intervene between creation and destruction, yet doth it seem less than the twinkle of an eye to The Absolute One."

And so the "Day and Night of Brahm" means only the statement of the alternating periods of Activity and Inactivity in some one particular Universe, amidst the Infinite Universality. You will find a mention of these periods of Activity and Inactivity in the "*Bhagavad Gita*," the great Hindu epic. The following quotations, and page references, relate to the edition published

322

by the Yogi Publication Society, which was compiled and adapted by the writer of these lessons. In that edition of the "*Bhagavad Gita*," on page 77, you will find these words attributed to *Krishna*, the Absolute One in human incarnation: "The worlds and universes—yea, even the world of Brahm, a single day of which is like unto a thousand *Yugas* (four billion years of the earth), and his night as much—these worlds must come and go... The Days of Brahm are succeeded by the Nights of Brahm. In these Brahmic Days all things emerge from invisibility, and become visible. And, on the coming of the Brahmic Night, all visible things again melt into invisibility. The Universe having once existed, melteth away; and lo! is again re-created."

And, in the same edition, on page 80, we find these words, attributed to the same speaker:

"At the end of a *Kalpa*—a Day of Brahm—a period of Creative Activity—I withdraw into my nature, all things and beings. And, at the beginning of another *Kalpa*, I emanate all things and beings, and re-perform my creative act."

We may say here, in passing, that Modern Science now holds to the theory of periods of Rhythmic Change; of Rise and Fall; of Evolution and Dissolution.

It holds that, beginning at some time in the past aeons of time, there was the beginning of an upward or evolutionary movement, which is now under way; and that, according to the law of Nature, there must come a time when the highest point will be reached, and then will come the beginning of the downward path, which in time must come to an end, being succeeded by a long period of inactivity, which will then be followed by the beginning of a new period of Creative Activity and Evolution—"a Day of Brahm."

This thought of this law of Rhythm, in its Universal form, has been entertained by the thinkers of all times and races. Herbert Spencer expressly held to it in his "First Principles," expressing it in many ways akin to this: "Evolution must come to a close in complete equilibrium or rest;" and again, "It is not inferable from the general progress towards equilibrium, that a state of universal quiescence or death will be reached; but that if a process of reasoning ends in that conclusion, a further process of reasoning points to renewals of activity and life;" and again, "Rhythm in the totality of changes—alternate eras of evolution and dissolution." The Ancient Western Philosophers also indulged in this idea. Heraclitus taught that the universe manifested itself in cycles, and the Stoics taught that "the world moves in an endless cycle, through the same stages." The followers of Pythagoras went even further, and claimed that "the succeeding worlds resemble each other, down to the minutest detail," this latter idea, however—the idea of the "Eternal Recurrence"—while held by a number of thinkers, is not held by the Yogi teachers, who teach infinite progression—an Evolution of Evolution, as it were. The Yogi teachings, in this last mentioned particular, are resembled more by the line of Lotze's thinking, as expressed in this sentence from his *Micro-cosmos:* "The series of Cosmic Periods, ... each link of which is bound together with every other; ... the successive order of these sections shall compose the unity of an onward-advancing melody." And, so through the pages of Heraclitus, the Stoics, the Pythagoreans, Empedocles, Virgil, down to the present time, in Nietzsche, and his followers, we find this thought of Universal Rhythm—that fundamental conception of the ancient Yogi Philosophy.

And, now, returning to the main path of our thought—let us stand here at the beginning of the dawn of a Day of Brahm. It is verily a beginning, for there is nothing to be seen—there is nothing but Space. No trace of Matter, Force or Mind, as we know these terms. In that portion of Infinite Space—that is, of course, in that "portion" of the Infinite Mind of the Absolute One, for even Space is a "conception" of that Mind, there is "Nothing." This is "the darkest moment, just before the dawn." Then comes the breaking of the dawn of the Brahmic Day. The Absolute begins the "creation" of a Universe. And, how does It create? There can be no creation of something out of nothing. And except the Absolute Itself there is but Nothing.

Therefore The Absolute must create the Universe out of Its own "substance," if we can use the word "substance" in this connection. "Substance" means, literally, "that which stands under," being derived from the two Latin words, *sub*, meaning "under," and *stare*, meaning "to stand." The English word

324

"understand" means, literally, "to stand under"—the two words really meaning the same. This is more than a coincidence.

So the Absolute must create the Universe from its own substance, we have seen. Well, what is this "substance" of the Absolute? Is it Matter? No! for Matter we know to be, in itself, merely a manifestation of Force, or Energy. Then, is it Force or Energy? No! because Force and Energy, in itself, cannot possess Mind, and we must think of the Absolute as possessing Mind, for it manifests Mind, and what is manifested must be in the Manifestor, or Manifesting Agent. Then this "substance" must be Mind? Well, yes, in a way—and yet not Mind as we know it, finite and imperfect. But something like Mind, only Infinite in degree and nature—something sufficiently greater than Mind as we know it, to admit of it being the Cause of Mind. But, we are compelled to think of it as "Infinite Mind," for our finite Minds can hold no higher conception. So we are content to say that this "substance" from which the Absolute must create the Universe is a something that we will call Infinite Mind. Fix this in your mind, please, as the first step in our conception.

But, how can the Infinite Mind be used to create finite minds, shapes, forms, and things, without it being lessened in quantity— how can you take something from something, and still have the original something left? An impossibility! And, we cannot think of the Absolute as "dividing Itself up" into two or more portions—for if such were the case, there would be two or more Absolutes, or else None. There cannot be two Absolutes, for if the Absolute were to divide itself so there would be no Absolute, but only two Relatives—two Finites instead of One Infinite. Do you see the absurdity?

Then how can this work of Creation be accomplished, in view of these difficulties which are apparent even to our finite minds? You may thresh this question over and over again in your minds—men have done so in all times—and you will not find the answer except in the fundamental Idea of the Yogi Teachings. And this Fundamental Idea is that the creation is purely a Mental Creation, and the Universe is the Mental Image, or Thought-Form, in the Mind of the Absolute—in the Infinite Mind, itself. No other "creation" is possible. And so this, say the Yogi Masters, this is the Secret of Universal Creation. The

Universe is *of*, and *in*, the Infinite Mind, and this is the only way it could be so. So, fix in your mind this second step in our conception.

But then, you ask us, from whence comes Force, Matter, and Finite Mind?

Well asked, good student—your answer shall be forthcoming. Here it is.

Finite Mind; Force or Energy; and Matter; in themselves have no existence. They are merely Mental Images, or Thought-Forms in the Infinite Mind of the Absolute. Their whole existence and appearance depends upon their Mental Conception and Retention in the Infinite Mind. In It they have their birth, rise, growth, decline and death.

Then what is Real about ME, you may ask—surely I have a vivid consciousness of Reality—is this merely an illusion, or shadow? No, not so! that sense of Reality which you possess and which every creature or thing possesses—that sense of "I Am"— is the perception by the Mental Image of the Reality of its Essence—and that Essence is the Spirit. And that Spirit is the SUBSTANCE OF THE ABSOLUTE embodied in Its conception, the Mental Image. It is the perception by the Finite, of its Infinite Essence. Or, the perception by the Relative of its Absolute Essence. Or, the perception by You, or I, or any other man or woman, of the Real Self, which underlies all the sham self or Personality. It is the reflection of the Sun, in the dew-drop, and thousands of dew-drops—seemingly thousands of Suns, and yet but One. And yet, that reflection of the Sun in the dewdrop is more than a "reflection," for it is the substance of the Sun itself—and yet the Sun shines on high, one and undivided, yet manifesting in millions of dew-drops. It is only by figures of speech that we can speak of the Unspeakable Reality.

To make it perhaps plainer to some of you, let us remind you that even in your finite Mental Images there is evident many forms of life. You may think of a moving army of thousands of men. And yet the only "I" in these men is your own "I." These characters in your mind move and live and have their being, and yet there is nothing in them except "You!" The characters of Shakespeare, Dickens, Thackeray, Balzac, and the rest, were such strong Mental Images that not only their creators were carried away by their power, and apparent ability, but even you who read of them, many years after, perhaps, feel the apparent reality, and weep, or smile, or grow angry over their actions. And, yet there was no Hamlet, outside of Shakespeare's mind; no Micawber outside of Dickens; no Pere Goriot outside of Balzac.

These illustrations are but finite examples of the Infinite, but still they will give you an idea of the truth that we are trying to unfold in your mind. But you must not imagine that You and I, and all others, and things, are but mere "imaginations," like *our* created characters—that would be a most unhappy belief. The mental creations held by You and I, and other finite minds, are but *finite creations of finite minds*, while WE, ourselves, are the finite creations of an INFINITE MIND. While our, and Dickens', and Balzac's, and Shakespeare's creations live and move and have their being, they have no other "I" than our Finite Minds, while we, the characters in the Divine Drama, Story, or Epic, have for our "I"—our Real Self—the ABSOLUTE REALITY. They have merely a background of our finite personalities, and minds, before which they may desport themselves. until, alas! the very background fades away to dust, and both background and shadows disappear. But, we have behind our personalities the Eternal Background of Reality, which changeth not, neither doth it Disappear. Shadows on a screen though our Personalities may be, yet the Screen is Real and Eternal. Take away the finite screen and the shadows disappear—but our Screen remains forever.

We *are* Mental Images in the Infinite Mind—the Infinite Mind holds us safe—we cannot be lost—we cannot be hurt—we can never disappear, unless we be absorbed in the Infinite Mind itself, and then we STILL ARE! The Infinite Mind never forgets—it never can overlook us—it is aware of our presence, and being, always. We are safe—we are secure—we ARE! Just as we could not be created from Nothing—so we cannot be converted into Nothing. We are in the All—and there is no outside.

At the dawn of the Brahmic Day, The Absolute begins the creation of a new Universe, or the recreation of one, just as you may care to state it. The highest Yogi Teachings inform us that the information relating to this event (which is, of course, beyond the personal knowledge of man as we know him) has been passed down to the race from teachers, who have received it from still higher teachers, and so on, and on and on, higher and higher, until it is believed to have originated with some of those wonderfully developed souls which have visited the earth from higher planes of Being, of which there are many. In these lessons we are making no claims of this sort, but pass on the teachings to you, believing that their truth will appeal to those who are ready for them, without any attempt to attribute to them an authority such as just mentioned. Our reference to this high source of the teachings was made because of its general acceptance in the Eastern countries, and by occultists generally.

The Yogi teachings inform us that, in the Beginning, The Absolute formed a Mental Image, or Thought-Form, of an Universal Mind—that is, of an Universal Principle of Mind. And here the distinction is made between this Universal Mind Principle, or Universal Mind-Stuff, as some have called it, and the Infinite Mind itself. The Infinite Mind is something infinitely above this creation of the Universal Mind Principle, the latter being as much an "emanation" as is Matter. Let there be no mistake about this. The Infinite Mind is Spirit—the Universal Mind Principle is "Mind-Stuff" of which all Finite Mind is a part. This Universal Mind Principle was the first conception of The Absolute, in the process of the creation of the Universe. It was the "Stuff" from which all Finite Mind forms, and is formed. It is the Universal Mental Energy. Know it as such—but do not confound it with Spirit, which we have called Infinite Mind, because we had no other term. There is a subtle difference here, which is most important to a careful understanding of the subject.

The Yogi teachings inform us that from this Mental Principle there was developed the Universal Principle of Force or Energy. And that from this Universal Force Principle there developed the Universal Principle of Matter. The Sanscrit terms for these Three Principles are as follows: *Chitta*, or the Universal Mind Substance, or Principle; *Prana*, or the Universal Energy Principle; and *Akasa*, or the Universal Principle of Matter. We have spoken of these Three Principles, or Three Great Manifestations, in our "Advanced Course" of lessons, which

328

followed our "Fourteen Lessons," several years ago, but it becomes necessary for us to refer to them again at this place in connection with the present presentation of the subject. As was stated in the lessons just mentioned, these Three Manifestations, or Principles, are really one, and shade into each other. This matter has been fully touched upon in the concluding lessons of the aforesaid "Advanced Course," to which we must refer you for further details, in order to avoid repetition here. You will find a wonderful correspondence between these centuries-old Yogi teachings, and the latest conceptions of Modern Science.

Well, to return to the main path once more, the Teachings inform us that The Absolute "thought" into being—that is, held the Mental Image, or Thought-Form, of—*Chitta*, or Universal Mind Principle. This *Chitta* was finite, of course, and was bound and governed by the Laws of Finite Mind, imposed upon it by the Will of The Absolute. Everything that is Finite is governed by Laws imposed by the great LAW which we call The Absolute. Then began the Great INVOLUTION which was necessary before Evolution was possible. The word "Involve," you know, means "to wrap up; to cover; to hide; etc.;" and the word "Evolve" means "to unwrap; to unfold; to un-roll; etc." Before a thing can be "evolved," or "unfolded," it must first have been "involved" or "folded-in, or wrapped up, etc." Everything must be "involved" before it can be "evolved;" remember this, please—it is true on all planes, mental, physical, and spiritual. A thing must be "put in" before it may be "taken out." This truth, if remembered and applied to metaphysical problems, will throw the clearest light upon the darkest problems. Make it your own. Therefore before the process of Evolution from the gross forms of Matter up to the higher, and then on to the Mental, from higher to higher, and then on the Spiritual plane—that Evolution which we see being performed before our sight today—before that Evolution became possible there was a necessary Involution, or "wrapping-up." The Spirit of the Absolute first "involved" itself in its Mental Image; Thought-Form, or Creation, of the Mind Principle, just as you may "involve" yourself in an earnest thought in deep meditation. Did you never "lose yourself" in thought, or "forget yourself" in an idea? Have you not spoken of yourself as having been "wrapped in thought?" Well, then you can see something of what is here meant, at least so far as the process of "involution" is concerned. You involve yourself in your meditations—the Absolute involves Itself in Its Mental Creations—but, remember the one is Finite, and the other Infinite, and the results are correspondingly weak or strong. Obeying the laws imposed upon it, the Mental Principle then involved itself in the Energy Principle, or *Prana*, and the Universal Energy sprang into existence. Then, in obedience to the same Laws, the *Prana*involved itself in the *Akasa*, or Universal Matter Principle. Of course each "involving" practically "created" the "wrapper," "sheath" of the lower Principle. Do you see this? Each, therefore, depends upon the Principle higher than itself, which becomes its "Parent Principle," as the Yogis express it. And in this process of Involution the extreme form of Matter was reached before the process of Evolution became possible. The extreme form of gross Matter is not known to us today, on this planet, for we have passed beyond it. But the teachings inform us that such forms were as much grosser that the grossest Matter that we know today, as the latter is gross in comparison with the most ethereal vapors known to Modern Science. The human mind cannot grasp this extreme of the scale, any more than it can the extreme high degree of manifestation.

At this point we must call your attention to certain occult teachings, widely disseminated, which the highest Yogi teachers discountenance, and contradict. We allude to the teaching that in the process of Involution there was a "degeneration" or "devolution" from higher to lower forms of life, until the gross state of Matter was reached. Such a teaching is horrible, when considered in detail. It would mean that The Absolute deliberately created high forms of life, arch-angels, and higher than these—gods in fact—and then caused them to "devolve" until the lowest state was reached. This would mean the exact opposite of Evolution, and would mean a "going down" in accordance with the Divine Will, just as Evolution is a "going up" in accordance with the Divine Will.

This is contrary to man's best instincts, and the advanced Yogi teachings inform us that it is but an illusion or error that men have created by endeavoring to solve spiritual mysteries by purely intellectual processes. The true teaching is that the process of Involution was accomplished by a Principle involving itself in the lower Principle created within itself, and so on until the lowest plane was reached. Note the difference—"Principles as Principles" did this, and not as Individual Forms of Life or Being. There was no more a "devolution" in this process than there was in The Absolute involving itself in the Mental Image of the Mind Principle. There was no "devolution" or "going down"—only an "involution" or "wrapping up," of Principle, within Principle—the Individual Life not having as yet appeared, and not being possible of appearance until the Evolutionary process began.

We trust that we have made this point clear to you, for it is an important matter. If the Absolute first made higher beings, and then caused them to "devolute" into lower and lower forms, then the whole process would be a cruel, purposeless thing, worthy only of some of the base conceptions of Deity conceived of by men in their ignorance. No! the whole effort of the Divine Will seems to be in the direction of "raising up" Individual Egos to higher and still higher forms. And in order to produce such Egos the process of "Involution" of Principles seems to have been caused, and the subsequent wonderful Evolutionary process instituted. What that "Reason" is, is Unknowable, as we have said over and over again. We cannot pry into the Infinite Mind of the Absolute, but we may form certain conclusions by observing and studying the Laws of the Universe, which seem to be moving in certain directions. From the manifested Will of the Divine One, we may at least hazard an idea as to its purposes. And these purposes seem to be always in an "upward" lifting and evolution. Even the coming of the "Night of Brahm" is no exception to this statement, as we shall see in future lessons. From the starting of the process of Involution from the Mental Principle, down to the extreme downward point of the grossest Manifestation of Matter, there were many stages. From the highest degree of the Finite Mind, down to lower and still lower degrees; then on to the plane of Force and Energy, from higher to lower degrees of Principle within Principle; then on to the plane of Matter, the Involutionary urge proceeded to work. When the plane of Matter was reached, it, of course, showed its highest degree of manifested Matter—the most subtle form of Ether, or *Akasa*. Then down, down, down, went the degrees of Matter, until the grossest possible form was reached, and then there was a moment's pause, before the Evolutionary process, or upward-movement, began. The impulse of the Original Will, or Thought, had exhausted its downward urge, and now began the upward urge or tendency. But here was manifested a new feature.

This new feature was "The Tendency toward Individualization." During the downward trend the movement was *en masse*, that is, by Principle as *Principle*, without any "splitting up" into portions, or centers. But with the first upward movement there was evidenced a tendency toward creating Centers of Energy, or Units of activity, which then manifested itself, as the evolutionary movement continued, from electrons to atoms; from atoms to man. The gross matter was used as material for the formation of finer and more complex forms; and these in turn combined, and formed higher, and so on, and on. And the forms of Energy operated in the same way. And the manifestations of centers of Mind or consciousness in the same way. But all in connection. Matter, Energy and Mind formed a Trinity of Principles, and worked in connection. And the work was always in the direction of causing higher and higher "forms" to arise— higher and higher Units—higher and higher Centers. But in every form, center or unit, there was manifested the Three Principles, Mind, Energy, and Matter. And within each was the ever present Spirit. For Spirit *must* be in All—just as All must be in Spirit.

And, so this Evolutionary process has continued ever since, and must continue for aeons yet. The Absolute is raising itself up into Itself higher and higher Egos, and is providing them with higher and higher sheaths in which to manifest. And, as we shall see in these lessons, as we progress, this evolution is not only along the physical lines, but also along the mental. And it concerns itself not only with "bodies," but with "souls," which also evolve, from time to time, and bodies are given these souls in order that they may work out their evolution. And the whole end and aim of it all seems to be that Egos may reach the stage where they are conscious of the Real Self—of the Spirit within them, and its relation to the Spirit of the Absolute, and then go on and on and on, to planes of life and being, and activities of which even the most advanced of the race may only dream.

As some of the Ancient Yogi Teachers have said: "Men are evolving into super-men; and super-men into gods; and gods into super-gods; and super-gods into Something still higher; until from the lowest bit of matter enclosing life, unto the highest being—yea, even unto The Absolute—there is an Infinite Ladder of Being—and yet the One Spirit pervades all; is in all, as the all is in It."

The Creative Will, of which we have spoken in these lessons, is in full operation all through Life. The Natural Laws are laws of Life imposed by The Absolute in his Mental Image. They are the Natural Laws of this Universe, just as other Universes have other Laws. But The Absolute Itself has no Laws affecting It—It, in Itself *is* LAW.

And these Laws of Life, and Nature, along its varying planes, Material, of Energy; and Mental; are also, in the Divine Mind, else they would not be at all, even in appearance. And when they are transcended, or apparently defied by some man of advanced development, it is only because such a man is able to rise above the plane upon which such laws are operative. But even this transcending is, in itself, in accordance with some higher law. And so, we see that All, high and low—good and bad—simple or complex—all are contained Within the Mind of the One. Gods, angels, adepts, sages, heavens, planes,—all, everything— is within the Universe, and the Universe is Within the Mind of the One. And all is proceeding in accordance with Law. And all is moving upward and onward, along the lines of Evolution. All is Well. We are held firmly in The Mind of the One.

And, just as the tendency was from the general Principle toward the particular Individual Soul, so is there a Reconciliation later on, for the Individual soul, as it develops and unfolds, loses its sense of Separateness, and begins to feel its identity with the One Spirit, and moves along the lines of unfoldment, until it becomes in Conscious Union with God. Spiritual Evolution does not mean the "growth of the Spirit," for the Spirit cannot grow—it is already Perfect. The term means the unfoldment of the

Individual Mind, until it can recognize the Spirit Within. Let us close this lesson with the
CENTRAL THOUGHT.
There is but ONE. That ONE is Spirit. In the Infinite Mind of that ONE SPIRIT there arose the Mental Image or Thought-Form of this Universe. Beginning with the Thought of the Principle in Mind; and passing on to the Principle of Energy; and then on to the Principle of Matter; proceeded the Involutionary Process of Creation. Then, upward began the Evolutionary Process, and Individual Centers or Units were formed. And the tendency, and evolutionary urge is ever in the direction of "unfolding" within the Ego of the Realization of the Indwelling Spirit. As we throw off sheath after sheath, we approach nearer and nearer to the SPIRIT within us, which is the One Spirit pervading all things. This is the Meaning of Life—the Secret of Evolution. All the Universe is contained Within the Mind of The One. There is Nothing outside of that Infinite Mind. There is no Outside, for the One is All in All; Space, Time, and Laws, being but Mental Images in that Mind, as are likewise all shapes and forms, and phenomena. And as the Ego unfolds into a realization of Itself—Its Real Self—so does its Wisdom and Power expand. It thus enters into a greater and greater degree of its Inheritance. Within the Mind of the One, is All there is. And I, and Thou, and All Things are HERE within that Infinite Mind. We are always "held in Mind" by The Absolute—are always safe here. There is nothing to harm us, in Reality, for our Real Self is the Real Self of the Infinite Mind. All is Within the Mind of the One. Even the tiniest atom is under the Law, and protected by the Law. And the LAW is All there Is. And in that Law we may rest Content and Unafraid. May this Realization be YOURS.
PEACE BE WITH YOU ALL.

THE SEVENTH LESSON - Cosmic Evolution

We have now reached a most interesting point in this course of lessons, and a period of fascinating study lies before us from now until the close of the course. We have acquainted ourselves with the fundamental principles, and will now proceed to witness these principles in active operation. We have studied the Yogi Teachings concerning the Truth underlying all things, and shall now pass on to a consideration of the process of Cosmic Evolution; the Cyclic Laws; the Law of Spiritual Evolution, or Reincarnation; the Law of Spiritual Cause and Effect, or *Karma*; etc. In this lesson we begin the story of the upward progress of the Universe, and its forms, shapes, and forces, from the point of the "moment's pause" following the ceasing of the process of Involution—the point at which Cosmic Evolution begins. Our progress is now steadily upward, so far as the evolution of Individual Centres is concerned. We shall see the principles returning to the Principle—the centres returning to the great Centre from which they emanated during the process of Involution. We shall study the long, gradual, but steady ascent of Man, in his journey toward god-hood. We shall see the Building of an Universe, and the Growth of the Soul.

In our last lesson we have seen that at the dawn of a Brahmic Day, the Absolute begins the creation of a new Universe. The Teachings inform us that in the beginning, the Absolute forms a Mental Image, or Thought-Form of an Universal Mind Principle, or Universal Mind-Stuff, as some of the teachers express it. Then this Universal Mind Principle creates within itself the Universal Energy Principle. Then this Universal Energy Principle creates within itself the Universal Matter Principle. Thus, Energy is a product of Mind; and Matter a product of Energy.

The Teachings then further inform us that from the rare, tenuous, subtle form of Matter in which the Universal Matter Principle first appeared, there was produced forms of Matter less rare; and so by easy stages, and degrees, there appeared grosser and still grosser forms of matter, until finally there could be no further involution into grosser forms, and the Involutionary Process ceased. Then ensued the "moment's pause" of which the Yogi

335

teachers tell us. At that point Matter existed as much grosser that the grossest form of Matter now known to us, as the latter is when compared to the most subtle vapors known to science. It is impossible to describe these lower forms of matter, for they have ages since disappeared from view, and we would have no words with which to describe them. We can understand the situation only by comparisons similar to the above.

Succeeding the moment's pause, there began the Evolutionary Process, or Cosmic Evolution, which has gone on ever since, and which will go on for ages to come. From the grossest forms of Matter there evolved forms a little more refined, and so on and on. From the simple elementarv forms, evolved more complex and intricate forms. And from these forms combinations began to be formed. And the urge was ever upward.

But remember this, that all of this Evolutionary Process is but a Returning Home. It is the Ascent after the Descent. It is not a Creation but an Unfoldment. The Descent was made by principles as principles—the Ascent is being made by Individualized Centres evolved from the principles. Matter manifests finer and finer forms, and exhibits a greater and greater subservience to Energy or Force. And Energy or Force shows a greater and greater degree of "mind" in it. But, remember this, that there is Mind in even the grossest form of Matter. This must be so, for what springs from a thing must contain the elements of its cause.

And the Cosmic Evolution continues, and must continue for aeons of time. Higher and higher forms of Mind are being manifested, and still higher and higher forms will appear in the scale, as the process continues. The evolution is not only along material lines, but has passed on to the mental planes, and is now operating along the spiritual lines as well. And the end, and aim seems to be that each Ego, after the experiences of many lives, may unfold and develop to a point where it may become conscious of its Real Self, and realize its identity with the One Life, and the Spirit.

At this point we may be confronted with the objection of the student of material science, who will ask why we begin our consideration of Cosmic Evolution at a point in which matter has reached the limit of its lowest vibrations, manifesting in the grossest possible form of matter. These students may point to the fact that Science begins its consideration of evolution with the *nebulae*, or faint cloudlike, vaporous matter, from which the planets were formed. But there is only an apparent contradiction here. The *nebulae* were part of the Process of Involution, and Science is right when it holds that the gross forms were produced from the finer. But the process of change from finer to grosser was *Involution*, not Evolution. Do you see the difference? Evolution begins at the point when the stage of Unfoldment commenced. When the gross forms begin to yield to the new upward urge, and unfold into finer forms—then begins Evolution.

We shall pass over the period of Evolution in which Matter was evolving into finer and still finer forms, until at last it reached a degree of vibration capable of supporting that which we call "life." Of course there is "life" in all matter—even in the atom, as we have shown in previous lessons. But when we speak of "life," as we now do, we mean what are generally called "living forms." The Yogi Teachings inform us that the lowest forms of what we call "life" were evolved from forms of high crystal life, which indeed they very much resemble. We have spoken of this resemblance, in the previous lessons of this series. And, so we shall begin at the point where "living forms" began.

Speaking now of our own planet, the Earth, we find matter emerging from the molten state in which it manifested for ages. Gradually cooling and stratifying, the Earth contained none of those forms that we call living forms. The temperature of the Earth in that period is estimated at about 15,000 times hotter than boiling water, which would, of course, render impossible the existence of any of the present known forms of life. But the Yogi Teachings inform us that even in the molten mass there were elementary forms that were to become the ancestral forms of the later living forms. These elementary forms were composed of a vaporous, peculiar form of matter, of minute size,—little more than the atoms, in fact, and yet, just a little more advanced. From these elementary forms, there gradually evolved, as the Earth cooled and solidified, other forms, and so on until at last the first "living form" manifested.

As the globe cooled at the poles, there was gradually created a tropical climate, in which the temperature was sufficiently cool to support certain rudimentary forms of life. In the rocks in the far northern latitudes, there are found abundant traces of fossils, which goes to prove the correctness of the Yogi Teachings of the origin of life at the north pole, from which the living forms gradually spread south toward the equator, as the Earth's surface cooled.

The elementary evolving life forms were of a very simple structure, and were but a degree above the crystals. They were composed of identically the same substance as the crystals, *the only difference being that they displayed a greater degree of mind.* For that matter, even the highest physical form known to us today is composed of simple chemical materials. And these chemical materials are obtained, either directly or indirectly, from the air, water, or earth. The principal materials composing the physical bodies of plants, animals, and man, are oxygen, carbon, hydrogen, nitrogen, with a still smaller proportion of sulphur and phosphorus, and traces of a few other elements. The material part of all living things is alike—the difference lies in the degree of Mind controlling the matter in which it is embodied.

Of these physical materials, carbon is the most important to the living forms. It seems to possess properties capable of drawing to it the other elements, and forcing them into service. From carbon proceeds what is called "protoplasm," the material of which the cells of animal and vegetable life is composed. From protoplasm the almost infinite varieties of living forms have been built up by the process of Evolution, working gradually and by easy stages. Every living form is made up, or composed, of a multitude of single cells, and their combinations. And every form originates in a single cell which rapidly multiplies and reproduces itself until the form of the amoeba; the plant; the animal; the man, is completed. All living forms are but a single cell multiplied. And every cell is composed of protoplasm. Therefore we must look for the beginning of life in the grade of matter called protoplasm. In this both modern Science and the Yogi Teachings agree fully.

In investigating protoplasm we are made to realize the wonderful qualities of its principal constituent—Carbon. Carbon is the wonder worker of the elements. Manifesting in various forms, as the diamond, graphite, coal, protoplasm—is it not entitled to respect? The Yogi Teachings inform vis that in Carbon we have that form of matter which was evolved as the physical basis of life. If any of you doubt that inorganic matter may be transformed into living forms, let us refer you to the plant life, in which you may see the plants building up cells every day from the inorganic, chemical or mineral substances, in the earth, air, and water. Nature performs every day the miracle of transforming chemicals and minerals into living plant cells. And when animal or man eats these plant cells, so produced, they become transformed into animal cells of which the body is built up. What it took Nature ages to do in the beginning, is now performed in a few hours, or minutes.

The Yogi Teachings, again on all-fours with modern Science, inform us that living forms had their beginning in water. In the slimy bed of the polar seas the simple cell-forms appeared, having their origin in the transitional stages before mentioned. The first living forms were a lowly form of plant life, consisting of a single cell. From these forms were evolved forms composed of groups of cells, and so proceeded the work of evolution, from the lower form to the higher, ever in an upward path.

As we have said, the single cell is the physical centre, or parent, of every living form. It contains what is known as the *nucleus*, or kernel, which seems to be more highly organized than the rest of the material of the cell—it may be considered as the "brain" of the cell, if you wish to use your imagination a little. The single cell reproduces itself by growth and division, or separation. Each cell manifests the functions of life, whether it be a single-celled creature, or a cell which with billions of others, goes to make up a higher form. It feels, feeds, grows, and reproduces itself. In the single-celled creature, the one cell performs all of the functions, of course. But as the forms become more complex, the many cells composing a form perform certain functions which are allotted to it, the division of labor resulting in a higher manifestation. This is true not only in the case of animal forms, but also in the case of plant forms. The cells in the bone, muscle,

339

nerve-tissue and blood of the animal differ according to their offices; and the same is true in the cells in the sap, stem, root, leaf, seed and flower of the plant.

As we have said, the cells multiply by division, after a period of growth. The cell grows by material taken into its substance, as food. When sufficient food has been partaken, and enough new material accumulated to cause the cell to attain a certain size, then it divides, or separates into two cells, the division being equal, and the point of cleavage being at the kernel or nucleus. As the two parts separate, the protoplasm *of* each groups itself around its nucleus, and two living forms exist where there was but one a moment before. And then each of the two cells proceed to grow rapidly, and then separate, and so on to the end, each cell multiplying into millions, as time passes.

Ascending in the scale, we next find the living forms composed of cell-groups. These cell-groups are formed by single cells dividing, and then subdividing, but instead of passing on their way they group themselves in clusters, or masses. There are millions of forms of these cell-group creatures, among which we find the sponges, polyps, etc.

In the early forms of life it is difficult to distinguish between the animal and the plant forms, in fact the early forms partake of the qualities of both. But as we advance in the scale a little there is seen a decided "branching out," and one large branch is formed of the evolving plant forms, and the other of the evolving animal forms. The plant-branch begins with the sea-weeds, and passes on to the fungi, lichens, mosses, ferns, pines and palm-ferns, grasses, etc., then to the trees, shrubs and herbs. The animal-branch begins with the *monera*, or single-cell forms, which are little more than a drop of sticky, glue-like protoplasm. Then it passes on to the *amoebae*, which begins to show a slight difference in its parts. Then on the *foraminifera*, which secretes a shell of lime from the water. Then on a step higher to the *polycystina*, which secretes a shell, or skeleton of flint-like material from the water. Then come the sponges. Then the coral-animals, anemones and jelly-fish. Then come the sea-lilies, star-fish, etc. Then the various families of worms. Then the crabs, spiders, centipedes, insects. Then come the mollusca, which include the oysters, clams and other shell-fish; snails, cuttle-fish, sea-squirts, etc. All of the above families of animal-forms are what are known as "invertebrates," that is, without a backbone. Then we come to the "vertebrates," or animals having a backbone. First we see the fish family with its thousands of forms. Then come the amphibia, which include the toads, frogs, etc. Then come the reptiles, which include the serpents, lizards, crocodiles, turtles, etc. Then come the great family of birds, with its wonderful variety of forms, sizes, and characteristics. Then come the mammals, the name of which comes from the Latin word meaning "the breast," the characteristic of which group comes from the fact that they nourish their young by milk, or similar fluid, secreted by the mother. The mammals are the highest form of the vertebrates.

First among the mammals we find the aplacentals, or those which bring forth immature young, which are grouped into two divisions, *i.e.*, (1) the *monotremes*, or one-vented animals, in which group belong the duck-bills, spiny ant-eaters, etc.; and (2) the *marsupials*, or pouched animals, in which group belong the kangaroo, opossum, etc.

The next highest form among the mammals are known as the *placentals*, or those which bring forth mature young. In this class are found the ant-eaters, sloth, manatee, the whale and porpoise, the horse, cow, sheep, and other hoofed animals; the elephant, seal, the dog, wolf, lion, tiger, and all flesh eating animals; the hares, rats, mice, and ail other gnawing animals; the bats, moles, and other insect-feeders; then come the great family of apes, from the small monkeys up to the orang-outang, chimpanzee, and other forms nearly approaching man. And then comes the highest, Man, from the Kaffir, Bush-man, Cave-man, and Digger Indian, up through the many stages until the highest forms of our own race are reached.

From the Monera to Man is a long path, containing many stages, but it is a path including all the intermediate forms. The Yogi Teachings hold to the theory of evolution, as maintained by modern Science, but it goes still further, for it holds not only that the physical forms are subject to the evolutionary process, but that also the "souls" embodied in these forms are subject to the evolutionary process. In other words the Yogi Teachings hold that there is a twin-process of evolution under way, the main object of which is to develop "souls," but which also finds it necessary to evolve higher and higher forms of physical bodies for these constantly advancing souls to occupy.

Let us take a hasty glance at the ascending forms of animal life, as they rise in the evolutionary scale. By so doing we can witness the growth of the soul, within them, as manifested by the higher and higher physical forms which are used as channels of expression by the souls within. Let us first study soul-evolution from the outer viewpoint, before we proceed to examine it from the inner. By so doing we will have a fuller idea of the process than if we ignored the outer and proceed at once to the inner. Despise not the outer form, for it has always been, and is now, the Temple of the Soul, which the latter is remodelling and rebuilding in order to accommodate its constantly increasing needs and demands.

Let us begin with the *Protozoa*, or one-celled forms—the lowest form of animal life. The lowest form of this lowest class is that remarkable creature that we have mentioned in previous lessons—the *Moneron*. This creature lives in water, the natural element in which organic life is believed to have had its beginning. It is a very tiny, shapeless, colorless, slimy, sticky mass—something like a tiny drop of glue—alike all over and in its mass, and without organs or parts of any kind. Some have claimed that below the field of the microscope there may be something like elementary organs in the Moneron, but so far as the human eye may discover there is no evidence of anything of the kind. It has no organs or parts with which to perform particular functions, as is the case with the higher forms of life. These functions, as you know, may be classed into three groups, *i.e.*, nutrition, reproduction, and relation—that is, the function of feeding, the function of reproducing its kind, and the function of receiving and responding to the impressions of the outside world. All of these three classes of functions the Moneron performs—but *with any part of its body, or with all of it*.

Every part, or the whole, of the Moneron absorbs food and oxygen—it is all mouth and lungs. Every part, or the whole, digests the food—it is all stomach. Every part, or the whole, performs the reproductive function—it is all reproductive

342

organism. Every part of it senses the impressions from outside, and responds to it—it is all organs of sense, and organs of motion. It envelops its prey as a drop of glue surrounds a particle of sand, and then absorbs the substance of the prey into its own substance. It moves by prolonging any part of itself outward in a sort of tail-like appendage, which it uses as a "foot," or "finger" with which to propel itself; draw itself to, or push itself away from an object. This prolongation is called a *pseudopod*, or "false-foot." When it gets through using the "false-foot" for the particular purpose, it simply draws back into itself that portion which had been protruded for the purpose.

It performs the functions of digestion, assimilation, elimination, etc., perfectly, just as the higher forms of life—but it has no organs for the functions, and performs them severally, and collectively with any, or all parts of its body. What the higher animals perform with intricate organs and parts—heart, stomach, lungs, liver, kidneys, etc., etc.—this tiny creature performs *without organs*, and with its entire body, or any part thereof. The function of reproduction is startlingly simple in the case of the Moneron. It simply divides itself in two parts, and that is all there is to it. There is no male or female sex in its case—it combines both within itself. The reproductive process is even far more simple than the "budding" of plants. You may turn one of these wonderful creatures inside out, and still it goes on the even tenor of its way, in no manner disturbed or affected. It is simply a "living drop of glue," which eats, digests, receives impressions and responds thereto, and reproduces itself. This tiny glue-drop performs virtually the same life functions as do the higher complex forms of living things. Which is the greater "miracle"—the Moneron or Man?

A slight step upward from the Moneron brings us to the *Amoeba*. The name of this new creature is derived from the Greek word meaning "change," and has been bestowed because the creature is constantly changing its shape. This continual change of shape is caused by a continuous prolongation and drawing-in of its pseudopods, or "false-feet," which also gives the creature the appearance of a "many-fingered" organism. This creature shows the first step toward "parts," for it has something like a membrane or "skin" at its surface, and a "nucleus" at its centre, and also an expanding and contracting cavity within its substance, which it uses for holding, digesting and distributing its food, and also for storing and distributing its oxygen—an elementary combination of stomach and lungs! So you see that the amoeba has taken a step upward from the moneron, and is beginning to appreciate the convenience of parts and organs. It is interesting to note, in this connection, that while the ordinary cells of the higher animal body resemble the *monera* in many ways, still the white corpuscles in the blood of man and the animals bear a startling resemblance to the *amoebae* so far as regards size, general structure, and movements, and are in fact known to Science as "amoeboids." The white corpuscles change their shape, take in food in an intelligent manner, and live a comparatively independent life, their movements showing independent "thought" and "will."

Some of the amoebae (the diatoms, for instance) secrete solid matter from the water, and build therefrom shells or houses, which serve to protect them from their enemies. These shells are full of tiny holes, through which the pseudopods are extended in their search for food, and for purposes of movement. Some of these shells are composed of secreted lime, and others of a flinty substance, the "selection" of these substances from the ether mineral particles in the water, evidencing a degree cf "thought," and mind, even in these lowly creatures. The skeletons of these tiny creatures form vast deposits of chalk and similar substances. Next higher in the scale are the *Infusoria*. These creatures differ from the amoebae inasmuch as instead of pseudopods, they have developed tiny vibrating filaments, or thread-like appendages, which are used for drawing in their prey and for moving about. These filaments are permanent, and are not temporary like the pseudopods of the monera or amoebae—they are the *first signs of permanent hands and feet*. These creatures have also discovered the possibilities of organs and parts, to a still greater degree than have their cousins the amoebae, and have evolved something like a mouth-opening (very rudimentary) and also a short gullet through which they pass their food and oxygen— *they have developed the first signs of a throat, wind-pipe and food-passage.*

Next come the family of Sponges, the soft skeletons of which form the useful article of everyday use. There are many forms who weave a home of far more delicacy and beauty than their more familiar and homely brothers. The sponge creature itself is a slimy, soft creature, which fills in the spaces in its spongy skeleton. It is fastened to one spot, and gathers in its food from the water around it (and oxygen as well), by means of numerous whip-like filaments called *cilia*, which flash through the water driving in the food and oxygen to the inner positions of its body. The water thus drawn in, as well as the refuse from the food, is then driven out in the same manner. It is interesting to note that in the organisms of the higher animals, including man, there are numerous *cilia* performing offices in connection with nutrition, etc. When Nature perfects an instrument, it is very apt to retain it, even in the higher forms, although in the latter its importance may be dwarfed by higher ones.

The next step in the ascending scale of life-forms is occupied by the *polyps*, which are found in water, fastened to floating matter. The polyps fasten themselves to this floating matter, with their mouths downward, from the latter dangling certain tentacles, or thin, long arms. These tentacles contain small thread-like coils in contact with a poisonous fluid, and enclosed in a cell. When the tentacles come in contact with the prey of the creature, or with anything that is sensed as a possible enemy, they contract around the object and the little cells burst and the tiny thread-like coils are released and twist themselves like a loop around the object, poisoning it with the secreted fluid. Some of the polyps secrete flint-like tubes, which they inhabit, and from the ends of which they emerge like flowers. From these parent polyps emerge clusters of young, resembling buds. These bud-like young afterwards become what are known as jelly-fishes, etc., which in turn reproduce themselves—but here is a wonder—the jelly-fish lay eggs, which when hatched produce stationary polyps like their grandparent, and not moving creatures like their parents. The jelly-fishes have a comparatively complex organism. They have an intricate system of canal-like passages with which to convey their food and oxygen to the various parts. They also have something like muscles, which contract and enable the creature to "swim." They also possess a "nervous system," and, most wonderful of all, they have *rudimentary eyes and ears*. Their tentacles, like those of the parent-polyp, secrete the poisonous fluid which is discharged into prey or enemy.

Akin to the polyps are the sea-anemones, with their beautiful colors, and still more complex structure and organism, the tentacles of which resemble the petals of a flower. Varying slightly from these are the coral-creatures, which form in colonies and the skeletons of which form the coral trees and branches, and other forms, with which we are familiar.

Passing on to the next highest family of life-forms, we see the spiny-bodied sea-creatures, such as the sea-urchin, star-fish, etc., which possess a thick, hard skin, covered by spines or prickly projections. These creatures abound in numerous species. The star-fish has rays projecting from a common centre, which gives it its name, while the sea-urchin resembles a ball. The sea-lilies, with their stems and flowers (so-called) belong to this family, as do also the sea-cucumbers, whose name is obtained from their shape and general appearance, but which are animals possessing a comparatively complex organism, one of the features of which is a stomach which may be discarded at will and replaced by a new one. These creatures have a well defined nervous system, and have eyes, and some of them even rudimentary eyelids.

Ascending the scale of life-forms, we next observe the great family of the *Annulosa*, or jointed creatures, which comprises the various families of the worm, the crab, the spider, the ant, etc. In this great family are grouped nearly four-fifths of the known life-forms. Their bodies are well formed and they have nervous systems running along the body and consisting of two thin threads, knotted at different points into ganglia or masses of nerve cells similar to those possessed by the higher animals. They possess eyes and other sense organs, in some cases highly developed. They possess organs, corresponding to the heart, and have a well-developed digestive apparatus. Note this advance in the nutritive organism: the *moneron* takes its food at any point of its body; the *amoeba* takes its food by means of its "false-feet," and drives it through its body by a rhythmic movement of its substance; the *polyp* distributes its food to its various parts by means of the water which it absorbs with the food; the *sea-urchin and star-fish* distribute their food by canals in their bodies

346

which open directly into the water; in the higher forms of the *annulosa*, the food is distributed by a fluid resembling blood, which carries the nourishment to every part and organ, and which carries away the waste matter, the blood being propelled through the body by a rudimentary heart. The oxygen is distributed by each of these forms in a corresponding way, the higher forms having rudimentary lungs and respiratory organs. Step by step the life-forms are perfected, and the organs necessary to perform certain definite functions are evolved from rudimentary to perfected forms.

The families of worms are the humblest members of the great family of the Annulosa. Next come the creatures called Rotifers, which are very minute. Then come the Crustacea, so called from their crustlike shell. This group includes the crabs, lobsters, etc., and closely resembles the insects. In fact, some of the best authorities believe that the insects and the crustacea spring from the same parent form, and some of the Yogi authorities hold to this belief, while others do not attempt to pass upon it, deeming it immaterial, inasmuch as all life-forms have a common origin. The western scientists pay great attention to outward details, while the Oriental mind is apt to pass over these details as of slight importance, preferring to seek the cause back of the outward form. On one point both the Yogi teachers and the scientists absolutely agree, and that is that the family of insect life had its origin in some aquatic creature. Both hold that the wings of the insect have been evolved from organs primarily used for breathing purposes by the ancestor when it took short aerial flights, the need for means of flight afterwards acting to develop these rudimentary organs into perfected wings. There need be no more wonder expressed at this change than in the case of the transformation of the insect from grub to chrysalis, and then to insect. In fact this process is a reproduction of the stages through which the life-form passed during the long ages between sea-creature and land-insect.

We need not take up much of your time in speaking of the wonderful complex organism of some of the insect family, which are next on the scale above the crustacea. The wonders of spider-life—the almost human life of the ants—the spirit of the beehive—and all the rest of the wonders of insect life are familiar to all of our readers. A study of some good book on the life of the higher forms of the insect family will prove of value to anyone, for it will open his or her eyes to the wonderful manifestation of life and mind among these creatures. Remember the remark of Darwin, that the brain of the ant, although not much larger than a pin point, "is one of the most marvelous atoms of matter in the world, perhaps more so than the brain of man."

Closely allied to the crustacea is the sub-family of the *mollusca*, which includes the oyster, clams, and similar creatures; also the snails, cuttle-fish, slugs, nautilus, sea-squirts, etc., etc. Some are protected by a hard shell, while others have a gristly outer skin, serving as an armor, while others still are naked. Those having shells secrete the material for their construction from the water. Some of them are fixed to rocks, etc., while others roam at will. Strange as it may appear at first sight, some of the higher forms of the mollusca show signs of a rudimentary vertebra, and science has hazarded the opinion that the sea-squirts and similar creatures were descended from some ancestor from whom also descended the vertebrate animals, of which man is the highest form known today on this planet. We shall mention this connection in our next lesson, where we will take up the story of "The Ascent of Man" from the lowly vertebrate forms.

And now, in closing this lesson, we must remind the reader that we are *not* teaching Evolution as it is conceived by modern science. We are viewing it from the opposite viewpoint of the Yogi Teaching. Modern Science teaches that Mind is a by-product of the evolving material forms—while the Yogi Teachings hold that there was Mind *involved* in the lowest form, and that that Mind constantly pressing forward for unfoldment *compelled* the gradual evolution, or unfoldment of the slowly advancing degrees of organization and function. Science teaches that "function precedes organization," that is, that a form performs certain functions, imperfectly and crudely, before it evolves the organs suitable for the functioning. For instance the lower forms digested food before they evolved stomachs—the latter coming to meet the need. But the Yogi Teachings go further and claim that "desire precedes function," that is, that the lowly life form "desires" to have digestive apparatus, in order to proceed in the evolutionary scale, before it begins the functioning that brings about the more complex organism. There is ever the "urge" of the Mind which craves unfoldment, and which the creature feels as a dim desire, which grows stronger and stronger as time goes on. Some yield more readily to the urge, and such become the parents of possible higher forms. "Many are called, but few are chosen," and so matters move along slowly from generation to generation, a few forms serving to carry on the evolutionary urge to their descendants. But is always the Evolutionary Urge of the imprisoned Mind striving to cast aside its sheaths and to have more perfect machinery with which, and through which, to manifest and express itself? This is the difference between the "Evolution" of Modern Science and the "Unfoldment" of the Yogi Teachings. The one is all material, with mind as a mere by-product, while the other is all Mind, with matter as a tool and instrument of expression and manifestation.

As we have said in this lesson—and as we shall point out to you in detail in future lessons—accompanying this evolution of bodies there is an evolution of "souls" producing the former. This evolution of souls is a basic principle of the Yogi Teachings, but it is first necessary that you acquaint yourselves with the evolution of bodies and forms, before you may fully grasp the higher teachings.

Our next lesson will be entitled "The Ascent of Man," in which the rise of man—that is, his body—from the lowly forms of the vertebrates is shown. In the same lesson we shall begin our consideration of the "evolution of souls." We trust that the students are carefully studying the details of each lesson, for every lesson has its part in the grand whole of the Teachings.

THE EIGHTH LESSON - The Ascent of Man

In our last lesson we led you by successive steps from the
beginnings of Life in living forms up to the creatures closely
resembling the family of vertebrates—the highest family of
living forms on this planet. In this present lesson we take up the
story of the "Ascent of Man" from the lowly vertebrate forms.
The large sub-family of forms called "The Vertebrates" are
distinguished from the Invertebrates by reason of the former
possessing an *internal* bony skeleton, the most important feature
of which is the vertebra or spinal column. The vertebrates, be it
remembered, possess practically the same organs as the lower
forms of life, but differ from them most materially by the
possession of the *internal* skeleton, the lower forms having
an *external* or outside *skeleton*, which latter is merely a
hardening of the skin.
The flexibility of the vertebra creates a wonderful strength of
structure, combined with an ease of movement peculiar to the
vertebrates, and which renders them the natural forms of life
capable of rapid development and evolution. By means of this
strength, and ease, these forms are enabled to move rapidly in
pursuit of their prey, and away from their pursuers, and also to
resist outside pressure or attack. They are protected in a way
similar to the invertebrates having shells, and yet have the
additional advantage of easy movement. Differing in shape and
appearance as do the numerous members of the sub-family of
vertebrates, still their structure is easily seen to spring from a
single form—all are modifications of some common pattern, the
differences arising from the necessities of the life of the animal,
as manifested through the desire and necessities of the species.
Science shows the direct relationship between the Vertebrates,
and the Invertebrates by means of several connecting-links, the
most noticeable of which is the Lancelot, a creature resembling
the fish-form, and yet also closely resembling the lower
(invertebrate) forms of life. This creature has no head, and but
one eye. It is semi-transparent, and possesses *cilia* for forcing in
the water containing its food. It has something like gills, and a
gullet like the lower forms. It has no heart, the blood being

circulated by means of contracting vessels or parts. Strictly speaking, it has no back-bone, or vertebra, but still Science has been compelled to class it among the vertebrates because is has a gristly cartilage where the back-bone is found in the higher forms. This gristle may be called an "elementary spine." It has a nervous system consisting of a single cord which spreads into a broadened end near the creature's mouth, and which may therefore be regarded as "something like a brain." This creature is really a developed form of Invertebrate, shaped like a Vertebrate, and showing signs of a rudimentary spine and nervous system of the latter. It is a "connecting-link."

The lowest forms of the true Vertebrates are the great families of Fishes. These Fish families include fishes of high and low degree, some of the higher forms being as different from the lowest as they (the highest) are different from the Reptile family. It is not necessary to go into detail regarding the nature of the fish families, for every student is more or less familiar with them.

Some peculiar forms of fish show a shading into the Reptile family, in fact they seem to belong nearly as much to the latter as to their own general family. Some species of fish known as the *Dipnoi* or "double-breathers," have a remarkable dual system of breathing. That is, they have gills for breathing while in the water, and also have a primitive or elementary "lung" in the shape of an air-bladder, or "sound," which they use for breathing on land. The Mud-fish of South America, and also other forms in Australia and other places, have a modification of fins which are practically "limbs," which they actually use for traveling on land from pond to pond. Some of these fish have been known to travel enormous distances in search of new pools of water, or new streams, having been driven from their original homes by droughts, or perhaps by instincts similar to the migrating instinct of birds. Eels are *fish* (although many commonly forget this fact) and many of their species are able to leave the water and travel on land from pond to pond, their breathing being performed by a peculiar modification of the gills. The climbing perch of India are able to live out of water, and have modified gills for breathing purposes, and modified fins for climbing and walking. So you see that without leaving the fish family proper, we have examples of land living creatures which are akin to "connecting links."

But there are real "connecting-links'" between the Fish and the Reptiles. Passing over the many queer forms which serve as links between the two families, we have but to consider our common frog's history for a striking example. The Tadpole has gills, has no limbs, uses its tail like a fish's fin, eats plants, etc. Passing through several interesting stages the Tadpole reaches a stage in which it is a frog with a tail—then it sheds its tail and is a full fledged Frog, with four legs; web-feet; no tail; and feeding on animals. The Frog is amphibious, that is, able to live on land or in water—and yet it is compelled to come to the surface of the water for air to supply its lungs. Some of the amphibious animals possess both lungs and gills, even when matured; but the higher vertebrates living in the water breathe through lungs which are evolved from the air-bladder of fishes, which in turn have been evolved from the primitive gullet of the lower forms. There are fishes known which are warm-blooded. Students will kindly remember that the Whale is not a fish, but an aquatic animal—a mammal, in fact, bringing forth its young alive, and suckling it from its breasts.

So we readily see that it is but a step, and a short step at that, between the land-traveling and climbing fishes and the lower forms of Reptiles. The Frog shows us the process of evolution between the two families, its life history reproducing the gradual evolution which may have required ages to perfect in the case of the species. You will remember that the embryo stages of all creatures reproduce the various stages of evolution through which the species has passed—this is true in Man as well as in the Frog.

We need not tarry long in considering the Reptile family of living forms. In its varieties of serpents, lizards, crocodiles, turtles, etc., we have studied and observed its forms. We see the limbless snakes; the lizards with active limbs; the huge, clumsy, slow crocodiles and alligators—the armor-bearing turtles and tortoises—all belonging to the one great family of Reptiles, and nearly all of them being degenerate descendants of the mighty Reptile forms of the geological Age of Reptiles, in which flourished the mighty forms of the giant reptiles—the monsters of land and water. Amidst the dense vegetation of that pre-historic age, surrounded by the most favorable conditions, these mighty creatures flourished and lived, their fossilized skeleton forms evidencing to us how far their descendants have fallen, owing to less favorable conditions, and the development of other life-forms more in harmony with their changed environment.

Next comes the great family of Birds. The Birds ascended from the Reptiles. This is the Eastern Teaching, and this is the teaching of Western Science It was formerly taught in the text-books that the line of ascent was along the family of winged reptiles which existed in the Age of Reptiles, in the early days of the Earth. But the later writers on the subject, in the Western world, have contradicted this. It is now taught that these ancient winged-reptiles were featherless, and more closely resembled the Bat family than birds. (You will remember that a Bat is neither a reptile nor a bird—it is a mammal, bringing forth its young alive, and suckling them at its breast. The Bat is more like a mouse, and its wings are simply membrane stretched between its fingers, its feet, and its tail.)

The line of ascent from Reptile to Bird was along the forms of the Reptiles that walked on land. There are close anatomical and physiological relations and correspondences between the two families (Reptiles and Birds) which we need not refer to here. And, of course, many modifications have occurred since the "branching-out." The scales of the reptiles, and the feathers of the birds, are known to be but modifications of the original outer skin, as are also the hair, claws, hoofs, nails, etc., of all animals. Even teeth arose in this way, strange as it may now seem—they are all secreted from the skin. What a wonderful field for thought—this gradual evolution from the filmy outer covering of the lowest living forms to the beautiful feathers, beaks, and claws of the bird!

The evolving of wings meant much to the ascending forms of life. The Reptiles were compelled to live in a narrow circle of territory, while the Birds were able to travel over the earth in wide flights. And travel always develops the faculties of observation, memory, etc., and cultivates the senses of seeing, hearing, etc. And the creature is compelled to exercise its evolving "thinking" faculties to a greater extent. And so the

353

Birds were compelled by necessity of their travels to develop a greater degree of thinking organism. The result is that among birds we find many instances of intelligent thought, which cannot be dismissed as "mere instinct." Naturalists place the Crow at the head of the family of Birds, in point of intelligence, and those who have watched these creatures and studied the mental processes, will agree that this is a just decision. It has been proven that Crows are capable of counting up to several figures, and in other ways they display a wonderful degree of almost human sagacity.

Next above the Bird family comes the highest form of all—the Mammals. But before we begin our consideration of these high forms, let us take a hasty glance at the "connecting-links" between the Birds and the Mammals. The lowest forms of the Mammals resemble Birds in many ways. Some of them are toothless, and many of them have the same primitive intestinal arrangements possessed by the birds, from which arises their name, *Monotremes*. These *Monotremes* may be called half-bird and half-mammal. One of the most characteristic of their family is the *Ornithorhynchus*, or Duck-bill, which the early naturalists first thought was a fraud of the taxidermists, or bird-stuffers, and then, when finally convinced, deemed it a "freak-of-nature." But it is not a freak creature, but a "connecting-link" between the two great families of creatures. This animal presents a startling appearance to the observer who witnesses it for the first time. It resembles a beaver, having a soft furry coat, but also has a horny, flat bill like a duck, its feet being webbed, but also furnished with claws projecting over the edge of the web-foot. It lays eggs in an underground nest—two eggs at a time, which are like the eggs of birds, inasmuch as they contain not only the protoplasm from which the embryo is formed, but also the "yolk." on which the embryo feeds until hatched. After the young Duck-bill is hatched, it feeds from teatless glands in the mother's body, the milk being furnished by the mother by a peculiar process. Consider this *miracle—an animal which lays eggs and then when her young are hatched nourishes them with milk*. The milk-glands in the mother are elementary "breasts." The above-mentioned animal is found in Australia, the land of many strange forms and "connecting-links," which have survived there while in other parts of the globe they have vanished gradually from existence, crowded out by the more perfectly evolved forms. Darwin has called these surviving forms "living fossils." In that same land is also found the *Echidna* or spiny ant-eater, which lays an egg and then hatches it in her pouch, after which she nourishes it on milk, in a manner similar to that of the Duck-bill. This animal, like the Duck-bill, is a Monotreme. Scientists are divided in theories as to whether the Monotremes are actually descended directly from the Reptiles or Birds, or whether there was a common ancestor from which Reptiles and Birds and Mammals branched off. But this is not important, for the relationship between Reptiles, Birds and Mammals is clearly proven. And the Monotremes are certainly one of the surviving forms of the intermediate stages.

The next higher step in the ascent of Mammal life above the Monotreme is occupied by the Marsupials, or *milk-giving, pouched animals*, of which family the opossum and kangaroo are well known members. The characteristic feature of this family of creatures is the possession of an external pouch in the female, in which the young are kept and nourished until they can take care of themselves as the young of other animals are able to do. The young of the Marsupials are brought forth, or born, in an imperfect condition, and undeveloped in size and strength. There are fossil remains of Marsupials showing that in past ages creatures of this kind existed which were as large as elephants. In the more common form of Mammals the young are brought forth fully formed, they having received "nourishment, before birth, from the mother's body, through the *placenta*, the appendage which connects the fetus with the parent. The Placental Mammals were the best equipped of all the life-forms for survival and development, for the reason that the young were nourished during their critical period, and the care that the mammal must of necessity give to her young operated in the direction of affording a special protection far superior to that of the other forms. This and other causes acted to place the Placentals in the "Royal line" from which Man was evolved. The following families of Placental Mammals are recognized by Science, each having its own structural peculiarities:

The *Edentata*, or Toothless creatures, among which are the sloths, ant-eaters, armadillos, etc. These animals seem to be closer to the Monotremes than they are to the Marsupials;

The *Sirenia*, so called by reason of their fanciful resemblance to the sirens of mythology, among which are the sea-cows, manatees, dugongs, etc., which are fish-like in structure and appearance, the fore-limbs being shaped like paddles, or fins, and the hind-limbs being absent or rudimentary;

The *Cetacea*, or Whale Family, including whales, Porpoises, dolphins, etc., which are quite fish-like in appearance and structure, their forms being adapted for life in the sea, although they are, of course, Mammals, bringing forth matured young which are suckled at the breast;

The *Ungulata*, or Hoofed Animals, which comprise many varied forms, such as the horse, the tapir, the rhinoceros, the swine, the hippopotamus, the camel, the deer, the sheep, the cow, etc., etc.;

The *Hyracoidea*, which is a small family, the principal member of which is the coney, or rock rabbit, which has teeth resembling those of the hoofed animals, in some ways, and those of the gnawing animals in the others.

The *Proboscidea*, or Trunked Animals, which family is represented in this age only by the families of elephants, which have a peculiar appendage called a "trunk," which they use as an additional limb;

The *Carnivora*, or Flesh-eaters, represented by numerous and various forms, such as the seal, the bear, the weasel, the wolf, the dog, the lion, the tiger, the leopard, etc. The wolf and similar forms belong to the sub-family of dogs; while the lion, tiger, etc., belong to the sub-family of cats;

The *Rodentia*, or Gnawers, comprising the rat, the hare, the beaver, the squirrel, the mouse, etc., etc.;

The *Insectivora*, or Insect Feeders, comprising the mole, the shrew, the hedgehog, etc.;

The *Chiroptera*, or Finger-Winged Animals, comprising the great family of Bats, etc., which are very highly developed animals;

The *Lemuroidea*, or Lemurs, the name of which is derived from the Latin word meaning a "ghost," by reason of the Lemur's habits of roaming about at night. The Lemur is a nocturnal animal, somewhat resembling the Monkey in general appearance, but with a long, bushy tail and sharp muzzle like a fox. It is akin to a small fox having hands and feet like a monkey, the feet being used to grasp like a hand, as is the case with the true Monkey family. These creatures are classed by some naturalists among the Monkeys by reason of being "four-handed," while others are disposed to consider as still more important their marked relationship with, and affinity to, the marsupials, gnawers and insect-feeders. On the whole, these creatures are strangely organized and come very near to being a "connecting-link" between other forms. One of the Lemurs is what is known as the *colugo*, or "flying lemur," which resembles a squirrel in many particulars, and yet has a membranous web extending from its hands, which enables it to make flying leaps over great distances. This last named variety seems to furnish a link between the insect-feeders and the Primates;

The *Primates*, which is a large family comprising the various forms of monkeys, baboons, man-apes, such as the gibbon, gorilla, chimpanzee, orang-outang, etc., all of which have big jaws, small brains, and a stooping posture. This family also includes MAN, with his big brain and erect posture, and his many races depending upon shape of skull, color of skin, character of hair, etc.

In considering the Ascent of Man (physical) from the lowly forms of the Monera, etc., up to his present high position, the student is struck with the continuity of the ascent, development and unfoldment. While there are many "missing-links," owing to the disappearance of the forms which formed the connection, still there is sufficient proof left in the existing forms to satisfy the fair-minded inquirer. The facts of embryology alone are sufficient proof of the ascent of Man from the lowly forms. Each and every man today has passed through all the forms of the ascent within a few months, from single cell to the new-born, fully formed infant.

Embryology teaches us that the eggs from which all animal forms evolve are all practically alike so far as one can ascertain by microscopic examination, no matter how diverse may be the forms which will evolve from them, and this resemblance is maintained even when the embryo of the higher forms begins to manifest traces of its future form. Von Baer, the German scientist, was the first to note this remarkable and suggestive fact. He stated it in the following words: "In my possession are two little embryos, preserved in alcohol, whose names I have omitted to attach, and at present I am unable to state to what class they belong. They may be lizards, or small birds, or very young mammals, so complete is the similarity in the mode of the formation of the head and trunk in these animals. The extremities, however, are still absent in these embryos. But even if they had existed in the earliest stage of their development, we should learn nothing, for the feet of lizards and mammals, the wings and feet of birds, no less than the hands and feet of man, all arise from the same fundamental form."

As has been said by Prof. Clodd, "the embryos of all living creatures epitomize during development the series of changes through which the ancestral forms passed if their ascent from the simple to the complex; the higher structures passing through the same stages as the lower structures up to the point when they are marked off from them, yet never becoming in detail the form which they represent for the time being. For example, the embryo of man has at the outset gill-like slits on each side of the neck, like a fish. These give place to a membrane like that which supersedes gills in the development of birds and reptiles; the heart is at first a simple pulsating chamber like that in worms; the backbone is prolonged into a movable tail; the great toe is extended, or opposable, like our thumbs, and like the toes of apes; the body three months before birth is covered all over with hair except on the palms and soles. At birth the head is relatively larger, and the arms and legs relatively longer than in the adult; the nose is bridgeless; both features, with others which need not be detailed, being distinctly ape-like. Thus does the egg from which man springs, a structure only one hundred and twenty-fifth of an inch in size, compress into a few weeks the results of millions of years, and set before us the history of his development from fish-like and reptilian forms, and of his more immediate descent from a hairy, tailed quadruped. That which is individual or peculiar to him, the physical and mental character inherited, is left to the slower development which follows birth."

This, then, in brief is the Western theory of Evolution—the Physical Ascent of Man. We have given it as fully as might be in the small space at our disposal in these lessons on the Yogi Philosophy. Why? Because we wish to prove to the Western mind, in the Western way, that Western Science corroborates the Ancient Yogi Teachings of the Unfoldment of Living Forms, from Monad to Man. The Eastern teachers scorn to "prove" anything to their pupils, who sit at the feet of teachers and accept as truth that which is taught them, and which has been handed down from the dim ages long past. But this method will never do for the Western student—he must have it "proven" to him by physical facts and instances, not by keen, subtle, intellectual reasoning alone. The Eastern student wishes to be "told"—the Western student wishes to be "shown." Herein lies the racial differences of method of imparting knowledge. And so we have recognized this fact and have heaped up proof after proof from the pages of Western Science, in order to prove to you the reasonableness, from the Western point of view, of the doctrine of Physical Unfoldment as taught for ages past by the Yogi *gurus* to their *chelas*. You have now the Eastern Teachings on the subject, together with the testimony of Western Science to the reasonableness of the idea.

But, alas! Western Science, while performing a marvelous work in piling up fact after fact to support its newly-discovered theory of Evolution, in a way utterly unknown to the Oriental thinker who seeks after principles by mental concentration— *within* rather than without—while actually proving by physical facts the *mental* conceptions of the Oriental Teachings, still misses the vital point of the subject-thought. In its materialistic tendencies it has failed to recognize *the mental cause of the physical unfoldment*. It is true that Lamark, the real Western discoverer of Evolution, taught that Desire and Mental Craving, was the real force behind Evolution, but his ideas were jeered at by his contemporaries, and are not regarded seriously by the majority of Evolutionists even today. And yet he was nearer to the truth than Darwin or any other Western Evolutionist. And time will show that Science has overlooked his genius, which alone throws the true light upon the subject.

In order to see just this difference between the Darwinian school and the Yogi Teachings let us examine into what causes the Western Evolutionists give for the fact of Evolution itself. We shall do this briefly.

The Darwinians start out to explain the causes of the "Origin of Species," with the statement that "no two individuals of the same species are exactly alike; each tends to vary." This is a self-evident fact, and is very properly used as a starting point for Variation. The next step is then stated as "variations are transmitted, and therefore tend to become permanent," which also is self-evident, and tends to prove the reasonableness of the gradual evolution of species. The next step in the argument is "as man produces new species and forms, by breeding, culture, etc., so has Nature in a longer time produced the same effect, in the same way." This also is reasonable, although it tends to personify Nature, and to give it a *mind* before the evolutionists admit "mind" was evolved.

It will be as well to quote Darwin himself on this point. He says; "As man can produce, and certainly has produced, a great result by his methodical and unconscious means of selection, what may not natural selection effect? Man can act only on external and visible characters, while Nature, if I may be allowed to personify the natural preservation or survival of the fittest, cares nothing for appearances except in so far as they are useful to any being. She can act on every internal organ, on every shade of constitutional difference, on the whole machinery of life. Man selects only for his own good; Nature only for the good of the being which she tends. Every selected character is fully exercised by her, as is implied by the fact of their selection. Man keeps the natives of many climates in the same country; he seldom exercises each selected character in some peculiar and fitting manner; he feeds a long-beaked and a short-beaked pigeon on the same food; he does not exercise a long-backed or long-legged quadruped in any peculiar manner; he exposes sheep with long hair and short wool in the same climate. He does not allow the most vigorous males to struggle for the females. He does not rigidly destroy all inferior animals, but protects during each varying season, so far as lies in his power, all his productions. He often begins his selection by some half-monstrous form, or at least by some modification prominent enough to catch the eye or to be plainly useful to him. Under Nature the slightest differences of structure or constitution may-well turn the nicely balanced scale in the struggle for life, and so be preserved. How fleeting are the wishes and efforts of man! how short his time! and consequently how poor will be his results, compared with those accumulated by nature during whole geological periods! Can we wonder, then, that Nature's productions should be far 'truer' in character than man's productions; that they should be infinitely better adapted to the most complex conditions of life, and should plainly bear the stamp of far higher workmanship?"

Darwin's theory of survival of the fittest is begun by the statement of the fact that the number of organisms that survive are very small compared with the number that are born. To quote his own words, "There is no exception to the rule that every organic being naturally increases at so high a rate that, if not destroyed, the earth would soon be covered by the progeny of a single pair. Even slow-breeding man has doubled in twenty-five years, and at this rate in less than a thousand years there would literally not be standing room for the progeny." It has been computed that if the offspring of the elephant, which is believed to be the slowest breeding animal known, were to survive, there would be about 20,000,000 elephants on the earth in 750 years. The roe of a single cod contains eight or nine millions of eggs, and if each egg were to hatch, and the fish survive, the sea would shortly become a solid mass of codfish. The house fly is said to have 20,000,000 descendants in a season, counting several generations of progeny, from its several broods. And some scientist has computed that the *aphis*, or plant-louse, breeds so rapidly, and in such enormous quantity, that the tenth generation of one set of parents would be so large that it would contain more ponderable animal matter than would the population of China, which is estimated at 500,000,000! And this without counting the progeny preceding the tenth generation!

The result of the above conditions is very plain. There must ensue a Struggle for Existence, which necessitates the Survival of the Fittest. The weak are crushed out by the strong; the swift out-distance the slow. The individual forms or species best adapted to their environment and best equipped for the struggle, be the equipment physical or mental, survive those less well equipped or less well adapted to environment. Animals evolving variations in structure that give them even a slight advantage over others not so favored, naturally have a better chance to survive. And this, briefly, is what Evolutionists call "The Survival of the Fittest."

As appertaining to the Struggle for Existence, color and mimicry are important factors. Grant Allen, in his work on Darwin, says concerning this, and also as illustrating "Natural Selection": "In the desert with its monotonous sandy coloring, a black insect or a white insect, still more a red insect or a blue insect, would be immediately detected and devoured by its natural enemies, the birds and the lizards. But any greyish or yellowish insects would be less likely to attract attention at first sight, and would be overlooked as long as there were any more conspicuous individuals of their own kind about for the birds and lizards to feed on. Hence, in a very short time the desert would be depopulated of all but the greyest and yellowest insects; and among these the birds would pick out those which differed most markedly in hue and shade from the sand around them. But those which happened to vary most in the direction of a sandy or spotty color would be more likely to survive, and to become the parents of future generations. Thus, in the course of long ages, all the insects which inhabit deserts have become sand-colored, because the less sandy were perpetually picked out for destruction by their ever-watchful foes, while the most sandy escaped, and multiplied and replenished the earth with their own likes."

Prof. Clodd, remarking upon this fact, adds: "Thus, then, is explained the tawny color of the larger animals that inhabit the desert; the stripes upon the tiger, which parallel with the vertical stems of bamboo, conceal him as he stealthily nears his prey; the brilliant green of tropical birds; the leaf-like form and colors of certain insects; the dried, twig-like form of many caterpillars; the bark-like appearance of tree-frogs; the harmony of the ptarmigan's summer plumage with the lichen-colored stones upon which it sits; the dusky color of creatures that haunt the night; the bluish transparency of animals which live on the surface of the sea; the gravel-like color of flat-fish that live at the bottom; and the gorgeous tints of those that swim among the coral reefs."

All this does not run contrary to the Yogi Philosophy, although the latter would regard these things as but the secondary cause for the variation and survival of species, etc. The Oriental teachings are that it is the *desire* of the animal that *causes* it to assume the colors and shapes in accordance with its environment, the desire of course operating along sub-conscious lines of physical manifestation. The mental influence, which is the real cause of the phenomena, and which is taught as such by the Yogis, is almost lost sight of by the Western Evolutionists, who are apt to regard Mind as a "by-product" of matter. On the contrary, *the Yogis regard Matter as the product of Mind.* But there is no conflict here as far as regards the law of the Survival of the Fittest. The insects that *most desired* to become sand-colored became so, and were thus protected, while their less "desireful" brethren were exterminated. The Western scientist explains the outward phenomena, but does not look for the *cause* behind it, which is taught by the Oriental sages.

The doctrine of "Sexual Selection" is another of the leading tenets of the Darwinists. Briefly, it may be expressed as the theory that in the rivalry and struggle of the males for the females the strongest males win the day, and thus transmit their particular qualities to their offspring. Along the same lines is that of the attraction exerted by bright colors in the plumage of the males of birds, etc., which give them an advantage in the eyes of the females, and thus, naturally, the bright colors are perpetuated.

This, then, is the brief outline of the Story of Man's Physical Evolution, as stated by Western Science, and compared with the Yogi Teachings. The student should compare the two ideas, that he may harmonize and reconcile them. It must be remembered, however, that Darwin did *not* teach that Man descended from the monkeys, or apes, as we know them now. The teaching of Western Evolution is that the apes, and higher forms of monkey life descended from some common ancestral form, which same ancestor was also the ancestor of Man. In other words, Man and Apes are the different branches that emerged from the common trunk ages ago. Other forms doubtless emerged from the same trunk, and perished because less adapted to their environments. The Apes were best adapted to their own environments, and Man was best adapted to his. The weaker branches failed.

One must remember that the most savage races known to us today are practically as far different from the highest American, European or Hindu types of Man as from the highest Apes. Indeed, it would seem far easier for a high Ape to evolve into a Kaffir, Hottentot, or Digger Indian, than for the latter to evolve into an Emerson, Shakespeare, or Hindu Sage. As Huxley has shown, the brain-structure of Man compared with that of the Chimpanzee shows differences but slight when compared with the difference between that of the Chimpanzee and that of the Lemur. The same authority informs us that in the important feature of the deeper brain furrows, and intricate convolutions, the chasm between the highest civilized man and the lowest savage is far greater than between the lowest savage and the highest man-like ape. Darwin, describing the Fuegians, who are among the very lowest forms of savages, says: "Their very signs and expressions are less intelligible to us than those of the domesticated animal. They are men who do not possess the instinct of those animals, nor yet appear to boast of human reason, or at least of arts consequent upon that reason." Professor Clodd, in describing the "primitive man," says: "Doubtless he was lower than the lowest of the savages of today—a powerful, cunning biped, with keen sense organs always sharper, in virtue of constant exercise, in the savage than in the civilized man (who supplements them by science), strong instincts, uncontrolled and fitful emotions, small faculty of wonder, and nascent reasoning power; unable to forecast tomorrow, or to comprehend yesterday, living from hand to mouth on the wild products of Nature, clothed in skin and bark, or daubed with clay, and finding shelter in trees and caves; ignorant of the simplest arts, save to chip a stone missile, and perhaps to produce fire; strong in his needs of life and vague sense of right to it and to what he could get, but slowly impelled by common perils and passions to form ties, loose and haphazard at the outset, with his kind, the power of combination with them depending on sounds, signs and gestures."

Such was the ancestral man. Those who are interested in him are referred to the two wonderful tales of the cave-man written in the form of stories by two great modern novelists. The books referred to are (1) "*The Story of Ab*," by Stanley Waterloo, and (2) "*Before Adam*," by Jack London. They may be obtained from any bookseller. Both are works of fiction, with the scientific facts cleverly interwoven into them.

And now in conclusion before we pass on the subject of "Spiritual Evolution," which will form the subject of our next lesson, we would again call your attention to the vital difference between the Western and the Eastern Teachings. The Western holds to a mechanical theory of life, which works without the necessity of antecedent Mind, the latter appearing as a "product" at a certain stage. The Eastern holds *that Mind is back of, under, and antecedent to all the work of Evolution*—the *cause*, not the effect or product. The Western claims that Mind was produced by the struggle of Matter to produce higher forms of itself. *The Eastern claims that the whole process of Evolution is caused by Mind striving, struggling and pressing forward toward expressing itself more fully—to liberate itself from the confining and retarding Matter—the struggle resulting in an Unfoldment which causes sheath after sheath of the confining material bonds to be thrown off and discarded, in the effort to release the confined Spirit which is behind even the Mind. The Yogi Teachings are that the Evolutionary Urge is the pressure of the confined Spirit striving to free itself from the fetters and bonds which sorely oppress it.*

The struggle and pain of Evolution is the parturition-pangs of the Spiritual deliverance from the womb of Matter. Like all birth it is attended by pain and suffering, but the end justifies it all. And as the human mother forgets her past suffering in the joy of witnessing the face, and form, and life, of her loved child, so will the soul forget the pain of the Spiritual birth by reason of the beauty and nobility of that which will be born to and from it.

Let us study well the story of Physical Evolution, but let us not lose ourselves in it, for it is but the preliminary to the story of the Unfoldment of the Soul.

Let us not despise the tale of the Body of Man—for it is the story of the Temple of the Spirit which has been built up from the most humble beginnings, until it has reached the present high stage. And yet even this is but the beginning, for the work will go on, and on, and on, in the spirit of those beautiful lines of Holmes:

"Build thee more stately mansions, oh, my soul!
As the swift seasons roll!
Leave thy low-vaulted past!
Let each new temple, nobler than the last,
Shut thee from heaven with a dome more vast,
Till thou at last *art free*,
Leaving thine outgrown shell by life's unresting sea."

THE NINTH LESSON - Metempsychosis

As we have said in our last lesson, while the Yogi Teachings throw an important light upon the Western theory of Evolution, still there is a vital difference between the Western scientific teachings on the subject and the Eastern theories and teachings. The Western idea is that the process is a mechanical, material one, and that "mind" is a "by-product" of Matter in its evolution. But the Eastern Teachings hold that Mind is under, back of, and antecedent to all the work of Evolution, and that Matter is a "by-product" of Mind, rather than the reverse.

The Eastern Teachings hold that Evolution is caused by Mind striving, struggling, and pressing forward toward fuller and fuller expression, using Matter as a material, and yet always struggling to free itself from the confining and retarding influence of the latter. The struggle results in an Unfoldment, causing sheath after sheath of the confining material bonds to be thrown off and discarded, as the Spirit presses upon the Mind, and the Mind moulds and shapes the Matter. Evolution is but the process of birth of the Individualized Spirit, from the web of Matter in which it has been confined. And the pains and struggles are but incidents of the spiritual parturition.

In this and following lessons we shall consider the "Spiritual Evolution, of the race—that is the Unfoldment of Individualized Spirit—just as we did the subject Physical Evolution in the last two
lessons.

We have seen that preceding Spiritual Evolution, there was a Spiritual Involution. The Yogi Philosophy holds that in the Beginning, the Absolute meditated upon the subject of Creation, and formed a Mental Image, or Thought-Form, of an Universal Mind—that is, of an Universal Principle of Mind. This Universal Principle of Mind is the Great Ocean of "Mind-Stuff" from which all the phenomenal Universe is evolved. From this Universal Principle of Mind, proceeded the Universal Principle of Force or Energy. And from the latter, proceeded the Universal Principle of Matter.

The Universal Principle of Mind was bound by Laws imposed upon it by the mental-conception of the Absolute—the Cosmic

Laws of Nature. And these laws were the compelling causes of the Great Involution. For before Evolution was possible, Involution was necessary. We have explained that the word "involve" means "to wrap up; to cover; to hide, etc." Before a thing can be "evolved," that is "unfolded," it must first be "involved," that is "wrapped up." A thing must be *put in*, before it may be *taken out*.

Following the laws of Involution imposed upon it, the Universal Mental Principle involved itself in the Universal Energy Principle; and then in obedience to the same laws, the latter involved itself in the Universal Material Principle. Each stage of Involution, or *wrapping-up*, created for itself (out of the higher principle which in being involved) the wrapper or sheath which is to be used to wrap-up the higher principle. And the higher forms of the Material Principle formed sheaths of lower forms, until forms of Matter were produced far more gross than any known to us now, for they have disappeared in the Evolutionary ascent. Down, down, down went the process of Involution, until the lowest point was reached. Then ensued a moment's pause, preceding the beginning of the Evolutionary Unfoldment.

Then began the Great Evolution. But, as we have told you, the Upward movement was distinguished by the "Tendency toward Individualization." That is, while the Involuntary Process was accomplished by Principles as Principles, the Upward Movement was begun by a tendency toward "splitting up," and the creation of "individual forms," and the effort to perfect them and build upon them higher and still higher succeeding forms, until a stage was reached in which the Temple of the Spirit was worthy of being occupied by Man, the self-conscious expression of the Spirit. For the coming of Man was the first step of a higher form of Evolution—the Spiritual Evolution. Up to this time there had been simply an Evolution of Bodies, but now there came the Evolution of Souls.

And this Evolution of Souls becomes possible only by the process of Metempsychosis (pronounced *me-temp-si-ko-sis*) which is more commonly known as Reincarnation, or Re-embodiment.

It becomes necessary at this point to call your attention to the general subject of Metempsychosis, for the reason that the public mind is most confused regarding this important subject. It has the most vague ideas regarding the true teachings, and has somehow acquired the impression that the teachings are that human souls are re-born into the bodies of dogs, and other animals. The wildest ideas on this subject are held by some people. And, not only is this so, but even a number of those who hold to the doctrine of Reincarnation, in some of its forms, hold that their individual souls were once the individual souls of animals, from which state they have evolved to the present condition. This last is a perversion of the highest Yogi Teachings, and we trust to make same plain in these lessons. But, first we must take a look at the general subject of Metempsychosis, that we may see the important part it has played in the field of human thought and belief.

While to many the idea of Metempsychosis may seem new and unfamiliar, still it is one of the oldest conceptions of the race, and in ages past was the accepted belief of the whole of the civilized race of man of the period. And even today, it is accepted as Truth by the majority of the race

The almost universal acceptance of the idea by the East with its teeming life, counterbalances its comparative non-reception by the Western people of the day. From the early days of written or legendary history, Metempsychosis has been the accepted belief of many of the most intelligent of the race. It is found underlying the magnificent civilization of ancient Egypt, and from thence it traveled to the Western world being held as the highest truth by such teachers as Pythagoras, Empedocles, Plato, Virgil and Ovid. Plato's Dialogues are full of this teaching. The Hindus have always held to it. The Persians, inspired by their learned Magi, accepted it implicitly. The ancient Druids, and Priests of Gaul, as well as the ancient inhabitants of Germany, held to it. Traces of it may be found in the remains of the Aztec, Peruvian and Mexican civilizations.

The Eleusinian Mysteries of Greece, the Roman Mysteries, and the Inner Doctrines of the Cabbala of the Hebrews all taught the Truths of Metempsychosis. The early Christian Fathers; the Gnostic and Manichaeans and other sects of the Early Christian people, all held to the doctrine. The modern German philosophers have treated it with the greatest respect, if indeed they did not at least partially accept it. Many modern writers have considered it gravely, and with respect. The following quotations will give an idea of "how the wind is blowing" in the West:

"Of all the theories respecting the origin of the soul, Metempsychosis seems to me the most plausible and therefore the one most likely to throw light on the question of a life to come."—*Frederick H. Hedge.*

"It would be curious if we should find science and philosophy taking up again the old theory of metempsychosis, remodelling' it to suit our present modes of religious and scientific thought, and launching it again on the wide ocean of human belief. But stranger things have happened in the history of human opinions."—*James Freeman Clarke.*

"If we could legitimately determine any question of belief by the number of its adherents, the —— would apply to metempsychosis more fitly than to any other. I think it is quite as likely to be revived and to come to the front as any rival theory."—*Prof. Wm. Knight.*

"It seems to me, a firm and well-grounded faith in the doctrine of Christian metempsychosis might help to regenerate the world. For it would be a faith not hedged around with many of the difficulties and objections which beset other forms of doctrine, and it offers distinct and pungent motives for trying to lead a more Christian life, and for loving and helping our brother-man."—*Prof. Francis Bowen.*

"The doctrine of Metempsychosis may almost claim to be a natural or innate belief in the human mind, if we may judge from its wide diffusion among the nations of the earth, and its prevalence throughout the historical ages."—*Prof. Francis Bowen.*

"When Christianity first swept over Europe, the inner thought of its leaders was deeply tinctured with this truth. The Church tried ineffectually to eradicate it, but in various sects it kept sprouting forth beyond the time of Erigina and Bonaventura, its mediaeval advocates. Every great intuitional soul, as Paracelsus, Boehme, and Swedenborg, has adhered to it. The Italian luminaries, Giordano Bruno and Campanella. embraced it. The best of German philosophy is enriched by it. In Schopenhauer, Lessing,

Hegel, Leibnitz, Herder, and Fichte, the younger, it is earnestly advocated. The anthropological systems of Kant and Schelling furnish points of contact with it. The younger Helmont, in *De Revolutione Animarum*, adduces in two hundred problems all the arguments which may be urged in favor of the return of souls into human bodies according to Jewish ideas. Of English thinkers, the Cambridge Platonists defended it with much learning and acuteness, most conspicuously Henry More; and in Cudsworth and Hume it ranks as the most rational theory of immortality. Glanvil's *Lux Orientalis* devotes a curious treatise to it. It captivated the minds of Fourier and Leroux. Andre Pezzani's book on *The Plurality of the Soul's Lives* works out the system on the Roman Catholic idea of expiation."—E.D. WALKER, in "*Re-Incarnation, a Study of Forgotten Truth.*"

And in the latter part of the Nineteenth Century, and this the early part of the Twentieth Century, the general public has been made familiar with the idea of Metempsychosis, under the name of Re-incarnation, by means of the great volume of literature issued by The Theosophical Society and its allied following. No longer is the thought a novelty to the Western thinker, and many have found within themselves a corroborative sense of its truth. In fact, to many the mere mention of the idea has been sufficient to awaken faint shadowy memories of past lives, and, to such, many heretofore unaccountable traits of character, tastes, inclinations, sympathies, dislikes, etc., have been explained. The Western world has been made familiar with the idea of the re-birth of souls into new bodies, under the term of "Re-incarnation," which means "a re-entry into flesh," the word "incarnate" being derived from the words "*in*," and "*carnis*," meaning flesh—the English word meaning "to clothe with flesh," etc. The word Metempsychosis, which we use in this lesson, is concerned rather with the "passage of the soul" from one tenement to another, the "fleshly" idea being merely incidental. The doctrine of Metempsychosis, or Re-incarnation, together with its accompanying doctrine, Karma, or Spiritual Cause and Effect, is one of the great foundation stones of the Yogi Philosophy, as indeed it is of the entire system of systems of Oriental Philosophy and Thought. Unless one understands Metempsychosis he will never be able to understand the Eastern

Teachings, for he will be without the Key. You who have read the *Bhagavad Gita*, that wonderful Hindu Epic, will remember how the thread of Re-Birth runs through it all. You remember the words of *Krishna* to *Arjuna*: "As the soul, wearing this material body, experienceth the stages of infancy, youth, manhood, and old age, even so shall it, in due time, pass on to another body, and in other incarnations shall it again live, and move and play its part." "These bodies, which act as enveloping coverings for the souls occupying them, are but finite things—things of the moment—and not the Real Man at all. They perish as all finite things perish—let them perish." "As a man throweth away his old garments, replacing them with new and brighter ones, even so the Dweller of the body, having quitted its old mortal frame, entereth into others which are new and freshly prepared for it. Weapons pierce not the Real Man, nor doth the fire burn him; the water affecteth him not, nor the wind drieth him nor bloweth him away. For he is impregnable and impervious to these things of the world of change—he is eternal, permanent, unchangeable, and unalterable—Real."

This view of life gives to the one who holds to it, an entirely different mental attitude. He no longer identifies himself with the particular body that he may be occupying, nor with any other body for that matter. He learns to regard his body just as he would a garment which he is wearing, useful to him for certain purposes, but which will in time be discarded and thrown aside for a better one, and one better adapted to his new requirements and needs. So firmly is this idea embedded in the consciousness of the Hindus, that they will often say "My body is tired," or "My body is hungry," or "My body is full of energy," rather than that "I am" this or that thing. And this consciousness, once attained, gives to one a sense of strength, security and power unknown to him who regards his body as himself. The first step for the student who wishes to grasp the idea of Metempsychosis, and who wishes to awaken in his consciousness a certainty of its truth, is to familiarize himself with the idea of his "I" being a thing independent and a part from his body, although using the latter as an abiding place and a useful shelter and instrument for the time being.

Many writers on the subject of Metempsychosis have devoted much time, labor and argument to prove the reasonableness of the doctrine upon purely speculative, philosophical, or metaphysical grounds. And while we believe that such efforts are praiseworthy for the reason that many persons must be first convinced in that way, still we feel that one must really *feel* the truth of the doctrine from something within his own consciousness, before he will really *believe* it to be truth. One may convince himself of the logical necessity of the doctrine of Metempsychosis, but at the same time he may drop the matter with a shrug of the shoulders and a "still, who knows?" But when one begins to feel within himself the awakening consciousness of a "something in the past," not to speak of the flashes of memory, and feeling of former acquaintance with the subject, then, and then only, does he begin to *believe.*

Many people have had "peculiar experiences" that are accountable only upon the hypothesis of Metempsychosis. Who has not experienced the consciousness of having *felt the thing before—having thought it some time in the dim past? Who has not witnessed new scenes that appear old, very old? Who has not met persons for the first time, whose presence awakened memories of a past lying far back in the misty ages of long ago? Who has not been seized at times with the consciousness of a mighty "oldness" of soul? Who has not heard music, often entirely new compositions, which somehow awakens memories of similar strains, scenes, places, faces, voices, lands, associations and events, sounding dimly on the strings of memory as the breezes of the harmony floats over them? Who has not gazed at some old painting, or piece of statuary, with the sense of having seen it all before? Who has not lived through events, which brought with them a certainty of being merely a repetition of some shadowy occurrences away back in lives lived long ago? Who has not felt the influence of the mountain, the sea, the desert, coming to them when they are far from such scenes— coming so vividly as to cause the actual scene of the present to fade into comparative unreality. Who has not had these experiences—we ask?*

Writers, poets, and others who carry messages to the world, have testified to these things—and nearly every man or woman who hears the message recognizes it as something having correspondence in his or her own life. Sir Walter Scott tells us in his diary: "I cannot, I am sure, tell if it is worth marking down, that yesterday, at dinner time, I was strangely haunted by what I would call the sense of preexistence, viz., a confused idea that nothing that passed was said for the first time; that the same topics had been discussed and the same persons had stated the same opinions on them. The sensation was so strong as to resemble what is called the mirage in the desert and a calenture on board ship." The same writer, in one of his novels, "Guy Mannering," makes one of his characters say: "Why is it that some scenes awaken thoughts which belong as it were, to dreams of early and shadowy recollections, such as old Brahmin moonshine would have ascribed to a state of previous existence. How often do we find ourselves in society which we have never before met, and yet feel impressed with a mysterious and ill-defined consciousness that neither the scene nor the speakers nor the subject are entirely new; nay, feel as if we could anticipate that part of the conversation which has not yet taken place." Bulwer speaks of "that strange kind of inner and spiritual memory which so often recalls to us places and persons we have never seen before, and which Platonists would resolve to be the unquenched consciousness of a former life." And again, he says: "How strange is it that at times a feeling comes over us as we gaze upon certain places, which associates the scene either with some dim remembered and dreamlike images of the Past, or with a prophetic and fearful omen of the Future. Every one has known a similar strange and indistinct feeling at certain times and places, and with a similar inability to trace the cause." Poe has written these words on the subject: "We walk about, amid the destinies of our world existence, accompanied by dim but ever present memories of a Destiny more vast—very distant in the bygone time and infinitely awful. We live out a youth peculiarly haunted by such dreams, yet never mistaking them for dreams. As memories we know them. During our youth the distinctness is too clear to deceive us even for a moment. But the doubt of manhood dispels these feelings as illusions."

Home relates an interesting incident in his life, which had a marked effect upon his beliefs, thereafter. He relates that upon an occasion when he visited a strange house in London he was shown into a room to wait. He says: "On looking around, to my astonishment everything appeared perfectly familiar to me. I seemed to recognize every object. I said to myself, 'What is this? I have never been here before, and yet I have seen all this, and if so, then there must be a very peculiar knot in that shutter.'" He proceeded to examine the shutter, and much to his amazement the knot was there.

We have recently heard of a similar case, told by an old lady who formerly lived in the far West of the United States. She states that upon one occasion a party was wandering on the desert in her part of the country, and found themselves out of water. As that part of the desert was unfamiliar even to the guides, the prospect for water looked very poor indeed. After a fruitless search of several hours, one of the party, a perfect stranger to that part of the country, suddenly pressed his hand to his head, and acted in a dazed manner, crying out "I know that a water-hole is over to the right—this way," and away he started with the party after him. After a half-hour's journey they reached an old hidden water-hole that was unknown even to the oldest man in the party. The stranger said that he did not understand the matter, but that he had somehow experienced a sensation of *having been there before*, and knowing just where the water-hole was located. An old Indian who was questioned about the matter, afterward, stated that the place had been well known to his people who formerly travelled much on that part of the desert; and that they had legends relating to the "hidden water-hole," running back for many generations. In this case, it was remarked that the water-hole was situated in such a peculiar and unusual manner, as to render it almost undiscoverable even to people familiar with the characteristics of that part of the country. The old lady who related the story, had it direct from the lips of one of the party, who regarded it as "something queer," but who had never even heard of Metempsychosis.

A correspondent of an English magazine writes as follows: "A gentleman of high intellectual attainments, now deceased, once told me that he had dreamed of being in a strange city, so vividly that he remembered the streets, houses and public buildings as distinctly as those of any place he ever visited. A few weeks later he was induced to visit a panorama in Leicester Square, when he was startled by seeing the city of which he had dreamed. The likeness was perfect, except that one additional church appeared in the picture. He was so struck by the circumstance that he spoke to the exhibitor, assuming for the purpose the air of a traveller acquainted with the place, when he was informed that the church was a recent erection." The fact of the addition of the church, seems to place the incident within the rule of awakened memories of scenes known in a past life, for clairvoyance, astral travel, etc., would show the scene as it was at the time of the dream, not as it had been years before.

Charles Dickens mentions a remarkable impression in his work "Pictures from Italy." "In the foreground was a group of silent peasant girls, leaning over the parapet of the little bridge, looking now up at the sky, now down into the water; in the distance a deep dell; the shadow of an approaching night on everything. If I had been murdered there in some former life I could not have seemed to remember the place more thoroughly, or with more emphatic chilling of the blood; and the real remembrance of it acquired in that minute is so strengthened by the imaginary recollection that I hardly think I could forget it."

We have recently met two people in America who had very vivid memories of incidents in their past life. One of these, a lady, has a perfect horror of large bodies of water, such as the Great Lakes, or the Ocean, although she was born and has lived the greater part of her life inland, far removed from any great body of water, She has a distinct recollection of falling from a large canoe-shape vessel, of peculiar lines, and drowning. She was quite overcome upon her first visit to the Field Museum in Chicago, where there were exhibited a number of models of queer vessels used by primitive people. She pointed out one similar in shape, and lines, to the one she remembers as having fallen from in some past life.

The second case mentioned is that of a married couple who met each other in a country foreign to both, on their travels. They fell in love with each other, and both have felt that their marriage was a reunion rather than a new attachment. The husband one day shortly after their marriage told his wife in a rather shamed-faced way that he had occasional flashes of memory of having held in his arms, in the dim past, a woman whose face he could not recall, but who wore a strange necklace, he describing the details of the latter. The wife said nothing, but after her husband had left for his office, she went to the attic and unpacked an old trunk containing some odds and ends, relics, heirlooms, etc., and drew from it an old necklace of peculiar pattern that her grandfather had brought back from India, where he had lived in his younger days, and which had been in the family ever since. She laid the necklace on the table, so that her husband would see it upon his return. The moment his eyes fell upon it, he turned white as death, and gasped "My God! *that's the necklace!*"

A writer in a Western journal gives the following story of a Southern woman. "When I was in Heidelberg, Germany, attending a convention of Mystics, in company with some friends I paid my first visit to the ruined Heidelberg Castle. As I approached it I was impressed with the existence of a peculiar room in an inaccessible portion of the building. A paper and pencil were provided me, and I drew a diagram of the room even to its peculiar floor. My diagram and description were perfect, when we afterwards visited the room. In some way, not yet clear to me, I have been connected with that apartment. Still another impression came to me with regard to a book, which I was made to feel was in the old library of the Heidelberg University. I not only knew what the book was, but even felt that a certain name of an old German professor would be found written in it. Communicating this feeling to one of the Mystics at the convention, a search was made for the volume, but it was not found. Still the impression clung to me, and another effort was made to find the book; this time we were rewarded for our pains. Sure enough, there on the margin of one of the leaves was the very name I had been given in such a strange manner. Other things at the same time went to convince me that I was in possession of the soul of a person who had known Heidelberg two or three centuries ago."

A contributor to an old magazine relates, among other instances, the following regarding a friend who remembers having died in India during the youth of some former life. He states: "He sees the bronzed attendants gathered about his cradle in their white dresses: they are fanning him. And as they gaze he passes into unconsciousness. Much of his description concerned points of which he knew nothing from any other source, but all was true to the life, and enabled me to fix on India as the scene which he recalled."

While comparatively few among the Western races are able to remember more than fragments of their past lives, in India it is quite common for a man well developed spiritually to clearly remember the incidents and details of former incarnations, and the evidence of the awakening of such power causes little more than passing interest among his people. There is, as we shall see later, a movement toward conscious Metempsychosis, and many of the race are just moving on to that plane. In India the highly developed individuals grow into a clear recollection of their past lives when they reach the age of puberty, and when their brains are developed sufficiently to grasp the knowledge locked up in the depths of the soul. In the meantime the individual's memory of the past is locked away in the recesses of his mind, just as are many facts and incidents of his present life so locked away, to be remembered only when some one mentions the subject, or some circumstance serves to supply the associative link to the apparently forgotten matter.

Regarding the faculty of memory in our present lives, we would quote the following from the pen of Prof. William Knight, printed in the Fortnightly Review. He says: "Memory of the details of the past is absolutely impossible. The power of the conservative faculty, though relatively great, is extremely limited. We forget the larger portion of experience soon after we have passed through it, and we should be able to recall the particulars of our past years, filling all the missing links of consciousness since we entered on the present life, before we were in a position to remember our ante-natal experience. Birth must necessarily be preceded by crossing the river of oblivion, while the capacity for fresh acquisition survives, and the garnered wealth of old experience determines the amount and character of the new."

Another startling evidence of the proof of Metempsychosis is afforded us in the cases of "infant prodigies," etc., which defy any other explanation. Take the cases of the manifestation of musical talent in certain children at an early age, for instance.

Take the case of Mozart who at the age of four was able to not only perform difficult pieces on the piano, but actually composed original works of merit. Not only did he manifest the highest faculty of sound and note, but also an instinctive ability to compose and arrange music, which ability was superior to that of many men who had devoted years of their life to study and practice. The laws of harmony—the science of commingling tones, was to him not the work of years, but a faculty born in him. There are many similar cases of record.

Heredity does not explain these instances of genius, for in many of the recorded cases, none of the ancestors manifested any talent or ability. From whom did Shakespeare inherit his genius? From whom did Plato derive his wonderful thought? From what ancestor did Abraham Lincoln inherit his character—coming from a line of plain, poor, hard-working people, and possessing all of the physical attributes and characteristics of his ancestry, he, nevertheless, manifested a mind which placed him among the foremost of his race. Does not Metempsychosis give us the only possible key? Is it not reasonable to suppose that the abilities displayed by the infant genius, and the talent of the men who spring from obscure origin, have their root in the experiences of a previous life?

Then take the cases of children at school. Children of even the same family manifest different degrees of receptivity to certain studies. Some "take to" one thing, and some to another. Some find arithmetic so easy that they almost absorb it intuitively, while grammar is a hard task for them; while their brothers and sisters find the exact reverse to be true. How many have found that when they would take up some new study, it is almost like recalling something already learned. Do you student, who are now reading these lines take your own case. Does not all this Teaching seem to you like the repetition of some lesson learned long ago? Is it not like remembering something already learned, rather than the learning of some new truth? Were you not attracted to these studies, in the first place, by a feeling that you had known it all before, somewhere, somehow? Does not your mind leap ahead of the lesson, and see what is coming next, long before you have turned the pages? These inward evidences of the fact of pre-existence are so strong that they outweigh the most skillful appeal to the intellect.

This intuitive knowledge of the truth of Metempsychosis explains why the belief in it is sweeping over the Western world at such a rapid rate. The mere mention of the idea, to many people who have never before heard of it, is sufficient to cause them to recognize its truth. And though they may not understand the laws of its operation, yet deep down in their consciousness they find a something that convinces them of its truth. In spite of the objections that are urged against the teaching, it is making steady headway and progress.

The progress of the belief in Metempsychosis however has been greatly retarded by the many theories and dogmas attached to it by some of the teachers. Not to speak of the degrading ideas of re-birth into the bodies of animals, etc., which have polluted the spring of Truth, there are to be found many other features of teaching and theory which repel people, and cause them to try to kill out of the minds the glimmer of Truth that they find there. The human soul instinctively revolts against the teaching that it is bound to the wheel or re-birth, *willy-nilly*, compulsorily, without choice—compelled to live in body after body until great cycles are past. The soul, perhaps already sick of earth-life, and longing to pass on to higher planes of existence, fights against such teaching. And it does well to so fight, for the truth is nearer to its hearts desire. There is no soul longing that does not carry with it the prophecy of its own fulfillment, and so it is in this case. It is true that the soul of one filled with earthly desires, and craving for material things, will by the very force of those desires be drawn back to earthly re-birth in a body best suited for the gratification of the longings, desires and cravings that it finds within itself. But it is likewise true that the earth-sick soul is not compiled to return unless its own desires bring it back. Desire is the key note of Metempsychosis, although up to a certain stage it may operate unconsciously. The sum of the desires of a soul regulate its re-birth. Those who have become sickened of all that earth has for them at this stage of its evolution, may, and do, rest in states of existence far removed from earth scenes, until the race progresses far enough to afford the resting soul the opportunities and environments that it so earnestly craves.

380

And more than this, when Man reaches a certain stage, the process of Metempsychosis no longer remains unconscious, but he enters into a conscious knowing, willing passage from one life to another. And when that stage is reached a full memory of the past lives is unfolded, and life to such a soul becomes as the life of a day, succeeded by a night, and then the awakening into another day with full knowledge and recollection of the events of the day before. We are in merely the babyhood of the race now, and the fuller life of the conscious soul lies before us. Yea, even now it is being entered into by the few of the race that have progressed sufficiently far on the Path. And you, student, who feel within you that craving for conscious re-birth and future spiritual evolution, and the distaste for, and horror of, a further blind, unconscious re-plunge into the earth-life—know you, that this longing on your part is but an indication of what lies before you. It is the strange, subtle, awakening of the nature within you, which betokens the higher state. Just as the young person feels within his or her body strange emotions, longings and stirrings, which betoken the passage from the child state into that of manhood or womanhood, so do these spiritual longings, desires and cravings betoken the passage from unconscious re-birth into conscious knowing Metempsychosis, when you have passed from the scene of your present labors.

In our next lesson we shall consider the history of the race as its souls passed on from the savage tribes to the man of to-day. It is the history of the race—the history of the individual—your own history, student—the record of that through which you have passed to become that which you now are. And as you have climbed step after step up the arduous path, so will you, hereafter climb still higher paths, but no longer in unconsciousness, but with your spiritual eyes wide open to the Rays of Truth pouring forth from the great Central Sun—the Absolute.

Concluding this lesson, we would quote two selections from the American poet, Whitman, whose strange genius was undoubtedly the result of vague memories springing from a previous life, and which burst into utterances often not more than half understood by the mind that gave them birth. Whitman says:

"Facing West from California's shores,
Inquiring, tireless, seeking what is yet unfound,

A, a child, very old, over waves, toward the house of
  maternity, the land of migrations, look afar,
Look off the shores of my Western sea, the circle
  almost circled:
For starting Westward from Hindustan, from the
  vales of Kashmere,
From Asia, from the north, from God, the sage, and
  the hero,
From the south, from the flowery peninsulas and
  spice islands,
Long having wandered since, round the earth having
  wandered,
Now I face home again, very pleased and joyous.
(But where is what I started for so long ago?
And why is it yet unfound?)"
* * * * *

"I know I am deathless.
  I know that this orbit of mine cannot be swept by a
    carpenter's compass;
  And whether I come to my own to-day, or in ten
    thousand or ten million years,
  I can cheerfully take it now or with equal cheerfulness
    can wait."
* * * * *

  "As to you, Life, I reckon you are the leavings of
    many deaths.
  No doubt I have died myself ten thousand times before."
* * * * *

"Births have brought us richness and variety, and other births
have brought us richness and variety."
* * * * *

And this quotation from the American poet N.P. Willis:
  "But what a mystery this erring mind?
  It wakes within a frame of various powers
  A stranger in a new and wondrous world.
  It brings an instinct from some other sphere,
  For its fine senses are familiar all,
  And with the unconscious habit of a dream
  It calls and they obey. The priceless sight

Springs to its curious organ, and the ear
Learns strangely to detect the articulate air
In its unseen divisions, and the tongue
Gets its miraculous lesson with the rest,
And in the midst of an obedient throng
Of well trained ministers, the mind goes forth
To search the secrets of its new found home."

THE TENTH LESSON - Spiritual Evolution

One of the things that repel many persons who have had their attention directed to the subject of Metempsychosis for the first time, is the idea that they have evolved *as a soul* from individual lowly forms, for instance that they have at one time been an individual plant, and then an individual animal form, and then an individual higher animal form, and so on until now they are the particular individual human form contemplating the subject. This idea, which has been taught by many teachers, is repellent to the average mind, for obvious reasons, and naturally so, for it has no foundation in truth.

While this lesson is principally concerned with the subject of the Spiritual Evolution of the human soul, since it became a human soul, still it may be as well to mention the previous phase of evolution, briefly, in order to prevent misconception, and to dispel previously acquired error.

The atom, although it possesses life and a certain degree of mind, and acts as an individual temporarily, has no permanent individuality that reincarnates. When the atom is evolved it becomes a centre of energy in the great atomic principle, and when it is finally dissolved it resolves itself back into its original state, and its life as an individual atom ceases, although the experience it has gained becomes the property of the entire principle. It is as if a body of water were to be resolved into millions of tiny dew-drops for a time, and each dew-drop was then to acquire certain outside material in solution. In that case, each dew-drop when it again returned to the body of water, would carry with it its foreign material, which would become the property of the whole. And subsequently formed dew-drops would carry in their substance a particle of the foreign matter brought back home by the previous generation of dewdrops, and would thus be a little different from their predecessors. And this process, continuing for many generations of dew-drops, would ultimately cause the greatest changes in the composition of the successive generations.

This, in short, is the story of the change and improving forms of life. From the atoms into the elements; from the lower elements into those forming protoplasm; from the protoplasm to the lower forms of animal life; from these lower forms on to higher forms—this is the story. But it is all a counterpart of the dew-drop and the body of water, *until the human soul is evolved.* The plants and the lower forms of animal life are not permanent individual souls, but each family is a *group-soul* corresponding to the body of water from which the dew-drop arose. From these family group-souls gradually break off minor groups, representing species, and so on into sub-species. At last when the forms reach the plane of man, the group-soul breaks itself up into *permanent individual souls*, and true Metempsychosis begins. That is, *each individual human soul becomes a permanent individual entity*, destined to evolve and perfect itself along the lines of spiritual evolution.

And from this point begins our story of Spiritual Evolution. The story of Man, the Individual, begins amidst humble surroundings. Primitive man, but little above the level of the lower animals in point of intelligence, has nevertheless that distinguishing mark of Individuality—"Self-Consciousness," which is the demarkation between Beast and Man. And even the lowest of the lowest races had at least a "trace" of this Self-Consciousness, which made of them individuals, and caused the fragment of the race-soul to separate itself from the general principle animating the race, and to fasten its "I" conscious upon itself, rather than upon the underlying race-soul, along instinctive lines. Do you know just what this Self-Consciousness is, and how it differs from the Physical Consciousness of the lower animals? Perhaps we had better pause a moment to consider it at this place.

The lower animals are of course conscious of the bodies, and their wants, feelings, emotions, desires, etc., and their actions are in response to the animating impulses coming from this plane of consciousness. But it stops there. They "know," but they do not "know that they know"; that is, they have not yet arrived at a state in which they can think of themselves as "I," and to reason upon their thoughts and mental operations. It is like the consciousness of a very young child, which feels and knows its sensations and wants, but is unable to think of itself as "I," and to turn the mental gaze inward. In another book of these series we have used the illustration of the horse which has been left standing out in the cold sleet and rain, and which undoubtedly feels and knows the unpleasant sensations arising therefrom, and longs to get away from the unpleasant environment. But, still, he is unable to analyze his mental states and wonder whether his master will come out to him soon, or think how cruel it is to keep him out of his warm comfortable stable; or wonder whether he will be taken out in the cold rain again tomorrow; or feel envious of other horses who are indoors; or wonder why he is kept out cold nights, etc., etc. In short, the horse is unable to think as would a reasoning man under just the same circumstances. He is aware of the discomfort, just as would be the man; and he would run away home, if he were able, just as would the man. But he is not able to pity himself, nor to think about his personality, as would a man—he is not able to wonder whether life is worth the living, etc., as would a man. He "knows" but is not able to reflect upon the "knowing."

In the above illustration, the principal point is that the horse does not "know himself" as an entity, while even the most primitive man is able to so recognize himself as an "I." If the horse were able to think in words, he would think "feel," "cold," "hurt," etc., but he would be unable to think "*I* feel; *I* am cold; *I* am hurt," etc. The thought "I" would be missing.

It is true that the "I" consciousness of the primitive man was slight, and was but a degree above the Physical Consciousness of the higher apes, but nevertheless it had sprung into being, never again to be lost. The primitive man was like a child a few years old—he was able to say "I," and to think "I." *He had become an individual soul.*

And this individual soul inhabited and animated a body but little removed from that of an ape. But this new consciousness began to mould that rude body and the ascent was begun. Each generation showed a physical improvement over that of the preceding one, according to the lines of physical evolution, and as the developing soul demanded more perfect and developed bodies the bodies were evolved to meet the demand, for the mental demand has ever been the cause of the physical form. The soul of the primitive man reincarnated almost immediately after the death of the physical body, because the experiences gained were mostly along the lines of the physical, the mental planes being scarcely brought into play, while the higher and spiritual faculties were almost entirely obscured from sight. Life after life the soul of the primitive man lived out in rapid succession. But in each new embodiment there was a slight advance over that of the previous one. Experience, or rather the result of experiences, were carried over, and profited by. New lessons were learned and unlearned, improved upon or discarded. And the race grew and unfolded.

After a time the number of advancing souls which had outstripped their fellows in progress became sufficiently large for sub-races to be formed, and so the branching off process began. In this way the various races and types were formed, and the progress of Mankind gained headway. At this point we may as well consider the history of the Races of Mankind, that we may see how the great tide-wave of Soul has ever pressed onward, marking higher and still higher stages of progress, and also how the various minor waves of the great wave pushed in and then receded, only to be followed by still higher waves. The story is most interesting.

The Yogi Teachings inform us that the Grand Cycle of Man's Life on the Earth is composed of Seven Cycles, of which we are now living in the third-seventh part of the Fifth Cycle. These Cycles may be spoken of as the Great Earth Periods, separated from each other by some great natural cataclysm which destroyed the works of the previous races of men, and which started afresh the progress called "civilization," which, as all students know, manifests a rise and fall like unto that of the tides.

Man in the First Cycle emerged from a gross animal-like state into a condition somewhat advanced. It was a slow progress, but nevertheless a distinct series of advances were made by the more progressive souls who passed over on to the Second Cycle, embodying themselves as the ruling races in the same, their less progressive brothers incarnating in the lower tribes of the Second Cycle. It must be remembered that the souls which do not advance during a Cycle reincarnate in the next Cycle among the lower races. So that even in this Fifth Cycle we have remnants of the previous cycles, the lives of the members of which give us an idea of what life in the earlier cycles must have been.

The Yogi Teachings give us but little information regarding the people of the First and Second Cycles, because of the low state of these ages. The tale, if told, would be the story of the Cave-dweller, and Stone-age people; the Fire-peoples, and all the rest of savage, barbarian crew; there was but little trace of anything like that which we call "civilization," although in the latter periods of the Second Cycle the foundations for the coming civilizations were firmly laid.

After the cataclysm which destroyed the works of Man of the Second Cycle, and left the survivors scattered or disorganized, awaiting the touch of the organizing urge which followed shortly afterward, there dawned the first period of the Third Cycle. The scene of the life of the Third Cycle was laid in what is known to Occultists as Lemuria. Lemuria was a mighty continent situated in what is now known as the Pacific Ocean, and parts of the Indian Ocean. It included Australia, Australasia, and other portions of the Pacific islands, which are in fact surviving portions of the great continent of Lemuria, its highest points, the lower portion having sunk beneath the seas ages and ages ago. Life in Lemuria is described as being principally concerned with the physical senses, and sensual enjoyment, only a few developed souls having broken through the fetters of materiality and reached the beginnings of the mental and spiritual planes of life. Some few indeed made great progress and were saved from the general wreck, in order to become the leaven which would lighten the mass of mankind during the next Cycle. These developed souls were the teachers of the new races, and were looked upon by the latter as gods and supernatural beings, and legends and traditions concerning them are still existent among the ancient peoples of our present day. Many of the myths of the ancient peoples arose in this way.

The Yogi traditions hold that just prior to the great cataclysm which destroyed the races of the Second Cycle, there was a body of the Chosen Ones which migrated from Lemuria to certain islands of the sea which are now part of the main land of India. These people formed the nucleus of the Occult Teachings of the Lemurians, and developed into the Fount of Truth which has

388

been flowing ever since throughout the successive periods and cycles.

When Lemuria passed away, there arose from the depths of the ocean the continent which was to be the scene of the life and civilization of the Fourth Cycle—the continent of Atlantis. Atlantis was situated in a portion of what is now known as the Atlantic Ocean, beginning at what is now known as the Caribbean Sea and extending over to the region of what is now known as Africa. What are now known as Cuba and the West Indies were among the highest points of the continent, and now stand like monuments to its departed greatness.

The civilization of Atlantis was remarkable, and its people attained heights which seem almost incredible to even those who are familiar with the highest achievements of man in our own times. The Chosen Ones preserved from the cataclysm which destroyed Lemuria, and who lived to a remarkably old age, had stored up within their minds the wisdom and learning of the races that had been destroyed, and they thus gave the Atlanteans an enormous starting-advantage. They soon attained great advancement along all the lines of human endeavor. They perfected mechanical inventions and appliances, reaching far ahead of even our present attainments. In the field of electricity especially they reached the stages that our present races will reach in about two or three hundred years from now. Along the lines of Occult Attainment their progress was far beyond the dreams of the average man of our own race, and in fact from this arose one of the causes of their downfall, for they prostituted the power to base and selfish uses, and Black Magic.

And, so the decline of Atlantis began. But the end did not come at once, or suddenly, but gradually. The continent, and its surrounding islands gradually sank beneath the waves of the Atlantic Ocean, the process occupying over 10,000 years. The Greeks and Romans of our own Cycle had traditions regarding the sinking of the continent, but their knowledge referred only to the disappearance of the small remainder—certain islands—the continent itself having disappeared thousands of years before their time. It is recorded that the Egyptian priests had traditions that the continent itself had disappeared nine thousand years before their time. As was the case with the Chosen Ones of

Lemuria, so was it with the Elect of Atlantis, who were taken away from the doomed land some time prior to its destruction. The few advanced people left their homes and migrated to portions of what are now South America and Central America, but which were then islands of the sea. These people have left their traces of their civilization and works, which our antiquaries are discovering to-day.

When the Fifth Cycle dawned (our own cycle, remember) these brave and advanced souls acted as the race-teachers and became as "gods" to those who came afterward. The races were very prolific, and multiplied very rapidly under the most favorable conditions. The souls of the Atlanteans were pressing forward for embodiment, and human forms were born to supply the demand. And now begins the history of our own Cycle—the Fifth Cycle.

But before we begin a consideration of the Fifth Cycle, let us consider for a moment a few points about the laws operating to cause these great changes.

In the first place, each Cycle has a different theatre for its work and action. The continent of Lemuria was not in existence during the Second Cycle, and arose from the ocean bed only when its appointed time came. And, likewise the continent of Atlantis reposed beneath the waves while the Lemurian races manifested during the Third Cycle, rising by means of a convulsion of the earth's surface to play its part during its own period—the Fourth Cycle—only to sink again beneath the waves to make way for the birth of the Fifth Cycle with its races. By means of these cataclysms the races of each Cycle were wiped out when the time came, the few Elect or Chosen ones, that is those who have manifested the right to live on, being carried away to some favorable environment where they became as leaven to the mass—as "gods" to the new races that quickly appear.

It must be remembered, however, that these Chosen Ones are not the only ones saved from the destruction that overtakes the majority of the race. On the contrary a few survivors are preserved, although driven away from their former homes, and reduced to "first principles of living" in order to become the parents of the new races. The new races springing from the fittest of these survivors quickly form sub-races, being composed of the better adapted souls seeking reincarnation, while the less fit sink into barbarism, and show evidences of decay, although a remnant drags on for thousands of years, being composed of the souls of those who have not advanced sufficiently to take a part in the life of the new races. These "left-overs" are in evidence in our own times in the cases of the Australian savages, and some of the African tribes, as well as among the Digger Indians and others of similar grade of intelligence.

In order to understand the advance of each race it must be remembered that the more advanced souls, after passing out of the body, have a much longer period of rest in the higher planes, and consequently do not present themselves for reincarnation until a period quite late when compared with the hasty reincarnation of the less advanced souls who are hurried back to rebirth by reason of the strong earthly attachments and desires. In this way it happens that the earlier races of each Cycle are more primitive folk than those who follow them as the years roll by. The soul of an earth-bound person reincarnates in a few years, and sometimes in a few days, while the soul of an advanced man may repose and rest on the higher planes for centuries—nay, even for thousands of years, until the earth has reached a stage in which the appropriate environment may be afforded it.

Observers, unconnected with Occultism, have noted certain laws which seem to regulate the rise and fall of nations—the procession of ruling races. They do not understand the law of Metempsychosis that alone gives the key to the problem, but nevertheless they have not failed to record the existence of the laws themselves. In order to show that these laws are recognized by persons who are not at all influenced by the Occult Teachings, we take the liberty of quoting from Draper's "History of the Intellectual Development of Europe."

Dr. Draper writes as follows: "We are, as we often say, the creatures of circumstances. In that expression there is a higher philosophy than might at first appear. From this more accurate point of view we should therefore consider the course of these events, recognizing the principle that the affairs of men pass forward in a determinate way, expanding and unfolding themselves. And hence we see that the things of which we have spoken as if they were matters of choice, were in reality forced upon their apparent authors by the necessity of the times. But in truth they should be considered as the presentation of a certain phase of life which nations in their onward course sooner or later assume. To the individual, how well we know that a sober moderation of action, an appropriate gravity of demeanor, belonging to the mature period of life, change from the wanton willfulness of youth, which may be ushered in, or its beginnings marked by many accidental incidents; in one perhaps by domestic bereavements, in another by the loss of fortune, in a third by ill-health. We are correct enough in imputing to such trials the change of character; but we never deceive ourselves by supposing that it would have failed to take place had these incidents not occurred. There runs an irresistible destiny in the midst of these vicissitudes. There are analogies between the life of a nation, and that of an individual, who, though he may be in one respect the maker of his own fortunes, for happiness or for misery, for good or for evil, though he remains here or goes there as his inclinations prompt, though he does this or abstains from that as he chooses, is nevertheless held fast by an inexorable fate—a fate which brought him into the world involuntarily, so far as he was concerned, which presses him forward through a definite career, the stages of which are absolutely invariable,— infancy, childhood, youth, maturity, old age, with all their characteristic actions and passions,—and which removes him from the scene at the appointed time, in most cases against his will. So also is it with nations; the voluntary is only the outward semblance, covering but hardly hiding the predetermined. Over the events of life we may have control, but none whatever over the law of its progress. There is a geometry that applies to nations an equation of their curve of advance. That no mortal man can touch."

This remarkable passage, just quoted, shows how the close observers of history note the rise and fall of the tides of human race progress, although ignorant of the real underlying causing energy or force. A study of the Occult Teachings alone gives one the hidden secret of human actions and throws the bright light of Truth upon the dark corners of phenomena.

At the beginning of the Fifth Cycle (which is the present one), there were not only the beginnings of the new races which always spring up at the beginning of each new cycle and which are the foundations for the coming races which take advantage of the fresh conditions and opportunities for growth and development—but there were also the descendants of the Elect Saved from the destruction of Atlantis by having been led away and colonized far from the scene of danger. The new races were the descendant of the scattered survivors of the Atlantean peoples, that is, the common run of people of the time. But the Elect few were very superior people, and imparted to their descendants their knowledge and wisdom. So that we see at the beginning of the Fifth Cycle hordes of new, primitive people in certain lands, and in other places advanced nations like the ancestors of the Ancient Egyptians, Persians, Chaldeans, Hindus, etc.

These advanced races were old souls—advanced souls—the progressed and developed souls of Ancient Lemuria and Atlantis, who lived their lives and who are now either on higher planes of life, or else are among us to-day taking a leading part in the world's affairs, striving mightily to save the present races from the misfortunes which overtook their predecessors.

The descendants of the people were the Assyrians and Babylonians. In due time the primitive new races developed and the great Roman, Grecian, and Carthaginian peoples appeared. Then came the rise of other peoples and nations down to the present time. Each race or nation has its rise, its height of attainment, and its decline. When a nation begins to decline it is because its more advanced souls have passed on, and only the less progressive souls are left. The history of all nations show the truth of the Occult the term. Men are forsaking old ideals, creeds and dogmas, and are running hither and thither seeking something they feel to be necessary, but of the nature of which they know nothing. They are feeling the hunger for Peace—the thirst for Knowledge—and they are seeking satisfaction in all directions.

This is not only the inevitable working of the Law of Evolution, but is also a manifestation of the power and love of the great souls that have passed on to higher planes of existence, and who have become as angels and arch-angels. These beings are filled with the love of the race, and are setting into motion influences that are being manifest in many directions, the tendency of which are to bring the race to a realization of its higher power, faculties, and destiny.

As we have said in other places, one of the greatest difficulties in the way of the seeker after Truth in his consideration of the question of Spiritual Evolution is the feeling that rebirth is being forced upon him, without any say on his part, and against his desires. But this is far from being correct. It is true that the whole process is according to the Great Law, but that Law operates through the force of Desire and Attraction. The soul is attracted toward rebirth by reason of its desire or rather the essence of its desires. It is reborn only because it has within itself the desire for further experience, and opportunity for unfoldment. And it is reborn into certain environments solely because it has within itself unsatisfied desires for those environments, etc. The process is just as regular and scientific as is the attraction of one atom of matter for another.

Each soul has within itself certain elements of desire and attraction, and it attracts to itself certain conditions and experiences, and is in turn attracted by these things. This is the law of life, in the body and out of it. And there is no injustice in the law it is the essence of justice itself, for it gives to each just what is required to fill the indwelling desires, or else the conditions and experiences designed to burn out the desires which are holding one back, and the destruction of which will make possible future advancement.

For instance, if one is bound by the inordinate desire for material wealth, the Law of Karma will attract him to a rebirth in conditions in which he will be surrounded by wealth and luxury until he becomes sickened with them and will find his heart filled with the desire to flee from them and toward higher and more satisfying things. Of course the Law of Karma acts in other ways, as we shall see in our next lesson—it deals with one's debts and obligations, also. The Law of Karma is closely connected with Metempsychosis, and one must be considered in connection with the other, always.

Not only is it true that man's rebirths are in strict accordance with the law of Attraction and Desire, but it is also true that after he attains a certain stage of spiritual unfoldment he enters into the conscious stage of rebirth, and thereafter he is reborn consciously and with full foreknowledge. Many are now entering into this stage of development, and have a partial consciousness of their past lives, which also implies that they have had at least a partial consciousness of approaching rebirth, for the two phases of consciousness run together.

Those individuals of a race who have outstripped their fellows in spiritual unfoldment, are still bound by the Karma of the particular race to which they belong, up to a certain point. And as the entire race, or at least a large proportion of it, must move forward as a whole, such individuals must needs wait also. But they are not compelled to suffer a tiresome round of continued rebirths amid environments and conditions which they have outgrown. On the contrary, the advanced individual soul is allowed to wait until the race reaches its own stage of advancement, when it again joins in the upward movement, in full consciousness, however. In the interim he may pass his well earned rest either on some of the higher planes of rest, or else in conscious temporary sojourn in other material spheres helping in the great work as a Teacher and worker for Good and Spiritual Evolution among those who need such help. In fact there are in the world to-day, individual souls which have reached similar stages on other planets, and who are spending their rest period here amidst the comparatively lower Earth conditions, striving to lift up the Earth souls to greater heights.

So long as people allow themselves to become attached to material objects, so long will they be reborn in conditions in which these objects bind them fast. It is only when the soul frees itself from these entangling obstructions that it is born in conditions of freedom. Some outgrow these material attachments by right thinking and reasoning, while others seem to be compelled to live them out, and thus outlive them, before they are free. At last when the soul realizes that these things are merely incidents of the lower personality, and have naught to do with the real individuality, then, and then only, do they fall from it like a wornout cloak, and are left behind while it bounds forward on The Path fresh from the lighter weight being carried. The Yogi Philosophy teaches that Man will live forever, ascending from higher to higher planes, and then on and on and on. Death is but the physical symbol of a period of Soul Rest, similar to sleep of the tired body, and is just as much to be welcomed and greeted with thanks. Life is continuous, and its object is development, unfoldment and growth. We are in Eternity now as much as we ever shall be. Our souls may exist out of the body as well as in it, although bodily incarnation is necessary at this stage of our development. As we progress on to higher planes of life, we shall incarnate in bodies far more ethereal than those now used by us, just as in the past we used bodies almost incredibly grosser and coarser than those we call our own to-day. Life is far more than a thing of three-score and ten years—it is really a succession of such lives, on an ascending scale, that which we call our personal self to-day being merely the essence of the experiences of countless lives in the past. The Soul is working steadily upward, from higher to higher, from gross to finer forms and manifestations. And it will steadily work for ages to come, always progressing, always advancing, always unfolding. The Universe contains many worlds for the Soul to inhabit, and then after it has passed on to other Universes, there will still be Infinitude before it. The destiny of the Soul of Man is of wondrous promise and possibilities—the mind to-day cannot begin to even dream of what is before the Soul. Those who have already advanced many steps beyond you—those Elder Brethren—are constantly extending to you aid in many directions. They are extending to you the Unseen Hand, which lifts you over many a hard place and dangerous crossing—but you recognize it not except in a vague way. There are now in existence, on planes infinitely higher than your own, intelligences of transcendent glory and magnificence—but they were once Men even as you are to-day. They have so far progressed upon the Path that they have become as angels and archangels when compared with you. And, blessed thought, even as these exalted ones were once even as you, so shall you, in due course of Spiritual Evolution, become even as these mighty ones.

The Yogi Philosophy teaches that You who are reading these lines have lived many lives previous to the present one. You have lived in the lower forms, and have worked your way arduously along the Path until now you are reaching the stage of Spiritual Consciousness in which the past and future will begin to appear plain to you for the first time. You have lived as the cave-man—the cliff-dweller—the savage—the barbarian. You have been the warrior—the priest—the Medieval scholar and occultist—the prince—the pauper. You have lived in Lemuria—in Atlantis—in India—in Persia—in Egypt—in ancient Rome and Greece—and are now playing your part in the Western civilization, associating with many with whom you have had relations in your past lives.

In closing this lesson, let us quote from a previous writing from the same pen that writes this lesson:

"Toward what goal is all this Spiritual Evolution tending? What does it all mean? From the low planes of life to the highest—all are on The Path. To what state or place does The Path lead? Let us attempt to answer by asking you to imagine a series of millions of circles, one within the other. Each circle means a stage of Life. The outer circles are filled with life in its lowest and most material stages—each circle nearer the Centre holds higher and higher forms—until Men (or what were once Men) become as gods. Still on, and on, and on. does the form of life grow higher, until the human mind cannot grasp the idea. But what is the Centre? The MIND of the entire Spiritual Body—the ABSOLUTE! And we are traveling toward that Centre!"

And again from the same source:

"But beyond your plane, and beyond mine, are plane after plane, connected with our earth, the splendors of which man cannot conceive. And there are likewise many planes around the other planets of our chain—and there are millions of other worlds—and there are chains of universes just as there are chains of planets—and then greater groups of these chains—and so on greater and grander beyond the power of man to imagine—on and on and on and on—higher and higher—to inconceivable heights. An infinity of infinities of worlds are before us. Our world and our planetary system and our system of suns, and our system of solar systems, are but as grains of sand on the beach of the mighty ocean. But then you cry, 'But what am I—poor mortal thing—lost among all this inconceivable greatness?' The answer comes that You are that most precious thing—a living soul. And if you were destroyed the whole system of universes would crumble, for you are as necessary as the greatest part of it—it cannot do without you—you cannot be lost or destroyed—you are a part of it all, and are eternal. 'But,' you ask, 'beyond all of this of which you have told me, what is there—what is the Centre of it All?' Your Teacher's face takes on a rapt expression—a light not of earth beams forth from his countenance. '*THE ABSOLUTE*!' he replies.

THE ELEVENTH LESSON - The Law of Karma

"Karma" is a Sanscrit term for that great Law known to Western thinkers as Spiritual Cause and Effect, or Causation. It relates to the complicated affinities for either good or evil that have been acquired by the soul throughout its many incarnations. These affinities manifest as characteristics enduring from one incarnation to another, being added to here, softened or altered there, but always pressing forward for expression and manifestation. And, so, it follows that what each one of us is in this life depends upon is what we have been and how we have acted in our past lives.

Throughout the operations of the Law of Karma the manifestation of Perfect Justice is apparent. We are not punished *for* our sins, as the current beliefs have it, but instead we are punished *by* our sins. We are not rewarded *for* our good acts, but we received our reward *through and by* characteristics, qualities, affinities, etc., acquired by reason of our having performed these good acts in previous lives. We are our own judges and executioners. In our present lives we are storing up good or bad Karma which will stick to us closely, and which will demand expression and manifestation in lives to come. When we fasten around ourselves the evil of bad Karma, we have taken to shelter a monster which will gnaw into our very vitals until we shake him off by developing opposite qualities. And when we draw to ourselves the good Karma of Duty well performed, kindness well expressed, and Good Deeds freely performed without hope of reward, then do we weave for ourselves the beautiful garments which we are destined to wear upon the occasion of our future lives.

The Yogi Teachings relating to the Law of Karma do not teach us that Sin is an offense against the Power which brought us into being, so much as it is an offense against ourselves. We cannot injure the Absolute, nor harm It in any way. But we may harm each other, and in so doing harm ourselves. The Yogis teach that Sin is largely a matter of ignorance and misunderstanding of our true nature, and that the lesson must be well learned until we are able to see the folly and error of our former course, and thus are able to remedy our past errors and to avoid their recurrence. By Karma the effects arising from our sins cling to us, until we become sick and weary of them, and seek their cause in our hearts. When we have discovered the evil cause of these effects, we learn to hate it and tear it from us as a foul thing, and are thence evermore relieved of it.

The Yogis view the sinning soul as the parent does the child who will persist in playing with forbidden things. The parent cautions the child against playing with the stove, but still the child persists in its disobedience, and sooner or later receives a burn for its meddling. The burn is not a *punishment* for the disobedience (although it may seem so to it) but comes in obedience to a natural law which is invariable. To child finds out that stoves and burns are connected, and begins to see some sense and reason in the admonitions of the parent. The love of the parent sought to save the child the pain of the burn, and yet the child-nature persisted in experimenting, and was taught the lesson. But the lesson once thoroughly learned, it is not necessary to forbid the child the stove, for it has learned the danger for itself and thereafter avoids it.

And thus it is with the human soul passing on from one life to another. It learns new lessons, gathers new experiences, and learns to recognize the pain that invariably comes from Wrong Action, and the Happiness that invariably comes from Right Action. As it progresses it learns how hurtful certain courses of action are, and like the burnt child it avoids them thereafter.

If we will but stop to consider for a moment the relative degrees of temptation to us and to others, we may see the operations of past Karma in former lives. Why is it that this thing is "no temptation" to you, while it is the greatest temptation to another. Why is it that certain things do not seem to have any attraction for him, and yet they attract you so much that you have to use all of your will power to resist them? It is because of the Karma in your past lives. The things that do not now tempt you, have been outlived in some former life, and you have profited by your own experiences, or those of others, or else through some teaching given you by one who had been attracted to you by your unfolding consciousness of Truth.

We are profiting to-day by the lessons of our past lives. If we have learned them well we are receiving the benefit, while if we have turned our backs on the words of wisdom offered us, or have refused to learn the lesson perfectly, we are compelled to sit on the same old school-benches and hear the same old lesson repeated until it is fairly driven into our consciousness. We wonder why it is that other persons can perform certain evil acts that seem so repulsive to us, and are apt to pride ourselves upon our superior virtue. But those who know, realize that their unfortunate brethren have not paid sufficient attention to the lesson of the past, and are having it repeated to them in a more drastic form this time. They know that the virtuous ones are simply reaping the benefit of their own application in the past, but that their lesson is not over, and that unless they advance and hold fast to that which they have attained, as well, they will be outstripped by many of those whose failure they are now viewing with wonder and scorn.

It is hard for us to fully realize that we are what we are because of our past experiences. It is difficult for us to value the experiences that we are now going through, because we do not fully appreciate the value of bitter experiences once lived out and outlived. Let us look back over the experiences of this present life, for instance. How many bitter episodes are there which we wish had never happened, and how we wish we could tear them out of our consciousness. But we do not realize that from these same bitter experiences came knowledge and wisdom that we would not part with under any circumstances. And yet if we were to tear away from us the cause of these benefits, we would tear away the benefits also, and would find ourselves back just where we were before the experience happened to us. What we would like to do is to hold on to the benefits that came from the experience—-the knowledge and wisdom that were picked from the tree of pain. But we cannot separate the effect from the cause in this way, and must learn to look back upon these bitter experiences as the causes from which our present knowledge, wisdom and attainment proceeded. Then may we cease to hate these things, and to see that good may come from evil, under the workings of the Law.

And when we are able to do this, we shall be able to regard the painful experiences of our present day as the inevitable outcome of causes away back in our past, but which will work surely toward increased knowledge, wisdom and attainment, if we will but see the Good underlying the working of the Law. When we fall in with the working of the Law of Karma we recognize its pain not as an injustice or punishment, but as the beneficent operation of a Law which, although apparently working Evil, has for its end and aim Ultimate Good.

Many object to the teachings of the Law of Karma by saying that the experiences of each life not being remembered, must be useless and without value. This is a very foolish position to take concerning the matter. These experiences although not fully remembered, are not lost to us at all—they are made a part of the material of which our minds are composed. They exist in the form of feelings, characteristics, inclinations, likes and dislikes, affinities, attractions, repulsions, etc., etc., and are as much in evidence as are the experiences of yesterday which are fresh in our memory. Look back over your present life, and try to remember the experiences of the past years. You will find that you remember but few of the events of your life. The pressing and constant experiences of each of the days that you have lived have been, for the most part, forgotten. Though these experiences may have seemed very vivid and real to you when they occurred, still they have faded into nothingness now, and they are to all intents and purposes *lost* to you. But *are* they lost? Not at all. You are what you are because of the results of these experiences. Your character has been moulded and shaped, little by little, by these apparently forgotten pains, pleasures, sorrows and happinesses. This trial strengthened you along certain lines; that one changed your point of view and made you see things with a broader sweep of vision. This grief caused you to feel the pain of others; that disappointment spurred you on to new endeavors. And each and every one of them left a permanent mark upon your personality—upon your character. All men are what they are by reason of what they have lived through and out. And though these happenings, scenes, circumstances, occurrences, experiences, have faded from the memory, their effects are indelibly imprinted upon the fabric of the character, and the man of to-day is different from what he would have been had the happening or experience not entered into his life.

And this same rule applies to the characteristics brought over from past incarnations. You have not the memory of the experiences, but you have the fruit in the shape of "characteristics," tastes, inclinations, etc. You have a tendency toward certain things, and a distaste for others. Certain things attract, while others repel you. All of these things are the result of your experiences in former incarnations. Your very taste and inclination toward occult studies which has caused you to read these lessons is your legacy from some former life in which some one spoke a word or two to you regarding the subject, and attracted your interest and desire. You learned some little about the subject then—perhaps much—and developed a desire for more knowledge along these lines, which manifesting in your present life has brought you in contact with further instruction. The same inclination will lead to further advancement in this life, and still greater opportunities in future incarnations. Nearly every one who reads these lines has felt that much of this occult instruction imparted is but a "re-learning" of something previously known, although many of the things taught have never been heard before in this life. You pick up a book and read something, and know at once that it is so, because in some vague way you have a consciousness of having studied and worked out the problem in some past period of your lives. All this is the working of the Law of Karma, which caused you to attract that for which you have an affinity, and which also causes others to be attracted to you.

Many are the reunions of people who have been related to each other in previous lives. The old loves, and old hates work out their Karmic results in our lives. We are bound to those whom we have loved, and also to those whom we may have injured. The story must be worked out to the end, although a knowledge of the Law undoubtedly relieves one of many entangling attachments and Karmic relationships, by pointing out the nature of the relation, and enabling one to free himself mentally from the bond, which process tends to dissolve much of the Karmic entanglements.

Life is a great school for the learning of lessons. It has many grades, many classes, many scales of progress. And the lessons must be learned whether we will or no. If we refuse or neglect to learn the lesson we are sent back to accomplish the task, again and again, until the lesson is finally learned. Nothing once learned is ever forgotten entirely. There is an indelible imprint of the lesson in our character, which manifests as predispositions, tastes, inclinations, etc. All that goes to make up that which we call "Character" is the workings of the Law of Karma. There is no such thing as Chance. Nothing ever "happens." All is regulated by the Law of Cause and Effect or Karma. As a man sows so shall he reap, in a literal sense. You are what you are to-day, by reason of what you were in your last life. And in your next life you will be what you are making of yourself to-day. You are your own judge, and executioner—your own bestower of rewards. But the Love of the Absolute is ever working to lead you upward to the Light, and to open your soul to that knowledge that, in the words of the Yogis, "burns up Karma," and enables you to throw off the burden of Cause and Effect that you have been carrying around with you, and which has weighted you down.

In the Fourteen Lessons we quoted from Mr. Berry Benson, a writer in the *Century Magazine* for May, 1894. The quotation fits so beautifully into this place, that we venture to reproduce it here once more, with your permission. It reads as follows:

"A little boy went to school. He was very little. All that he knew he had drawn in with his mother's milk. His teacher (who was God) placed him in the lowest class, and gave him these lessons to learn: Thou shalt not kill. Thou shalt do no hurt to any living thing. Thou shalt not steal. So the man did not kill; but he was cruel, and he stole. At the end of the day (when his beard was gray—when the night was come) his teacher (who was God) said: Thou hast learned not to kill, but the other lessons thou hast not learned. Come back tomorrow.

"On the morrow he came back a little boy. And his teacher (who was God) put him in a class a little higher, and gave him these lessons to learn: Thou shalt do no hurt to any living thing. Thou shalt not steal. Thou shalt not cheat. So the man did no hurt to any living thing; but he stole and cheated. And at the end of the day (when his beard was gray—when the night was come) his teacher (who was God) said: Thou hast learned to be merciful. But the other lessons thou hast not learned. Come back tomorrow.

"Again, on the morrow, he came back, a little boy. And his teacher (who was God) put him in a class yet a little higher, and gave him these lessons to learn: Thou shalt not steal. Thou shalt not cheat. Thou shalt not covet. So the man did not steal; but he cheated and he coveted. And at the end of the day (when his beard was gray—when the night was come) his teacher (who was God) said: Thou hast learned not to steal. But the other lessons thou hast not learned. Come back, my child, tomorrow.

"This is what I have read in the faces of men and women, in the book of the world, and in the scroll of the heavens, which is writ with stars."

Under the operation of the Law of Karma every man is master of his own destiny—he rewards himself—he punishes himself—he builds, tears down and develops his character, always, however, under the brooding influence of the Absolute which is Love Infinite and which is constantly exerting the upward spiritual urge, which is drawing the soul toward its ultimate haven of rest. Man must, and does, work out his own salvation and destiny, but the upward urge is always there—never tiring—never despairing—knowing always that Ultimate Victory belongs to the soul.

Under the Law of Karma every action, yea, every thought as well, has its Karmic effect upon the future incarnations of the soul. And, not exactly in the nature of punishment or rewards, in the general acceptation of the term, but as the invariable operation of the Law of Cause and Effect. The thoughts of a person are like seeds which seek to press forward into growth, bud, blossom and fruit. Some spring into growth in this life, while others are carried over into future lives. The actions of this life may represent only the partial growth of the thought seed, and future lives may be necessary for its full blossoming and fruition. Of course, the individual who understands the Truth, and who has mentally divorced himself from the fruits of his actions—who has robbed material Desire of its vital force by seeing it as it is, and not as a part of his Real Self—his seed-thoughts do not spring into blossom and fruit in future lives, for he has killed their germ. The Yogis express this thought by the illustration of the baked-seeds. They show their pupils that while ordinary seeds sprout, blossom and bear fruit, still if one bakes the seeds their vitality is gone, and while they may serve the purposes of a nourishing meal still they can never cause sprout, blossom or fruit. Then the pupil is instructed in the nature of Desire, and shown how desires invariably spring into plant, blossom and fruit, the life of the person being the soil in which they flourish. But Desires understood, and set off from the Real Man, are akin to baked-seeds—they have been subjected to the heat of spiritual wisdom and are thus robbed of their vitality, and are unable to bear fruit. In this way the understood and mastered Desire bears no Karmic fruit of future action.

The Yogis teach that there are two great principles at work in the matter of Karmic Law affecting the conditions of rebirth. The first principle is that whereby the prevailing desires, aspirations, likes, and dislikes, loves and hates, attractions and repulsions, etc., press the soul into conditions in which these characteristics may have a favorable and congenial soil for development. The second principle is that which may be spoken of as the urge of the unfolding Spirit, which is always urging forward toward fuller expression, and the breaking down of confining sheaths, and which thus exerts a pressure upon the soul awaiting reincarnation which causes it to seek higher environments and conditions than its desires and aspiration, as well as its general characteristics, would demand. These two apparently conflicting (and yet actually harmonious) principles acting and reacting upon each other, determine the conditions of rebirth, and have a very material effect upon the Karmic Law. One's life is largely a conflict between these two forces, the one tending to hold the soul to the present conditions resulting from past lives, and the other ever at work seeking to uplift and elevate it to greater heights.

The desires and characteristics brought over from the past lives, of course, seek fuller expression and manifestation upon the lines of the past lives. These tendencies simply wish to be let alone and to grow according to their own laws of development and manifestation. But the unfolding Spirit, knowing that the soul's best interests are along the lines of spiritual unfoldment and growth, brings a steady pressure to bear, life after life, upon the soul, causing it to gradually kill out the lower desires and characteristics, and to develop qualities which tend to lead it upward instead of allowing it to remain on its present level, there to bring to blossom and fruit many low thoughts and desires. Absolute Justice reigns over the operations of the Law of Karma, but back of that and superior even to its might is found the Infinite Love of the absolute which tends to Redeem the race. It is that love that is back of all the upward tendencies of the soul, and which we all feel within our inner selves in our best moments. The light of the Spirit (Love) is ever there.

Our relationship to others in past lives has its effect upon the working of the Law of Karma. If in the past we have formed attachments for other individuals, either through love or hate; either by kindness or cruelty; these attachments manifest in our present life, for these persons are bound to us, and we to them, by the bonds of Karma, until the attachment is worn out. Such people will in the present life have certain relationships to us, the object of which is the working out of the problems in which we are mutually concerned, the adjustment of relationship, the "squaring up" of accounts, the development of both. We are apt to be placed in a position to receive hurts from those whom we have hurt in past lives, and this not through the idea of revenge, but by the inexorable working out of the Law of Compensation in Karmic adjustments. And when we are helped, comforted and receive favors from those who we helped in past lives, it is not merely a reward, but the operation of the same law of Justice. The person who hurts us in this way may have no desire to do so, and may even be distressed because he is used as an instrument in this way, but the Karmic Law places him in a position where he unwittingly and without desire acts so that you receive pain through him. Have you not felt yourselves hurting another, although you had no desire and intention of so doing, and, in fact, were sorely distressed because you could not prevent the pain? This Is the operation of Karma. Have you not found yourself placed where you unexpectedly were made the bestower of favors upon some almost unknown persons? This is Karma. The Wheel turns slowly, but it makes the complete circle.

Karma is the companion law to Metempsychosis. The two are inextricably connected, and their operations are closely interwoven. Constant and unvarying in operation, Karma manifests upon and in worlds, planets, races, nations, families and persons Everywhere in space is the great law in operation in some form. The so-called mechanical operations called Causation are as much a phase of Karma as is the highest phases manifest on the higher planes of life, far beyond our own. And through it all is ever the urge toward perfection—the upward movement of all life. The Yogi teachings regard the Universe as a mighty whole, and the Law of Karma as the one great law operating and manifesting through that whole.

How different is the workings of this mighty Law from the many ideas advanced by man to account for the happenings of life. Mere Chance is no explanation, for the careful thinker must inevitably come to the conclusion that in an Universe governed by law, there can be no room for Chance. And to suppose that all rewards and punishments are bestowed by a personal deity, in answer to prayers, supplications, good behavior, offerings, etc., is to fall back into the childhood stage of the race thought. The Yogis teach that the sorrow, suffering and affliction witnessed on all sides of us, as well as the joy, happiness and blessings also in evidence, are not caused by the will or whim of some capricious deity to reward his friends and punish his enemies—but by the working of an invariable Law which metes out to each his measure of good and ill according to his Karmic attachments and relationships.

Those who are suffering, and who see no cause for their pain, are apt to complain and rebel when they see others of no apparent merit enjoying the good things of life which have been denied their apparently more worthy brethren. The churches have no answer except "It is God's will," and that "the Divine motive must not be questioned." These answers seem like mockery, particularly when the idea of Divine Justice is associated with the teaching. There is no other answer compatible with Divine Justice other than the Law of Karma, which makes each person responsible for his or her happiness or misery. And there is nothing so stimulating to one as to know that he has within himself the means to create for himself newer and better conditions of life and environment. We are what we are to-day by reason of what we were in our yesterdays. We will be in our tomorrows that which we have started into operation to-day. As we sow in this life, so shall we reap in the next—we are now reaping that which we have sown in the past. St. Paul voiced a world truth when he said: "Brethren, be not deceived. God is not mocked, for whatsoever a man soweth that shall he also reap." The teachers divide the operation of Karma into three general classes, as follows: (1) The Karmic manifestations which are now under way in our lives, producing results which are the effects of causes set into motion in our past lives. This is the most common form, and best known phase of Karmic manifestation.

(2) The Karma which we are now acquiring and storing up by reason of our actions, deeds, thoughts and mental and spiritual relationships. This stored up Karma will spring into operation in future lives, when the body and environments appropriate for its manifestation presents itself or is secured; or else when other Karma tending to restrict its operations is removed. But one does not necessarily have to wait until a future life in order to set into operation and manifestation the Karma of the present life. For there come times in which there being no obstructing Karma brought over from a past life, the present life Karma may begin to manifest.

(3) The Karma brought over from past incarnations, which is not able to manifest at the present time owing to the opposition presented by other Karma of an opposite nature, serves to hold the first in check. It is a well known physical law, which likewise manifests on the mental plane, that two opposing forces result in neutralization, that is, both of the forces are held in check. Of course, though, a more powerful Karma may manage to operate, while a weaker is held in check by it.

Not only have individuals their own Karma, but families, races, nations and worlds have their collective Karma. In the cases of races, if the race Karma generated in the past be favorable on the whole, the race flourishes and its influence widens. If on the contrary its collective Karma be bad, the race gradually disappears from the face of the earth, the souls constituting it separating according to their Karmic attractions, some going to this race and some to another. Nations are bound by their Karma, as any student of history may perceive if he studies closely the tides of national progress or decline.

The Karma of a nation is made up of the collective Karma of the individuals composing it, so far as their thoughts and acts have to do with the national spirit and acts. Nations as nations cease to exist, but the souls of the individuals composing them still live on and make their influence felt in new races, scenes and environments. The ancient Egyptians, Persians, Medes, Chaldeans, Romans, Grecians and many other ancient races have disappeared, but their reincarnating souls are with us to-day. The modern revival of Occultism is caused by an influx of the souls of these old peoples pouring in on the Western worlds.

The following quotation from *The Secret Doctrine*, that remarkable piece of occult literature, will be interesting at this point:

"Nor would the ways of Karma be inscrutable were men to work in union and harmony instead of disunion and strife. For our ignorance of those ways—which one portion of mankind calls the ways of Providence, dark and intricate, while another sees in them the action of blind fatalism, and a third simple Chance with neither gods nor devils to guide them—would surely disappear if we would but attribute all these to their correct cause. With right knowledge, or at any rate with a confident conviction that our neighbors will no more work harm to us than we would think of harming them, two-thirds of the world's evil would vanish into thin air. Were no man to hurt his brother, Karma-Nemesis would have neither cause to work for, nor weapons to act through ... We cut these numerous windings in our destinies daily with our own hands, while we imagine that we are pursuing a track on the royal road of respectability and duty, and then complain of those ways being so intricate and so dark. We stand bewildered before the mystery of our own making and the riddles of life that we will not solve, and then accuse the great Sphinx of devouring us. But verily there is not an accident in our lives, not a misshapen day or a misfortune, that could not be traced back to our own doings in this or another life ... Knowledge of Karma gives the conviction that if—

    'Virtue in distress and vice in triumph
    Makes atheists of Mankind,'
it is only because that mankind has ever shut its eyes to the great
truth that man is himself his own savior as his own destroyer;
that he need not accuse heaven, and the gods, fates and
providence, of the apparent injustice that reigns in the midst of
humanity. But let him rather remember that bit of Grecian
wisdom which warns man to forbear accusing THAT which 'Just
though mysterious, leads us on unerring Through ways
unmarked from guilt to punishment'—which are now the ways
and the high road on which move onward the great European
nations. The Western Aryans have every nation and tribe like
their eastern brethren of the fifth race, their Golden and their Iron
ages, their period of comparative irresponsibility, or the Satya
age of purity, while now several of them have reached their Iron
Age, the *Kali Yuga*, an age black with horrors. This state will last
… until we begin acting from within instead of ever following
impulses from without. Until then the only palliative is union
and harmony—a Brotherhood in *actu* and *altruism* not simply in
name."

Edwin Arnold, in his wonderful poem, "The Light of Asia,"
which tells the story of the Buddha, explains the doctrine of
Karma from the Buddhist standpoint. We feel that our students
should become acquainted with this view, so beautifully
expressed, and so we herewith quote the passages referred to:

    "Karma—all that total of a soul
      Which is the things it did, the thoughts it had,
    The 'self' it wove with woof of viewless time
      Crossed on the warp invisible of acts.

* * * * *

    "What hath been bringeth what shall be, and is,
      Worse—better—last for first and first for last;
    The angels in the heavens of gladness reap
      Fruits of a holy past.
    "The devils in the underworlds wear out
      Deeds that were wicked in an age gone by.
    Nothing endures: fair virtues waste with time,
      Foul sins grow purged thereby.

411

"Who toiled a slave may come anew a prince
  For gentle worthiness and merit won;
Who ruled a king may wander earth in rags
  For things done and undone.
"Before beginning, and without an end,
  As space eternal and as surety sure,
Is fixed a Power divine which moves to good,
  Only its laws endure.
"It will not be contemned of any one:
  Who thwarts it loses, and who serves it gains;
The hidden good it pays with peace and bliss,
  The hidden ill with pains.
"It seeth everywhere and marketh all:
  Do right—it recompenseth! Do one wrong—
The equal retribution must be made,
  Though DHARMA tarry long.
"It knows not wrath nor pardon; utter-true
  Its measures mete, its faultless balance weighs;
Times are as naught, to-morrow it will judge,
  Or after many days.
"By this the slayer's knife did stab himself;
  The unjust judge hath lost his own defender;
The false tongue dooms its lie; the creeping thief
  And spoiler rob, to render.
"Such is the law which moves to righteousness,
  Which none at last can turn aside or stay;
The heart of it is love, the end of it
  Is peace and consummation sweet. Obey!

* * * * *

"The books say well, my brothers! each man's life
  The outcome of his former living is;
The bygone wrongs bring forth sorrow and woes,
  The bygone right breeds bliss.
"That which ye sow ye reap. See yonder fields!
  The sesamum was sesamum, the corn
Was corn. The silence and the darkness knew;
  So is a man's fate born.
"He cometh, reaper of the things he sowed,
  Sesamum, corn, so much cast in past birth;

And so much weed and poison-stuff, which mar
  Him and the aching earth.
"If he shall labor rightly, rooting these,
  And planting wholesome seedlings where they grew,
Fruitful and fair and clean the ground shall be,
  And rich the harvest due.
"If he who liveth, learning whence woe springs,
  Endureth patiently, striving to pay
His utmost debt for ancient evils done
  In love and truth always;
If making none to lack, he thoroughly purge
  The lie and lust of self forth from his blood;
Suffering all meekly, rendering for offence
  Nothing but grace and good:
"If he shall day by day dwell merciful,
  Holy and just and kind and true; and rend
Desire from where it clings with bleeding roots,
  Till love of life have end:
"He—dying—leaveth as the sum of him
  A life-count closed, whose ills are dead and quit,
Whose good is quick and mighty, far and near,
  So that fruits follow it.
"No need hath such to live as ye name life;
  That which began in him when he began
Is finished: he hath wrought the purpose through
  Of what did make him man.
"Never shall yearnings torture him, nor sins
  Stain him, nor ache of earthly joys and woes
Invade his safe eternal peace; nor deaths
  And lives recur. He goes
"Unto NIRVANA. He is one with Life
  Yet lives not. He is blest, ceasing to be.
OM, MANI PADME OM! the dewdrop slips
  Into the shining sea!
"This is the doctrine of the Karma. Learn!
  Only when all the dross of sin is quit,
Only when life dies like a white flame spent.
  Death dies along with it."

413

And so, friends, this is a brief account of the operations of the Law of Karma. The subject is one of such wide scope that the brief space at our disposal enables us to do little more than to call your attention to the existence of the Law, and some of its general workings. We advise our students to acquaint themselves thoroughly with what has been written on this subject by ourselves and others. In our first series of lessons— the *"Fourteen Lessons"*—the chapter or lesson on Spiritual Cause and Effect was devoted to the subject of Karma. We advise our students to re-study it. We also suggest that Mr. Sinnett's occult story entitled *"Karma"* gives its readers an excellent idea of the actual working of Karma in the everyday lives of people of our own times. We recommend the book to the consideration of our students. It is published at a popular price, and is well worth the consideration of every one interested in this wonderful subject of Reincarnation and Karma.

THE TWELFTH LESSON - Occult Miscellany

In this, the last lesson of this series, we wish to call your attention to a variety of subjects, coming under the general head of the Yogi Philosophy, and yet apparently separated from one another. And so we have entitled this lesson "Occult Miscellany," inasmuch as it is made up of bits of information upon a variety of subjects all connected with the general teaching of the series. The lesson will consist of answers to a number of questions, asked by various students of the courses in Yogi Philosophy coming from our pen. While these answers, of necessity, must be brief, still we will endeavor to condense considerable information into each, so that read as a whole the lesson will give to our students a variety of information upon several important subjects.

QUESTION 1: *"Are there any Brotherhoods of Advanced Occultists in existence, in harmony with the Yogi Teachings? And if so, what information can you give regarding them?"*

ANSWER: Yes, there are a number of Occult Brotherhoods, of varying degrees of advancement, scattered through the various countries of the earth. These Brotherhoods agree in principle with the Yogi Teachings, although the methods of interpretation may vary somewhat. There is but one TRUTH, which becomes apparent to all deep students of Occultism, and therefore all true Occultists have a glimpse of that Truth, and upon this glimpse is founded their philosophies and teachings. These Occult Brotherhoods vary in their nature. In some, the members are grouped together in retired portions of the earth, dwelling in the community life. In others the headquarters are in the large cities of the earth, their membership being composed of residents of those cities, with outlying branches. Others have no meeting places, their work being managed from headquarters, their members being scattered all over the face of the earth, the communication being kept up by personal correspondence and privately printed and circulated literature. Admission to these true Occult Brotherhoods is difficult. They seek their members, not the members them. No amount of money, or influence, or energy can gain entrance to these societies. They seek to impart information and instruction only to those who are prepared to receive it—to those who have reached that stage of spiritual unfoldment that will enable them to grasp and assimilate the teachings of the Inner Circles. While this is true, it is also true that these Societies or Brotherhoods are engaged in disseminating Occult Knowledge, suited to the minds of the public, through various channels, and cloaked in various disguises of name, authority and style. Their idea is to gradually open the mind of the public to the great truths underlying and back of all of these various fragmentary teachings. And they recognize the fact that one mind may be reached in a certain way, and another mind in a second way, and so on. And, accordingly, they wrap their teachings in covers likely to attract the attention of various people, and to cause them to investigate the contents. But, under and back of all of these various teachings, is the great fundamental TRUTH. It has often been asked of us how one might distinguish the real Brotherhoods from the spurious ones which have assumed the name and general style of the true societies, for the purpose of exploiting the public, and making money from their interest in the great occult truths. Answering this, we would say that the true Occult Brotherhoods and Societies *never sell their knowledge*. It is given free as water to those who seek for it, and is never sold for money. The true adept would as soon think of selling his soul as selling Spiritual Knowledge for gain. While money plays its proper place in the world, and the laborer is worthy of his hire; and while the Masters recognize the propriety of the sale of books on Occultism (providing the price is reasonable and not in excess of the general market price of books) and while they also recognize the propriety of having people pay their part of the expenses of maintaining organizations, magazines, lecturers, instructors, etc., still the idea stops there—it does not extend to the selling of the Inner Secrets of Occultism for silver or gold. Therefore if you are solicited to become a member of any so-called Brotherhood or Occult Society for a consideration of money, you will know at once that the organization is not a true Occult Society, for it has violated one of the cardinal principles at the start. Remember the old occult maxim: "When the Pupil is ready, the Master appears"—and so it is with the Brotherhoods and Societies—if it is necessary for your growth, development, and attainment, to be connected with one of these organizations then, when the time comes—when you are ready—you will receive your call, and then will know for a certainty that those who call are the true messengers of Truth.

QUESTION II: "*Are there any exalted human beings called Masters, or*

Adepts, or are the tales regarding them mere fables, etc?"

ANSWER: Of a truth there are certain highly developed, advanced and exalted souls in the flesh, known as Masters and Adepts, although many of the tales told concerning them are myths, or pure fiction originating in the minds of some modern sensational writers. And, moreover, these souls are members of the Great Lodge, an organization composed of these almost super-human beings—these great souls that have advanced so very far on THE PATH. Before beginning to speak of them, let us answer a question often asked by Western people, and that is, "Why do not these people appear to the world, and show their powers?" Each of you may answer that question from your own experiences. Have you ever been foolish enough to open your soul to the crowd, and have it reveal the sacred Truth that rests there? Have you ever attempted to impart the highest teachings known to you, to persons who had not attained sufficient spiritual development to even understand the meaning of your words? Have you ever committed the folly of throwing spiritual pearls to material swine? If you have had these experiences, you may begin to faintly imagine the reasons of these illumined souls for keeping away from the crowd—for dwelling away from the multitude. No one who has not suffered the pain of having the vulgar crowd revile the highest spiritual truths to him, can begin to understand the feelings of the spiritually illumined individuals. It is not that they feel that they are better or more exalted than the humblest man—for these feelings of the personality have long since left them. It is because they see the folly of attempting to present the highest truths to a public which is not prepared to understand even the elementary teachings. It is a feeling akin to that of the master of the highest musical conceptions attempting to produce his wonderful compositions before a crowd fit only for the "rag-time" and slangy songs of the day.

Then again, these Masters have no desire to "work miracles" which would only cause the public to become still more superstitious than they now are. When one glances back over the field of religions, and sees how the miraculous acts of some of the great leaders have been prostituted and used as a foundation for the grossest credulity and basest superstition, he may understand the wisdom of the masters in this respect. There is another reason for the non-appearance of the Masters, and that is that there is no occasion for it. The laws of Spiritual Evolution are as regular, constant and fixed as are the laws of Physical Evolution, and any attempt to unduly force matters only results in confusion, and the abortive results soon fade away. The world is not ready for the appearance of the Masters. Their appearance at this time would not be in accordance with The Plan.

The Masters or Adepts are human beings who have passed from lower to higher planes of consciousness, thus gaining wisdom, power and qualities that seem almost miraculous to the man of the ordinary consciousness. A Hindu writer speaking of them has said: "To him who hath traveled far along The Path, sorrow ceases to trouble; fetters cease to bind; obstacles cease to hinder. Such an one is free. For him there is no more fever or sorrow. For him there are no more unconscious re-births. His old Karma is exhausted, and he creates no new Karma. His heart is freed from the desire for future life. No new longings arise within his soul. He is like a lamp which burneth from the oil of the Spirit, and not from the oil of the outer world." Lillie in his work on Buddhism, tells his readers: "Six supernatural faculties were expected of the ascetic before he could claim the grade of *Arhat*. They are constantly alluded to in the *Sutras* as the six supernatural faculties, usually without further specification…. In this transitory body the intelligence of Man is enchained. The ascetic finding himself thus confused, directs his mind to the creation of *Manas*. He represents to himself, in thought, another body created from this material body,—a body with a form, members and organs. This body in relation to the material body is like a sword and the scabbard, or a serpent issuing from a basket in which it is confined. The ascetic then, purified and perfected, begins to practice supernatural faculties. He finds himself able to pass through material obstacles, walls, ramparts, etc.; he is able to throw his phantasmal appearance into many places at once. He acquires the power of hearing the sounds of the unseen world as distinctly as those of the phenomenal world—more distinctly in point of fact. Also by the power of *Manas* he is able to read the most secret thoughts of others, and to tell their characters."

These great Masters are above all petty sectarian distinctions. They may have ascended to their exalted position along the paths of the many religions, or they may have walked the path of no-denomination, sect, or body. They may have mounted to their heights by philosophical reasoning alone, or else by scientific investigation. They are called by many names, according to the viewpoint of the speaker, but at the last they are of but one religion; one philosophy; one belief—TRUTH.

The state of Adeptship is reached only after a long and arduous apprenticeship extending over many lives. Those who have reached the pinnacle were once even as You who read these lines. And some of you—yes, perhaps even You who are now reading these words may have taken the first steps along the narrow path which will lead you to heights equally as exalted as those occupied by even the highest of these great beings of whom we are speaking. Unconsciously to yourself, the urge of the Spirit has set your feet firmly upon The Path, and will push you forward to the end. In order to understand the occult custom that finds its full fruit in the seclusion of the Masters, one needs to be acquainted with the universal habit among true occultists of refraining from public or vulgar displays of occult power. While the inferior occultists often exhibit some of the minor manifestations to the public, it is a fact that the true advanced occultists scrupulously refrain from so doing. In fact, among the highest teachers, it is a condition imposed upon the pupil that he shall refrain from exhibitions of his developing powers among the uninitiated public. "The Neophyte is bound over to the most inviolable secrecy as to everything connected with his entrance and further progress in the schools. In Asia, in the same way, the *chela*, or pupil of occultism, no sooner becomes a *chela* than he ceases to be a witness on behalf of the reality of occult knowledge," says Sinnett in his great work on "Esoteric Buddhism," And he then adds: "I have been astonished to find, since my own connection with the subject, how numerous such *chelas* are. But it is impossible to imagine any human act more improbable than the unauthorized revelation by any such *chela*, to persons in the outer world, that he is one; and so the great esoteric school of philosophy guards its seclusion."

QUESTION III: "*Does the Yogi Philosophy teach that there is a place corresponding to the 'Heavens' of the various religions? Is there any basis for the belief that there is a place resembling 'Heaven'?*"

ANSWER: Yes, the Yogi Philosophy *does* teach that there is a real basis for the popular religious beliefs in "Heaven," and that there are states of being, the knowledge of which has filtered through to the masses in the more or less distorted theories regarding "heavens."

But the Yogis do not teach that these "heavens" are *places* at all. The teaching is that they are *planes of existence*. It is difficult to explain just what is meant by this word "plane." The nearest approach to it in English is the term or word "State." A portion of space may be occupied by several planes at the same time, just as a room may be filled with the rays of the sun, those of a lamp. X-rays, magnetic and electric vibrations and waves, etc., each interpenetrating each other and yet not affecting or interfering with each other.

On the lower planes of the Astral World there are to be found the earth-bound souls which have passed out from their former bodies, but which are attracted to the earthly scenes by strong attractions, which serve to weight them down and to prevent them from ascending to the higher planes. On the higher planes are souls that are less bound by earthly attractions, and who, accordingly, are relieved of the weight resulting therefrom. These planes rise in an ascending scale, each plane being higher and more spiritual than the one lower than itself. And dwelling on each plane are the souls fitted to occupy it, by reason of their degree of spiritual development, or evolution. When the soul first leaves the body it falls into a sleep-like stage, from which it awakens to find itself on the plane for which it is fitted, by reason of its development, attractions, character, etc. The particular plane occupied by each soul is determined by the progress and attainment it has made in its past lives. The souls on the higher planes may, and often do, visit the planes lower in the scale than their own, but those on the lower planes may not visit those higher than their own. Quoting from our own writings on this subject, published several years ago, we repeat: This prohibition regarding the visiting of higher planes is not an arbitrary rule, but a law of nature. If the student will pardon the commonplace comparison, he may get an understanding of it, by imagining a large screen, or series of screens, such as used for sorting coal into sizes. The large coal is caught by the first screen; the next size by the second; and so on until the tiny coal is reached. Now, the large coal cannot get into the receptacle of the smaller sizes, but the small sizes may easily pass through the screen and join the larger sizes, if force be imparted to them. Just so in the Astral World, the soul with the greatest amount of materiality, and gross nature, is stopped by the spiritual screen of a certain plane, and cannot pass on to the higher ones, while other souls have cast off some of the confining and retarding material sheaths, and readily pass on to higher and finer planes. And it may be readily seen that those souls which dwell on the higher planes are able to re-visit the lower and grosser planes, while the souls on the grosser cannot penetrate the higher boundries of their plane, being stopped by the spiritual screen. The comparison is a crude one, but it almost exactly pictures the existing conditions on the spiritual world.

Souls on the upper planes, may, and often do, journey to the lower planes for the purpose of "visiting" the souls of friends who may be dwelling there, and thus affording them comfort and consolation. In fact, the teaching is that in many cases a highly developed soul visits souls on the lower planes in whom it is interested, and actually imparts spiritual teaching and instruction to those souls, so that they may be re-born into much better conditions than would have been the case otherwise. All of the planes have Spiritual Instructors from very high planes, who sacrifice their well-earned rest and happiness on their own planes in order that they may work for the less-developed souls on the lower planes.

As we have said, the soul awakens on the plane to which it is suited. It finds itself in the company of congenial souls, in whose company it is enabled to pursue those things which were dear to its heart when alive. It may be able to make considerable advancement during its sojourn in "heaven," which will result to its benefit when it is reborn on earth. There are countless sub-planes, adapted to the infinite requirements of the advancing souls in every degree of development, and each soul finds an opportunity to develop and enjoy to the fullest the highest of which it is capable, and to also perfect itself and to prepare itself for future development, so that it may be re-born under the very best possible conditions and circumstances in the next earth life. But, alas, even in this higher world, all souls do not live up to the best that is in them, and instead of making the best of their opportunities for development, and growing spiritually, they allow the attractions of their material natures to draw them downward, and too often spend much of their time on the planes beneath them, not to help and assist, but to live the less spiritual lives of their friends on the lower planes. In such cases the soul does not reap the benefit of the sojourn in the "after-life," but is born again according to the attractions of its lower, instead of its higher nature, and is compelled to learn its lesson over again. The Yogi teachings inform us that the lower planes of the Astral World are inhabited by souls of a very gross and degraded type, undeveloped and animal-like. These low souls live out the tendencies and characteristics of their former earth lives, and reincarnate rapidly in order to pursue their material attractions. Of course, there is slowly working even in these undeveloped souls an upward tendency, but it is so slow as to be almost imperceptible. In time these undeveloped souls grow sick and tired of their materiality, and then comes the chance for a slight advance. Of course these undeveloped souls have no access to the higher planes of the Astral world, but are confined to their own degraded plane and to the sub-planes which separate the Astral World from the material world. They cling as closely as possible to the earthly scenes, and are separated from the material world by only a thin screen (if we may use the word). They suffer the tantalizing condition of being within sight and hearing of their old material scenes and environments, and yet unable to manifest on them. These souls form the low class of "spirits" of which we hear so much in certain circles. They hang around their old scenes of debauchery and sense gratification, and often are able to influence the minds of living persons along the same line and plane of development. For instance, these creatures hover around low saloons and places of ill-repute, influencing the sodden brains of living persons to participate in the illicit gratifications of the lower sensual nature.

Souls on the higher planes are not bound by these earthly and material attractions, and take advantage of their opportunities to improve themselves and develop spiritually. It is a rule of the Astral World that the higher the plane occupied by a soul, the longer the sojourn there between incarnations. A soul on the lowest planes may reincarnate in a very short time, while on the higher planes hundreds and even thousands of years may elapse before the soul is called upon to experience re-birth. But re-birth comes to all who have not passed on to other spheres of life. Sooner or later the soul feels that inward urge toward re-birth and further experience, and becomes drowsy and falls into a state resembling sleep, when it is caught up in the current that is sweeping on toward re-birth, and is gradually carried on to re-birth in conditions chosen by its desires and characteristics, in connection with the operation of the laws of Karma. From the soul-slumber it passes through what may be called a "death" on the Astral plane, when it is re-born on the earth plane. But, remember this, the soul, when it is re-born on earth, does not fully awaken from its Astral sleep. In infancy and in early childhood the soul is but slowly awakening, gradually from year to year, the brain being built to accommodate this growth. The rare instances of precocious children, and infant genius are cases in which the awakening has been more rapid than ordinary. On the other hand, cases are known where the soul does not awaken as rapidly as the average, and the result is that the person does not show signs of full intellectual activity until nearly middle age. Cases are known when men seemed to "wake up" when they were forty years of age, or even later in life, and would then take on a freshened activity and energy, surprising those who had known them before.

On some of the planes of the Astral world the souls dwelling there do not seem to realize that they are "dead," but act and live as if they were in the flesh.

They have a knowledge of the planes beneath them, just as we on earth know of conditions beneath us (spiritually), but they seem to be in almost absolute ignorance of the planes above them, just as many of us on earth cannot comprehend the existence of beings more highly developed spiritually than ourselves. This, of course, is only true of the souls who have not been made acquainted with the meaning and nature of life on the Astral Plane. Those who have acquired this information and knowledge readily understand their condition and profit thereby. It will be seen from this that it is of the greatest importance for persons to become acquainted with the great laws of Occultism in their present earth life, for the reason that when they pass out of the body and enter some one of the Astral Planes they will not be in ignorance of the condition, but will readily grasp the meaning and nature of their surroundings and take advantage of the same in order to develop themselves more rapidly.

It will be seen from what has been written by us here and elsewhere that there are planes after planes on the Astral side of life. All that has been dreamt of Heaven, Purgatory or Hell has its correspondence there, although not in the literal sense in which these things have been taught. For instance, a wicked man dying immersed in his desires and longings of his lower nature, and believing that he will be punished in a future life for sins committed on earth—such a one is very apt to awaken on the lower planes or sub-planes, in conditions corresponding with his former fears. He finds the fire and brimstone awaiting him, although these things are merely figments of his own imagination, and having no existence in reality. Murderers may roam for ages (apparently) pursued by the bleeding corpses of their victims, until such a horror of the crime arises in the mind that at last sinking from exhaustion into the soul-sleep, their souls pass into re-birth with such a horror of bloodshed and crime as to make them entirely different beings in the new life. And, yet the "hell" that they went through existed only in their imaginations. They were their own Devil and Hell. Just as a man in earth life may suffer from *delirium tremens*, so some of these souls on the Astral plane suffer agonies from their delirium arising from their former crimes, and the belief in the punishment therefor which has been inculcated in them through earth teachings. And these mental agonies, although terrible, really are for their benefit, for by reason of them the soul becomes so sickened with the thought and idea of crime that when it is finally re-born it manifests a marked repulsion to it, and flies to the opposite. In this connection we would say that the teaching is that although the depraved soul apparently experiences ages of this torment, yet, in reality, there is but the passage of but a short time, the illusion arising from the self-hypnotization of the soul, just as arises the illusion of the punishment itself.

In the same way the soul often experiences a "heaven" in accordance with its hopes, beliefs and longings of earth-life. The "heaven" that it has longed for and believed in during its earth-life is very apt to be at least partially reproduced on the Astral plane, and the pious soul of any and all religious denominations finds itself in a "heaven" corresponding to that in which it believed during its earth-life. The Mohammedan finds his paradise; the Christian finds his; the Indian finds his—but the impression is merely an illusion created by the Mental Pictures of the soul. But the illusion tends to give pleasure to the soul, and to satisfy certain longings which in time fade away, leaving the soul free to reach out after higher conceptions and ideals. We cannot devote more space to this subject at this time, and must content ourselves with the above statements and explanations. The principal point that we desire to impress upon your minds is the fact that the "heaven-world" is not a place or state of permanent rest and abode for the disembodied soul, but is merely a place or temporary sojourn between incarnations, and thus serves as a place of rest wherein the soul may gather together its forces, energies, desires and attractions preparatory to re-birth. In this answer we have merely limited ourselves to a general statement of the states and conditions of the Astral World, or rather of certain planes of that world. The subject itself requires far more extensive treatment.

QUESTION IV: "*Is Nirvana a state of the total extinction of consciousness; and is it a place, state or condition?*"

ANSWER: The teaching concerning *Nirvana*, the final goal of the soul, has been much misunderstood, and much error has crept into the teaching even among some very worthy teachers. To conceive of *Nirvana* as a state of extinction of consciousness would be to fall into the error of the pessimistic school of philosophy which thinks of life and consciousness as a curse, and regards the return into a total unconsciousness as the thing to be most desired. The true teaching is that *Nirvana* is a state of the fullest consciousness—a state in which the soul is relieved of all the illusion of separateness and relativity, and enters into a state of Universal Consciousness, or Absolute Awareness, in which it is conscious of Infinity, and Eternity—of all places and things and time. *Nirvana* instead of being a state of Nothingness, is a state of "Everythingness." As the soul advances along the Path it becomes more and more aware of its connection with, relation to, and identity with the Whole. As it grows, the Self enlarges and transcends its former limited bounds. It begins to realize that it is more than the tiny separated atom that it had believed itself to be, and it learns to identify itself in a constantly increasing scale with the Universal Life. It feels a sense of Oneness in a fuller degree, and it sets its feet firmly upon the Path toward *Nirvana*. After many weary lives on this and other planets—in this and other Universes—after it has long since left behind it the scale of humanity, and has advanced into god-like states, its consciousness becomes fuller and fuller, and time and space are transcended in a wonderful manner. And at last the goal is attained—the battle is won—and the soul blossoms into a state of Universal Consciousness, in which Time and Place disappear and in which every place is Here; every period of Time is Now; and everything is "I." This is *Nirvana*.

QUESTION V: "*What is that which Occultists call 'an Astral Shell,' or similar name? Is it an entity, or force, or being?*"

ANSWER: When the soul passes out from the body at the moment of death it carries with it the "Astral Body" as well as the higher mental and spiritual principles (see the first three lessons in the "Fourteen Lessons"). The Astral Body is the counterpart of the material or physical body, although it is composed of matter of a much finer and ethereal nature than is the physical body. It is invisible to the ordinary eye, but may be seen clairvoyantly. The Astral Body rises from the physical body like a faint, luminous vapor, and for a time is connected with the dying physical body by a thin, vapory cord or thread, which finally breaks entirely and the separation becomes complete. The Astral Body is some time afterward discarded by the soul as it passes on to the higher planes, as we have described a few pages further back, and the abandoned Astral Body becomes an "Astral Shell," and is subject to a slow disintegration, just as is the physical body. It is no more the soul than is the physical body— it is merely a cast off garment of fine matter. It will be seen readily that it is not an entity, force or being—it is only cast off matter—a sloughed skin. It has no life or intelligence, but floats around on the lower Astral Plane until it finally disintegrates. It has an attraction toward its late physical associate—the physical body—and often returns to the place where the latter is buried, where it is sometimes seen by persons whose astral sight is temporarily awakened, when it is mistaken for a "ghost" or "spirit" of the person. These Astral Shells are often seen floating around over graveyards, battlefields, etc. And sometimes these shells coming in contact with the psychic magnetism of a medium become "galvanized" into life, and manifest signs of intelligence, which, however, really comes from the mind of the medium. At some seances these re-vitalized shells manifest and materialize, and talk in a vague, meaningless manner, the shell receiving its vitality from the body and mind of the medium instead of speaking from any consciousness of its own. This statement is not to be taken as any denial of true "spirit return," but is merely an explanation of certain forms of so-called "spiritualistic phenomena" which is well understood by advanced "spiritualists," although many seekers after psychic phenomena are in ignorance of it.

QUESTION VI: *What is meant by "the Days and Nights of Brahm"; the*
"Cycles"; the "Chain of Worlds", etc., etc.?

ANSWER: In Lesson Sixth, of the present series, you will find a brief mention of the "Days and Nights of Brahm"—those vast periods of the In-breathing and Out-breathing of the Creative Principle which is personified in the Hindu conception of *Brahma*. You will see mentioned there that universal philosophical conception of the Universal Rhythm, which manifests in a succession of periods of Universal Activity and Inactivity.

The Yogi Teachings are that all Time is manifested in Cycles. Man calls the most common form of Cyclic Time by the name of "a Day," which is the period of time necessary for the earth's revolution on its axis. Each Day is a reproduction of all previous Days, although the incidents of each day differ from those of the other—all Days are but periods of Time marked off by the revolution of the earth on its axis. And each Night is but the negative side of a Day, the positive side of which is called "day." There is really no such thing as a Day, that which we call a "Day" being simply a record of certain physical changes in the earth's position relating to its own axis.

The second phase of Cyclic Time is called by man by the name "a Month," by which is meant certain changes in the relative positions of the moon and the earth. The true month consists of twenty-eight lunar days. In this Cycle (the Month) there is also a light-time or "day," and a dark-time or "night," the former being the fourteen days of the moon's visibility, and the second being the fourteen days of the moon's invisibility.

The third phase of Cyclic Time is that which we call "a Year," by which is meant the time occupied by the earth in its revolution around the sun. You will notice that the year has its positive and negative periods, also, known as Summer and Winter.

But the Yogis take up the story where the astronomers drop it, at the Year. Beyond the Year there are other and greater phases of Cyclic Time. The Yogis know many cycles of thousands of years in which there are marked periods of Activity and Inactivity. We cannot go into detail regarding these various cycles, but may mention another division common to the Yogi teachings, beginning with the Great Year. The Great Year is composed of 360 earth years. Twelve thousand Great Years constitute what is known as a Great Cycle, which is seen to consist of 4,320,000 earth years. Seventy-one Great Cycles compose what is called a *Manwantara*, at the end of which the earth becomes submerged under the waters, until not a vestige of land is left uncovered. This state lasts for a period equal to 71 Great Cycles. A *Kalpa* is composed of 14 Manwantaras. The largest and grandest Cycle manifested is known as the *Maya-Praylaya*, consisting of 36,000 *Kalpas*when the Absolute withdraws into Itself its entire manifestations, and dwells alone in its awful Infinity and Oneness, this period being succeeded by a period equally long—the two being known as the Days and Nights of Brahm.

You will notice that each of these great Cycles has its "Day" period

and its "Night" period—its Period of Activity. and its Period of Inactivity. From Day to Maya-Praylaya, it is a succession of Nights and

Days—Creative Activity and Creative Cessation.

The "Chain of Worlds," is that great group of planets in our own solar system, seven in number, over which the Procession of Life passes, in Cycles. From globe to globe the great wave of soul life passes in Cyclic Rhythm. After a race has passed a certain number of incarnations upon one planet, it passes on to another, and learns new lessons, and then on and on until finally it has learned all of the lessons possible on this Universe, when it passes on to another Universe, and so on, from higher to higher until the human mind is unable to even think of the grandeur of the destiny awaiting each human soul on THE PATH. The various works published by the Theosophical organizations go into detail regarding these matters, which require the space of many volumes to adequately express, but we think that we have at last indicated the general nature of the question, pointing out to the student the nature of the subject, and indicating lines for further study and investigation.

CONCLUSION

May The Peace be with you all, now and forever, even unto
NIRVANA, which is PEACE itself.

And now, dear students, we have reached the end of this series of lessons. You have followed us closely for the past four years, many of you having been with us as students from the start. We feel many ties of spiritual relationship binding you to us, and the parting, although but temporary, gives a little pang to us—a little pull upon our heart strings. We have tried to give to you a plain, practical and simple exposition of the great truths of this world-old philosophy—have endeavored to express in plain simple terms the greatest truths known to man on earth to-day, *the Yogi Philosophy*. And many have written us that our work has not been in vain, and that we have been the means of opening up new worlds of thought to them, and have aided them in casting off the old material sheaths that had bound them for so long, and the discarding of which enabled them to unfold the beautiful blossom of Spirituality. Be this as it may, we have been able merely to give you the most elementary instruction in this world-philosophy, and are painfully conscious of the small portion of the field that we have tilled, when compared with the infinite expanse of Truth still untouched. But such are the limitations of Man—he can speak only of that which lies immediately before him, leaving for others the rest of the work which is remote from his place of abode. There are planes upon planes of this Truth which every soul among you will some day make his or her own. It is yours, and you will be impelled to reach forth and take that which is intended for you. Be not in too much haste—be of great patience—and all will come to you, for it is your own.

Mystic Christianity

We have here to make an announcement that will please our readers, judging from the many letters that we have received during the several years of our work. We will now enter upon a new phase of our work of presenting the great truths underlying life, as taught by the great minds of centuries ago, and carefully transmitted from master to student from that time unto our own. We have concluded our presentation of the mystic teachings underlying the Hindu Philosophies, and shall now pass on to a consideration and presentation of the great Mystic Principles underlying that great and glorious creed of the Western world—the religion, teachings, and philosophy of JESUS THE CHRIST. These teachings, too, as we should remember, are essentially Eastern in their origin, and source, although their effects are more pronounced in the Western world. Underlying the teaching and philosophy of the Christ are to be found the same esoteric principles that underlie the other great systems of philosophies of

430

the East. Covered up though the Truth be by the additions of the Western churches and sects, still it remains there burning brightly as ever, and plainly visible to one who will brush aside the rubbish surrounding the Sacred Flame and who will seek beneath the forms and non-essentials for the Mystic Truths underlying Christianity.

We realize the importance of the work before us, but we shrink not from the task, for we know that when the bright Light of the Spirit, which is found as the centre of the Christian philosophy, is uncovered, there will be great rejoicing from the many who while believing in and realizing the value of the Eastern Teachings, still rightly hold their love, devotion and admiration for Him who was in very Truth the Son of God, and whose mission was to raise the World spiritually from the material quagmire into which it was stumbling.

And now, dear pupils, we must close this series of lessons on the Yogi
Philosophy. We must rest ere we so soon engage upon our new and great
work. We must each take a little rest, ere we meet again on The Path of
Attainment. Each of these temporary partings are milestones upon our
Journey of Spiritual Life. Let each find us farther advanced.

And now we send you our wishes of Peace. May The Peace be with you all, now and forever, even unto NIRVANA, which is PEACE itself.

THE DHAMMAPADA

A Collection of Verses
Canonical Buddhism

Translated from Pali by F. Max Muller

Initially published in 1823.

Chapter I.

The Twin-Verses

1. All that we are is the result of what we have thought: it is founded on our thoughts, it is made up of our thoughts. If a man speaks or acts with an evil thought, pain follows him, as the wheel follows the foot of the ox that draws the carriage.

2. All that we are is the result of what we have thought: it is founded on our thoughts, it is made up of our thoughts. If a man speaks or acts with a pure thought, happiness follows him, like a shadow that never leaves him.

3. "He abused me, he beat me, he defeated me, he robbed me,"—in those who harbour such thoughts hatred will never cease.

4. "He abused me, he beat me, he defeated me, he robbed me,"—in those who do not harbour such thoughts hatred will cease.

5. For hatred does not cease by hatred at any time: hatred ceases by love, this is an old rule.

6. The world does not know that we must all come to an end here;—but those who know it, their quarrels cease at once.

7. He who lives looking for pleasures only, his senses uncontrolled, immoderate in his food, idle, and weak, Mara (the tempter) will certainly overthrow him, as the wind throws down a weak tree.

8. He who lives without looking for pleasures, his senses well controlled, moderate in his food, faithful and strong, him Mara will certainly not overthrow, any more than the wind throws down a rocky mountain.

9. He who wishes to put on the yellow dress without having cleansed himself from sin, who disregards temperance and truth, is unworthy of the yellow dress.

10. But he who has cleansed himself from sin, is well grounded in all virtues, and regards also temperance and truth, he is indeed worthy of the yellow dress.

11. They who imagine truth in untruth, and see untruth in truth, never arrive at truth, but follow vain desires.

12. They who know truth in truth, and untruth in untruth, arrive at truth, and follow true desires.

13. As rain breaks through an ill-thatched house, passion will break through an unreflecting mind.

14. As rain does not break through a well-thatched house, passion will not break through a well-reflecting mind.

15. The evil-doer mourns in this world, and he mourns in the next; he mourns in both. He mourns and suffers when he sees the evil of his own work.

16. The virtuous man delights in this world, and he delights in the next; he delights in both. He delights and rejoices, when he sees the purity of his own work.

17. The evil-doer suffers in this world, and he suffers in the next; he suffers in both. He suffers when he thinks of the evil he has done; he suffers more when going on the evil path.

18. The virtuous man is happy in this world, and he is happy in the next; he is happy in both. He is happy when he thinks of the good he has done; he is still more happy when going on the good path.

19. The thoughtless man, even if he can recite a large portion (of the law), but is not a doer of it, has no share in the priesthood, but is like a cowherd counting the cows of others.

20. The follower of the law, even if he can recite only a small portion (of the law), but, having forsaken passion and hatred and foolishness, possesses true knowledge and serenity of mind, he, caring for nothing in this world or that to come, has indeed a share in the priesthood.

Chapter II.

On Earnestness

21. Earnestness is the path of immortality (Nirvana), thoughtlessness the path of death. Those who are in earnest do not die, those who are thoughtless are as if dead already.

22. Those who are advanced in earnestness, having understood this clearly, delight in earnestness, and rejoice in the knowledge of the Ariyas (the elect).

23. These wise people, meditative, steady, always possessed of strong powers, attain to Nirvana, the highest happiness.

24. If an earnest person has roused himself, if he is not forgetful, if his deeds are pure, if he acts with consideration, if he restrains himself, and lives according to law,—then his glory will increase.

25. By rousing himself, by earnestness, by restraint and control, the wise man may make for himself an island which no flood can overwhelm.

26. Fools follow after vanity, men of evil wisdom. The wise man keeps earnestness as his best jewel.

27. Follow not after vanity, nor after the enjoyment of love and lust! He who is earnest and meditative, obtains ample joy.

28. When the learned man drives away vanity by earnestness, he, the wise, climbing the terraced heights of wisdom, looks down upon the fools, serene he looks upon the toiling crowd, as one that stands on a mountain looks down upon them that stand upon the plain.

29. Earnest among the thoughtless, awake among the sleepers, the wise man advances like a racer, leaving behind the hack.

30. By earnestness did Maghavan (Indra) rise to the lordship of the gods. People praise earnestness; thoughtlessness is always blamed.

31. A Bhikshu (mendicant) who delights in earnestness, who looks with fear on thoughtlessness, moves about like fire, burning all his fetters, small or large.

32. A Bhikshu (mendicant) who delights in reflection, who looks with fear on thoughtlessness, cannot fall away (from his perfect state)—he is close upon Nirvana.

Chapter III.

Thought

33. As a fletcher makes straight his arrow, a wise man makes straight his trembling and unsteady thought, which is difficult to guard, difficult to hold back.

34. As a fish taken from his watery home and thrown on dry ground, our thought trembles all over in order to escape the dominion of Mara (the tempter).

35. It is good to tame the mind, which is difficult to hold in and flighty, rushing wherever it listeth; a tamed mind brings happiness.

36. Let the wise man guard his thoughts, for they are difficult to perceive, very artful, and they rush wherever they list: thoughts well-guarded bring happiness.

37. Those who bridle their mind which travels far, moves about alone, is without a body, and hides in the chamber (of the heart), will be free from the bonds of Mara (the tempter).

38. If a man's thoughts are unsteady, if he does not know the true law, if his peace of mind is troubled, his knowledge will never be perfect.

39. If a man's thoughts are not dissipated, if his mind is not perplexed, if he has ceased to think of good or evil, then there is no fear for him while he is watchful.

40. Knowing that this body is (fragile) like a jar, and making this thought firm like a fortress, one should attack Mara (the tempter) with the weapon of knowledge, one should watch him when conquered, and should never rest.

41. Before long, alas! this body will lie on the earth, despised, without understanding, like a useless log.

42. Whatever a hater may do to a hater, or an enemy to an enemy, a wrongly-directed mind will do us greater mischief.

43. Not a mother, not a father will do so much, nor any other relative; a well-directed mind will do us greater service.

Chapter IV.

Flowers

44. Who shall overcome this earth, and the world of Yama (the lord of the departed), and the world of the gods? Who shall find out the plainly shown path of virtue, as a clever man finds out the (right) flower?

45. The disciple will overcome the earth, and the world of Yama, and the world of the gods. The disciple will find out the plainly shown path of virtue, as a clever man finds out the (right) flower.

46. He who knows that this body is like froth, and has learnt that it is as unsubstantial as a mirage, will break the flower-pointed arrow of Mara, and never see the king of death.

47. Death carries off a man who is gathering flowers and whose mind is distracted, as a flood carries off a sleeping village.

48. Death subdues a man who is gathering flowers, and whose mind is distracted, before he is satiated in his pleasures.

49. As the bee collects nectar and departs without injuring the flower, or its colour or scent, so let a sage dwell in his village.

50. Not the perversities of others, not their sins of commission or omission, but his own misdeeds and negligences should a sage take notice of.

51. Like a beautiful flower, full of colour, but without scent, are the fine but fruitless words of him who does not act accordingly.

52. But, like a beautiful flower, full of colour and full of scent, are the fine and fruitful words of him who acts accordingly.

53. As many kinds of wreaths can be made from a heap of flowers, so many good things may be achieved by a mortal when once he is born.

54. The scent of flowers does not travel against the wind, nor (that of) sandal-wood, or of Tagara and Mallika flowers; but the odour of good people travels even against the wind; a good man pervades every place.

55. Sandal-wood or Tagara, a lotus-flower, or a Vassiki, among these sorts of perfumes, the perfume of virtue is unsurpassed.

56. Mean is the scent that comes from Tagara and sandal-wood;—the perfume of those who possess virtue rises up to the gods as the highest.

57. Of the people who possess these virtues, who live without thoughtlessness, and who are emancipated through true knowledge, Mara, the tempter, never finds the way.

58, 59. As on a heap of rubbish cast upon the highway the lily will grow full of sweet perfume and delight, thus the disciple of the truly enlightened Buddha shines forth by his knowledge among those who are like rubbish, among the people that walk in darkness.

Chapter V.

The Fool

60. Long is the night to him who is awake; long is a mile to him who is tired; long is life to the foolish who do not know the true law.

61. If a traveller does not meet with one who is his better, or his equal, let him firmly keep to his solitary journey; there is no companionship with a fool.

62. "These sons belong to me, and this wealth belongs to me," with such thoughts a fool is tormented. He himself does not belong to himself; how much less sons and wealth?

63. The fool who knows his foolishness, is wise at least so far. But a fool who thinks himself wise, he is called a fool indeed.

64. If a fool be associated with a wise man even all his life, he will perceive the truth as little as a spoon perceives the taste of soup.

65. If an intelligent man be associated for one minute only with a wise man, he will soon perceive the truth, as the tongue perceives the taste of soup.

66. Fools of little understanding have themselves for their greatest enemies, for they do evil deeds which must bear bitter fruits.

67. That deed is not well done of which a man must repent, and the reward of which he receives crying and with a tearful face.

68. No, that deed is well done of which a man does not repent, and the reward of which he receives gladly and cheerfully.

69. As long as the evil deed done does not bear fruit, the fool thinks it is like honey; but when it ripens, then the fool suffers grief.

70. Let a fool month after month eat his food (like an ascetic) with the tip of a blade of Kusa grass, yet he is not worth the sixteenth particle of those who have well weighed the law.

71. An evil deed, like newly-drawn milk, does not turn (suddenly); smouldering, like fire covered by ashes, it follows the fool.

72. And when the evil deed, after it has become known, brings sorrow to the fool, then it destroys his bright lot, nay, it cleaves his head.

73. Let the fool wish for a false reputation, for precedence among the Bhikshus, for lordship in the convents, for worship among other people!

74. "May both the layman and he who has left the world think that this is done by me; may they be subject to me in everything which is to be done or is not to be done," thus is the mind of the fool, and his desire and pride increase.

75. "One is the road that leads to wealth, another the road that leads to Nirvana;" if the Bhikshu, the disciple of Buddha, has learnt this, he will not yearn for honour, he will strive after separation from the world.

Chapter VI.

The Wise Man (Pandita)

76. If you see an intelligent man who tells you where true treasures are to be found, who shows what is to be avoided, and administers reproofs, follow that wise man; it will be better, not worse, for those who follow him.

77. Let him admonish, let him teach, let him forbid what is improper!—he will be beloved of the good, by the bad he will be hated.

78. Do not have evil-doers for friends, do not have low people for friends: have virtuous people for friends, have for friends the best of men.

79. He who drinks in the law lives happily with a serene mind: the sage rejoices always in the law, as preached by the elect (Ariyas).

80. Well-makers lead the water (wherever they like); fletchers bend the arrow; carpenters bend a log of wood; wise people fashion themselves.

81. As a solid rock is not shaken by the wind, wise people falter not amidst blame and praise.

82. Wise people, after they have listened to the laws, become serene, like a deep, smooth, and still lake.

83. Good people walk on whatever befall, the good do not prattle, longing for pleasure; whether touched by happiness or sorrow wise people never appear elated or depressed.

84. If, whether for his own sake, or for the sake of others, a man wishes neither for a son, nor for wealth, nor for lordship, and if he does not wish for his own success by unfair means, then he is good, wise, and virtuous.

85. Few are there among men who arrive at the other shore (become Arhats); the other people here run up and down the shore.

86. But those who, when the law has been well preached to them, follow the law, will pass across the dominion of death, however difficult to overcome.

87, 88. A wise man should leave the dark state (of ordinary life), and follow the bright state (of the Bhikshu). After going from his home to a homeless state, he should in his retirement look for enjoyment where there seemed to be no enjoyment. Leaving all pleasures behind, and calling nothing his own, the wise man should purge himself from all the troubles of the mind.

89. Those whose mind is well grounded in the (seven) elements of knowledge, who without clinging to anything, rejoice in freedom from attachment, whose appetites have been conquered, and who are full of light, are free (even) in this world.

Chapter VII.

The Venerable (Arhat).

90. There is no suffering for him who has finished his journey, and abandoned grief, who has freed himself on all sides, and thrown off all fetters.

91. They depart with their thoughts well-collected, they are not happy in their abode; like swans who have left their lake, they leave their house and home.

92. Men who have no riches, who live on recognised food, who have perceived void and unconditioned freedom (Nirvana), their path is difficult to understand, like that of birds in the air.

93. He whose appetites are stilled, who is not absorbed in enjoyment, who has perceived void and unconditioned freedom

(Nirvana), his path is difficult to understand, like that of birds in the air.

94. The gods even envy him whose senses, like horses well broken in by the driver, have been subdued, who is free from pride, and free from appetites.

95. Such a one who does his duty is tolerant like the earth, like Indra's bolt; he is like a lake without mud; no new births are in store for him.

96. His thought is quiet, quiet are his word and deed, when he has obtained freedom by true knowledge, when he has thus become a quiet man.

97. The man who is free from credulity, but knows the uncreated, who has cut all ties, removed all temptations, renounced all desires, he is the greatest of men.

98. In a hamlet or in a forest, in the deep water or on the dry land, wherever venerable persons (Arhanta) dwell, that place is delightful.

99. Forests are delightful; where the world finds no delight, there the passionless will find delight, for they look not for pleasures.

Chapter VIII.

The Thousands

100. Even though a speech be a thousand (of words), but made up of senseless words, one word of sense is better, which if a man hears, he becomes quiet.

101. Even though a Gatha (poem) be a thousand (of words), but made up of senseless words, one word of a Gatha is better, which if a man hears, he becomes quiet.

102. Though a man recite a hundred Gathas made up of senseless words, one word of the law is better, which if a man hears, he becomes quiet.

103. If one man conquer in battle a thousand times thousand men, and if another conquer himself, he is the greatest of conquerors.

104, 105. One's own self conquered is better than all other people; not even a god, a Gandharva, not Mara with Brahman could change into defeat the victory of a man who has vanquished himself, and always lives under restraint.

106. If a man for a hundred years sacrifice month after month with a thousand, and if he but for one moment pay homage to a man whose soul is grounded (in true knowledge), better is that homage than sacrifice for a hundred years.

107. If a man for a hundred years worship Agni (fire) in the forest, and if he but for one moment pay homage to a man whose soul is grounded (in true knowledge), better is that homage than sacrifice for a hundred years.

108. Whatever a man sacrifice in this world as an offering or as an oblation for a whole year in order to gain merit, the whole of it is not worth a quarter (a farthing); reverence shown to the righteous is better.

109. He who always greets and constantly reveres the aged, four things will increase to him, viz. life, beauty, happiness, power.

110. But he who lives a hundred years, vicious and unrestrained, a life of one day is better if a man is virtuous and reflecting.

111. And he who lives a hundred years, ignorant and unrestrained, a life of one day is better if a man is wise and reflecting.

112. And he who lives a hundred years, idle and weak, a life of one day is better if a man has attained firm strength.

113. And he who lives a hundred years, not seeing beginning and end, a life of one day is better if a man sees beginning and end.

114. And he who lives a hundred years, not seeing the immortal place, a life of one day is better if a man sees the immortal place.

115. And he who lives a hundred years, not seeing the highest law, a life of one day is better if a man sees the highest law.

Chapter IX.

Evil

116. If a man would hasten towards the good, he should keep his thought away from evil; if a man does what is good slothfully, his mind delights in evil.

117. If a man commits a sin, let him not do it again; let him not delight in sin: pain is the outcome of evil.

118. If a man does what is good, let him do it again; let him delight in it: happiness is the outcome of good.

119. Even an evil-doer sees happiness as long as his evil deed has not ripened; but when his evil deed has ripened, then does the evil-doer see evil.

120. Even a good man sees evil days, as long as his good deed has not ripened; but when his good deed has ripened, then does the good man see happy days.

121. Let no man think lightly of evil, saying in his heart, It will not come nigh unto me. Even by the falling of water-drops a water-pot is filled; the fool becomes full of evil, even if he gather it little by little.

122. Let no man think lightly of good, saying in his heart, It will not come nigh unto me. Even by the falling of water-drops a water-pot is filled; the wise man becomes full of good, even if he gather it little by little.

123. Let a man avoid evil deeds, as a merchant, if he has few companions and carries much wealth, avoids a dangerous road; as a man who loves life avoids poison.

124. He who has no wound on his hand, may touch poison with his hand; poison does not affect one who has no wound; nor is there evil for one who does not commit evil.

125. If a man offend a harmless, pure, and innocent person, the evil falls back upon that fool, like light dust thrown up against the wind.

126. Some people are born again; evil-doers go to hell; righteous people go to heaven; those who are free from all worldly desires attain Nirvana.

127. Not in the sky, not in the midst of the sea, not if we enter into the clefts of the mountains, is there known a spot in the whole world where death could not overcome (the mortal).

Chapter X.

Punishment

129. All men tremble at punishment, all men fear death; remember that you are like unto them, and do not kill, nor cause slaughter.

130. All men tremble at punishment, all men love life; remember that thou art like unto them, and do not kill, nor cause slaughter.

131. He who seeking his own happiness punishes or kills beings who also long for happiness, will not find happiness after death.

132. He who seeking his own happiness does not punish or kill beings who also long for happiness, will find happiness after death.

133. Do not speak harshly to anybody; those who are spoken to will answer thee in the same way. Angry speech is painful, blows for blows will touch thee.

134. If, like a shattered metal plate (gong), thou utter not, then thou hast reached Nirvana; contention is not known to thee.

135. As a cowherd with his staff drives his cows into the stable, so do Age and Death drive the life of men.

136. A fool does not know when he commits his evil deeds: but the wicked man burns by his own deeds, as if burnt by fire.

137. He who inflicts pain on innocent and harmless persons, will soon come to one of these ten states:

138. He will have cruel suffering, loss, injury of the body, heavy affliction, or loss of mind,

139. Or a misfortune coming from the king, or a fearful accusation, or loss of relations, or destruction of treasures,

140. Or lightning-fire will burn his houses; and when his body is destroyed, the fool will go to hell.

141. Not nakedness, not platted hair, not dirt, not fasting, or lying on the earth, not rubbing with dust, not sitting motionless, can purify a mortal who has not overcome desires.

142. He who, though dressed in fine apparel, exercises tranquillity, is quiet, subdued, restrained, chaste, and has ceased to find fault with all other beings, he indeed is a Brahmana, an ascetic (sramana), a friar (bhikshu).

143. Is there in this world any man so restrained by humility that he does not mind reproof, as a well-trained horse the whip?

144. Like a well-trained horse when touched by the whip, be ye active and lively, and by faith, by virtue, by energy, by meditation, by discernment of the law you will overcome this

great pain (of reproof), perfect in knowledge and in behaviour, and never forgetful.

145. Well-makers lead the water (wherever they like); fletchers bend the arrow; carpenters bend a log of wood; good people fashion themselves.

Old Age

146. How is there laughter, how is there joy, as this world is always burning? Why do you not seek a light, ye who are surrounded by darkness?
147. Look at this dressed-up lump, covered with wounds, joined together, sickly, full of many thoughts, which has no strength, no hold!
148. This body is wasted, full of sickness, and frail; this heap of corruption breaks to pieces, life indeed ends in death.
149. Those white bones, like gourds thrown away in the autumn, what pleasure is there in looking at them?
150. After a stronghold has been made of the bones, it is covered with flesh and blood, and there dwell in it old age and death, pride and deceit.
151. The brilliant chariots of kings are destroyed, the body also approaches destruction, but the virtue of good people never approaches destruction,—thus do the good say to the good.
152. A man who has learnt little, grows old like an ox; his flesh grows, but his knowledge does not grow.
153, 154. Looking for the maker of this tabernacle, I shall have to run through a course of many births, so long as I do not find (him); and painful is birth again and again. But now, maker of the tabernacle, thou hast been seen; thou shalt not make up this tabernacle again. All thy rafters are broken, thy ridge-pole is sundered; the mind, approaching the Eternal (visankhara, nirvana), has attained to the extinction of all desires.
155. Men who have not observed proper discipline, and have not gained treasure in their youth, perish like old herons in a lake without fish.
156. Men who have not observed proper discipline, and have not gained treasure in their youth, lie, like broken bows, sighing after the past.

Chapter XII.

Self

157. If a man hold himself dear, let him watch himself carefully; during one at least out of the three watches a wise man should be watchful.

158. Let each man direct himself first to what is proper, then let him teach others; thus a wise man will not suffer.

159. If a man make himself as he teaches others to be, then, being himself well subdued, he may subdue (others); one's own self is indeed difficult to subdue.

160. Self is the lord of self, who else could be the lord? With self well subdued, a man finds a lord such as few can find.

161. The evil done by oneself, self-begotten, self-bred, crushes the foolish, as a diamond breaks a precious stone.

162. He whose wickedness is very great brings himself down to that state where his enemy wishes him to be, as a creeper does with the tree which it surrounds.

163. Bad deeds, and deeds hurtful to ourselves, are easy to do; what is beneficial and good, that is very difficult to do.

164. The foolish man who scorns the rule of the venerable (Arahat), of the elect (Ariya), of the virtuous, and follows false doctrine, he bears fruit to his own destruction, like the fruits of the Katthaka reed.

165. By oneself the evil is done, by oneself one suffers; by oneself evil is left undone, by oneself one is purified. Purity and impurity belong to oneself, no one can purify another.

166. Let no one forget his own duty for the sake of another's, however great; let a man, after he has discerned his own duty, be always attentive to his duty.

Chapter XIII.

The World

167. Do not follow the evil law! Do not live on in thoughtlessness! Do not follow false doctrine! Be not a friend of the world.

168. Rouse thyself! do not be idle! Follow the law of virtue! The virtuous rests in bliss in this world and in the next.

169. Follow the law of virtue; do not follow that of sin. The virtuous rests in bliss in this world and in the next.

170. Look upon the world as a bubble, look upon it as a mirage: the king of death does not see him who thus looks down upon the world.

171. Come, look at this glittering world, like unto a royal chariot; the foolish are immersed in it, but the wise do not touch it.

172. He who formerly was reckless and afterwards became sober, brightens up this world, like the moon when freed from clouds.

173. He whose evil deeds are covered by good deeds, brightens up this world, like the moon when freed from clouds.

174. This world is dark, few only can see here; a few only go to heaven, like birds escaped from the net.

175. The swans go on the path of the sun, they go through the ether by means of their miraculous power; the wise are led out of this world, when they have conquered Mara and his train.

176. If a man has transgressed one law, and speaks lies, and scoffs at another world, there is no evil he will not do.

177. The uncharitable do not go to the world of the gods; fools only do not praise liberality; a wise man rejoices in liberality, and through it becomes blessed in the other world.

178. Better than sovereignty over the earth, better than going to heaven, better than lordship over all worlds, is the reward of the first step in holiness.

Chapter XIV.

The Buddha (The Awakened)

179. He whose conquest is not conquered again, into whose conquest no one in this world enters, by what track can you lead him, the Awakened, the Omniscient, the trackless?

180. He whom no desire with its snares and poisons can lead astray, by what track can you lead him, the Awakened, the Omniscient, the trackless?

181. Even the gods envy those who are awakened and not forgetful, who are given to meditation, who are wise, and who delight in the repose of retirement (from the world).

182. Difficult (to obtain) is the conception of men, difficult is the life of mortals, difficult is the hearing of the True Law, difficult is the birth of the Awakened (the attainment of Buddhahood).

183. Not to commit any sin, to do good, and to purify one's mind, that is the teaching of (all) the Awakened.

184. The Awakened call patience the highest penance, long-suffering the highest Nirvana; for he is not an anchorite (pravragita) who strikes others, he is not an ascetic (sramana) who insults others.

185. Not to blame, not to strike, to live restrained under the law, to be moderate in eating, to sleep and sit alone, and to dwell on the highest thoughts,—this is the teaching of the Awakened.

186. There is no satisfying lusts, even by a shower of gold pieces; he who knows that lusts have a short taste and cause pain, he is wise;

187. Even in heavenly pleasures he finds no satisfaction, the disciple who is fully awakened delights only in the destruction of all desires.

188. Men, driven by fear, go to many a refuge, to mountains and forests, to groves and sacred trees.

189. But that is not a safe refuge, that is not the best refuge; a man is not delivered from all pains after having gone to that refuge.

190. He who takes refuge with Buddha, the Law, and the Church; he who, with clear understanding, sees the four holy truths:—

191. Viz. pain, the origin of pain, the destruction of pain, and the eightfold holy way that leads to the quieting of pain;—

192. That is the safe refuge, that is the best refuge; having gone to that refuge, a man is delivered from all pain.

193. A supernatural person (a Buddha) is not easily found, he is not born everywhere. Wherever such a sage is born, that race prospers.

194. Happy is the arising of the awakened, happy is the teaching of the True Law, happy is peace in the church, happy is the devotion of those who are at peace.

195, 196. He who pays homage to those who deserve homage, whether the awakened (Buddha) or their disciples, those who have overcome the host (of evils), and crossed the flood of sorrow, he who pays homage to such as have found deliverance and know no fear, his merit can never be measured by anybody.

Happiness

197. Let us live happily then, not hating those who hate us! among men who hate us let us dwell free from hatred!
198. Let us live happily then, free from ailments among the ailing! among men who are ailing let us dwell free from ailments!
199. Let us live happily then, free from greed among the greedy! among men who are greedy let us dwell free from greed!
200. Let us live happily then, though we call nothing our own! We shall be like the bright gods, feeding on happiness!
201. Victory breeds hatred, for the conquered is unhappy. He who has given up both victory and defeat, he, the contented, is happy.
202. There is no fire like passion; there is no losing throw like hatred; there is no pain like this body; there is no happiness higher than rest.
203. Hunger is the worst of diseases, the body the greatest of pains; if one knows this truly, that is Nirvana, the highest happiness.
204. Health is the greatest of gifts, contentedness the best riches; trust is the best of relationships, Nirvana the highest happiness.
205. He who has tasted the sweetness of solitude and tranquillity, is free from fear and free from sin, while he tastes the sweetness of drinking in the law.
206. The sight of the elect (Arya) is good, to live with them is always happiness; if a man does not see fools, he will be truly happy.
207. He who walks in the company of fools suffers a long way; company with fools, as with an enemy, is always painful; company with the wise is pleasure, like meeting with kinsfolk.
208. Therefore, one ought to follow the wise, the intelligent, the learned, the much enduring, the dutiful, the elect; one ought to follow a good and wise man, as the moon follows the path of the stars.

Pleasure

209. He who gives himself to vanity, and does not give himself to meditation, forgetting the real aim (of life) and grasping at pleasure, will in time envy him who has exerted himself in meditation.

210. Let no man ever look for what is pleasant, or what is unpleasant. Not to see what is pleasant is pain, and it is pain to see what is unpleasant.

211. Let, therefore, no man love anything; loss of the beloved is evil. Those who love nothing and hate nothing, have no fetters.

212. From pleasure comes grief, from pleasure comes fear; he who is free from pleasure knows neither grief nor fear.

213. From affection comes grief, from affection comes fear; he who is free from affection knows neither grief nor fear.

214. From lust comes grief, from lust comes fear; he who is free from lust knows neither grief nor fear.

215. From love comes grief, from love comes fear; he who is free from love knows neither grief nor fear.

216. From greed comes grief, from greed comes fear; he who is free from greed knows neither grief nor fear.

217. He who possesses virtue and intelligence, who is just, speaks the truth, and does what is his own business, him the world will hold dear.

218. He in whom a desire for the Ineffable (Nirvana) has sprung up, who is satisfied in his mind, and whose thoughts are not bewildered by love, he is called urdhvamsrotas (carried upwards by the stream).

219. Kinsmen, friends, and lovers salute a man who has been long away, and returns safe from afar.

220. In like manner his good works receive him who has done good, and has gone from this world to the other;—as kinsmen receive a friend on his return.

Chapter XVII.

Anger

221. Let a man leave anger, let him forsake pride, let him overcome all bondage! No sufferings befall the man who is not attached to name and form, and who calls nothing his own.

222. He who holds back rising anger like a rolling chariot, him I call a real driver; other people are but holding the reins.

223. Let a man overcome anger by love, let him overcome evil by good; let him overcome the greedy by liberality, the liar by truth!

224. Speak the truth, do not yield to anger; give, if thou art asked for little; by these three steps thou wilt go near the gods.

225. The sages who injure nobody, and who always control their body, they will go to the unchangeable place (Nirvana), where, if they have gone, they will suffer no more.

226. Those who are ever watchful, who study day and night, and who strive after Nirvana, their passions will come to an end.

227. This is an old saying, O Atula, this is not only of to-day: `They blame him who sits silent, they blame him who speaks much, they also blame him who says little; there is no one on earth who is not blamed.'

228. There never was, there never will be, nor is there now, a man who is always blamed, or a man who is always praised.

229, 230. But he whom those who discriminate praise continually day after day, as without blemish, wise, rich in knowledge and virtue, who would dare to blame him, like a coin made of gold from the Gambu river? Even the gods praise him, he is praised even by Brahman.

231. Beware of bodily anger, and control thy body! Leave the sins of the body, and with thy body practice virtue!

232. Beware of the anger of the tongue, and control thy tongue! Leave the sins of the tongue, and practise virtue with thy tongue!

233. Beware of the anger of the mind, and control thy mind! Leave the sins of the mind, and practise virtue with thy mind!

234. The wise who control their body, who control their tongue, the wise who control their mind, are indeed well controlled.

Impurity

235. Thou art now like a sear leaf, the messengers of death (Yama) have come near to thee; thou standest at the door of thy departure, and thou hast no provision for thy journey.

236. Make thyself an island, work hard, be wise! When thy impurities are blown away, and thou art free from guilt, thou wilt enter into the heavenly world of the elect (Ariya).

237. Thy life has come to an end, thou art come near to death (Yama), there is no resting-place for thee on the road, and thou hast no provision for thy journey.

238. Make thyself an island, work hard, be wise! When thy impurities are blown away, and thou art free from guilt, thou wilt not enter again into birth and decay.

239. Let a wise man blow off the impurities of his self, as a smith blows off the impurities of silver one by one, little by little, and from time to time.

240. As the impurity which springs from the iron, when it springs from it, destroys it; thus do a transgressor's own works lead him to the evil path.

241. The taint of prayers is non-repetition; the taint of houses, non-repair; the taint of the body is sloth; the taint of a watchman, thoughtlessness.

242. Bad conduct is the taint of woman, greediness the taint of a benefactor; tainted are all evil ways in this world and in the next.

243. But there is a taint worse than all taints,—ignorance is the greatest taint. O mendicants! throw off that taint, and become taintless!

244. Life is easy to live for a man who is without shame, a crow hero, a mischief-maker, an insulting, bold, and wretched fellow.

245. But life is hard to live for a modest man, who always looks for what is pure, who is disinterested, quiet, spotless, and intelligent.

246. He who destroys life, who speaks untruth, who in this world takes what is not given him, who goes to another man's wife;

247. And the man who gives himself to drinking intoxicating liquors, he, even in this world, digs up his own root.

248. O man, know this, that the unrestrained are in a bad state; take care that greediness and vice do not bring thee to grief for a long time!

249. The world gives according to their faith or according to their pleasure: if a man frets about the food and the drink given to others, he will find no rest either by day or by night.

250. He in whom that feeling is destroyed, and taken out with the very root, finds rest by day and by night.

251. There is no fire like passion, there is no shark like hatred, there is no snare like folly, there is no torrent like greed.

252. The fault of others is easily perceived, but that of oneself is difficult to perceive; a man winnows his neighbour's faults like chaff, but his own fault he hides, as a cheat hides the bad die from the gambler.

253. If a man looks after the faults of others, and is always inclined to be offended, his own passions will grow, and he is far from the destruction of passions.

254. There is no path through the air, a man is not a Samana by outward acts. The world delights in vanity, the Tathagatas (the Buddhas) are free from vanity.

255. There is no path through the air, a man is not a Samana by outward acts. No creatures are eternal; but the awakened (Buddha) are never shaken.

Chapter XIX.

The Just

256, 257. A man is not just if he carries a matter by violence; no, he who distinguishes both right and wrong, who is learned and leads others, not by violence, but by law and equity, and who is guarded by the law and intelligent, he is called just.

258. A man is not learned because he talks much; he who is patient, free from hatred and fear, he is called learned.

259. A man is not a supporter of the law because he talks much; even if a man has learnt little, but sees the law bodily, he is a supporter of the law, a man who never neglects the law.

260. A man is not an elder because his head is grey; his age may be ripe, but he is called `Old-in-vain.'

261. He in whom there is truth, virtue, love, restraint, moderation, he who is free from impurity and is wise, he is called an elder.

262. An envious greedy, dishonest man does not become respectable by means of much talking only, or by the beauty of his complexion.

263. He in whom all this is destroyed, and taken out with the very root, he, when freed from hatred and wise, is called respectable.

264. Not by tonsure does an undisciplined man who speaks falsehood become a Samana; can a man be a Samana who is still held captive by desire and greediness?

265. He who always quiets the evil, whether small or large, he is called a Samana (a quiet man), because he has quieted all evil.

266. A man is not a mendicant (Bhikshu) simply because he asks others for alms; he who adopts the whole law is a Bhikshu, not he who only begs.

267. He who is above good and evil, who is chaste, who with knowledge passes through the world, he indeed is called a Bhikshu.

268, 269. A man is not a Muni because he observes silence (mona, i.e. mauna), if he is foolish and ignorant; but the wise who, taking the balance, chooses the good and avoids evil, he is a Muni, and is a Muni thereby; he who in this world weighs both sides is called a Muni.

270. A man is not an elect (Ariya) because he injures living creatures; because he has pity on all living creatures, therefore is a man called Ariya.

271, 272. Not only by discipline and vows, not only by much learning, not by entering into a trance, not by sleeping alone, do I earn the happiness of release which no worldling can know. Bhikshu, be not confident as long as thou hast not attained the extinction of desires.

Chapter XX

The Way

273. The best of ways is the eightfold; the best of truths the four words; the best of virtues passionlessness; the best of men he who has eyes to see.

274. This is the way, there is no other that leads to the purifying of intelligence. Go on this way! Everything else is the deceit of Mara (the tempter).

275. If you go on this way, you will make an end of pain! The way was preached by me, when I had understood the removal of the thorns (in the flesh).

276. You yourself must make an effort. The Tathagatas (Buddhas) are only preachers. The thoughtful who enter the way are freed from the bondage of Mara.

277. `All created things perish,' he who knows and sees this becomes passive in pain; this is the way to purity.

278. `All created things are grief and pain,' he who knows and sees this becomes passive in pain; this is the way that leads to purity.

279. `All forms are unreal,' he who knows and sees this becomes passive in pain; this is the way that leads to purity.

280. He who does not rouse himself when it is time to rise, who, though young and strong, is full of sloth, whose will and thought are weak, that lazy and idle man will never find the way to knowledge.

281. Watching his speech, well restrained in mind, let a man never commit any wrong with his body! Let a man but keep these three roads of action clear, and he will achieve the way which is taught by the wise.

282. Through zeal knowledge is gotten, through lack of zeal knowledge is lost; let a man who knows this double path of gain and loss thus place himself that knowledge may grow.

283. Cut down the whole forest (of lust), not a tree only! Danger comes out of the forest (of lust). When you have cut down both the forest (of lust) and its undergrowth, then, Bhikshus, you will be rid of the forest and free!

284. So long as the love of man towards women, even the smallest, is not destroyed, so long is his mind in bondage, as the calf that drinks milk is to its mother.

285. Cut out the love of self, like an autumn lotus, with thy hand! Cherish the road of peace. Nirvana has been shown by Sugata (Buddha).

286. `Here I shall dwell in the rain, here in winter and summer,' thus the fool meditates, and does not think of his death.

287. Death comes and carries off that man, praised for his children and flocks, his mind distracted, as a flood carries off a sleeping village.

288. Sons are no help, nor a father, nor relations; there is no help from kinsfolk for one whom death has seized.

289. A wise and good man who knows the meaning of this, should quickly clear the way that leads to Nirvana.

Chapter XXI.

Miscellaneous

290. If by leaving a small pleasure one sees a great pleasure, let a wise man leave the small pleasure, and look to the great.

291. He who, by causing pain to others, wishes to obtain pleasure for himself, he, entangled in the bonds of hatred, will never be free from hatred.

292. What ought to be done is neglected, what ought not to be done is done; the desires of unruly, thoughtless people are always increasing.

293. But they whose whole watchfulness is always directed to their body, who do not follow what ought not to be done, and who steadfastly do what ought to be done, the desires of such watchful and wise people will come to an end.

294. A true Brahmana goes scatheless, though he have killed father and mother, and two valiant kings, though he has destroyed a kingdom with all its subjects.

295. A true Brahmana goes scatheless, though he have killed father and mother, and two holy kings, and an eminent man besides.

296. The disciples of Gotama (Buddha) are always well awake, and their thoughts day and night are always set on Buddha.

297. The disciples of Gotama are always well awake, and their thoughts day and night are always set on the law.

298. The disciples of Gotama are always well awake, and their thoughts day and night are always set on the church.

299. The disciples of Gotama are always well awake, and their thoughts day and night are always set on their body.

300. The disciples of Gotama are always well awake, and their mind day and night always delights in compassion.

301. The disciples of Gotama are always well awake, and their mind day and night always delights in meditation.

302. It is hard to leave the world (to become a friar), it is hard to enjoy the world; hard is the monastery, painful are the houses; painful it is to dwell with equals (to share everything in common) and the itinerant mendicant is beset with pain. Therefore let no man be an itinerant mendicant and he will not be beset with pain.

303. Whatever place a faithful, virtuous, celebrated, and wealthy man chooses, there he is respected.

304. Good people shine from afar, like the snowy mountains; bad people are not seen, like arrows shot by night.

305. He alone who, without ceasing, practises the duty of sitting alone and sleeping alone, he, subduing himself, will rejoice in the destruction of all desires alone, as if living in a forest.

Chapter XXII.

The Downward Course

306. He who says what is not, goes to hell; he also who, having done a thing, says I have not done it. After death both are equal, they are men with evil deeds in the next world.

307. Many men whose shoulders are covered with the yellow gown are ill-conditioned and unrestrained; such evil-doers by their evil deeds go to hell.

308. Better it would be to swallow a heated iron ball, like flaring fire, than that a bad unrestrained fellow should live on the charity of the land.

309. Four things does a wreckless man gain who covets his neighbour's wife,—a bad reputation, an uncomfortable bed, thirdly, punishment, and lastly, hell.

310. There is bad reputation, and the evil way (to hell), there is the short pleasure of the frightened in the arms of the frightened, and the king imposes heavy punishment; therefore let no man think of his neighbour's wife.

311. As a grass-blade, if badly grasped, cuts the arm, badly-practised asceticism leads to hell.

312. An act carelessly performed, a broken vow, and hesitating obedience to discipline, all this brings no great reward.

313. If anything is to be done, let a man do it, let him attack it vigorously! A careless pilgrim only scatters the dust of his passions more widely.

314. An evil deed is better left undone, for a man repents of it afterwards; a good deed is better done, for having done it, one does not repent.

315. Like a well-guarded frontier fort, with defences within and without, so let a man guard himself. Not a moment should escape, for they who allow the right moment to pass, suffer pain when they are in hell.

316. They who are ashamed of what they ought not to be ashamed of, and are not ashamed of what they ought to be ashamed of, such men, embracing false doctrines enter the evil path.

317. They who fear when they ought not to fear, and fear not when they ought to fear, such men, embracing false doctrines, enter the evil path.

318. They who forbid when there is nothing to be forbidden, and forbid not when there is something to be forbidden, such men, embracing false doctrines, enter the evil path.

319. They who know what is forbidden as forbidden, and what is not forbidden as not forbidden, such men, embracing the true doctrine, enter the good path.

Chapter XXIII.

The Elephant

320. Silently shall I endure abuse as the elephant in battle endures the arrow sent from the bow: for the world is ill-natured.

321. They lead a tamed elephant to battle, the king mounts a tamed elephant; the tamed is the best among men, he who silently endures abuse.

322. Mules are good, if tamed, and noble Sindhu horses, and elephants with large tusks; but he who tames himself is better still.

323. For with these animals does no man reach the untrodden country (Nirvana), where a tamed man goes on a tamed animal, viz. on his own well-tamed self.

324. The elephant called Dhanapalaka, his temples running with sap, and difficult to hold, does not eat a morsel when bound; the elephant longs for the elephant grove.

325. If a man becomes fat and a great eater, if he is sleepy and rolls himself about, that fool, like a hog fed on wash, is born again and again.

326. This mind of mine went formerly wandering about as it liked, as it listed, as it pleased; but I shall now hold it in thoroughly, as the rider who holds the hook holds in the furious elephant.

327. Be not thoughtless, watch your thoughts! Draw yourself out of the evil way, like an elephant sunk in mud.

328. If a man find a prudent companion who walks with him, is wise, and lives soberly, he may walk with him, overcoming all dangers, happy, but considerate.

329. If a man find no prudent companion who walks with him, is wise, and lives soberly, let him walk alone, like a king who has left his conquered country behind,—like an elephant in the forest.

330. It is better to live alone, there is no companionship with a fool; let a man walk alone, let him commit no sin, with few wishes, like an elephant in the forest.

331. If an occasion arises, friends are pleasant; enjoyment is pleasant, whatever be the cause; a good work is pleasant in the hour of death; the giving up of all grief is pleasant.

332. Pleasant in the world is the state of a mother, pleasant the state of a father, pleasant the state of a Samana, pleasant the state of a Brahmana.

333. Pleasant is virtue lasting to old age, pleasant is a faith firmly rooted; pleasant is attainment of intelligence, pleasant is avoiding of sins.

Chapter XXIV.

Thirst

334. The thirst of a thoughtless man grows like a creeper; he runs from life to life, like a monkey seeking fruit in the forest.
335. Whomsoever this fierce thirst overcomes, full of poison, in this world, his sufferings increase like the abounding Birana grass.
336. He who overcomes this fierce thirst, difficult to be conquered in this world, sufferings fall off from him, like water-drops from a lotus leaf.
337. This salutary word I tell you, `Do ye, as many as are here assembled, dig up the root of thirst, as he who wants the sweet-scented Usira root must dig up the Birana grass, that Mara (the tempter) may not crush you again and again, as the stream crushes the reeds.'
338. As a tree, even though it has been cut down, is firm so long as its root is safe, and grows again, thus, unless the feeders of thirst are destroyed, the pain (of life) will return again and again.
339. He whose thirst running towards pleasure is exceeding strong in the thirty-six channels, the waves will carry away that misguided man, viz. his desires which are set on passion.
340. The channels run everywhere, the creeper (of passion) stands sprouting; if you see the creeper springing up, cut its root by means of knowledge.
341. A creature's pleasures are extravagant and luxurious; sunk in lust and looking for pleasure, men undergo (again and again) birth and decay.
342. Men, driven on by thirst, run about like a snared hare; held in fetters and bonds, they undergo pain for a long time, again and again.
343. Men, driven on by thirst, run about like a snared hare; let therefore the mendicant drive out thirst, by striving after passionlessness for himself.

344. He who having got rid of the forest (of lust) (i.e. after having reached Nirvana) gives himself over to forest-life (i.e. to lust), and who, when removed from the forest (i.e. from lust), runs to the forest (i.e. to lust), look at that man! though free, he runs into bondage.

345. Wise people do not call that a strong fetter which is made of iron, wood, or hemp; far stronger is the care for precious stones and rings, for sons and a wife.

346. That fetter wise people call strong which drags down, yields, but is difficult to undo; after having cut this at last, people leave the world, free from cares, and leaving desires and pleasures behind.

347. Those who are slaves to passions, run down with the stream (of desires), as a spider runs down the web which he has made himself; when they have cut this, at last, wise people leave the world free from cares, leaving all affection behind.

348. Give up what is before, give up what is behind, give up what is in the middle, when thou goest to the other shore of existence; if thy mind is altogether free, thou wilt not again enter into birth and decay.

349. If a man is tossed about by doubts, full of strong passions, and yearning only for what is delightful, his thirst will grow more and more, and he will indeed make his fetters strong.

350. If a man delights in quieting doubts, and, always reflecting, dwells on what is not delightful (the impurity of the body, &c.), he certainly will remove, nay, he will cut the fetter of Mara.

351. He who has reached the consummation, who does not tremble, who is without thirst and without sin, he has broken all the thorns of life: this will be his last body.

352. He who is without thirst and without affection, who understands the words and their interpretation, who knows the order of letters (those which are before and which are after), he has received his last body, he is called the great sage, the great man.

353. 'I have conquered all, I know all, in all conditions of life I am free from taint; I have left all, and through the destruction of thirst I am free; having learnt myself, whom shall I teach?'

354. The gift of the law exceeds all gifts; the sweetness of the law exceeds all sweetness; the delight in the law exceeds all delights; the extinction of thirst overcomes all pain.

355. Pleasures destroy the foolish, if they look not for the other shore; the foolish by his thirst for pleasures destroys himself, as if he were his own enemy.

356. The fields are damaged by weeds, mankind is damaged by passion: therefore a gift bestowed on the passionless brings great reward.

357. The fields are damaged by weeds, mankind is damaged by hatred: therefore a gift bestowed on those who do not hate brings great reward.

358. The fields are damaged by weeds, mankind is damaged by vanity: therefore a gift bestowed on those who are free from vanity brings great reward.

359. The fields are damaged by weeds, mankind is damaged by lust: therefore a gift bestowed on those who are free from lust brings great reward.

Chapter XXV.

The Bhikshu (Mendicant)

360. Restraint in the eye is good, good is restraint in the ear, in the nose restraint is good, good is restraint in the tongue.

361. In the body restraint is good, good is restraint in speech, in thought restraint is good, good is restraint in all things. A Bhikshu, restrained in all things, is freed from all pain.

362. He who controls his hand, he who controls his feet, he who controls his speech, he who is well controlled, he who delights inwardly, who is collected, who is solitary and content, him they call Bhikshu.

363. The Bhikshu who controls his mouth, who speaks wisely and calmly, who teaches the meaning and the law, his word is sweet.

364. He who dwells in the law, delights in the law, meditates on the law, follows the law, that Bhikshu will never fall away from the true law.

365. Let him not despise what he has received, nor ever envy others: a mendicant who envies others does not obtain peace of mind.

366. A Bhikshu who, though he receives little, does not despise what he has received, even the gods will praise him, if his life is pure, and if he is not slothful.

367. He who never identifies himself with name and form, and does not grieve over what is no more, he indeed is called a Bhikshu.

368. The Bhikshu who acts with kindness, who is calm in the doctrine of Buddha, will reach the quiet place (Nirvana), cessation of natural desires, and happiness.

369. O Bhikshu, empty this boat! if emptied, it will go quickly; having cut off passion and hatred thou wilt go to Nirvana.

370. Cut off the five (senses), leave the five, rise above the five. A Bhikshu, who has escaped from the five fetters, he is called Oghatinna, 'saved from the flood.'

371. Meditate, O Bhikshu, and be not heedless! Do not direct thy thought to what gives pleasure that thou mayest not for thy heedlessness have to swallow the iron ball (in hell), and that thou mayest not cry out when burning, 'This is pain.'

372. Without knowledge there is no meditation, without meditation there is no knowledge: he who has knowledge and meditation is near unto Nirvana.

373. A Bhikshu who has entered his empty house, and whose mind is tranquil, feels a more than human delight when he sees the law clearly.

374. As soon as he has considered the origin and destruction of the elements (khandha) of the body, he finds happiness and joy which belong to those who know the immortal (Nirvana).

375. And this is the beginning here for a wise Bhikshu: watchfulness over the senses, contentedness, restraint under the law; keep noble friends whose life is pure, and who are not slothful.

376. Let him live in charity, let him be perfect in his duties; then in the fulness of delight he will make an end of suffering.

377. As the Vassika plant sheds its withered flowers, men should shed passion and hatred, O ye Bhikshus!

378. The Bhikshu whose body and tongue and mind are quieted, who is collected, and has rejected the baits of the world, he is called quiet.

379. Rouse thyself by thyself, examine thyself by thyself, thus self-protected and attentive wilt thou live happily, O Bhikshu!

380. For self is the lord of self, self is the refuge of self; therefore curb thyself as the merchant curbs a good horse.

381. The Bhikshu, full of delight, who is calm in the doctrine of Buddha will reach the quiet place (Nirvana), cessation of natural desires, and happiness.

382. He who, even as a young Bhikshu, applies himself to the doctrine of Buddha, brightens up this world, like the moon when free from clouds.

Chapter XXVI.

The Brahmana (Arhat)

383. Stop the stream valiantly, drive away the desires, O Brahmana! When you have understood the destruction of all that was made, you will understand that which was not made.

384. If the Brahmana has reached the other shore in both laws (in restraint and contemplation), all bonds vanish from him who has obtained knowledge.

385. He for whom there is neither this nor that shore, nor both, him, the fearless and unshackled, I call indeed a Brahmana.

386. He who is thoughtful, blameless, settled, dutiful, without passions, and who has attained the highest end, him I call indeed a Brahmana.

387. The sun is bright by day, the moon shines by night, the warrior is bright in his armour, the Brahmana is bright in his meditation; but Buddha, the Awakened, is bright with splendour day and night.

388. Because a man is rid of evil, therefore he is called Brahmana; because he walks quietly, therefore he is called Samana; because he has sent away his own impurities, therefore he is called Pravragita (Pabbagita, a pilgrim).

389. No one should attack a Brahmana, but no Brahmana (if attacked) should let himself fly at his aggressor! Woe to him who strikes a Brahmana, more woe to him who flies at his aggressor!

390. It advantages a Brahmana not a little if he holds his mind back from the pleasures of life; when all wish to injure has vanished, pain will cease.

391. Him I call indeed a Brahmana who does not offend by body, word, or thought, and is controlled on these three points.

392. After a man has once understood the law as taught by the Well-awakened (Buddha), let him worship it carefully, as the Brahmana worships the sacrificial fire.

393. A man does not become a Brahmana by his platted hair, by his family, or by birth; in whom there is truth and righteousness, he is blessed, he is a Brahmana.

394. What is the use of platted hair, O fool! what of the raiment of goat-skins? Within thee there is ravening, but the outside thou makest clean.

395. The man who wears dirty raiments, who is emaciated and covered with veins, who lives alone in the forest, and meditates, him I call indeed a Brahmana.

396. I do not call a man a Brahmana because of his origin or of his mother. He is indeed arrogant, and he is wealthy: but the poor, who is free from all attachments, him I call indeed a Brahmana.

397. Him I call indeed a Brahmana who has cut all fetters, who never trembles, is independent and unshackled.

398. Him I call indeed a Brahmana who has cut the strap and the thong, the chain with all that pertains to it, who has burst the bar, and is awakened.

399. Him I call indeed a Brahmana who, though he has committed no offence, endures reproach, bonds, and stripes, who has endurance for his force, and strength for his army.

400. Him I call indeed a Brahmana who is free from anger, dutiful, virtuous, without appetite, who is subdued, and has received his last body.

401. Him I call indeed a Brahmana who does not cling to pleasures, like water on a lotus leaf, like a mustard seed on the point of a needle.

402. Him I call indeed a Brahmana who, even here, knows the end of his suffering, has put down his burden, and is unshackled.

403. Him I call indeed a Brahmana whose knowledge is deep, who possesses wisdom, who knows the right way and the wrong, and has attained the highest end.

404. Him I call indeed a Brahmana who keeps aloof both from laymen and from mendicants, who frequents no houses, and has but few desires.

405. Him I call indeed a Brahmana who finds no fault with other beings, whether feeble or strong, and does not kill nor cause slaughter.

406. Him I call indeed a Brahmana who is tolerant with the intolerant, mild with fault-finders, and free from passion among the passionate.

407. Him I call indeed a Brahmana from whom anger and hatred, pride and envy have dropt like a mustard seed from the point of a needle.

408. Him I call indeed a Brahmana who utters true speech, instructive and free from harshness, so that he offend no one.

409. Him I call indeed a Brahmana who takes nothing in the world that is not given him, be it long or short, small or large, good or bad.

410. Him I call indeed a Brahmana who fosters no desires for this world or for the next, has no inclinations, and is unshackled.

411. Him I call indeed a Brahmana who has no interests, and when he has understood (the truth), does not say How, how? and who has reached the depth of the Immortal.

412. Him I call indeed a Brahmana who in this world is above good and evil, above the bondage of both, free from grief from sin, and from impurity.

413. Him I call indeed a Brahmana who is bright like the moon, pure, serene, undisturbed, and in whom all gaiety is extinct.

414. Him I call indeed a Brahmana who has traversed this miry road, the impassable world and its vanity, who has gone through, and reached the other shore, is thoughtful, guileless, free from doubts, free from attachment, and content.

415. Him I call indeed a Brahmana who in this world, leaving all desires, travels about without a home, and in whom all concupiscence is extinct.

416. Him I call indeed a Brahmana who, leaving all longings, travels about without a home, and in whom all covetousness is extinct.

417. Him I call indeed a Brahmana who, after leaving all bondage to men, has risen above all bondage to the gods, and is free from all and every bondage.

418. Him I call indeed a Brahmana who has left what gives pleasure and what gives pain, who is cold, and free from all germs (of renewed life), the hero who has conquered all the worlds.

419. Him I call indeed a Brahmana who knows the destruction and the return of beings everywhere, who is free from bondage, welfaring (Sugata), and awakened (Buddha).

420. Him I call indeed a Brahmana whose path the gods do not know, nor spirits (Gandharvas), nor men, whose passions are extinct, and who is an Arhat (venerable).

421. Him I call indeed a Brahmana who calls nothing his own, whether it be before, behind, or between, who is poor, and free from the love of the world.

422. Him I call indeed a Brahmana, the manly, the noble, the hero, the great sage, the conqueror, the impassible, the accomplished, the awakened.

423. Him I call indeed a Brahmana who knows his former abodes, who sees heaven and hell, has reached the end of births, is perfect in knowledge, a sage, and whose

Made in United States
North Haven, CT
13 May 2022

19139360R00286